# COMMON LISP

# COMMON LISP
## A TUTORIAL

Wendy L. Milner
Hewlett-Packard Company

Prentice Hall
Englewood Cliffs, New Jersey 07632

LIBRARY OF CONGRESS
Library of Congress Cataloging-in-Publication Data

Milner, Wendy L.
  Common Lisp : a tutorial / Wendy L. Milner
    p. cm.
  Includes index.
  ISBN 0-13-152844-0
  1. COMMON LISP (Computer program language) I. Title.
QA76.73.L23M55 1988                                    87-32053
005.13'3--dc19                                         CIP

Editorial/production supervision
  and interior design: *Carolyn Fellows*
Cover design: *Photo Plus Art*
Back cover photo: *Daniel Ashton*
Manufacturing buyer: *Lorraine Fumoso*

COVER ART

The photograph on the cover is taken from the screen of an HP 9000. Colin Cantwell is the software designer and Everit Darco of HP is the photographer. It depicts the Mandelbrot Set of numbers, which is the set of complex numbers that remain finite when a formula is applied to them recursively. The formula is $z^2 + c$. The first iteration of the formula gives $z = 0$ and $c =$ the chosen complex number. At each further iteration, $z$ is given the result of the previous iteration of $z^2 + c$. If after a large number of iterations the absolute value of the result is relatively small, that point in the complex plane is painted black. The number $c$ is part of the Mandelbrot Set. If the absolute value of the result of the iterations rapidly approaches infinity, the number c is not part of the Mandelbrot Set. Pictures are produced by assigning colors to these numbers based on how rapidly they approach infinity and by choosing values of $c$ around one point in the complex plane at certain intervals. As colors, points, and intervals are changed, different pictures are produced. Refer to *Scientific American* (August 1985) for more information on this set of numbers.

 Published by Prentice-Hall, Inc.
A division of Simon & Schuster
Englewood Cliffs, New Jersey 07632

Printed in the United of America
10   9   8   7   6   5   4   3   2   1

ISBN 0-13-152844-0   025

Prentice-Hall International (UK) Limited, *London*
Prentice-Hall of Australia Pty. Limited, *Sydney*
Prentice-Hall Canada Inc., *Toronto*
Prentice-Hall Hispanoamericana, S.A., *Mexico*
Prentice-Hall of India Private Limited, *New Delhi*
Prentice-Hall of Japan, Inc., *Tokyo*
Simon & Schuster Asia Pte. Ltd., *Singapore*
Editora Prentice-Hall do Brasil, Ltda., *Rio de Janeiro*

*To the family
for their understanding of late dinners,
missed appointments, and general neglect.*

*And to Mary Lee Milner,
for her faith and phone calls,
asking if the book was done yet.*

# Contents

# *Preface*

## AUDIENCE

This book is intended for those wishing to learn Common Lisp. While programming knowledge is not required, it is recommended that the reader be familiar with computer terminology. It is assumed that the reader has an understanding of computer programming or has access to instruction on computer programming.

## A NOTE ABOUT EXAMPLES

All of the examples and problems in this book have been tested. Because of differing implementations of Common Lisp, there may be some variance in the answers between what is shown in this book and what the readers may get on their systems. (For example, the precision of a floating-point number.) The results shown here are from a Hewlett-Packard 9000, Series 300 computer with a HP-UX operating system and a Common Lisp Development Environment. A note is given wherever implementation-dependent results are shown.

## HOW TO USE THIS BOOK

There are four parts to this book. Part 1 includes general information on Lisp and introduces the concept of functions. It is important that everyone learning Lisp read this part before going on to the rest of the book. Part 2 describes the many ways in which functions can be structured. Many concepts on programming are covered. Part 3 devotes a chapter to each of the many data types in Lisp. Each chapter is independent of the others in this part. Part 4 deals with Input and Output. It describes the method Lisp uses for I/O. The chapters should be read consecutively. This part may be read at any point where more than simple I/O is needed. Previous parts describe the basic I/O needed for their chapters.

There are extensive examples and exercises throughout the book. Where possible, the examples use only the functions that have been described in that chapter or in the first two parts. If functions from other chapters are used, a comment about the function and where it is fully described is included. Also, the exercises only require knowledge presented in the current chapter or in the first two parts. The answers to all the exercises are found in the back of the book.

## ACKNOWLEDGMENTS

Thanks is given to the Hewlett-Packard Company for use of their equipment. Both the Common Lisp software and the word processing equipment were used in the creation of this book. To Jaci Engle of Computer Documentation International for editing. To Richard Arts for his expertise in Pascal programming.

# COMMON LISP

# PART 1
# Lisp Concepts

# 1

# Introduction

What is Lisp and how do you program in Lisp? This first section introduces you to the concepts necessary to begin programming. From what is symbolic programming to how do you name a function, the chapters lead you through the first steps.

In the remaining sections, you will learn the specifics of the many functions of Lisp, the blocking constructs, and the input and output functions. The final section of the book gives you a complete reference to all the functions in Lisp.

If you are learning Lisp, you should begin with this first section. Read each chapter in sequence. If you already know Lisp and want information on specific functions, you can jump ahead to the chapter that describes those functions.

## SYMBOLIC PROGRAMMING VS. NUMERIC PROGRAMMING

In the beginning, there was counting on fingers and toes. Then came mechanical calculators such as stones in a box, the abacus, and other technological advancements. Finally came the electronic calculator that developed into a computer. While calculato, s were advancing, so was mathematics. It was no longer enough to count the number of sheep in the pasture, the problem was now as abstract as one of genetics and how many sheep would be in the pasture assuming various conditions. And this led to more abstract discussions of numbers, which, since they weren't connected with anything, were simply symbols. The poor fledgling computer, with only Fortran to work for it, just couldn't cope with anything except numbers. Mathematics can be very abstract.

John McCarthy developed Lisp in the late 1950s to help computers cope with such problems as symbolic differentiation and integration of algebraic expressions. In fact, lambda calculus is at the heart of Lisp. McCarthy conceived Lisp as a formalism of recursion equations. The first Lisp interpreter was implemented at MIT. Lisp is the second oldest computer language (Fortran is the oldest).

## LISP — COMMON OR OTHERWISE

Lisp has evolved over the years, mostly in the education research labs. Lisp is flexible. It has adapted to encompass ideas of program design. Several dialects have developed: MacLisp, Interlisp, Portable Standard Lisp, Zetalisp, Spicelisp, Nil, and Scheme, among others. Each dialect shares many of the same characteristics as the first implementation of Lisp.

While Lisp stayed in the academic environment, diverse evolution in multiple areas flourished with few consequences. When industry began using the language, the search for the one perfect dialect began. A gang of computer scientists led by Guy L. Steele, Jr. developed a written standard for Lisp called *Common Lisp*. It too is evolving.

The difference between Common Lisp and the other dialects is perhaps its widespread conception. The "gang" members are associated with universities and corporations all over the United States. MIT, CMU, Stanford, Symbolics, TI, DEC, and many more contributed to the development of Common Lisp. In this development, they took the best parts from the existing dialects and combined them into a language that many institutions could accept. Perhaps, in part, this acceptance has occurred because Common Lisp is not based on one set of hardware. It was developed independent of the hardware. Because of this, many computer companies can implement the language on their own hardware. In addition, since a group of independents created the language, there are no problems associated with copyrighted software.[1]

This book uses Common Lisp because it is becoming the standard Lisp dialect. Unless otherwise noted, this book adheres to the written standard *Common LISP: The Language*, by Guy Steele, Jr., first edition, 1984.

As stated, even Common Lisp is evolving. The network of Lisp users and implementors have commented on the first edition and changes are being made. At the writing of this book, a second edition of the standard has not been made.

---

[1] Compare this with UNIX® (a trademark of Bell Laboratories), where even to mention the name, you must refer to the owner of the copyright, and to implement the operating system requires a licensing agreement.

## ARTIFICIAL INTELLIGENCE

The term *artificial intelligence* brings images of "intelligent" computers to mind—robots like Robbie the Robot, who could do anything from driving the car, to cooking dinner, and still have time for making torpedo juice; worlds managed by one central computer that controls the weather, controls traffic flow, and advises the president on economic matters; science fiction fantasies that might someday come true. *Someday* is the magic word.

Artificial intelligence is concerned with human reasoning. That is, how does a human, as opposed to a computer, reason? Can we instill human reasoning into a computer? If we could put everything that makes human reasoning into a computer, we would have the androids of science fiction. That is a long way off.

Humans reason symbolically, not numerically. A child learns to speak before learning to count. You learn to drive, not by the numbers, but by watching, listening, and practicing. All these activities use symbols, not numbers. In contrast, most computers use numbers—not symbols—to solve problems. Artificial intelligence is a method of programming a computer so that the computer uses symbols instead of numbers. It isn't as exciting put that way—No R2-D2 and no C-3PO. Just plain straightforward programming. However, this programming lays the groundwork for all the science fiction computers of the future.

## RULE-BASED PROGRAMMING

We can determine how one person reasons on one problem. By taking many people and seeing how they reason on the same problem, we can set up rules that a computer can follow. The computer can then apply these rules to the same problem. Unlike some people, the computer can also tell how it got the answer.

*Rule-based programming* is one use of artificial intelligence. There is nothing magical about the methodology. Using standard numeric programming you could obtain the same results, but it would take more lines of code and a longer time to compute an answer. By using a language designed for manipulating symbols instead of numbers, the approach for reaching a solution is simpler.

## EXPERT SYSTEMS

An *expert system* is a computer system that contains the knowledge of an expert on some subject and the rules the expert uses for arriving at a solution to a problem within that subject.

When you first learn a skill, you follow the rules. When you are learning to drive a car, your driving instructor tells you how far you should stay from the car in front of you, how far in advance you should use your turn signals, and how fast you should drive. You practice using these rules. As you gain skill, you learn the many exceptions to the rules. To avoid an accident, you change lanes; you do not use your signals because it would take too much time. On a rainy day, you drive slower than on a sunny day because it takes longer to stop the car. Through your experience, you add to the rules that your driving instructor gave you. You use these rules without thinking about them.

In the same way, experts use rules for making decisions about their area of expertise. They begin by following the rules that everyone knows. Then, through years of experience, they add to the rules. They are the experts because they know more than the nonexperts. They have the knowledge to solve problems that few others have. When you put all this knowledge into a computer, you have an expert system.

One large mainframe computer may be devoted to solving problems on one subject. It is expensive, so why not just go to the expert? Expert systems preserve perishable expertise and distribute the expertise. When the expert retires or goes on vacation, the expertise is still available. Expert systems preserve the knowledge of the expert.

## WHERE DOES THIS LEAD?

Just learning to program in Lisp does not qualify you to write an expert system. Nor does this book make the attempt. Lisp is one of the languages that uses symbolic rather than numeric programming. Once you learn how to program using this language, then you can tackle the problem of expert systems and other symbolic programming problems.

To make an android, you must put all the expert systems together—vision, natural language, pattern recognition, voice, motion, and knowledge. It is no simple task, but one that is accomplishable. You are standing at the threshold of a cave with many twisty turns. This book could be your map through the cave.

# 2

# *The Structure*
# *of the Language*

As a programmer, you are familiar with line numbers, line labels, subroutines, statements, functions, variables, and constants. You know how to construct a program that performs operations. You know the difference between executing a statement and storing the statement for future execution within a program. You look for keywords or reserved words when learning a new language. Lisp offers new concepts along with new terms. This chapter introduces you to some of the concepts and terms and familiarizes you with Lisp programs.

You should be able to answer the following questions when you have finished reading this chapter:

- What makes up a *form*?

- How are *functions* defined?

- What is a *keyword*?

- What are the *primitives* of Lisp?

- How does Lisp *read-eval-print* a form?

## FORMS AND PARENTHESES

Program isn't exactly the right term. In Lisp you deal more often with individual forms[1] and functions. A *form* is a single complete unit in a program. It can be only a single line, or it can be many lines. A *function* is an action to be performed on arguments. In most languages, functions, called *keywords* in many cases, are predefined. In Lisp, most functions are defined by the programmer.

### Looking at Individual Forms

The look of a Lisp program is quite different from other languages. Parentheses give Lisp programs a distinctive look. As you glance through this book or any Lisp program, you will see them. Parentheses set off one form from another. Look at a simple form:

```
(+ 2 3)
```

This form adds the numbers 2 and 3. It is not very interesting and probably would never be found in any program. Instead, you might see one that uses variables:

```
(+ a b)
```

This form adds two numbers together. The values of the arguments would be determined somewhere else in the program.

In the simple example, you can see the three parts of the form: parentheses, operator and arguments. The *operator* always comes immediately after the opening *parenthesis*. The *arguments* follow the operator. The ordering of the operator followed by the arguments is called *prefix notation*. There might be two arguments as in the example, or there might be one argument, nine arguments, or none. The number of arguments is determined by the needs of the operator.

An argument can be supplied by another form.

```
(+ (* 2 2) (* 3 3))
```

In this example, the number 2 is squared and sent as the first argument to the addition operator. The number 3 is squared and sent as the second argument. Then 4 and 9 are added. Notice that each form has the same structure: parentheses surround the form, an operator is the first element of the form, and arguments follow the operator. In this addition form example, the arguments are supplied by another form. This is normal in Lisp.

The previous example is the sum of the squares. If you wanted to use this form more than once, you would define a new function:

---

[1] Forms are also called symbolic expressions in other literature.

```
(defun sum-of-squares (a b)
   (+ (* a a)(* b b)))
```

The `defun` macro *defines functions*. The name of the function being defined is `sum-of-squares`. `(a b)` are the two arguments `sum-of-squares` uses. `(+ (* a a)(* b b))` is the body of the new function.

Then, whenever you needed the function, you would call it exactly as if the function was predefined in Lisp:

```
(sum-of-squares 2 3)
```

Again, these are the parts of the form: parentheses, an operator (the defined function), and the arguments. To Lisp it does not matter if the function is part of the Lisp language or if you defined it. Once you begin writing programs, you will find that most of the programming time is spent developing new functions. There are several chapters later in the book that are devoted to writing your own functions.

## OPERATORS

The first item after the open parenthesis is an operator. Operators can be functions, macros, or special forms.

### Functions

A *function* is an operator in the classic sense. It has a definition and returns a value. Its arguments are evaluated before they are passed to the function. A function is a separate entity that is applied to arguments.

The `defun` macro defines new functions.

### Macros

*Macros* expand into a form that is translated into function calls or special forms. The arguments are not evaluated before they are passed to the macro. The macro returns a form that is handled by the evaluator before being passed to the interpretor or compiler.

The `defmacro` macro defines a new macro.

### Special Forms

*Special forms* handle program control and bindings. These forms include `if`, `setq`, `quote`, and `progn`.

There is no way to define new special forms.

## quote

quote is a special form that returns its arguments unevaluated. If you have already looked at some of the examples in this book, you will have noticed that some of the forms ignore the rule that an operator is the first thing to appear in an expression. You may also have noticed that those forms have a quote, ' , in front of them. This is short-hand notation for the quote special form. For example,

```
(+ 2 2)
⇒    4

(quote (+ 2 2))
⇒     (+ 2 2)

'(+ 2 2)
⇒     (+ 2 2)
```

---

### Note

The symbol ⇒ indicates the returned value.

---

In the above example, the inner form, (+ 2 2), was not evaluated when quote was placed in the outer form.

quote is used when it is necessary to pass a literal value to a function without evaluation. The following is one simple case:

```
(defun print-it (x)
  (print x)
  nil)

(print-it 1)
⇒    1
     NIL

(print-it a)
⇒    Error: the symbol A has no value.

(print-it (quote a))
⇒    A
     NIL
```

```
(print-it 'a)
⇒    A
     NIL

(print-it '(a b c))
⇒    (A B C)
     NIL

(print-it '(+ 2 2))
⇒    (+ 2 2)
     NIL
```

There are many functions that take other functions as arguments. quote is used frequently so that the argument functions are not evaluated before they are given to the other function.

In addition, many functions want lists as arguments. '(a b c) is an example of a list. a may or may not be a function. In either case, you do not want the form to be evaluated before it gets to the function. quote prevents evaluation.


## KEYWORDS THAT AREN'T

Functions are not keywords[2]. Neither are they reserved words. The names of functions are symbols. In all of Lisp, there are only a handful of functions that you cannot redefine. The symbol that names a function can be re-bound to any function definition. This is the nature of Lisp. As you saw previously, you can define your own functions any time. You can also redefine just about anything in the language.

A keyword in Lisp is a special symbol that defines how arguments are used in a function. *Lambda keywords* determine whether an argument is required, optional, to be gathered into a list, or is a keyword itself. When an argument is a keyword, the call to the function must include the keyword and its value. This process is completely described in Chapter 4.


## EVERYTHING IS SUBJECT TO CHANGE

The power of Lisp comes from its flexibility. It has been referred to as a plastic language. You can stretch it, mold it, fold it, build it, tear it down, and start over again.

It is because of this flexibility that there are so many versions of Lisp. Every programmer defines functions dear to that programmer's heart. In some cases, the name of a function was displeasing, and so was changed. In other cases, new functions were added. Or, modifications were made to existing functions. It is easy to do.

---

[2] Keywords are used in *lambda expressions*, which are described in Chapter 4.

## car, cdr, AND cons

While everything is subject to change, three functions are fairly constant among all Lisps. These are called *primitive functions*.

In numeric programming you have +, −, *, and /. These functions deal with numbers. In Lisp, you have `car`, `cdr` and `cons`. These deal with lists. In a *Lisp machine* these functions are hardwired into the computer just as addition is hardwired into other computers.

`car` gives the first element of a list. `cdr` (pronounced *could'er*) gives the rest of the list. `cons` builds lists. In later chapters, you will see more of these three functions.

For example,

```
(car '(a b c))
⇒     A

(cdr '(a b c))
⇒     (B C)

(cons 'a '(b c))
⇒     (A B C)

(car (cdr '(a b c)))
⇒     B
```

`car`, `cdr`, and `cons` are the basis for all Lisp functions. In an earlier example, you saw how the function `sum-of-squares` was built from the functions + and *. While this is a simple function, it does show how functions are built in Lisp. All Lisp functions are built from a handful of primitive functions, which include `car`, `cdr`, and `cons`.

Complex functions are built on other functions that use other functions, that use other functions, etc. An interesting exercise is to look at the source code of your Lisp to see how some functions are defined. Unless you have unlimited time, you won't be able to look at all of them. There are nearly 700 functions defined in Lisp.

While the language may be huge, do not despair of learning it. The rest of this book is devoted to teaching you Lisp. Each chapter takes a small portion and shows you with many examples how to program in Lisp.

## read-eval-print

When you type in a form and evaluate[3] it, Lisp reads the form, sends the form to the interpreter for evaluation, which sends the results to the printer to output. This process is referred to as the *read-eval-print* loop.

---

[3] There may be a Lisp-EVAL key, or control sequence to do this. Check your system to determine the key sequence to use.

When you begin writing functions, this process is done interactively. You write a function, evaluate it, and test it. You do not need to compile, link, and load the function as you must do in some other languages. Once you determine that the function is correct, you can compile it for better performance.

Since most functions have multiline definitions, the [RETURN] key is different from the [EXECUTE] key. You could type the following function definition:

```
( defun          sum-of-squares
   (a
          b)
                  (+
(*   a     a
)  (* b b)
) )
))
```

This is difficult to read. However, Lisp will read the function any way you type it.

To evaluate the form, Lisp reads the form and sends it to the interpreter, which tries to evaluate it. If there are no errors, after evaluation, the result is returned. In the case of `defun`, the name of the newly defined function is printed. When you evaluate `sum-of-squares`, the value of the function is returned.

If the function is an argument to another function, the result is not printed. Instead, the result is sent to the outer function. For example,

```
(* 2 2)
```

returns 4.

```
(+ (* 2 2) (* 3 3))
```

returns 13. It does not return 4, 9, and 13.

---

**Exercise 2-1**

Now that you are beginning to learn what Lisp is, it is time to use the computer. Try the following exercise to begin learning the system.

**1.** Use the operating instructions for your computer to log in and get Lisp running.

**2.** Type the `sum-of-squares` function and evaluate it.

```
(defun sum-of-squares (a b)
   (+ (* a a) (* b b)))
```

If you do it correctly, the result is SUM-OF-SQUARES.

**3.** Evaluate the following forms:

```
(sum-of-squares 2 3)
(sum-of-squares 0 0)
(sum-of-squares -4 -20)
(sum-of-squares -99 35)
```

**4.** Try your own numbers for `sum-of-squares`.

**5.** Try using a letter instead of a number in the `sum-of-squares` function. You will get an error and enter the debugger.

**6.** Correct the error by entering a number or giving the letter a value.

**7.** Use a letter in the function again. This time exit the debugger without correcting the error.

**8.** Type and evaluate the following form:

```
(defun double (a b)
     (* 2 (sum-of-squares a b))
```

**9.** Evaluate the following forms:

```
(double 2 4)
(double 3 5)
```

**10.** Make up some simple functions. Evaluate them and try some values.

**11.** Save your work in a file. There is no Lisp function to save the file. Use your computer's operating instructions to save the file.

**12.** Log off the computer.

## SUMMARY

- What makes up a *form*?
  A form is a single complete unit in a program. It begins and ends with parentheses. Within the parentheses are the function name and arguments. Arguments may themselves be the result of other forms.

- How are *functions* defined?
  The `defun` macro defines new functions. Functions themselves are made up of other functions.

- What is a *keyword*?
  The term *keyword* is reserved for special words within a lambda expression. The names of functions are symbols. The value of the symbols can be changed.

- What are the *primitives* of Lisp?
  The three basic primitives are `car`, `cdr` and `cons`. These functions put together and take apart lists.

- How does Lisp *read-eval-print* a form?

  The listener reads a form and sends it to the interpreter. The interpreter evaluates the form and sends the result to the printer for output. The result may be displayed on the screen or sent to another function for use as an argument.

# 3

# *The Parts*

# *of the Language*

When learning a computer language, you have to find out two important things: the types of data the language can manipulate and how to go about that manipulation. This chapter tells of the data types supported by Common Lisp and begins to show the functions that manipulate those data types.

In this chapter you will learn:

- What data types are available in Common Lisp?
- How can you determine the type of data?
- How can you determine if data is a subtype of another data type?
- Which functions operate on each type of data?

## DATA TYPES

Common Lisp supports literally an infinite number of data types. While there is a finite number of predefined types, you can define as many other types as you need. The following list shows the predefined Common Lisp data types. The indentations show the hierarchy of subtypes. Also notice that some types are subtypes of more than one other type.

Common
   Numbers
      Rational
         Integers
            Fixnums
               (mod n)
            Bignums
            Signed byte
               Bit
            Unsigned byte
               Bit
         Ratios
      Floating-point numbers
         Short
         Single
         Double
         Long
      Complex numbers
   Characters
      String characters
         Standard characters
   Symbols
      Null
   Lists
      Null
      Conses
   Arrays
      General arrays
      Simple arrays
      Vectors
         General vectors
         Simple vectors
         Strings
            Simple strings
         Bit vectors
            Simple bit vectors
   Sequences
      Vectors
      Lists
   Atom
   Keyword
   Hash tables
   Readtables
   Packages
   Pathnames

Streams
Random states
Structures
Functions
Compiled functions

There are two more data types: T and NIL. All the data types shown are subtypes of
type T. Conversely, NIL is a subtype of everything.

## Type Functions

To determine the type of an argument, use the type-of function.

```
(type-of 7)
⇒     FIXNUM

(type-of 7.2)
⇒     FLOAT

(type-of 7/2)
⇒     RATIO

(type-of "abc")
⇒     (SIMPLE-STRING 3)

(type-of '(a b b))
⇒     CONS

(type-of '#(a b))
⇒     (SIMPLE-VECTOR 2)

(type-of #\a)
⇒     STANDARD-CHAR
```

type-of returns the most specific type it can. While 7 is a number, it is also a
fixnum.

If you know the type, or want to determine if an object is a particular type, you
can use the typep function.

```
(typep 7 'number)
⇒     T

(typep '(a b c) 'list)
⇒     T

(typep 7/2 'ratio)
⇒     T
```

```
(typep 7/2 'rational)
⇒    T

(typep 7/2 'number)
⇒    T

(typep 7/2 'string)
⇒    NIL
```

The `typep` function returns T for an object not only if it is the specified type, but also if the object is a subtype of the one specified.

The `subtypep` function determines if one type is a subtype of another type.

```
(subtypep 'integer 'number)
⇒    T
     T

(subtypep 'vector 'array)
⇒    T
     T

(subtypep 'list 'number)
⇒    NIL
     T
```

Two values are returned. The second value indicates whether or not `subtypep` could determine a relationship between the two types. If the value is T, then the first value indicates whether or not the first type is a subtype of the second type. To determine if one object is a subtype of a type, you can use `type-of` and `subtypep` together.

```
(subtypep (type-of 7) 'number)
⇒    T
     T

(subtypep (type-of '(a b c)) 'list)
⇒    T
     T
```

---

**Exercise 3-1**

**1.** What is the most specific data type for the following?

```
"abc"
'(1 2 3)
1/2
10
:start
'a
```

**2.** Name all the types in which the following are members:

```
"abc"
'(1 2 3)
5.43
3
'a
nil
```

---

## NUMBERS

Lists may be the heart of Common Lisp, but real-world problems still deal with numbers. For these problems, Lisp provides four types of numbers: integers, ratios, floating-point numbers, and complex numbers.

### Integers

Integers represent the mathematical integers 0, 1, 2, 3, etc. and −0, −1, −2, −3, etc. The largest integer is `most-positive-fixnum` and is limited by the implementation.

Integers are usually represented in base 10; however, any other radix can be used. The radix is shown in the following manner:

```
#nnrdddd
```

where `nn` is the radix and `dddd` is the number. The `#` and `r` are used to indicate a radix.

For example,

```
#2r1001      ≡ radix-2 number 1001
#16ra4b3     ≡ radix-16 number a4b3
#32r123adg   ≡ radix-32 number 123adg
```

---

### Note

`#` is a macro character. It informs Lisp that the character that follows has a special meaning.

---

   Three radices are used frequently enough that they have a special notation.   #b is binary, equivalent to #2r. #o is octal, equivalent to #8r. #x is hexadecimal, equivalent to #16r.

.

| #b1001 | ⇒ | #2r1001 | ⇒ | 9 |
| #o11 | ⇒ | #8r11 | ⇒ | 9 |
| #x1a | ⇒ | #161a | ⇒ | 27 |

---

**Exercise 3-2**

   **1.** Translate the following numbers into base ten:

      #b110 _=6_
      #8r11 _=9_
      #o14 _= 12_
      #xf _= 15_
      #10r25 _25_

   **2.** Translate the following integers from base ten to the indicated radix:    _400_

      Radix 2: 2, 4, 8   _2r10 , 2r100, 2r1000_
      Radix 8: 1, 8, 10, 64 _8r1, 8r10, 8r12, 8r100_
      Radix 16: 1, 16, 12, 256, 4096 _16r1, 16r10, 16rc, 16rd0, 16r1000_

   **3.** Use the computer to translate the following integers to base ten:

      10
      #2r10
      #xadfb
      #9r158
      #o7777
      #3r122211

   **4.** For the curious, find a way for the computer to translate from decimal to octal.

---

## Ratios

Ratios are numbers represented by two integers, a numerator and a denominator. Some ratios, such as 4/2, represent integers. Other ratios, such as 1/3, cannot be represented as integers. The set of all ratios and integers make up the rational data type.

   A *ratio* consists of a sign, a positive numerator, a /, and a positive denominator. The denominator cannot be signed and must be greater than zero.

   For example,

```
4/5
4/2
-5/2
12098/3327893
```

A ratio may contain a radix indicator.

```
#xa/b
#o-71/16
#b1001/1100
```

The functions `numerator` and `denominator` return the numerator and denominator of a ratio.

```
(numerator 4/5)
⇒    4

(denominator #b100/110)
⇒    3

(numerator -16/17)
⇒    -16
```

---

**Exercise 3-3**

Which of the following "ratios" are legal and which are not?

```
1/2
1.2/3.4
7/-2
#b100/110
100/#b110
-5/100
#x1/c
```

---

## Floating Point

There are four types of floating-point numbers: long, short, single, and double. Each type can have a different precision. Within this book, the four types will be treated as simply floating-point numbers. There will be no distinction between them.

A *floating-point number* consists of a sign, an integer, a decimal point, and at least one digit following the decimal point. No radix is allowed.
For example,

```
12.4
3.1415
0.3
```

```
+99.9
-12.0
-1.141414
```

Most numeric functions will take any type of noncomplex number. The result
type will vary depending on the type of the arguments.

```
(+  1  2)
⇒    3

(+  1.0  2)
⇒    3.0

(+  1/2  2/3)
⇒    7/6

(+  0.5  0.66666)
⇒    1.16666

(/  3  2)
⇒    3/2

(/  3.0  2)
⇒    1.5
```

---

### Exercise 3-4

Create the function `make-float` that forces the result of any math operation to
return a floating-point value. Note that the value returned from a math operation
is always a number.

Remember to define a function you use the `defun` macro.

```
(defun name (arguments)
         (body of function) )
```

For example,

```
(+  1  2)
⇒    3

(make-float (+  1  2))
⇒    3.0

(+  1/2  2/2)
⇒    3/2
```

```
(make-float (+ 1/2 2/2))
⇒   1.5
```

## Complex

*Complex numbers* have two parts, an imaginary and a real part. The notation for complex numbers is:

```
#c(realpart imagpart)
```

For example,

```
#c(2 3)
#c(-4.5 7)
#c(7/6 2468)
#c(999 -7.9)
```

Each part of a complex number can be any type of number (except complex). Many of the number functions operate on complex numbers.

```
(+ #c(2 3) #c(5 9))
⇒   #C(7 12)

(- #c(7.6 9) 2)
⇒   #C(5.6 9.0)

(* #c(0 1) #c(0 1))
⇒   -1

(/ #c(42 24) 2.0)
⇒   #C(21.0 12.0)

(sqrt -2.0)
⇒   #C(0.0 1.414213562373095)
```

In addition, there are functions that only operate on complex numbers. The `realpart` and `imagpart` functions return the parts of a complex number.

```
(realpart #c(2 3))
⇒   2

(realpart #c(-4.5 7))
⇒   -4.5

(realpart #c(7/6 2468))
⇒   7/6
```

```
(imagpart #c(2 3))
⇒    3

(imagpart #c(-4.5 7))
⇒    7.0

(imagpart #c(7/6 2468))
⇒    2468

(imagpart #c(999 -7.9))
⇒    -7.9
```

## CHARACTERS

Characters have a special syntax to differentiate them from symbols.

```
#\character
```

For example,

```
#\a
#\A
#\8
#\Control-A
#\Meta-c
#\?
#\backspace
```

A *character* has three parts: the character code, font, and bit attribute. There is a different character code for each character on the keyboard. Some systems can support alternate keyboards, such as Katakana or Roman. The character code for a is different than the character code for A.

*Font* specifies how the character is printed. This includes height, width, slant, color, boldness, and any other attribute the system supports. Not all implementations support fonts.

The *bit attribute* specifies if the character is a control, meta, super, or hyper character. If the character has the bit attribute set, the word control, meta, super, or hyper appears before the character in the printed representation. The bit attribute allows extra coding to be added to a character.

The char-int function returns the integer encoding of a character. This integer is implementation dependent.

```
(char-int #\a)
⇒    97

(char-int #\A)
⇒    65
```

```
(char-int #\control-a)
⇒    16777281
```

```
(char-int #\Meta-A)
⇒    33554497
```

---

**Exercise 3-5**

Which of the following are characters?

```
#\a
'a
(#\a)
#\tab
#\control
#\meta-A
'meta-a
```

---

## SYMBOLS

*Symbols* are used to name functions and variables. In addition, symbols have a print name of their own. They can also have a property list associated with them.

A symbol name can contain letters, digits, and some special characters. The name cannot contain spaces or delimiting characters.

The following special characters are allowed:

```
+ - * \ @ $ % ^ & _ / < > ~ .
```

The following delimiting characters and other characters are not allowed:

```
? ! [ ] { } ( ) |
```

While the name is usually composed of uppercase letters, you do not have to enter the name in uppercase. The reader translates lowercase letters to uppercase letters. You have seen this in previous examples where you evaluate a function you named `fun` and the result is `FUN`.

For example, the following notations all name the same symbol.

```
HELLO-THERE
hello-there
Hello-There
HELLO-there
HeLLo-THeRe
```

If you want lowercase letters in the name, use the \ macro character. The \ character specifies that the next character, while normally not allowed, can be used.

```
\a\b\c          ; the symbol abc
ab\c            ; the symbol ABc
7y\x            ; the symbol 7Yx
```

The name can include digits; however, if the name is the same as a number, it is interpreted as a number, not as a symbol.

```
a1              ; the symbol A1
1a              ; the symbol 1A
103s4           ; the short floating-point number 103s4
103\s4          ; the symbol 103s4
25              ; the number 25
\25             ; the symbol 25
```

You can also use the \ character to include the space, parenthesis, or other character not normally allowed.

```
\(ab\)          ; the symbol (AB)
\\a\ b          ; the symbol \A B
\'\(\)          ; the symbol '()
```

If there are multiple characters that need the \ character, the | character can be used around the name.

```
|a b c|         ; the symbol a b c
|(123)|         ; the symbol (123)
|XbcD|          ; the symbol XbcD
|/users|        ; the symbol /users
|(ab \\ cd)|    ; the symbol (ab \ cd)
                ;    the \ must still have another \
|\|(ab)\||      ; the symbol |(ab)|
                ;    the | must be preceded by a \
```

When using symbols, you must determine whether you want the symbol or what the symbol names. For example,

```
(list 'a 'b 'c)
⇒    (A B C)
```

The symbol list names the function list. The symbols a, b, and c are used as symbol names. There is a quote in front of the symbol name.

```
(setq x 5)
⇒    5
```

```
(list x 'a)
⇒    (5 A)
```

The symbols `setq` and `list` name functions. The symbol x names a variable that has a value, 5. The symbol a is only a name. When you list the values x `'`a, the value of the variable x is listed along with the symbol a. x is not quoted. a is quoted.

---

**Exercise 3-6**

What symbol is specified by the following?

```
|abc|
'abc
|#\a|
#\a
555-1212
555
(ab)
|(ab)|
```

---

## LISTS

A *list* is a structure that contains zero or more elements. A list begins and ends with parentheses. The following are lists.

```
(list 'a 'b)
(a b c)
()
(* (+ 1 3) 9)
```

A list is made up of *cons* cells. A cons cell has a `car` and a `cdr`. Each car is an element of the list. Each cdr is the rest of the list.

```
(a b (c d) e)
```

This list has four elements, a, b, (c d), and e. The car of the list is a. The cdr of the list is (b (c d) e). If you take the cdr of the list four times, you will see the following:

```
(cdr '(a b (c d) e))
⇒    (B (C D) E)

(cdr (cdr '(a b (c d) e)))
⇒    ((C D) E)
```

```
(cdr (cdr (cdr '(a b (c d) e))))
⇒    (E)

(cdr (cdr (cdr (cdr '(a b (c d) e)))))
⇒    NIL
```

The last cdr of the list is NIL. This is true of every list except dotted lists.

a, b, and e are *atoms* in the list. (c d) is another list. An atom is any non-list element. A symbol is an atom. So is a number.

The following are atoms:

```
a
43.21
any-symbol
*k4*
&*$@
name
set
```

A cons cell can contain a cdr with the value nil or with the value of an atom. A cons cell that contains an atom is called a *dotted pair*. The list is called a *dotted list*.

```
(a b . c)
(7 k (n 9) . y)
(1 . 2)
```

If you take the cdr of the list (1 . 2), you will find that the last element is not NIL. It is the atom 2.

```
(cdr '(1 . 2))
⇒    2
```

A *tree* is a list that has *branches* and *leaves*. There is no structural difference between a tree and other lists. The concept is used by functions that operate on lists. This is discussed in Chapter 10.

---

**Exercise 3-7**

Which of the following are lists, atoms, or neither?

```
a
nil
(a b)
(a (b c))
()
((((A))))
(#\a)
(a (b)
(1 2 a b)
```

## ARRAYS

An *array* is an object that is composed of other objects. The objects are arranged in a Cartesian coordinate system. The indexing of arrays is zero-based. The array can have any number of dimensions and any number of elements up to the limits set by the implementation. The elements can be any type of data structure.

In an array, the number of dimensions precedes a nested list of the elements. For example,

```
#2A((1 2 3)(4 5 6))
```

This is a two-dimensional array. The first dimension contains three elements, 1, 2, and 3. The second dimension contains three elements, 4, 5, and 6. The 1 element is element (0 0), 2 is (0 1), 3 is (0 2), 4 is (1 0), 5 is (1 1), and 6 is (1 2).

```
#3A(((1)(2))
    ((3)(4))
    ((5)(6)))
```

This array is a 3-by-2-by-1 array.

The size and shape of an array can be adjusted. The elements of arrays can be shared or displaced.

### Vectors

A one dimensional array is also called a *vector*. A vector can have a *fill pointer*. The fill pointer is used by some function to find the last element of a vector, to point to the location where the next element can be added to the vector, or to determine the size of the vector.

```
#(1 2 3 4)
```

### Bit Vectors

A *bit vector* is a vector that contains only 1s and 0s.

```
#*101100
#*1
#*00001
#*1111111
#*0000
#*
```

## Strings

A *string* is a vector that contains only characters. When printed, the string is surrounded by double quotes.

```
"string string Strings"
"ab\"CD"
"123456"
"" .
";lkjasdf
   qwerqwerqwer"
"as90+12bv"
```

## OTHER TYPES

**Hash Tables.**    A *hash table* is a mapping of one object to an associated object. It is a strategy that allows rapid access to objects.

**Readtables.**    The *readtable* is a map for the Lisp parser to character syntax types. The readtable indicates macro characters and their functions. You have already seen several macro characters: #, (), |, and \. Another macro character of general interest is ;. The semicolon is the comment character in a function. Anything on the line following the semicolon is not evaluated.

**Packages.**    *Packages* are maps from symbol names to symbols. Symbols in one package can be exported to other packages.

**Pathnames.**    *Pathnames* are mappings from symbols to an external file system.

**Streams.**    A *stream* is an interface to an external I/O device. It is through a stream that characters are read and data is written to files. Most I/O functions use streams.

**Random States.**    The pseudorandom-number generator uses random-state objects for state information.

**Structures.**    A *structure* is a user-defined data type. It is similar to a Pascal record. The structure has a fixed number of named components. It also has functions that are defined for that structure.

**Functions.**    *Functions* are also data types. They are any object that can be executed as program code.

## FUNCTIONS

There are nearly 700 forms in Common Lisp. They each operate on one or more of the data types previously given. The chapters in Part 3 show the functions and give examples in detail. The next few pages show a few functions used frequently in examples. They are shown here so that you do not have to refer to the later chapters.

### On Numbers

You have already encountered several number functions. The basic arithmetic functions, addition, subtraction, multiplication, and division, are all included in Lisp. Also, finding the absolute value, square root, and exponentiation are included. Numbers can also be compared with one another.

The `abs` function returns the absolute value of a number.

```
(abs 4.5)
⇒    4.5
```

```
(abs -6/7)
⇒    6/7
```

```
(abs #c(-8 -2))
⇒    8.246211251235321
```

The `sqrt` function returns the square root of a number.

```
(sqrt 10)
⇒    3.162277660168379
```

```
(sqrt -2)
⇒    #C(0.0 1.414213562373095)
```

```
(sqrt 256)
⇒    15.999999999999998
```

The `expt` function returns the result of one number raised to the power of another number.

```
(expt 2 0)
⇒    1
```

```
(expt 3 2)
⇒    9
```

```
(expt 2 -2)
⇒    1/4
```

```
(expt #c(0 1) 2)
⇒    -1

(expt 10.0 4)
⇒    10000.0

(expt 7 1/2)
⇒    2.6457513110645903

(expt 3/4 2)
⇒    9/16
```

Numbers of any type can be compared using the following functions.

```
(< 1 2)
⇒    T

(> 5 3)
⇒    T

(<= 8 3 9)
⇒    NIL

(>= 9 7 7 3)
⇒    T

(< 1 3 5 7 9 234 345 456)
⇒    T

(= 3 3.0 3/1 #c(3 0))
⇒    T
```

The equal function tests the value of the objects and ignores the type.

The rounding function in Lisp is a little different than those found in other languages. round changes a number to the nearest even integer when the number is halfway between integers (at 0.5). In other cases, the nearest integer is returned. Two numbers are returned, the nearest integer and a remainder.

```
(round 3.5)
⇒    4
     -0.5

(round 2.5)
⇒    2
     0.5
```

```
(round 2.1)
⇒     2
      0.1

(round 7.9)
⇒     8
      -0.1

(round 4/5)
⇒     1
      -1/5
```

## On Lists

car and cdr are functions that return the car and cdr of a list.

```
(car '(a b c))
⇒     A

(cdr '(a b c))
⇒     (B C)

(car '((a b)(c d)(e f)))
⇒     (A B)

(cdr '((a b)(c d)(e f)))
⇒     ((C D) (E F))
```

The cons function creates a list.

```
(cons 'a 'b)
⇒     (A . B)

(cons 'a '(b))
⇒     (A B)

(cons 'a nil)
⇒     (A)

(cons '(a) '(b))
⇒     ((A) B)
```

The list function makes a list of all the arguments.

```
(list 'a 'b)
⇒     (A B)
```

```
(list 'a '(b) 1 nil)
⇒    (A (B) 1 NIL)

(list 1 2 3)
⇒    (1 2 3)
```

The `length` function returns the number of elements in the list. It does not return the number of atoms.

```
(length '(a b c))
⇒    3

(length '(a (b c) d))
⇒    3

(length '((a b)(c d)))
⇒    2
```

## Predicates

A *predicate* is a function that returns either nil or a non-nil value. A nil value means false and a *non-nil* value means true. The following predicates, as shown in the table, determine if a data structure meets a particular requirement. The predicate function returns NIL if the data structure fails the requirement and returns a non-nil value if the data structure meets the requirement.

**TABLE 3.1** PREDICATES

| Function | Meaning |
|---|---|
| numberp | Is the object a number? |
| listp | Is the object a list? |
| zerop | Is the object the number zero? |
| arrayp | Is the object an array? |
| consp | Is the object a cons? |
| characterp | Is the object a character? |
| floatp | Is the object a floating-point number? |

```
(numberp 'a)
⇒    NIL

(numberp 4.3)
⇒    T
```

```
(characterp #\a)
⇒    T


(arrayp #2A((1 2)(3 4)))
⇒    T


(floatp 4/5)
⇒    NIL


(floatp 4.5)
⇒    T
```

In the above predicates, the returned value is NIL or T. This is not the case with all predicates. For example, the member function returns NIL or a list. and returns NIL if a clause is nil or the value of the last clause. or returns the value of the first clause that is non-nil or NIL.

```
(member 'a '(b c a d))
⇒    (A D)


(member 4 '(1 2 3 4 5 6))
⇒    (4 5 6)


(member 9 '(1 2 3))
⇒    NIL


(and (+ 3 4)
     (- 4 2))
⇒    2


(and '(1 2)
     '(a b c)
     '(1 a b))
⇒    (1 A B)


(and 0
     nil)
⇒    NIL


(or '(1 2)
    nil)
⇒    (1 2)


(or nil
    (+ 3 4)
    '(a b c))
⇒    7
```

Equal is a predicate that has several forms, as shown in Table 3.2.

**TABLE 3.2** EQUAL PREDICATES

| Function | Meaning |
|----------|---------|
| eq | Two objects are identical. |
| eql | Two objects are identical, or numbers of the same type have the same value, or characters represent the same character. |
| equal | Two objects are structurally similar. |
| equalp | Numbers of different types have same value. |
| = | Numbers only, ignore type. |
| string-equal | Strings only, ignore character case. |
| string= | Strings only, do not ignore case. |
| char-equal | Characters only, ignore case. |
| char= | Characters only, do not ignore case. |

eq through equalp are listed in order. If two objects satisfy eq, they must satisfy eql, equal, and equalp. If two objects satisfy equal, they must satisfy equalp and may satisfy eq and eql.

```
(eq 'a 'a)
⇒    T

(eq '(a b) '(a b))
⇒    NIL

(equal '(a b) '(a b))
⇒    T

(eq 3.0 3.0)
⇒    NIL

(eql 3.0 3.0)
⇒    T

(eql 3 3.0)
⇒    NIL

(equal 3 3.0)
⇒    NIL

(equalp 3 3.0)
⇒    T

(= 3 3.0)
⇒    T
```

```
(eq "Abc" "abc")
⇒    NIL

(equalp "Abc" "abc")
⇒    T
```

Whenever you test for equality, consider the type of data you are testing and how precise you wish to be. In addition, when testing numbers, if any manipulation has been done with them, it is sometimes best to test whether they are close rather than equal.

```
(= .3333 1/3)
⇒    NIL

(< (- .3333 1/3) .001)
⇒    T
```

## Coercion

One data type can be changed to another in some cases. Any number (except complex) can be converted to a floating-point number or a complex number. A floating-point number can be changed to a ratio.

```
(float 9)
⇒    9.0

(float 5/6)
⇒    0.8333333333333334

(rationalize .3333)
⇒    3333/10000

(coerce "a" 'character)
⇒    #\a

(coerce "a" 'list)
⇒    (#\a)
```

## DEFINING NEW TYPES

The types and, or, not, member, and satisfies specify data types not in the table. The deftype macro gives each of these types a name.

The following example creates the type color.

```
(deftype color () '(member red blue green yellow orange purple))
⇒    COLOR
```

An object is of this type if the symbol is a member of the list.

```
(typep 'purple 'color)
⇒    (PURPLE)

(typep 'green 'color)
⇒    (GREEN YELLOW ORANGE PURPLE)
```

The `member` type returns as its nonnil value the remaining values in the list.
Every object that is not a list can be specified by:

```
(typep 'a '(not list))
⇒    T

(typep '(a) '(not list))
⇒    NIL
```

Every object that is either an alphabetic character or a number can be specified
by:

```
(typep #\a '(satisfies alphanumericp))
⇒    T

(typep #\& '(satisfies alphanumericp))
⇒    NIL
```

You can specify a type of integer between zero and ten with the following:

```
(deftype zero-ten () '(member 0 1 2 3 4 5 6 7 8 9 10))
```

or

```
(deftype zero-ten (x) (and (> x -1) (< x 11) (integerp x)))
```

Several "functions" have more than one meaning. The meaning depends upon how they
are used. Here, `and`, `or`, `not`, and `member` specify types. In the previous section,
they were predicates.

---

**Exercise 3-8**

1. Write a function that determines if an object is a number or a character.
2. If the number is zero, the function should return the symbol `'zero`.
3. If the argument is a character, return that character.
4. If the argument is not a number or a character, return a message that says
   so.

---

## SUMMARY

- What data types are available in Common Lisp?

  There are many data types predefined in Lisp. In addition, you can define your own types.

- How can you determine the type of data? How can you determine if data is a subtype of another data type?

  There are functions that determine the type of data and whether one object is a subtype of another object.

- Which functions operate on each type of data?

  With 700 functions available, many functions operate on each data type.

# 4

## Naming

This chapter is divided into four sections. The first section discusses variable names. The second section discusses functions and how they are defined. The third section examines the scope and extent of variable bindings. The fourth section looks at how variables may be shared between functions.

- What is the difference between sequential and parallel assignments?
- How is a symbol *bound* to a name?
- How is a name bound to a variable?
- What is *binding*?
- How do you define a function?
- Where are variables bound in time and place?
- What happens to variables when they are passed to a function?

### VARIABLE NAMES

Since you usually refer to a data object more than once, it is convenient to name the object rather than having to recalculate the value or rebuild the object. The name is a *symbol.* A *bound* symbol has a value, a memory location. The memory location holds another value, the value of the variable.

The setq special form assigns a value to a variable.

```
(setq {variable form}*)
```

You can set the symbol a to the number 1.

```
(setq a 1)
⇒    1


a
⇒    1
```

Unlike many languages, the type of the data within a variable can change in Lisp. The variable itself does not have a type.

You can rebind the value of a to the string "1".

```
(setq a "1")
⇒     "1"


a
⇒     "1"
```

You can rebind the value of a to the symbol ′ a.

```
(setq a ′a)
⇒     A


a
⇒     A
```

You can rebind the value of a to the list (1).

```
(setq a ′(1))
⇒     (1)


a
⇒     (1)
```

You can rebind the value of a as many times as you wish. It does not matter if the value is a string or a symbol. The value can be any data type.

There are few constraints on the name of a variable. It can be any set of alphanumeric characters. Because it is a symbol, the letters will be printed uppercase. Thus, a and A are the same symbol.

```
(setq a 'b)
⇒    B

(setq A 'c)
⇒    C


a
⇒    C


A
⇒    C
```

The name is a symbol. Thus, any character that can be used in a symbol can be used as the name. The \ character allows characters not normally permitted in a symbol to be used. There is no limit on the length of the name, other than memory limits and practicality.

Here are some examples of variable names.

```
A          B          C
Happy      merry      new-year
miles-per-gallon      12th-night
start-time            end-time
state-1    state-2    state-3
```

Names should be descriptive, where possible, to aid in debugging and later modifications to programs. You might remember while programming that a1 is the mean time between errors, but six months from now you'll probably forget. Part of documenting programs is to use names that most programmers can understand. If your functions become part of a larger program, it is possible that you will not be the one who has to update it later. Make the next programmer's job easier by using descriptive names.

---

**Exercise 4-1**

Which of the following are legal names for variables?

```
a99
open
#\a
99
a-5
12s5
```

```
start-time
|99|
&other
H*@$
```

---

## Numbers

Many times you calculate a number and want to refer to it later. If the calculation is only used once, you need not save the value; however, it is faster to name a variable than to recalculate its value.

When you use constant values in your program, it is often useful to give a variable that value. In this way, if you have to change the value of the constant, you only have to do it once, instead of looking throughout the program for every place the value is used.

Once a symbol is given a value, it can be used instead of the number it represents in all functions.

```
(setq age 20)
⇒    20

(setq time-to-21 (- 21 age))
⇒    1

(setq time-to-21 (- 21 20))
⇒    1
```

You can give values to more than one variable in a single setq form.

```
(setq a 1 b 2 c 3)
⇒    3
```

The value returned by setq is the last value assigned.

In addition to setq, which sets values *sequentially*, there is the psetq macro, which sets values in *parallel*.

```
(setq a 1 b 2)
⇒    2

(psetq a b b a)        ;; set a to the value b (2) and set b to the value a (1)
⇒    NIL

a
⇒    2
```

```
b
⇒    1

(setq a b b a)        ;; set a to the value b (1) then set b to the
⇒    1                ;; value a (1)

a
⇒    1

b
⇒    1
```

## Lists

A variable can represent a list as well as a number.

```
(setq m '(a b c))
⇒    (A B C)

(setq n '((1 2)(a b)))
⇒    ((1 2)(A B))

(setq p (list m n))
⇒    ((A B C)((1 2)(A B)))
```

In this example, the new list p has two elements. Each element is bound by another variable. Thus, if you change an element of the list m, the list p also changes.

```
(setf (car m) 'z)        ;; car returns the first element of a list.
                         ;; setf is similar to setq.  It has the added
                         ;; feature of being able to change a single
                         ;; element of a list.
⇒    Z

p
⇒    ((Z B C) ((1 2) (A B)))
```

Changing an atom of p also changes the related list.

```
(setf (car (car p)) 'p)
⇒    P

p
⇒    ((P B C) ((1 2) (A B)))

m
⇒    (P B C)
```

## makunbound

Once a variable has a value, you can refer to that value for as long as the variable is bound. When you are using a lot of data, you might not need the data after a certain point. To reclaim the memory, you must unbind the variable. The makunbound function does this.

```
(setq a '(a b c))
⇒    (A B C)


a
⇒    (A B C)


(makunbound 'a)
⇒    A


a
⇒    !!!!! Error: The symbol A has no value.
```

## FUNCTION NAMES

In most languages, the names of functions are reserved words. The functions are defined by the implementors of the language, and there is no way to add more. You can write subroutines, subprograms, or procedures, but this isn't the same as creating a new function.

Lisp is built on the principle that you can and should create functions to do everything you want to do. The built-in functions are supplied to get you started.

### Defining a Function

The defun macro is the heart of defining functions. defun defines a function. It binds a name to the function definition. Then you can call the function. For example,

```
(defun cube (x)
  "This function returns the cube of the argument."
  (* x x x))
⇒    CUBE
```

The name cube is the name of the function. It takes one argument. Within the function, this argument is x. The quoted string is the documentation for the function. The body of the function does the work. In this case, it multiplies the argument three times. The returned value is the name of the function.

To use this function, you do the following:

```
(cube 3)
⇒    27

(cube 2)
⇒    8

(cube 9.6)
⇒    884.736

(setq a 12)
⇒    12

(cube a)
⇒    1728
```

If you send a non-number to cube, you get an error.

```
(cube 'b)
⇒      Error:  The argument B is not of type NUMBER.
```

To avoid this problem, you could test if the argument was a number before trying to multiply.

```
(defun cube (x)
   "This function returns the cube of a number."
   (if (numberp x)(* x x x)
                  (list x 'is 'not 'a 'number)))
⇒    CUBE
```

The `if` special form evaluates the first form `(numberp x)`. If the form returns a true value, the next form `(* x x x)` is evaluated. If the first form returns `nil`, the third form `(list x 'is 'not 'a 'number)` is evaluated.

```
(cube 3)
⇒    27

(cube 'b)
⇒    (B IS NOT A NUMBER)
```

There are, of course, more sophisticated methods of error trapping, but they are discussed elsewhere.

## Return Value

A function executes each form in its body. The value returned by the last form is the value returned by the function. In the case of the first cube function, the result of cubing a number is returned. When the `if` special form was added, the result of the `if` was returned.

When you want to see intermediate results, you must ask for them using an output function such as `print`. If `print` is the last form in the function, you will see the output produced by `print` and the result of `print`, which is the result of the function. For example,

```
(defun new-cube (x)
  (print x)
  (* x x x))
⇒    NEW-CUBE


(new-cube 3)
⇒    3              ;; value of x
     27             ;; returned value

(defun miss-cube (x)
  (* x x x)
  (print x))
⇒    MISS-CUBE


(miss-cube 3)
⇒    3              ;; value of x
     3              ;; returned value
```

The result of `(* x x x)` is not output because it was not the last form in the function. The value of x is printed once and the output is the value of the function. `miss-cube` does not do anything right.

## Building Functions

As stated earlier, Lisp functions are built from other Lisp functions. There are a few primitive functions; the remainder of the 700 or so functions are built from the primitives. Similarly, the functions you define will be built from other functions you have defined.

To define a sum-of-squares function, you begin by defining a square function.

```
(defun square (x)
  (* x x))
⇒    SQUARE

(square 2)
⇒    4

(square 32.5)
⇒    1056.25
```

The sum-of-squares function uses the square function.

```
(defun sum-of-squares (x y)
  (+ (square x) (square y)))
⇒     SUM-OF-SQUARES

(sum-of-squares 2 3)
⇒     13

(sum-of-squares 32.5 16)
⇒     1312.25
```

Once a function has been defined, it is available for use as if it were a part of the system. In fact, it is a part of the system until you explicitly remove it or until you end the session.

A function can call itself. The following example shows Newton's Method for finding a square root. (There is a square root function defined in Lisp, so this function is called my-sqrt.)

```
(defun my-sqrt (root x)
  (if (closep root x) root              ;; if the root is close, return it.
    (my-sqrt (improve root x) x)))      ;; else, improve the root approximation
                                        ;; and try again.
⇒     MY-SQRT

(defun closep (root x)                  ;; close is within .001
  (< (abs (- (square root) x)) .001))
⇒     CLOSEP

(defun improve (root x)
  (/ (+ root (/ x root)) 2))            ;; take the average of the root and
                                        ;; the quotient of the number and root.
⇒     IMPROVE
```

To get the square root, you send my-sqrt two values. The first value is your first guess at the value of the root. The second value is the number for which you want the square root.

```
(my-sqrt 1.0 4)
⇒     2.0000000929222947

(my-sqrt 1.0 9)
⇒     3.00009155413138

(my-sqrt 3.0 9)
⇒     3.0
```

```
(my-sqrt 1.0 94)
⇒     9.695393872857231


(sqrt 94)                              ;; system-defined square root function.
⇒     9.695359714832657
```

## Redefining Functions

As with variables, you can change the value or definition of a function. You might decide that closep should be .00001. To do this, simply change the value and reevaluate the function.

---

### Caution

Changing functions is easy. You can attach any name to a function. Be careful not to change the value of a built-in function. Trying to change the value of a built-in function is an error and unexpected results may occur. Your system may have a function that prevents you from changing system functions. Even if it doesn't, when you choose names for your functions, use care. Attaching your name or my before the function name will prevent you from redefining system functions.

---

### fmakunbound

As with variables, you can unbind a function. The fmakunbound function unbinds a symbol from its function definition.

```
(defun nothing ()
  (print "nothing"))
⇒     NOTHING


(nothing)
⇒     "nothing"
      "nothing"


(fmakunbound 'nothing)
⇒     NOTHING


(nothing)
⇒     !!!! Continuable error: Undefined function `NOTHING' applied or called.
```

## defun Syntax

The defun macro has the following syntax:

(defun *name lambda-list* {*declaration*|*doc-string*}* {*form*}*)

While the syntax may look formidable, you have already defined several functions using defun.

| | |
|---|---|
| ***name*** | is the name of the function you are defining. The name can contain as many characters as needed. Letters, numbers, and most keyboard symbols can be used in the name. |
| ***lambda-list*** | is an expression that lists all the variables the function will use. |
| ***declarations*** | contain information about the types of variables. There can be zero or more declarations. |
| ***doc-string*** | is a documentation string that describes the function, variables, or any other comments you want to place in the string. The documentation function returns the *doc-string* of any function. There can be only one documentation string. |
| ***form*** | is the body of the function. The asterisk, *, means there can be zero or more forms. |

In its simplest form, a function definition could look this way:

(defun name ())

This function does nothing. A complex definition could take up several pages. However, most functions fall between the extremes.

## Lambda List

When you define a function using defun, you use the lambda list in the definition. The syntax is

```
({var}*
    [&optional {var| (var [initform [svar]]) }*]
    [&rest var]
    [&key {var| ({var| (keyword var) } [initform [svar]]) }*
            [&allow-other-keys]]
    [&aux {var| (var [initform]) }*])
```

The variables are processed from left to right. First, the required variables are given values from the argument list, then the optional variables are given values, then rest, and key variables.

The variables are not typed.  That is, they can take values of any data type.

**Required Variables.**   The first line, ({*var*}*, is a list of variables that the function requires.  These are the names of the variables that the function uses, not the names of variables that are passed to the function.  There can be zero or more of these variables.  For example,

```
(defun ex-1 (a b c d) ... )

(defun ex-2 (name date address phone) ...)

(defun ex-3 () ...)
```

When the first example function is called, the arguments could look as follows:

```
(ex-1 1 2 3 4)

(ex-1 'a 'b 'c 'd)

(ex-1 () 0 (+ a b) 'hello)
```

**&optional.**   The &optional variables are optional.  There can be zero or more optional variables.

> [&optional {*var*| (*var* [*initform* [*svar*]]) }*]

There can be variable names, variable names followed by initial values, and variable names, initial values followed by a boolean variable that indicates if the variable is using the initial value or one supplied in the call.

```
(defun ex-1 (a b c d &optional e (f 1) (g 3 g-flag))
   (list a b c d e f g g-flag))

(defun ex-2 (&optional (name nil counter)) ...)
```

In calling the first example function, any of the following could be used.

```
(ex-1 1 2 3 4)
⇒    (1 2 3 4 NIL 1 3 NIL)
```

e has the value nil, f has the default value 1, g has the default value 3, and g-flag has the value nil because g used the default value.

```
(ex-1 1 2 3 4 5)
⇒    (1 2 3 4 5 1 3 NIL)
```

e has the value 5, f has the default value 1, g has the default value 3, and g-flag has the value nil.

```
(ex-1 1 2 3 4 5 6)
⇒    (1 2 3 4 5 6 3 NIL)
```

e has the value 5, f has the value 6, g has the default value 3, and g-flag has the value nil.

```
(ex-1 1 2 3 4 5 6 7)
⇒    (1 2 3 4 5 6 7 T)
```

e has the value 5, f has the value 6, g has the value 7, and g-flag has the value t because g was passed a value.

**&rest.**     The &rest variable collects all the remaining arguments into a list. There is only one variable.

[&rest *var*]

```
(defun ex-1 (a b &optional c (d 1 d-flag) &rest e)
  (list a b c d d-flag e))

(defun ex-2 (&rest a) ...)

(defun ex-3 (a b &rest c) ...)
```

The first example could be called as followed:

```
(ex-1 1 2 3 4)
⇒    (1 2 3 4 T NIL)
```

a has the value 1, b has the value 2, c has the value 3, d has the value 4, d-flag has the value t, and e has the value NIL.

```
(ex-1 1 2 3 4 5 6 7 8)
⇒    (1 2 3 4 T (5 6 7 8))
```

e has the value (5 6 7 8).

```
(ex-1 1 2 3 4 5 '(a b) 'd)
⇒    (1 2 3 4 T (5 (A B) D))
```

e has the value (5 (A B) D).

**&key.**   The &key variables specify keywords.  There can be zero or more keywords.  &allow-other-keys specifies if keywords that are not specified in the
definition are also allowed.

[&key {var| ({var| (keyword var)} [initform [svar]]) }*
  [&allow-other-keys]]

There can be variable names, keywords followed by variable names, and these can be
followed by initial values and a supplied-variable flag.  For example,

```
(defun ex-1 (&key start end) ...)

(defun ex-2 (a b &key ((:start start) (:end end))) ...)

(defun ex-3 (&rest a &key (fun 'a) ((:stt begin) 0) ((:finish end)))
       (list a fun begin end))

(defun ex-4 (&optional a &key b &allow-other-keys)
       (list a b))
```

To call the function, the keywords do not have to be used in order, nor do they all have
to be specified.
    In the third example, the call to the function could look as follows:

```
(ex-3  :fun 'd :stt 2 :finish 3)
⇒    ((:FUN D :STT 2 :FINISH 3) "D" 2 3)

(ex-3)
⇒    (NIL "A" 0 NIL)

(ex-3 :stt 5)
⇒    ((:STT 5) "A" 5 NIL)
```

In the fourth example, the call could look as follows:

```
(ex-4 1 :b 2 :xyz 3)
⇒    (1 2)
```

a has the value 1 and b has the value 2. :xyz 3 is ignored.

```
(ex-4 :b 'a)
⇒    !!!!! Error: No value for keyword A
```

This will cause an error. a gets the value :b. The next argument is not a keyword pair. Whenever &optional appears before &key, the optional values must be specified if any keyword values are specified.

**&aux.** The &aux variables are auxiliary. The function call cannot supply values to these variables. These variables are local to the function.

```
[&aux {var| (var [initform]) }*])

(ex-1 (a &optional b &rest c &key d &aux e (f 1) (g 2)) ...)
```

## Lambda Expressions

The lambda expression consists of lambda, a lambda list, and a body. The *lambda expression* defines an unnamed function. You can use a lambda expression wherever a function name is required. Thus, if you are going to use a function only once, you do not have to define the function; instead, you can use a lambda expression.

```
(lambda lambda-list . body)
```

The lambda expression is also a method by which you can explore how to use the lambda list.

```
((lambda (a b c) (list a b c)) 1 2 3)
⇒    (1 2 3)
```

The unnamed function is passed three values, 1, 2, and 3. The function lists the values. The following examples show how values are used in the lambda list.

```
((lambda (a &optional b &rest c &key d) (list a b c d)) 1 2 :d 3)
⇒    (1 2 (:D 3) 3)

((lambda (a &optional b &rest c &key d) (list a b c d)) 1 :d 3)
⇒    !!!!! Error: No value for keyword 3

((lambda (a b &optional (c 1 d) e &rest f &key (g 1)((:s k) 5))
   (list a b c d e f g k) )
   1 2)
⇒    (1 2 1 NIL NIL NIL 1 5)

((lambda (a b &optional (c 1 d) e &rest f &key (g 1)((:s k) 5))
   (list a b c d e f g k) )
   'a 'b 'c 'e :g 10)
⇒    (A B C T E (:G 10) 10 5)
```

```
((lambda (a b &optional (c 1 d) e &rest f &key (g 1)((:s k) 5))
   (list a b c d e f g k) )
  ·1 2 ' (a b) 'a :s 3)
⇒    (1 2 (A B) T A (:S 3) 1 3)

((lambda (a b &optional (c 1 d) e &rest f &key (g 1)((:s k) 5))
   (list a b c d e f g k) )
   1 2 3 4 :g 5 :s 6)
⇒    (1 2 3 T 4 (:G 5 :S 6) 5 6)

((lambda (&key a (b 1) ((:c d) 4) &allow-other-keys)
   (list a b d))
   :a 1 :b 2 :c 3 :d 4 :e 5)
⇒    (1 2 3)
```

---

**Exercise 4-2**

What do the following lambda expressions return?

1.  ```
    ((lambda (x &optional y &rest z &key a)
        (list x y z a))
        1 2 :a 3)
    ```

2.  ```
    ((lambda (&optional (a 1) &key r)
        (list a r))
        :r 'r)
    ```

3.  ```
    ((lambda (&optional (a 1) &key r)
        (list a r))
        12 :r 'r)
    ```

4.  ```
    ((lambda (&rest a &key (m 'def x) ((:q n)))
        (list a m x n))
        :m 12 :q 5)
    ```

5.  ```
    ((lambda (&rest a &key (m 'def x) ((:q n)))
        (list a m x n)))
    ```

6.  ```
    ((lambda (&optional a (b 'c) (d 1 r))
        (list a b d r)))
    ```

7.  ```
    ((lambda (&optional a (b 'c) (d 1 r))
        (list a b d r))
        1 2)
    ```

8.  ```
    ((lambda (&optional a (b 'c) (d 1 r))
        (list a b d r))
        'a 'b 'c)
    ```

Write a lambda list that takes the following arguments and prints them.

**9.** Three arguments are required. One additional argument can be supplied.

**10.** One argument is required. The keyword test is optional; its value is held by the variable x.

**11.** The variable x holds a list of all the arguments passed. Three keywords can be supplied. Their default values are 1, 2, and 3.

## Declarations

Declarations state how a function is going to use its arguments. You can also make declarations that specify how the interpreter and compiler look at the function. For example,

```
(defun ex (a)
  "a is always a fixnum,
   speed is very important"
  (declare (type fixnum a)
           (optimize (speed 3))))
  ...
  )
```

type specifies that the variables that follow are a specified data type. This allows the interpreter and compiler to make assumptions about the variables. Depending on the implementation, space allocations for the variables could be made differently than if the variables were left with no declaration.

optimize specifies where the interpreter and compiler can take "liberties" to optimize the speed, compilation-speed, space, or safety of the code. A zero value means the quality is not important. A three value means the quality is very important.

ftype specifies that when functions are called from this function, they require a particular number and type of variables and they will return a particular type of value. For example,

```
(defun ex()
  (declare (ftype (function (number) number) sin)
           (ftype (function (list number) list) my-fun2))
  ...)
```

This example shows that the sin function requires one numeric argument and returns a numeric result. The my-fun2 function requires two arguments, a list and a numeric, and returns a list.

special names the variables as special. They can be used by functions called from this function. (More on the scope and the extent in the next section.) For example,

```
(defun ex (a)
  (declare (special a))
  (ex2)
  ...)
```

In this example, ex2 can use the variable a as if the variable were bound outside of any function. The next section shows how this is not normally the case.

## SCOPE AND EXTENT

When a variable appears in a lambda list, the symbol naming the variable is bound to the variable while the function is executing. When control leaves the function, the same symbol can be unbound or bound to another variable. For example,

```
(defun test (x)
   x)
⇒    TEST

(setq x 3)     ;; give x the value 3
⇒   3

(test 10)      ;; while in function test, x has the value 10
⇒    10        ;; this is the result of the test function

x              ;; after leaving test, x has the value 3
⇒   3


(defun test2 (x y)
  (test y)
  (print x)
   y)           ;; if print were used here, the value of y would be output twice,
                ;; once as the result of print and once as the result of test2.
⇒    TEST2

(setq x 10)
⇒   10

(setq y 20)
⇒   20

(test2 1 2)
⇒    2          ; within test, x has the value 2
     1          ; within test2, x has the value 1
     2          ; within test2, y has the value 2
```

```
x
⇒    10            ; outside the functions, x has the value 10


y
⇒    20            ; outside the functions, y has the value 20
```

The above functions show that the symbols naming variables within the lambda list are independent of the same symbol naming variables outside the function.

While in a function, a symbol that does not appear in the lambda list retains its value in the function.

```
(defun another-test (a)
  (print a)
   b)
⇒    ANOTHER-TEST

(setq a 10)
⇒    10

(setq b 'name)
⇒    NAME

(another-test 'phone)
⇒    PHONE            ; a has the value 'phone
     NAME             ; b still has the value 'name
```

You can change the value of a parameter within the function and not change the value of any variable outside the function.

```
(defun ex-1 (a b)
  (print a)
  (setq a (+ a b))
  (print a)
   b)
⇒    EX-1

(setq a 1 b 2)
⇒    2

(ex-1 10 20)
⇒    10
     30
     20

a
⇒    1
```

```
b
⇒    2
```

If the symbol within the lambda list has no value outside the function, it still has no value when the function completes execution.

```
(defun why? (nothing)
  (print nothing))
⇒    WHY?

(why? 'blank)
⇒    BLANK
      BLANK

nothing
⇒    !!!!! Error: The symbol NOTHING has no value.
```

You can check if a symbol is bound to a value using the boundp function.

```
(boundp 'nothing)
⇒    NIL

(boundp 'x)
⇒    T
```

If a symbol has a value outside of the function and the same symbol is not included in the parameter list, the symbol maintains its outside value.

```
(defun ex-2 ()
  (print outside)
  nil)
⇒    EX-2

(setq outside 12)
⇒    12

(ex-2)
⇒    12
      NIL

(defun ex3 ()
  (setq a 3))
⇒    EX3

(ex3)
⇒    3

a
⇒    3
```

## Scope — Textual Area

The scope of an object is the area within a program that can refer to the object. There are two terms that describe scope: lexical scope and indefinite scope. A *lexical scope* symbol is one that can only be used within the construct that defined it, for example, within a function. An *indefinite scope* symbol is one that can be used anywhere, for example, all predefined Lisp symbols.

In the following diagram, the functions can refer to any object defined in any region below them; that is, in the user package, the system environment, and, if the implementation supports it, the operating system.

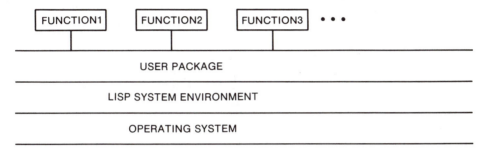

**Figure 4-1**

The user package is the area that you have been using that is not inside a function. When you set values to variables outside a function, you were in the user package. The name of the package can change with implementations. In the author's system, the default package is the user package. Other packages can also be used. If two people are using the same system for their work, they may wish to be in two different packages. In that way, the variables defined in one package do not conflict with variables defined in the other package. The functions defined in one package belong to that package. (Chapter 18 describes more on packages.)

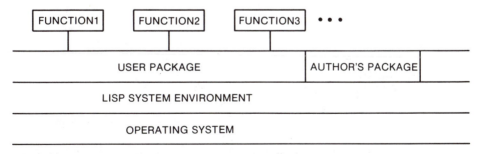

**Figure 4-2**

When a symbol is used within a function, a value is looked for first in the function, then in the package, and then in the system environment. When a value is found, the search stops and that value is used. If the symbol has no value, that is, it is unbound, an error occurs.

If one function calls another function, the called function cannot see the symbols in the calling function. When looking for values, if the function does not have a value, the next place to look is the package, not the calling function.

The next example shows symbols being bound and used in two functions. The diagram that follows places the symbols at the proper level.

```
(defun fun1 (a b)
  (list a b c))
⇒    FUN1

(defun fun2 (b c)
  (fun1 d b))
⇒    FUN2

(setq a 'a b 'b c 'c d 'd)
⇒    D

(list a b c d)
⇒    (A B C D)

(fun2 a d)
⇒    (D A C)
```

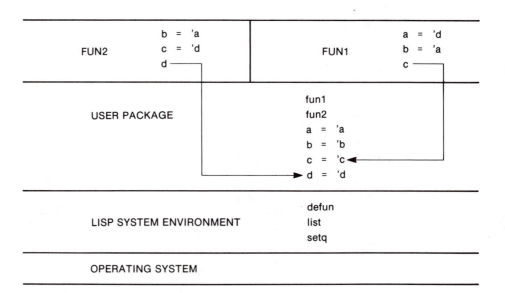

**Figure 4-3**

## Extent — Time

The *extent* of an object is the length of time during which it can be accessed. Again, there are two terms that describe extent: indefinite extent and dynamic extent. *Indefinite extent* pertains to objects that exist as long as it is possible to refer to them, for example, function parameters. *Dynamic extent* refers to objects that can be referenced any time from when they are first established to when they are explicitly disestablished, for example, variables in a package.

There are other ways to establish dynamic extent variables. A function can create a *closure*, which allows a variable to exist longer than the function. In this way, a calling function can share an object with the called function.

```
(setq a 'a)
⇒    A

(defun test (a)
  (declare (special a))
    (test2 )))
⇒    TEST

(defun test2 ()
  (list a))

(test 1)
⇒    (1)

a
⇒    A
```

When test2 lists the value of variable a, it looks back to the global value of a, which is temporarily the value test gave to it. After test finishes, the value of a returns to A.

---

### Exercise 4-3

Use the following functions to answer the questions.

```
(setq a 1 b 2 c 3)
⇒    3

(defun ex1 ()
  (print b)
  (ex3))
⇒    EX1
```

```
(defun ex2 (b)
  (declare (special b))
  (ex1)
  (ex3)
  (print b))
⇒     EX2

(defun ex3 ()
  (print c))
⇒     EX3
```

1. Given the functions above, what are the printed values?

```
(ex3)
(ex2 a)
(ex1)
```

2. In ex3, what does c refer to?
3. In ex1, what does b refer to?
4. If ex1 is changed,

```
(defun ex1 ()
  (print b)
  (setq b 5)
  (ex3))
⇒     EX1
```

What is the printed result of the following?

```
(ex2 a)
```

5. What is the value of b outside the functions?
6. Why?

---

## THE let SPECIAL FORM

When you use setq within a defun, if the variable is not in the lambda list, it is a global variable. This is shown in ex-1 in the fourth exercise in Exercise 4-3. In most cases, it is not desirable to make a global variable from within a function. If you do, the function cannot be used within a larger program because there could be conflicts with the variables. The let special form provides a means of giving a variable a value without making a global variable.

```
(let ({var| (var value) }*) {declarations}* {forms}*)
```

`let` evaluates the forms with the variables specified set to specific values. When `let` is done, the variables are no longer bound or are re-bound to previous values.

For example,

```
(setq a 1)
⇒    1

(setq c 'empty)
⇒    EMPTY

(let (a b (c 1))
  (setq b '(1 2 3))
  (setq a (list (+ c (car b)) (+ c (cadr b)) (+ c (caddr b))))
  (print a)
  (print b)
   c)
⇒    (2 3 4)
     (1 2 3)
     1


a
⇒    1


b
⇒    !!!!! Error: The symbol B has no value.


c
⇒    EMPTY
```

Within the `let`, the variables are set to values. Outside the `let`, they retain the values they had before the `let`.

`let` can appear within a function. For example,

```
(defun shuffle-deck (deck)
   (cond ((equal nil deck) nil)
         (t (let ((index (random (length deck))))
              (cons (nth index deck)
                    (shuffle-deck (append (subseq deck 0 index)
                                          (subseq deck (1+ index)))))))))
```

In this function, the variable index is used three times. Because `random` generates a different number each time it is called, it is not possible to use the `random` function wherever the index is needed. In addition, you do not want the calling function to have to supply a variable for the index. Thus, there are two ways to provide this variable without making it a global variable. (1) the `&aux` lambda variable supplies a variable with no value and  (2) the `let` special form supplies a variable and in this case gives it a value.

Another use of `let` allows two functions to share a variable without making the variable special.

```
(let ((count 0))
  (defun count-one (n)
    (if (equal (car n) t) (setq count (+ 1 count)))
    (count-two n))
  (defun count-two (x)
    (if (equal (cadr x) t) (setq count (+ 2 count)))
    count))
⇒    COUNT-TWO

(count-one '(t nil))
⇒    1

(count-one '(t t))
⇒    4

(count-one '(t nil))
⇒    5
```

The variables specified within `let` has lexical scope and indefinite extent.  Only `count-one` and `count-two` can "see" the variable count.  Since the variable has indefinite extent, it is available at any time (i.e., its value is not reset at each call to either function.) Outside the functions, the variable has no value.

```
count
⇒    !!!!! Error: The symbol COUNT has no value.
```

## SUMMARY

There were several topics covered in this chapter.

- *Variable Names.*  The name of a variable is a symbol.  This symbol can take any value, any data type, and can be changed at will.
- *Function Names.*  Function names are also symbols.  You should not redefine a system function.  Once you define your own functions, Lisp treats them as if they were system functions.
- *Defining Functions.*  The `defun` macro defines new functions.  Within this definition you can declare variables used by the function to be a specific type or special.  You can give the interpreter or compiler information about the function. You describe the arguments the function expects when called.  And, finally, you list the forms to be evaluated when the function is called.

- *Scope and Extent.* This refers to symbols with values and what those values are. A variable bound in one function is not necessarily bound in another function. The declarations in a function can change the scope of a variable.

# 5

## The Environment

### LISP REMEMBERS EVERYTHING YOU DO

When you evaluate a function definition, Lisp remembers the definition. When you give a value to a variable, Lisp remembers the value. You can enter a file of functions, evaluate them, change variable values, save files, read files, and do most anything except turn off the power. Lisp remembers each function and variable. Once evaluated, the functions and variables have a meaning unless you explicitly tell Lisp to forget (with `fmakunbound` or `makunbound`).

Each time you make a list or refer to a symbol, Lisp keeps all the information available so you can refer to that same list or symbol later.

Because Lisp can be run interactively, you can write functions and debug them without having to worry about compiling. Once you have a function that satisfies you, you can go on to the next function and debug it. The first function remains in memory. The second function can refer to it. There is no problem with linking and loading. If you find a problem (read bug) in the first function, you can go back and change that function. The second function does not necessarily have to be changed because of a bug in the first function. (If the first function is actually a macro, then any function that refers to the macro will have to be reevaluated. This is the nature of macros.)

## GARBAGE COLLECTION

Whenever Lisp does a cons, it uses memory. Much of what is consed is not needed past the current operation. This is referred to as garbage. When you unbind a function or variable, there is no longer a way to refer to that function or variable, yet the definition or value is still taking up memory. More garbage.

Garbage collection is an operation that cleans up the mess. It can occur when there is no free memory available or at specific times. This is implementation dependent. Anything to which a function can no longer refer is considered garbage and is collected. That area of memory is marked as free for other use. At the same time, other memory management tasks can be done.

The method of garbage collection and the tasks done are implementation dependent. When garbage collection occurs, everything else stops. If you are running a program, execution halts until the garbage collection is complete. In Common Lisp, there is no way to force a garbage collection. Many implementations have added a function that causes the garbage collection to occur. This function can be used before a sensitive piece of code, such as benchmarks or any code requiring timing.

## FOR PROGRAMMERS OF OTHER LANGUAGES

If you have ever programmed in C, Fortran, Pascal, Basic, or any of the other numeric programming languages, you have already noticed many differences between Lisp and the other languages. Parenthesis are one difference. No line numbers are another difference.

### Sequential, Numeric Programming

Top-down programming and structured programming are two terms frequently used to describe well-constructed numeric programs. In Basic, you can write a nice main program that refers to subprograms that appear later in the program. In Pascal, you have declarations at the beginning of the program, the main program and procedures. In Lisp, each subprogram or procedure is a function. And the functions generally appear in the reverse order of subprograms or procedures. (The examples will show this later.) In addition, in Lisp if you have a function that loads another file, the old functions still reside in memory and can be used by the new file. Lisp does not care where the functions come from. Whether they are user-defined or system-defined, Lisp simply looks up the symbol and tries to get a definition for that function.

### Programs

There are no programs in Lisp. Instead, you write functions and macros to do the work of a program. While macros must be defined before the functions that use them, the order in which functions are defined is not important.

There is no END statement in Lisp.  There is also no BEGIN.  Because there are no programs, there is no need to delimit the beginning and end of a sequence of steps. A function simply begins with an opening parentheses and ends with a closing parentheses.

The following programs all do approximately the same thing.  They shuffle a deck of cards and print the result.  The program is written in Basic, Pascal, and Lisp.  Use this example program to compare the way in which programs are written.

## The BASIC Program

```
100 REM PROGRAM CARD DEAL
105
110 REM NUMBER OF CARDS IN A DECK
115 LET SIZE = 52
120
125 REM ARRAY OF CARDS
130 DIM DECK(52)
135
140 REM FIND THE RANK NUMBER OF THE CARD
145 DEF GET-RANK(CARD) = CARD - 13*INT((CARD-S)/13)
150
155 REM FIND THE SUIT NUMBER OF THE CARD
160 DEF GET-SUIT(CARD) = INT((CARD-1)/13) + 1
165
170 REM ******** MAIN PROGRAM ***********************************
175
180 FOR I = 1 TO SIZE
185     LET DECK(I) = I
190 NEXT I
195
200 GO SUB 265
205
210 FOR I = 1 TO SIZE
215     LET CARD = DECK(I)
220     GO SUB 330
225     GO SUB 640
230     PRINT RANK$; " OF "; SUIT$; "    ";
235 NEXT I
240
245 STOP
250
255 REM ********** SHUFFLE SUBROUTINE  ****************************
260
265
270 LET INDEX = 0
275 LET TEMP-CARD = 0
280
285 FOR I = SIZE TO 1 STEP -1
```

```
290    LET INDEX = INT(RND*I + 1)
295    LET TEMP-CARD = DECK(INDEX)
300    LET TEMP-DECK(INDEX) = DECK(I)
305    LET DECK(I) = TEMP-CARD
310 NEXT I
315
320 RETURN
325
330 REM **************** RANK SUBROUTINE ********************
340
350 LET RANK = GET-RANK (CARD)
355 IF RANK > 7 THEN 365
360    ON R GOTO 375, 395, 415, 435, 455, 475
365    ON R GOTO 495, 515, 535, 555, 575, 595, 615
370
375 REM RANK=1 ACE
380    LET RANK$ = "ACE"
385    GOTO 630
390
395 REM RANK=2 DUCE
400    LET RANK$ = "TWO"
405    GOTO 630
410
415 REM RANK=3 THREE
420    LET RANK$ = "THREE"
425    GOTO 630
430
435 REM RANK=4 FOUR
440    LET RANK$ = "FOUR"
445    GOTO 630
450
455 REM RANK=5 FIVE
460    LET RANK$ = "FIVE"
465    GOTO 630
470
475 REM RANK=6 SIX
480    LET RANK$ = "SIX"
485    GOTO 630
490
495 REM RANK=7 SEVEN
500    LET RANK$ = "SEVEN"
505    GOTO 630
510
515 REM RANK=8 EIGHT
520    LET RANK$ = "EIGHT"
525    GOTO 630
530
535 REM RANK=9 NINE
540    LET RANK$ = "NINE"
```

```
545      GOTO 630
550
555 REM RANK=10 TEN
560      LET RANK$ = "TEN"
565      GOTO 630
570
575 REM RANK=11 JACK
580      LET RANK$ = "JACK"
585      GOTO 630
590
595 REM RANK=12 QUEEN
600      LET RANK$ = "QUEEN"
605      GOTO 630
610
615 REM RANK=13 KING
620      LET RANK$ = "KING"
625
630 RETURN
635
640 REM ***************** SUIT SUBROUTINE **********************
650
660 LET SUIT = GET-SUIT(CARD)
665 ON SUIT GOTO  675, 695, 715, 735
670
675 REM SUIT=1 CLUBS
680      LET SUIT$ = "CLUBS"
685      GOTO 750
690
695 REM SUIT=2 DIAMONDS
700      LET SUIT$ = "DIAMONDS"
705      GOTO 750
710
715 REM SUIT=3 HEARTS
720      LET SUIT$ = "HEARTS"
725      GOTO 750
730
735 REM SUIT=4 SPADES
740      LET SUIT$ = "SPADES"
745
750 RETURN
755
760 REM ***********************************************************
765 END
```

## The Pascal Program

```pascal
PROGRAM deck_of_cards(input,output);

CONST
   size=52;                          {52 cards in a deck}
TYPE
   rank_type = (bad_rank,ace,two,three,four,five,six,
                seven,eight,nine,ten,jack,queen,king);
   suit_type = (bad_suit,spades,hearts,clubs,diamonds);
   card_type = RECORD
                  rank : rank_type;
                  suit : suit_type;
               END;
   deck_type = ARRAY[0..size] OF card_type; {extra card "slot" 0}
VAR
   deck : deck_type;


{External Random Number Function}
FUNCTION $alias '_rand'$ random(s : integer): integer; external;

PROCEDURE initialize_deck;   {make initial card-slot assignments}
VAR
   i : integer;
BEGIN
  FOR i := 0 TO size DO
    BEGIN
      CASE ((i MOD 13) + 1) OF
       0 : deck[i].rank := bad_rank;
       1 : deck[i].rank := ace;
       2 : deck[i].rank := two;
       3 : deck[i].rank := three;
       4 : deck[i].rank := four;
       5 : deck[i].rank := five;
       6 : deck[i].rank := six;
       7 : deck[i].rank := seven;
       8 : deck[i].rank := eight;
       9 : deck[i].rank := nine;
      10 : deck[i].rank := ten;
      11 : deck[i].rank := jack;
      12 : deck[i].rank := queen;
      13 : deck[i].rank := king;
      END;
```

```
      CASE (((i DIV 13) MOD 4) + 1) OF
        0 : deck[i].suit := bad_suit;
        1 : deck[i].suit := spades;
        2 : deck[i].suit := hearts;
        3 : deck[i].suit := clubs;
        4 : deck[i].suit := diamonds;
      END;
    END;
END; {procedure}


PROCEDURE shuffle_deck;
VAR
  i,r : INTEGER;
BEGIN
  FOR i := 1 TO size DO           {for every card do}
    BEGIN
      REPEAT
        r := random(1) MOD size; {get random number}
      UNTIL r > 0;               {make sure it is non-zero}
      deck[0] := deck[i];        {use 0 slot to hold card}
      deck[i] := deck[r];        {swap with random card}
      deck[r] := deck[0];        {put held card back in deck}
    END;
END; {procedure}


PROCEDURE print_card(x : INTEGER);
BEGIN
  write(deck[x].rank:8,' of ',deck[x].suit:8);
END; {procedure}


PROCEDURE print_deck;
VAR
   i : integer;
BEGIN
  for i := 1 to size do print_card(i);
  writeln;
END; {procedure}


BEGIN {main}
  initialize_deck;
  print_deck;
  shuffle_deck;
  print_deck;
END.
```

## The Lisp "Program"

```
;;;;;;;;;;;;;;;;;;;;;;;;;;;;;;;;;;;;;;;;;;;;;;;;;;;;;;;;;;;;;;;;;
;
; File:          chapter5
; SCCS:          %A% %G% %U%
; Description:   The basic shuffle program in Lisp
; Author:        Wendy L. Milner
; Created:       3-Nov-86
; Modified:
; Language:      Lisp
; Package:       USER
; Status:        Experimental (Do Not Distribute)
;
; (c) Copyright 1986, Wendy L. Milner, all rights reserved.
;
;;;;;;;;;;;;;;;;;;;;;;;;;;;;;;;;;;;;;;;;;;;;;;;;;;;;;;;;;;;;;;;;;



;;
;; shuffle lists all the available cards.
;; It calls shuffle-deck to do the actual shuffling.

(defun shuffle ()
  "shuffle returns a list of 52 cards which are in random order"
  (shuffle-deck '((two spades) (three spades) (four spades) (five spades)
                 (six spades) (seven spades) (eight spades) (nine spades)
                 (ten spades) (jack spades) (queen spades) (king spades)(ace spades)
                 (two diamonds) (three diamonds) (four diamonds) (five diamonds)
                 (six diamonds) (seven diamonds) (eight diamonds) (nine diamonds)
                 (ten diamonds) (jack diamonds) (queen diamonds) (king diamonds)
                 (ace diamonds)
                 (two hearts) (three hearts) (four hearts) (five hearts)
                 (six hearts) (seven hearts) (eight hearts) (nine hearts)
                 (ten hearts) (jack hearts) (queen hearts) (king hearts)(ace hearts)
                 (two clubs) (three clubs) (four clubs) (five clubs)
                 (six clubs) (seven clubs) (eight clubs) (nine clubs)
                 (ten clubs) (jack clubs) (queen clubs) (king clubs) (ace clubs))))

;;
;; shuffle-deck begins with the full deck.
;; A random card is taken from the deck and placed on the shuffled deck.
;; shuffle-deck is called with the remaining deck.
;;
```

```
(defun shuffle-deck (deck)
  (cond ((equal nil deck) nil)
        (t  (let ((index (random (length deck))))
              (cons (nth index deck)
                    (shuffle-deck (append (subseq deck 0 index)
                                          (subseq deck (1+ index)))))))))))))
```

```
;;
;; get-suit looks at the second element of the symbols which identify
;; a card '(five clubs).
;;
```

```
(defun get-suit (card)
  (cadr card))
```

```
;;
;; get-rank looks at the first element of the symbols which identify
;; a card.
;;
```

```
(defun get-rank (card)
  (car card))
```

```
;;
;; print-card prints the name of the rank and the name of the suit.
;; It prints a carriage return so each card is printed on a new line.
;;
```

```
(defun print-card (card)
  (format t "~a of ~a~%" (get-rank card) (get-suit card)))
```

```
;;
;; print-deck sends print-card a card and removes that card from
;; the deck.  print-deck is called with the remaining deck.
;;
```

```
(defun print-deck (deck)
  (cond ((equal nil deck) nil)
        (t (print-card (car deck))
           (print-deck (cdr deck)))))
```

```
;;
;; card-deal is the "main" program.
;; To run this set of function, evaluate (card-deal)
;;
```

```
(defun card-deal ()
  (print-deck (shuffle)))
```

## What To Compare

The three programs are presented here mainly so that you can see what a Lisp "program" looks like and compare it with either a Basic or Pascal program. The functionality of all three programs is equivalent. The approach to programming in all three is different. In addition, you might compare code size and ease of programming.

*Code Size.* Count the number of lines of code that do work (leave out comments and blanks).

    Basic  - 64
    Pascal - 77
    Lisp   - 29

The Lisp program is less than half the size of the Basic and Pascal programs. Also, the Lisp program is broken down into small pieces, which makes it easier to debug.

*Ease of Use.* The Lisp functions do not change the value of **any** variable. Thus, you could take one of the functions and insert it into another "program" without having to worry about name conflicts. In addition, you could write a function, for example, to deal "hands" instead of dealing the entire deck, which could be added to the "program" file without having to change any of the other functions.

Because the Basic subroutines change the values of variables, it would not be easy to lift the routines and place them in other programs. Similarly, adding a new function would mean changing the entire program.

The Pascal program uses fewer global variables, so adding procedures or porting them to another program is not difficult. However, Pascal programs must be compiled before they are run. Lisp functions can be run without compiling. Once each function is known to be correct, they can be compiled for increased execution speed.

## SUMMARY

Each programming language has its own unique features. Each language also has a set of problems that it handles better than other languages. Lisp is a list-processing language. Basic and Pascal are more number oriented. This does not mean Lisp doesn't do numbers. It simply means that given a problem with lists, Lisp does it better.

# PART 2
## Programming Constructs

**6**

# *Blocking Constructs*

If you drive a car to work, you pick the shortest route to get there. If you ride your bike, you may use a different route, one based on less traffic and smoother roads. If you walk, you probably use some shortcuts. The problem remains the same whether you drive, ride, or walk. You have to go from home to work. The route you take can vary, but the results are the same. You get to work on time. (You hope.)

A similar situation arises in computer programming. You have a problem to solve. It may be to translate a cryptogram or to determine the feasibility of a shuttle launch. There are many ways to solve the problem. You can use brute force, iteration, recursion, a straightforward approach, or little tricks and shortcuts. If you come up with a solution, you have solved the problem.

While there are many ways to solve problems, there are some methods that lend themselves better to certain types of problems. Recursion is great when a large problem can be repeatedly broken down into a single small problem and the rest of the problem. Iteration is useful when the same procedure is repeated multiple times.

Part 2 contains chapters on different methods of solving problems. Chapter 6 introduces how segments of functions can be blocked. This is not football blocking, but rather indicating a beginning and end of a segment that can be entered and exited. Chapter 7 explains how blocks of code can be conditionally evaluated. Chapter 8 shows how a block can be repeated multiple times. Chapter 9 introduces recursion.

## SYNTAX FORMAT

The following chapters describe the functions, macros, special forms, variables, and constants that constitute Common Lisp. A specific format is used to show the syntax of the forms. In order for you to understand the forms, you must understand the symbols and type fonts used to show the syntax.

### Constants

A *constant* has a value that cannot be changed. For example, `pi` has an approximate value of $\pi$. Trying to change the value of `pi`, or trying to bind the constant to another value causes an error. When the constant is shown in text, it appears in `this type font`.

```
example-constant
```

If the constant is used as a form, parentheses do not appear around the constant name. (If you want the value of `pi`, you type `pi` and execute the form. You do not put `pi` within parentheses.)

### Variables

A *system variable* has a value that can be changed. For example, `*print-circle*` has a value that if true directs the reader to check for circular structures before printing, and if `nil` directs the reader to print without checking for circular structures. The user can set the value of `*print-circle*` depending on whether or not checking is desired. When the variable is shown in text, it appears in `this type font`.

```
*example-variable*
```

If the variable is used as a form, parentheses do not appear around the variable name. (If you want the value of `*print-circle*`, you type `*print-circle*` and execute the form. You do not put `*print-circle*` within parentheses.)

### Functions

A *function* has a definition and returns a value. Its parameters are evaluated before the function is called. There are several elements to the format used to describe a function. The function name appears in `this type font`. Parameters to the function appear in *this type font*. Keywords appear in `this type font`. Lambda keywords (&key, &optional, and &rest) appear in the normal text font.

(example-function *parameter1 parameter2* &key :key1 :key2)

When the function is used as a form, it is enclosed in parentheses. Thus, the syntax shows the function within parentheses. This is a different notation from what appears in the Steele[1] book. The meaning has not changed, only the method of representing the function has been changed, and then the added parentheses are the only change.

The lambda keywords are described fully in a previous chapter about defun. When you see a lambda keyword in the syntax of a function, it is a description of the parameters that follow.

&optional    Indicates that all parameters that follow are optional. When you type the function, you do not type the word &optional. The optional parameters have default values. If you do not specify an optional parameter, its default value is used by the function.

If the syntax for the function is:

(opt-function &optional *para1 para2*)

you can type:

```
(opt-function)
(opt-function first-var)
(opt-function first-var second-var)
```

where first-var and second-var have some value acceptable to the function.

&rest    Indicates that the parameter that follows can be repeated an indefinite number of times. Whatever values appear are collected in a list and given to the function.

If the syntax for the function is:

(res-function *para1* &rest *para2*)

you can type:

```
(res-function first-var)
(res-function first-var second-var)
(res-function first-var second-var third-var fourth fifth sixth)
```

where the variables have some value acceptable to the function.

&key    Indicates that keywords are accepted. The accepted keywords are given. You type the keyword and a value. You do not have to specify all the keywords, nor do you have to specify them in the order shown. Keywords that are not specified have a default value.

If &optional parameters precede &key parameters, the &optional parameters **must** be specified in order to specify the &key parameters.

If the syntax for the function is:

---

[1]    *Common Lisp: The Language* by Guy Steele, Jr.

```
(key-function para1 &optional para2 &key :key1 :key2)
```

you can type:

```
(key-function first-var)
(key-function first-var second-var)
(key-function first-var second-var :key1 key-var1)
(key-function first-var second-var :key2 key-var2)
(key-function first-var second-var :key1 key-var1 :key2 key-var2)
```

where the variables have some value acceptable to the function.

## Macros and Special Forms

A macro expands into a form that is translated into function calls or special forms. Its parameters are not evaluated before they are passed to the macro.

A special form deals with program control or bindings.

When the macro or special form is used as a form, it is enclosed in parentheses. Macros and special forms use the same format symbols.

{ }    Braces surround an item or set of items that can be followed by an asterisk or plus, and can contain a bar. You do not type the braces.

*       An asterisk indicates that the preceding item can be repeated zero or more times. Do not type the asterisk.

If the syntax for the macro is:

```
(mac {para1 para2}*)
```

you can type:

```
(mac)
(mac var1 var2)
(mac var1 var2 var3 var4)
(mac var1 var2 var3 var4 var5 var6 var7 var8)
```

Because there are two parameters within the brace, the arguments must appear in pairs.

+       A plus indicates that the preceding item can be repeated one or more times. Do not type the plus.

If the syntax for the macro is:

```
(mac para1+)
```

you can type:

```
(mac var1)
(mac var1 var2)
(mac var1 var2 var3 var4 var5)
```

[ ]        Brackets indicate that the enclosed item can appear zero or one times. Do not type the brackets.

If the syntax for the macro is:

```
(mac [para1])
```

you can type:

```
(mac)
(mac var1)
```

|          A bar indicates that the items it separates are mutually exclusive. Only one of the items can appear. Do not type the bar.

For example, if the syntax for the macro is:

```
(mac {para1|para2})
```

you can type:

```
(mac var1)
(mac var2)
```

---

Up till now, you have been executing functions one at a time. In the exercises where you created your own functions, the body of the defun listed the functions in the order they were to be executed. The first function was executed first; the second, second; and so forth through the last. After the last function, the defun was exited. This top-down method of programming is perhaps the easiest to learn. However, it doesn't always solve the problems. There are times when you want to exit the defun before all the functions are executed. Or, you might want to jump over one section of code and execute another section.

This chapter looks at four blocking constructs: blocks, catch and throw, tagbodies and protection blocks (as opposed to protection rackets).

## BLOCKS AND RETURNS

A block is a section of code that can have a name. Within a defun, the entire body is implicitly declared a block with the name being the same as the function's name. You can also declare you own blocks.

The block special form provides a named structure. The forms are evaluated, and the value of the last form is returned as the value of block. If a return-from or return is encountered, the *result* value is returned, and the block is exited.

```
(block name {form}*)
```

```
(return-from name [result])
```

```
(return [result])
```

return exits a block named NIL. return-from exits a block that matches the *name*. The return must occur lexically within the block. For example,

```
(block name
  ...
  ...
  (if x (return-from name))
  ...
  )
```

*name* must be a symbol. It is not evaluated in either the block or return-from.

In the following example, a block named nil is created. Since there is no return, all the functions within the block are executed in order. The value returned by the block in this case is the value of the last form.

```
(block nil
   (print 'abc)
   (print 'ghi))
⇒     ABC
      GHI
      GHI
```

In the next example, a return causes execution to skip over the forms after the return. The value of the block in this case is the result of the return.

```
(block nil
   (print 'abc)
   (return 'def)
   (print 'ghi))
⇒     ABC
      DEF
```

When the block is named, a return-from is necessary (rather than a return) to exit the block.

```
(block name1
  (print 'abc)
  (block name2
    (print 'def)
    (return-from name2 'finish)
    (print 'ghi))
  'end)
⇒    ABC
     DEF
     END

(block name1
  (print 'abc)
  (block name2
    (print 'def)
    (return-from name1 'finish)
    (print 'ghi))
  'end)
⇒    ABC
     DEF
     FINISH
```

*name* is lexically scoped. Thus, from within the block name2, you can exit the block name1 or name2.

## Implicit Blocks

Several functions create an implicit block around the body of their forms.

defun puts a block around the body of the function. The name of the block is the same as the name of the function. Thus, you can use return-from to exit the function.

```
(defun max-rate (x)
  (if (not (numberp x)) (return-from max-rate 'not-a-number))
  (* (- 220 x) .75))
⇒    MAX-RATE

(max-rate 31)
⇒    141.75

(max-rate 'style)
⇒    NOT-A-NUMBER
```

do and prog establish unnamed blocks. A return or return-from nil can exit these constructs. prog is discussed later in this chapter. do is discussed in Chapter 8.

**Exercise 6-1**

Write a function that takes two arguments, a number, and a list.

1. If the number argument was not passed a number value, exit the function with an appropriate message.
2. Within a block, `cons` the square of the number to the list.
3. If the `cdr` of the list is not a list, exit from the block and return the list.
4. Add the length of the list to the front of the list and return the list.

## CATCH AND THROW

Within a `block`, the name is lexically bound. Thus, the return must be within the block. The `catch` and `throw` special forms provide a dynamically scoped block. Thus, as long as the catcher is visible, you can throw to it.

(catch *tag* {*form*}*)

(throw *tag* *result*)

*tag* is evaluated to produce an object. This is different from the name of a block, which must be a symbol.

In the simple case, the `catch` and `throw` can duplicate the effects of a `block` and `return`.

```
(catch 'exit
  (print 'abc)
  (print 'def)
  (throw 'exit 'done)
  (print 'hij))
⇒    ABC
     DEF
     DONE
```

In a more complex case, the `throw` can be in a function separate from the `catch`.

```
(defun main (x)
  (if (not (or (eq x 'first) (eq x 'second)))
    (return-from  main "not a valid argument"))
  (print "beginning the function")
  (catch 'first
```

```
      (print "inside the first catch")
      (catch 'second
        (print "inside the second catch")
        (sub x)
        (print "leaving the second catch"))
      (print "leaving the first catch")))
⇒    MAIN

(defun sub (y)
  (throw y 'end))
⇒    SUB

(main 'first)
⇒    "beginning the function"
     "inside the first catch"
     "inside the second catch"
     END

(main 'second)
⇒    "beginning the function"
     "inside the first catch"
     "inside the second catch"
     "leaving the first catch"
     "leaving the first catch"

(main 'wrong)
⇒    "not a valid argument"
```

The result of the catch is returned just after the catcher is disestablished. That is, after the catch has completed, you cannot throw to it again.

---

### Exercise 6-2

```
(defun throwing (flag)
  (if flag (throw global-value "end of throw"))
  (print "exiting the throw"))
⇒    THROWING

(defun catching (flag-1)
  (print "where am i")
  (catch global-value
    (print "catch the global-value")
    (catch 'symbol
      (print "catch the symbol")
      (throwing flag-1)
      (print "exit symbol"))
    (print "exit global"))
```

```
        (print "leaving it all behind"))
  ⇒     CATCHING


   (setq global-value 'name)
  ⇒     NAME
```

**1.** Using the above functions, what are the results of the following?

```
        (catching t)
        (catching nil)
        (catching 'symbol)
```

**2.** If you change the value of global-value to symbol, does it change the results? Why?

---

## tagbody AND go

In the cases of a block and a catch, you can exit the structure or you can evaluate all of the enclosed functions. Within a tagbody, you can evaluate all of the enclosed functions in order or you can evaluate them in an order to be determined.

```
(tagbody {tag|statement}*)
(go tag)
```

The go special form transfers control to a *tag* within the tagbody. The *tag* is not evaluated. It must be a symbol.

```
(tagbody
    (setq a 1)
  1                                  ;; the tag 1
    (setq a (+ a 1))
    (if (> a 5) (go second))
    (print "a <= 5")
    (go 1)
  second                             ;; the tag second
    (print 'done))
  ⇒    "a <= 5"
       "a <= 5"
       "a <= 5"
       "a <= 5"
     DONE
     NIL
```

The *tag* can appear before or after the go, however, it must be lexically visable to the go. This means, that tagbodies can be nested and a go inside one tagbody can skip over several tagbodies to match a *tag*. It can also skip over a catch or other block.

```
(defun convoluted (x)
  (tagbody
      (print "inside tagbody")
      (tagbody
          (block one
          (print "inside block")
          (catch 'two
              (print "inside catch")
              (if (eql x 'first)(go first))
              (if (eql x 'second) (go second))
              (if (eq x 'one) (return-from one (print "returning to block")))
              (if (eq x 'two) (throw 'two (print "return to catch")))
              (print "end of catch"))
          (print "end of block"))
          second
          (print "end of second tagbody"))
      first
      (print "end of first tagbody"))
  'end)
⇒    CONVOLUTED


(convoluted 'first)
⇒    "inside tagbody"
     "inside block"
     "inside catch"
     "end of first tagbody"
    END


(convoluted 'second)
⇒    "inside tagbody"
     "inside block"
     "inside catch"
     "end of second tagbody"
     "end of first tagbody"
    END


(convoluted 'one)
⇒    "inside tagbody"
     "inside block"
     "inside catch"
     "returning to block"
     "end of second tagbody"
     "end of first tagbody"
    END
```

```
(convoluted 'two)
⇒    "inside tagbody"
     "inside block"
     "inside catch"
     "return to catch"
     "end of block"
     "end of second tagbody"
     "end of first tagbody"
   END

(convoluted 'nil)
⇒    "inside tagbody"
     "inside block"
     "inside catch"
     "end of catch"
     "end of block"
     "end of second tagbody"
     "end of first tagbody"
   END
```

Similarly, a throw can jump over tagbodies and blocks to match with a catcher, and a return-from can jump over tagbodies and catches to match with a block.

Using go in a Lisp function is not stylistically desirable. There are many programming constructs from which to choose. There is usually one that can do what you want without resorting to go. Indiscriminate use of go can cause problems in determining what your code is doing.

---

**Exercise 6-3**

Write a function that takes two numeric arguments. If the first argument is 1, return the second argument. If the first argument is 2, return the square of the second argument. If the first argument is 3, return the cube of the argument. If the first argument is not 1, 2, or 3, return an error message.

---

## Program

The prog macro evaluates a sequence of forms. The body of the prog is an implicit block from which you can exit with a return. You can also use tags within the body, and you can bind variables within the prog.

(prog ({var | (var[init]) }*) {declaration}* {tag | statement}*)

For example,

```
(defun simple (x y)
  (prog ((a x)(b y))
    (if (numberp a)(go a))
    (print "a is not a number")
    (return)                        ; leave the prog
   a
    (setq a (exp a a))
    (if (numberp b)(go b))
    (print "b is not a number")
    (return)                        ; leave the prog
   b
    (setq b (exp b b))
    (print a)
    (print b))
  nil)                              ; return nil
⇒    SIMPLE

(simple 2 3)
⇒    7.38905609893065
     20.085536923187668
     NIL
```

As stated before, the use of `go` is not recommended for programming; however, it is not the only reason for `prog`. `prog` is frequently used for structuring. The previous example could be written as follows.

```
(defun simple2 (x y)
  (if (numberp x)
    (prog ()
      (if (numberp y)
        (prog ()
          (print (exp x x))
          (print (exp y y)))
        (return-from simple2 "y is not a number")))
    (return-from simple2 "x is not a number")))
⇒    SIMPLE2

(simple2 2 3)
⇒    7.38905609893065
     20.085536923187668
     NIL

(simple 'a 'b)
⇒    "a is not a number"
     NIL

(simple2 'x 'y)
⇒    "x is not a number"
```

```
(simple 2 'b)
⇒    "b is not a number"
    NIL

(simple2 2 'y)
⇒    "y is not a number"
```

## unwind-protect

The `unwind-protect` special form provides a method of "protecting" a form. This function accepts two arguments, each of which is a form. The first form is evaluated. Regardless of how the first form exits, the second argument is evaluated. This is true whether the first form executes a throw outside the `unwind-protect` or causes an error to occur.

> (`unwind-protect` *protected-form* {*cleanup-form*})

Because each argument must be a single form, this is a perfect place to use `prog`. The `prog` is a single form that evaluates other forms.

```
(defun test (flag)
  (unwind-protect
   (prog ()
     (setq flag t)
     (print "testing"))
   (setq flag nil)))
⇒    TEST
```

In this example, regardless of what functions are evaluated within the `prog`, the flag is always reset to nil.

## SUMMARY

All the "functions" described in this chapter are special forms. These special forms determine the order in which functions are evaluated.

- You can specify a section of code to be a block from which you can exit before all the functions are evaluated.
- You can set up tags and jump to them to alter the order of evaluation.
- You can set up nonlocal catches and jump to them from other functions.
- You can specify a section of code to be a single function in which you can bind variables, and have tags and returns.
- You can specify a function to be protected and have another function alway execute regardless of how the protected function exits.

# 7

## *Conditional Constructs*

In the previous chapter, you saw how to block sections of code. These blocks could be evaluated sequentially or they could be exited at specified points. In this chapter, the concept of blocking is taken a step further. Based on a set of conditions, you might want to evaluate one of several blocks. Or you might want to evaluate a block only if certain conditions are met. There are several *conditional* functions that allow you to do this.

The macros and special forms that are described in this chapter conditionally evaluate forms. They can evaluate an initial form and based on the result evaluate one or more other forms. Or they can look through a list of forms for a match. Each of the conditional forms controls the flow of evaluation of forms.

This chapter looks at five sequencing constructs: `if`, `cond`, `case`, `when`, and `unless`.

## BOOLEAN VALUES

A boolean value is either true or false. Many of the conditional functions use a boolean value to determine which forms to evaluate. Lisp considers a `nil` value to be false and anything else to be true. Symbols, numbers, non-empty lists, and structures are true values. Any non-nil value is true.

There are three functions that look at one or more objects and, using the boolean value for that object, return another boolean value. These function are and, not, and or.

## and

The and macro looks at the forms and determines if none of them is nil. It evaluates the forms in the order given. If a form returns nil, and returns nil. It does not evaluate the remaining forms. If none of the forms returns nil, and returns the value of the last form.

```
(and {form}*)

(setq class '(tom larry lary moe joe))
⇒    (TOM LARRY LARY MOE JOE)


(and (member 'tom class))
⇒    (TOM LARRY LARY MOE JOE)


(and (member 'sue class))
⇒    NIL


(and (member 'lary class)
     (member 'tom class)
     (member 'joe class))
⇒    (JOE)
```

## not

The not function evaluates its argument and inverts the value. If the argument is nil, not returns t. If the argument is t, not returns nil.

```
(not argument)

(not (member 'joe class))
⇒    NIL


(not (member 'sue class))
⇒    T
```

## or

The or macro looks at the forms and determines if at least one of them is true. It evaluates the forms in the order given. When a non-nil result is found, or returns that value. It does not evaluate the remaining forms.

```
(or {form}*)

(or    (member 'joe class)
       (member 'sue class))
  ⇒    (JOE)


(or    (member 'sue class)
       (member 'mary class)
       (member 'rick class)
       (member 'tom class))
  ⇒    (TOM LARRY LARY MOE JOE)
```

The three functions can be combined to make not-and (at least one form is nil), not-or (none of the forms is true), and other variations.

```
(and (member 'joe class)
     (member 'larry class))
  ⇒    (LARRY LARY MOE JOE)


(not (and (member 'joe class)
          (member 'larry class)))
  ⇒    NIL


(or (not (member 'joe class))
    (not (member 'larry class))
    (not (member 'sue class)))
  ⇒    T


(and (or (member 'sue class)
         (member 'joe class))
     (not (member 'mary class)))
  ⇒    T
```

---

**Exercise 7-1**

1. Create three lists: class1, class2, and class3. Each class has students. Some students are in one class, some are in two classes, and some are in three classes.
2. Create a function that determines if a student is in all three classes.
3. Create a function that determines if a student is in exactly two classes.
4. Create a function that determines if a student is in exactly one class.
5. Create a function that determines if a student is in no class.

**if**

`if` is a special form. It evaluates a test form. The result of the test form is a boolean; it has a nil (false) or non-nil (true) value. If the result is non-nil, the next form is evaluated. This is the *then* clause. If the result is nil, the form after the then clause is evaluated. This is the *else* clause. The else clause is optional.

(`if` *test then* [*else*])

For example,

```
(setq a t)
⇒   T

(if a "a is true"
     "a is false")
⇒    "a is true"

(if (eql a 'test) (setq b 'passed)
                    (setq b 'failed))
⇒    FAILED

(if 0 (setq flag 'passed)
      (setq flag 'failed))
⇒    PASSED

(if nil (setq flag 'passed)
        (setq flag 'failed))
⇒    FAILED
```

You can use `if` when you are choosing between one of two forms or if you want to evaluate a form only if a condition is met.

```
(if (typep a 'number) (sqrt a))
⇒    NIL

(if (typep a 'number) (sqrt a) "a is not a number")
⇒    "a is not a number"

(setq class '(john mary dana lee karen))
⇒    (JOHN MARY DANA LEE KAREN)

(if (not (member 'sue class)) (cons 'sue class))
⇒    (SUE JOHN MARY DANA LEE KAREN)

(if (not (member 'john class)) (cons 'john class))
⇒    NIL

class
⇒    (JOHN MARY DANA LEE KAREN)
```

The then and else forms can be any form. They can call another function. They can also nest the `if` special form.

**Exercise 7-2**

Create a function that when given a name returns the number of classes in which the student appears.

## cond

The `cond` macro selects one form out of many.

```
(cond { (test {form}*) }*)
```

The *test* form returns a boolean value. If the value is non-nil, the next set of forms is evaluated and the remaining test forms are not evaluated. If the value is nil, the next test form is evaluated. If none of the test forms is non-nil, `cond` returns nil. For example,

```
(setq p 3)
⇒    3

(cond ((eql 1 p) (list 'p '= 1))
      ((eql 2 p) (list 'p '= 2))
      ((eql 3 p) (list 'p '= 3))
      (t (list 'p 'does 'not 'equal 1 2 'or 3)))
⇒    (P = 3)
```

Unlike `if`, any number of forms can appear in the clause following the test.

```
(cond ((typep p 'number) (setq ap (sqrt p))
                         (print ap)
                         (setq p (* p p))))
⇒    3.0
      81
```

If none of the tests is true, `cond` returns nil.

```
(cond ((= 1 2) 'weird)
      ((= 2 3) 'convoluted))
⇒    NIL
```

You can use an "else" clause in `cond`, so that if none of the tests is true, the "else" clause will be evaluated. The "else" clause is simply `t`, because `t` always evaluates to true.

```
(cond ((= 1 2) 'weird)
      ((= 2 3) 'convoluted)
      (t (list 'this 'will 'always 'be 'listed))))
⇒   (THIS WILL ALWAYS BE LISTED)
```

---

**Exercise 7-3**

Use cond to rewrite the num-classes function.

---

## case

The case macro, like cond, picks one clause out of many to evaluate. Instead of selecting the non-nil value, the test or *key* value must match a *keyform* exactly. The *key* must be a literal object. It is not evaluated like the test of cond.

(case *keyform* { ( { ( {*key*}*) | *key* } {*form*}*) }*)

The *keyform* can be any form. The *keys* must be literal values. There can be a single key or multiple keys in a list. There can also be an otherwise or t key that matches any keyform.

```
(case 'a
  (b (print "the key is b"))
  ((c d e) (print "the key is either c d or e"))
  (a (print "the key is a"))
  (otherwise (print "can not find the key")))
⇒   "the key is a"
    "the key is a"

(case (type-of 'a)
  (number (list 'a 'is 'a 'number))
  (list (list 'a 'is 'a 'list))
  (symbol (list 'a 'is 'a 'symbol)))
⇒   (A IS A SYMBOL)
```

If none of the clauses is chosen, case returns nil.

```
(case 4
  (1 'one)
  (2 'two))
⇒   NIL
```

## ccase and ecase

There are two macros that signal a continuable error, `ccase`, or a noncontinuable error, `ecase`, when none of the keys match the keyform. No `otherwise` or `t` key is allowed.

```
(ccase keyplace { ({ ({key}*) |key} {form}) }*)
```

```
(ecase keyform { ({ ({key}*)|key} {form}) }*)
```

For example,

```
(setq smith 'smith)
⇒   SMITH
(ccase smith
  (jones (print 'alias))
  ((tom john ryan) (print 'name)))
⇒   !!!! Continuable error: The key value SMITH does not correspond to
                          any of the case keys (RYAN JOHN TOM JONES).
        If continued: prompts for a new key value.

(ecase smith
  (jones (print 'alias))
  ((tom john ryan) (print 'name)))
⇒   !!!!! Error: The key value SMITH does not correspond to any of the
              case keys (RYAN JOHN TOM JONES).
```

The keys are used to create the error message. The exact message is implementation dependent.

---

**Exercise 7-4**

Write a function of one argument. The argument is the name of a class. The function returns a list of all the students in that class.

---

## typecase

`typecase` is similar to `case`, except that instead of looking for a matching key, `typecase` looks for a matching type. The type of the result returned by the *keyform* is compared to the specified types in the clauses.

```
(typecase keyform { (type {form}*) }*)
```

Notice that only one type can be specified for each form, not multiple keys, such as `case` allows. You can still have multiple forms after the type key.

```
(typecase (* 2 2.0)
   (integer (list 'result 'is 'integer))
   (float (list 'result 'is 'float))
   (number (list 'result 'is 'number))
   (otherwise (list 'result 'is 'not 'a 'number)))
⇒    (RESULT IS FLOAT)
```

The table of types in Chapter 3 shows the hierarchical structure of types. `typecase` picks the first type that matches the type of the keyform or of which keyform is a subtype.

```
(typecase (* 2 2.0)
   (integer (list 'result 'is 'integer))
   (number (list 'result 'is 'number))
   (float (list 'result 'is 'float))
   (otherwise (list 'result 'is 'not 'a 'number)))
⇒    (RESULT IS NUMBER)
```

If you are using subtypes within `typecase`, list the most specific type first and then move to the most general type. In the example above, the `float` clause is never evaluated because if an object is a float, it is also a number and only the `number` clause is evaluated.

### ctypecase and etypecase

Again similar to `case`, the `typecase` macro has a `ctypecase`, continuable error, and `etypecase`, noncontinuable error, equivalent.

```
(ctypecase keyplace { (type {form}*) }*)
```

```
(etypecase keyform { (type {form}*) }*)
```

## when

The `when` macro evaluates a test form. If the result of the test is non-nil, `when` evaluates the rest of the forms and returns the value of the last form. If the result of the test form is nil, `when` does not evaluate the rest of the forms and returns nil.

```
(when test {form}*)


(setq time-of-day 1200)
⇒    1200


(when (> time-of-day 1700)
  (print "Quiting Time"))
⇒    NIL  .


(setq time-of-day 1701)
⇒    1701


(when (> time-of-day 1700)
  (print "Quiting Time"))
⇒    "Quiting Time"
     "Quiting Time"
```

## unless

The unless macro evaluates a test form.  If the result is nil, unless evaluates the remaining forms and returns the results of the last form.  If the result is non-nil, unless returns nil without evaluating the rest of the forms.  This is the opposite of when.

```
(unless test {form}*)


(setq time-of-day 1200)
⇒    1200


(unless (> time-of-day 1700)
  (print "more to do"))
⇒    "more to do"
     "more to do"


(setq time-of-day 1701)
⇒    1701


(unless (> time-of-day 1700)
  (print "more to do"))
⇒    NIL
```

**Exercise 7-5**

The following function sends a form letter to students.

```
(defun form1 (name reason)
  (cond ((equal reason 'register)
         (format t "Dear ~a, ~% It has come to our attention that
            you have not registered for classes.~%" name))
        ((equal reason 'too-many)
         (format t "Dear ~a, ~% You are registered for too many
            classes.  Please get the dean's signature." name))))
```

1. If a student is in no classes, write the student a letter. Tell the student that he or she must register for a class. Use `when` to test for this case.
2. If a student is in more than two classes, write the student a letter. Tell the student they must get the dean's signature for having too many classes. Use `unless` for this.

## SUMMARY

There are many ways to write a function. To obtain the same result, you could use any or all the functions shown in this chapter. There is no correct method to solving the problems. Instead, there may be better ways. Chose the methods that seem to fit the problems.

| | |
|---|---|
| if | Choose one of two forms. The test is a boolean value. |
| cond | Choose one of many forms. The test is a boolean value. |
| case | Choose one of many forms. The test is matching of symbols. |
| typecase | Choose one of many forms. The test is matching of types. |
| when | Do the forms if the test is true. |
| unless | Do the forms if the test is false. |

# 8

## Iteration

Iteration means repeating the same forms over and over again. The iteration can be for a specific number of times, until a condition is met, or once for every value in a list.

This chapter looks at several Lisp constructs for looping: `loop`, `do`, `do*`, `dotimes`, and `do-list`; and several constructs that apply functions to a sequence of arguments: `apply`, `mapcar`, `mapcan`, `mapc`, `maplist`, and `mapcon`.

### loop

The `loop` macro repeatedly evaluates a series of forms. A `return` or `throw` exits a `loop`.

```
(loop {form}*)
```

For example,

```
(defun count-down (x)
  (loop
    (print x)
    (setq x (- x 1))
    (if (zerop x) (return "lift off"))))
⇒    COUNT-DOWN
```

```
(count-down 10)
⇒     10
       9
       8
       7
       6
       5
       4
       3
       2
       1
      "lift off"
```

---

**Exercise 8-1**

Write a function that prints each element of a list.

---

## DO CONSTRUCTS

The do constructs bind variables to values, rebind the variables to new values at each iteration, and have a test form to determine when to stop the loop. The do's are surrounded by an implicit unnamed block. The body of the do constructs is in an implicit tagbody. Thus, you can return from the do's at any time and you can have gos within the body of the construct.

There are four do's: do, do*, dotimes, and dolist.

### do

The do macro repeatedly evaluates a series of forms until an end condition is met.

```
(do  ({ (variable [initial-value [step-form]]) }*)
     (end-test {result}*)
     {declaration}*
     {tag | statement}*)
```

There can be any number of variables that are bound in the do loop. The default *initial-value* is nil. If *step-form* is not specified, the variable does not change value at each iteration unless the loop explicitly gives it another value. The variables are bound to values for the duration of the loop; they are not assigned the values. On exit from the loop, the variables retain the values they had before entering the loop.

The result of `end-test` is interpreted as a boolean value. If the value is true, non-nil, the *result* forms are evaluated and the `do` loop exits. If the value is nil, the body of the loop is evaluated. For example,

```
(defun count-down-2 (x)        ;; similar to the loop count-down
  (do ((a x (1- a)))           ;; the subtraction is done automatically
      ((zerop a) "lift-off")   ;; no if, no return
      (print a)))
⇒    COUNT-DOWN-2


(count-down-2 5)
⇒    5
     4
     3
     2
     1
     "lift-off"
```

The variables are given their initial values in parallel. On evaluation of the step forms, all forms are evaluated before any variable is bound to the new value. Therefore, the old values of the variables are available to all the step forms. Then the binding of the variables to the new values is done in parallel.

```
(defun building (x)
  (do ((a '() (cons b a))
       (b 1 (1+ b)))
      ((> b x) (return a))))
⇒    BUILDING


(building 3)
⇒    (3 2 1)


(building 0)
⇒    NIL


(building 5)
⇒    (5 4 3 2 1)
```

## do*

The `do*` macro is similar to `do`. The variables are bound to the initial values and to the step values sequentially. For example,

```
(defun around (z)
  (do*
    ((x z (cdr x))
     (result (list (car x)) (cons (car x) result)))
    ((eql (length z)(length result)) result)
    (print result)))
```
⇒     AROUND

```
(around '(a b c))
```
⇒     (A)
      (B A)
      (C B A)

While in a do* loop, the variables are bound to the initial values and then to the step values. The first initial value can refer to the assigned value of the variable. Because binding is done seqentially, other initial values will refer to the new binding of the variables. The step values always refers to the binding of the variables.

```
(defun round2 (z)
  (do*
    ((z z (cdr z))        ;; the first z is the variable,
                          ;; the second z refers to the assigned value
                          ;; the third z refers to the binding of z

     (result (list (car z)) (cons (car z) result))
                          ;; the first (car z) refers to the first binding of z
                          ;; the second (car z) refers to the second binding of z

     (finish (length z))) ;; (length z) is the length of the binding of z
                          ;; there is no step value

    ((eql finish (length result)) (print result))
                          ;; you can't use (length z) to replace finish because
                          ;; the length of z changes at each iteration
    (print result))
  z)                      ;; the assigned value of z after the do* loop
```
⇒     ROUND2

```
(round2 '(a b c))
```
⇒     (A)
      (B A)
      (C B A)
      (A B C)

This function would not work with do. The (cons (car z) result) form refers to the current binding of z, not the one that is about to be assigned. This is because do assigns values in parallel whereas do* assigns values sequentially.

```
(defun wrong-round2 (z)
  (do
    ((z z (cdr z))
     (result (list (car z)) (cons (car z) result))
     (finish (length z)))
    ((eql finish (length result)) (print result))
    (print result))
  z)
⇒    WRONG-ROUND2


(wrong-round2 '(a b c))
⇒    (A)
     (A A)
     (B A A)
     (A B C)
```

## dotimes

The dotimes macro repeatedly evaluates a series of forms for a specified number of times.

```
(dotimes  (variable countform [resultform])
          {declaration}* {tag | statement}*)
```

The variable is bound to zero on the first iteration of the body of dotimes. Each time through, 1 is added to the variable. It is tested against the value of countform. If the variable is less than the countform, the body of the loop is evaluated. If the variable and the value of countform are equal, the *resultform* is evaluated. If there is no *result-form*, nil is returned. For example,

```
(defun count-up (x)
  (dotimes (y x "go")
    (print y)))
⇒    COUNT-UP


(count-up 5)
⇒    0
     1
     2
     3
     4
     "go"
```

```
(defun round-3 (x)
  (let ((result '()))
    (dotimes (n (length x) result)
      (setq result (cons (car (nthcdr n x)) result))  ;; nthcdr takes the
      (print result))))                                          :: cdr n times
⇒    ROUND-3

(round-3 '(a b c))
⇒    (A)
     (B A)
     (C B A)
     (C B A)
```

## dolist

The `dolist` macro repeatedly evaluates a series of forms, once for each element in a list.

```
(dolist  (variable listform [resultform])
         {declaration}* {tag | statement}*)
```

The *listform* provides a list. The *variable* is bound to the first element of the list. Then the body of the loop is evaluated. The variable is bound to the next element of the list, etc. When all the elements of the list have been used, the *resultform* is evaluated. For example,

```
(defun round-4 (x)
  (let ((result '()))
    (dolist (a x result)
      (setq result (cons a result))
      (print result))))
⇒    ROUND-4

(round-4 '(a b c))
⇒    (A)
     (B A)
     (C B A)
     (C B A)
```

---

**Exercise 8-2**

**1.** Write a function using `do` that builds a list. The function takes one argument, which specifies the number of x's to put in the list.

**2.** Write the same function using `dotimes`.

**3.** Write a function that takes a list of numbers. Each number specifies the number of x's in an element of the list being built. Use `dolist` to create this function. For example,

```
(build-it '(1 2 3))
⇒    ((x)(x x)(x x x))
```

---

## MAPPING

The mapping functions apply a specified function to pieces of a sequence. The result is a sequence containing the results of the function application.

### apply

The `apply` function applies a function to a list of arguments. It returns a single value.

(apply *function argument* &rest *more-arguments*)

The *function* cannot be the name of a special form or macro. It must be a function. The macro characters `#'` specify that the function value of the symbol be used rather than the symbol value.

The arguments are gathered by `list*` to make one list. The function is applied to this list. For example,

```
(apply #'+ '(1 2 3))
⇒    6
```

The steps involved in this are:

```
(list* '(1 2 3))
⇒    (1 2 3)

(+ 1 2 3)
⇒    6
```

Here is another example of `apply`.

```
(apply #'cons '(1 2 3) '(a b d) nil)
⇒    ((1 2 3) A B D)

(list* '(1 2 3) '(a b d) nil)
⇒    ((1 2 3) (A B D))
```

```
(cons '(1 2 3) '(a b c))
⇒    ((1 2 3) A B C)
```

The `apply` function is used by the mapping functions.

## mapcar

The `mapcar` function applies a function to each element of a list. It returns a list of results.

> (mapcar *function list* &rest *more-lists*)

The first element of each list is given to the *function* as the function's arguments. The *function* must take the number of arguments supplied. The *function* cannot be a symbol that names a macro or special form.

For example, if there is one list, the function must accept one argument.

```
(mapcar #'1+ '(1 2 3))
⇒    (2 3 4)
```

This is equivalent to:

```
(list (1+ 1)
      (1+ 2)
      (1+ 3))
```

If there are two lists, the function must accept two arguments.

```
(mapcar #'+ '(1 2 3) '(4 5 6))
⇒    (5 7 9)
```

This is equivalent to:

```
(list (+ 1 4)
      (+ 2 5)
      (+ 3 6))
⇒    (5 7 9)
```

If the lists are of unequal lengths, the shortest list determines the number of elements used in all lists.

```
(mapcar #'list '(a b c) '(1 2 3) '(sue mary sam kelly))
⇒    ((A 1 SUE) (B 2 MARY) (C 3 SAM))
```

This is equivalent to:

```
(list (list 'a 1 'sue)
      (list 'b 2 'mary)
      (list 'c 3 'sam))
⇒    ((A 1 SUE) (B 2 MARY) (C 3 SAM))
```

When the function is applied to the arguments, it may produce side effects. For example,

```
(mapcar #'print '(a b c))
⇒    A                ;; side effect
     B                ;; side effect
     C                ;; side effect
     (A B C)          ;; value returned by mapcar

(mapcar #'set '(a b c) '(1 2 3))
⇒    (1 2 3)          ;; returned by mapcar


a
⇒    1                ;; side effect of set


b
⇒    2                ;; side effect of set


c
⇒    3                ;; side effect of set
```

## mapcan

The `mapcan` function is similar to `mapcar`. Instead of using `list` to create the result list, `mapcan` uses `nconc`. `nconc` concatenates its arguments, which must be lists.

```
(mapcan function list &rest more-lists)

(setq a '(1 2 3))
⇒    (1 2 3)

(setq b '(a b c))
⇒    (A B C)

(mapcan #'list a b)
⇒    (1 A 2 B 3 C)

(mapcar #'list a b)
⇒    ((1 A) (2 B) (3 C))
```

The `mapcan` example is equivalent to:

```
(apply #'nconc (mapcar #'list a b))
⇒    (1 A 2 B 3 C)
```

That is,

```
(nconc (list 1 'a)
       (list 2 'b)
       (list 3 'c))
⇒    (1 A 2 B 3 C)
```

## mapc

The `mapc` function is similar to `mapcar`. It produces the same side effects, however, it only returns the second argument.

```
(mapc #'set '(a b c) '(1 2 3))
⇒    (A B C)

a
⇒    1

b
⇒    2

c
⇒    3
```

`mapc` is used to produce side effects when the returned value is not important.

## maplist

The `maplist` function applies a function to each list, the cdr of the list, the cdr of the cdr of the list, etc. For example,

```
(maplist #'print '(a b c d))
⇒    (A B C D)
     (B C D)
     (C D)
     (D)
     ((A B C D) (B C D) (C D) (D))
```

This is equivalent to:

```
(list (print '(a b c d))
      (print '(b c d))
      (print '(c d))
      (print '(d)))
⇒    (A B C D)                        ;; side effect of print
      (B C D)                         ;; side effect of print
      (C D)                           ;; side effect of print
      (D)                             ;; side effect of print
      ((A B C D) (B C D) (C D) (D))   ;; result of list

(maplist #'cdr '(a b c d))
⇒    ((B C D) (C D) (D) NIL)
```

This is equivalent to:

```
(list (cdr '(a b c d))
      (cdr '(b c d))
      (cdr '(c d))
      (cdr '(d)))
⇒    ((B C D) (C D) (D) NIL)

(maplist #'list '(a b c d) '(1 2 3 4))
⇒    (((A B C D) (1 2 3 4)) ((B C D) (2 3 4)) ((C D) (3 4)) ((D) (4)))
```

This is equivalent to:

```
(list (list '(a b c d) '(1 2 3 4))
      (list '(b c d) '(2 3 4))
      (list '(c d) '(3 4))
      (list '(d) '(4)))
⇒    (((A B C D) (1 2 3 4)) ((B C D) (2 3 4)) ((C D) (3 4)) ((D) (4)))
```

## mapcon

The `mapcon` function is similar to `maplist`, except it uses `nconc` to accumulate the result.

```
(mapcon #'list '(a b c d) '(1 2 3 4))
⇒    ((A B C D) (1 2 3 4) (B C D) (2 3 4) (C D) (3 4) (D) (4))
```

## mapl

The `mapl` function is similar to `maplist`, except it returns the second argument. Use `mapl` for the side effects it produces.

```
(mapl #'print '(a b c d) )
⇒    (A B C D)
     (B C D)
     (C D)
     (D)
     (A B C D)
```

## map

The `map` function applies a function to arguments constructed from the argument sequences.

> (map *result-type function sequence* &rest *more-sequences*)

The *result-type* is a symbol that specifies the type of sequence returned by `map`. The type can be any subtype of sequence. Lists and vectors are subtypes of sequence.

The *function* must take as many arguments as there are sequences. For example,

```
(map 'vector #'+ '(1 2 3) '(4 5 6))
⇒    #(5 7 9)

(map 'string #'code-char '(97 122 35))
⇒    "az#"

(map 'list #'char-code "abc")
⇒    (97 98 99)
```

The first element of each sequence is passed to the function as its arguments. Then the next element of each sequence is used, etc., until all the elements of the shortest sequence are used.

```
(map 'list #'- '(1 2 3 4))
⇒    (-1 -2 -3 -4)
```

This is equivalent to:

```
(list (- 1)
      (- 2)
      (- 3)
      (- 4))
⇒    (-1 -2 -3 -4)

(map 'list #'- '(1 2 3) '(3 2 1))
⇒    (-2 0 2)
```

This is equivalent to:

```
(list (- 1 3)
      (- 2 2)
      (- 3 1))
  ⇒    (-2 0 2)
```

---

**Exercise 8-3**

1. Write a function that `applys` the minus function (−) to every element in a list of numbers.
2. Write a function that returns a list where the minus function has been applied to each element. Use `mapcar`.
3. Write a function that returns a list where every number in the list is negative. Use `mapcar`.
4. Use `maplist` to rewrite the round function. This function will reverse the elements in a list.
5. Write a function that given a list of numbers returns their average.

---

## SUMMARY

As with the previous chapters, there is no one right way in which to do iteration. Several constructs were presented in this chapter. You can choose the one that seems most suited to the problem to be solved.

| | |
|---|---|
| `loop` | Repeat forms until a return is evaluated. |
| `do` | Repeat forms until an exit condition is met. |
| `dolist` | Repeat forms once for each element in a list. |
| `dotime` | Repeat forms a specific number of times. |
| `mapcar` | Apply a function to each element of a list. |
| `maplist` | Apply a function to each list, and successive cdr of the list. |
| `map` | Apply a function to arguments constructed from the argument sequences. |

# 9

## Recursion

There is a definition for recursion that reads:

```
Recursion: see recursion.
```

This chapter looks at recursion. A function that calls itself, even indirectly, is called a *recursive function*. There are no specific functions to make a recursive function (such as looping functions or conditional functions). Instead, a function simply calls itself.

There are three criteria for writing a recursive function.

**1.** There must be a way to tell when you are done recursing.
**2.** The procedure must break down to a small operation and the rest.
**3.** Each time through the function, the rest gets smaller.

There are several terms used to describe different types of recursion: linear recursive, linear iterative, and tree recursion. These are each discussed in this chapter.

For example, consider the problem of cleaning your room. You have a list of tasks that have to be done. Being a logical person, you read the first task from the list and do it. Then you go back to the list and place a check next to the first task. Now, the second task on the list is the next task to be done. You continue until there are no tasks on the list to be done.

```
(defun clean-room (tasks)
   (if (null tasks) (return-from clean-room 'done))   ;; how to tell when you're done.
   (print (car tasks))                                ;; do some procedure.
   (clean-room (cdr tasks)))                           ;; recurse back to the function
                                                      ;; using a smaller list.
⇒    CLEAN-ROOM


(clean-room '(make-bed vacuum pick-up-clothes))
⇒    MAKE-BED
     VACUUM
     PICK-UP-CLOTHES
     DONE
```

This simple example shows the basics of recursion.


## LINEAR RECURSIVE

Consider the factorial function. The *factorial* of a number is the product of all the numbers from 1 to that number.

```
5! = 1 × 2 × 3 × 4 × 5
4! = 1 × 2 × 3 × 4
3! = 1 × 2 × 3
2! = 1 × 2
1! = 1
```

Notice that $5! = 4! \times 5$, and $4! = 3! \times 4$. In fact, $n! = (n-1)! \times n$, for any number $n$. This lends itself very well to recursion.

```
5! = 4! × 5
4! = 3! × 4
3! = 2! × 3
2! = 1! × 2
1! = 1
```

To write a recursive function, remember the three rules:

**1.** The stopping point is 1!.
**2.** The single step is one multiplication. $n \times (n - 1)!$.
**3.** The next time through the function, use $(n - 1)$ rather than $n$.

Because the factorial function only works on positive numbers, make sure the initial number is positive.

```
(defun factorial (n)
   (cond  ((> 1 n) 'error)               ;; you can only get the factorial of a
                                         ;;   positive number
          ((equal 1 n) 1)                ;; stop when n = 1
                                         ;;   the return value is (1! = 1)
          (t (* n (factorial (- n 1))))))) ;; multiply n time the factorial of
                                         ;;   the next smallest number
⇒     FACTORIAL


(factorial 5)
⇒     120


(factorial 3)
⇒     6


(factorial 10)
⇒     3628800


(factorial 0)
⇒     ERROR


(factorial -1)
⇒     ERROR
```

In the `factorial` function, enter the function five times for a factorial of 5. However, because not all the information necessary to compute a factorial is passed, it is necessary to return with a value for additional operations.

```
(factorial 5)
(* 5 (factorial 4))
(* 5 (* 4 (factorial 3)))
(* 5 (* 4 (* 3 (factorial 2))))
(* 5 (* 4 (* 3 (* 2 (factorial 1)))))
(* 5 (* 4 (* 3 (* 2 1))))
(* 5 (* 4 (* 3 2)))
(* 5 (* 4 6))
(* 5 24)
120
```

## Tracing a Function

One way to look at recursion is through the `trace` function.

```
(trace factorial)
⇒     (FACTORIAL)
```

```
(factorial 5)
⇒     FACTORIAL entry:
      |   Arg 1: 5
      |   FACTORIAL reentry (# 2):
      |   |   Arg 1: 4
      |   |   FACTORIAL reentry (# 3):
      |   |   |   Arg 1: 3
      |   |   |   FACTORIAL reentry (# 4):
      |   |   |   |   Arg 1: 2
      |   |   |   |   FACTORIAL reentry (# 5):
      |   |   |   |   |   Arg 1: 1
      |   |   |   |   FACTORIAL (# 5) return value = 1
      |   |   |   FACTORIAL (# 4) return value = 2
      |   |   FACTORIAL (# 3) return value = 6
      |   FACTORIAL (# 2) return value = 24
      FACTORIAL return value = 120
      120


(untrace factorial)
⇒     (FACTORIAL)
```

The trace function shows what is happening in the recursive calls. (You can also use trace on nonrecursive calls.) trace shows what function has been called, the arguments sent to that function, other functions called, and what the function(s) returns.

In this case, the value returned by each call to factorial is the factorial of smaller (starting with 1) numbers to the final factorial of the original number.

---

**Exercise 9-1**

1. Write a recursive countdown function. Given the value 5, the function should print:

```
5
4
3
2
1
"lift off"
```

2. Write a function that puts the numbers into a list rather than printing them.

---

## LINEAR ITERATIVE

When you started thinking about the factorial problem, you began with n! = n × (n − 1) ! . A different way to approach the factorial problem is to start with the factorial of 1 and go up to the factorial of the original number.

In the linear iterative method of recursion, you pass all the pertinent information to the function each time the function is called. In the factorial case, the information is the original number and the results tabulated. Because you are going to start with the factorial of 1 and go up, you also need to know how many times you have called the function. Thus, you will have three arguments going to the new factorial function.

The `fact` function has three arguments: the product so far, the counter, and the original number.

```
(defun fact (product counter original)
```

When the counter is greater than the original number, stop.

```
(cond ((> counter original) product)
```

If the counter is not greater than the original number, multiply the counter by the current product and pass that number as the new product to the `fact` function. Increment the counter by 1 and pass that as the new counter. The original number does not change.

```
(t (fact (* counter product)(+ 1 counter) original))))
```

The `fact` function looks this way:

```
(defun fact (product counter original)
  (cond ((> counter original) product)
        (t (fact (* counter product)(+ 1 counter) original))))
⇒    FACT
```

Because you do not want the caller of this function to have to put in the product and counter, you can add another function that does this. The initial values should be 1 for the product and 1 for the counter.

```
(defun factorial2 (n)
  (if (> 0 n)(return-from factorial2 'error))   ;; check for positive number
  (fact 1 1 n))
⇒    FACTORIAL2

(factorial2 5)
⇒    120

(trace factorial2)
⇒    (FACTORIAL2)
```

```
(trace fact)
⇒    (FACT)

(factorial2 5)
⇒    FACTORIAL2 entry:
     |   Arg 1: 5
     |  FACT entry:
     |  |   Arg 1: 1
     |  |   Arg 2: 1
     |  |   Arg 3: 5
     |  |  FACT reentry (# 2):
     |  |  |   Arg 1: 1
     |  |  |   Arg 2: 2
     |  |  |   Arg 3: 5
     |  |  |  FACT reentry (# 3):
     |  |  |  |   Arg 1: 2
     |  |  |  |   Arg 2: 3
     |  |  |  |   Arg 3: 5
     |  |  |  |  FACT reentry (# 4):
     |  |  |  |  |   Arg 1: 6
     |  |  |  |  |   Arg 2: 4
     |  |  |  |  |   Arg 3: 5
     |  |  |  |  |  FACT reentry (# 5):
     |  |  |  |  |  |   Arg 1: 24
     |  |  |  |  |  |   Arg 2: 5
     |  |  |  |  |  |   Arg 3: 5
     |  |  |  |  |  |  FACT reentry (# 6):
     |  |  |  |  |  |  |   Arg 1: 120
     |  |  |  |  |  |  |   Arg 2: 6
     |  |  |  |  |  |  |   Arg 3: 5
     |  |  |  |  |  |  FACT (# 6) return value = 120
     |  |  |  |  |  FACT (# 5) return value = 120
     |  |  |  |  FACT (# 4) return value = 120
     |  |  |  FACT (# 3) return value = 120
     |  |  FACT (# 2) return value = 120
     |  FACT return value = 120
     FACTORIAL2 return value = 120
     120
```

Notice that the return values of all functions are the same.

If you were to write the steps to this function, they would look something like this.

```
(factorial2 5)
(fact 1 1 5)
(fact 1 2 5)
(fact 2 3 5)
(fact 6 4 5)
```

```
(fact 24 5 5)
(fact 120 6 5)
120
```

When the counter is greater than the original number, you have the final product. There is no need to do any more multiplication. You have all the information required to return the answer.

In fact, at any point in time, you could stop the recursion and have all the information needed to determine an answer. In the original factorial problem, there was no way to determine where you were if you halted the recursion. In a linear iterative recursive process, the state of the process is totally captured by the three state variables. Using these variables, you could begin the process again and determine the answer. In a linear recursive process, the values of several variables remains on a stack waiting until other values are returned from the recursive function.

---

**Exercise 9-2**

1. Rewrite the count-list program using the linear iterative method.
2. Write a function that reverses the order of elements in a list.

---

## TREE RECURSION

Consider the following problem. Suppose you were given the choice of working for $100 a day for a year or starting at 1 cent and doubling your salary each day for a year. Which would you take? If you're smart, you'll start at 1 cent. Why? Look at the following example and see how much you would be making after only three weeks.

```
* 100 7)
⇒    700        ;; each week

(+ .01 .02 .04 .08 .16 .32 .64)
⇒    1.27       ;; first week

(+ 1.28 2.56 5.12 10.24 20.48 40.96 81.92)
⇒    162.56     ;; second week

(+ 163.84 327.68 655.36 1310.72 2621.44 5242.88 10485.76)
⇒    20807.68  ;; third week
```

At the 1-cent rate, the first two weeks you would make less than $700. After that, your salary would skyrocket. You would probably break the bank after another couple of weeks.

So what does this have to do with recursion?

Consider the fibonacci function. The fibonacci sequence of numbers is

$$0 \quad 1 \quad 1 \quad 2 \quad 3 \quad 5 \quad 8 \quad 13 \quad 21 \quad 34 \quad 56 \quad ...$$

Beginning with 0 and 1, each succeeding number is the sum of the two previous numbers.

```
(defun fib (x)
  (cond ((= 0 x) 0)
        ((= 1 x) 1)
        (t (+ (fib (- x 1))
              (fib (- x 2)))))))
⇒    FIB
```

When x is 1, fib is called 1 time.

When x is 2, fib is called 3 times.

When x is 3, fib is called 5 times.

When x is 4, fib is called 9 times.

Do you see the progression?

When x is 7, fib is called 65 times.

When x is 14, fib is called 8192 times.

When x is 21, fib is called 2080769 times.

Fib is called fib(x) + 1 times for any x > 1.

```
(fib 5)
(+ (fib 4) (fib 3))
(+ (+ (fib 3) (fib 2)) (+ (fib 2) (fib 1)))
(+ (+ (+ (+ (fib 2) (fib 1)) (+ (fib 1) (fib 0))) (+ (fib 1) (fib 0))) 1)
(+ (+ (+ (+ (fib 1) (fib 0)) 1) (+ 1 0)) (+ 1 0 1))
(+ (+ (+ (+ 1 0) 1) 1) 2)
3
```

Not only does this function call itself many times, it calls itself for the same numbers many times. For (fib 5), (fib 3) is called twice, (fib 2) is called three times, and (fib 1) is called five times. This uses a lot of resources, especially time. If you try to determine the fibonacci number of a large number, you will wait a long time and possibly run out of computer memory.

```
(trace fib)
⇒    (FIB)
```

```
(fib 5)
⇒    FIB entry:
     |   Arg 1: 5
     |  FIB reentry (# 2):
     |  |   Arg 1: 4
     |  |  FIB reentry (# 3):
     |  |  |   Arg 1: 3
     |  |  |  FIB reentry (# 4):
     |  |  |  |   Arg 1: 2
     |  |  |  |  FIB reentry (# 5):
     |  |  |  |  |   Arg 1: 1
     |  |  |  |  FIB (# 5) return value = 1
     |  |  |  |  FIB reentry (# 5):
     |  |  |  |  |   Arg 1: 0
     |  |  |  |  FIB (# 5) return value = 0
     |  |  |  FIB (# 4) return value = 1
     |  |  |  FIB reentry (# 4):
     |  |  |  |   Arg 1: 1
     |  |  |  FIB (# 4) return value = 1
     |  |  FIB (# 3) return value = 2
     |  |  FIB reentry (# 3):
     |  |  |   Arg 1: 2
     |  |  |  FIB reentry (# 4):
     |  |  |  |   Arg 1: 1
     |  |  |  FIB (# 4) return value = 1
     |  |  |  FIB reentry (# 4):
     |  |  |  |   Arg 1: 0
     |  |  |  FIB (# 4) return value = 0
     |  |  FIB (# 3) return value = 1
     |  FIB (# 2) return value = 3
     |  FIB reentry (# 2):
     |  |   Arg 1: 3
     |  |  FIB reentry (# 3):
     |  |  |   Arg 1: 2
     |  |  |  FIB reentry (# 4):
     |  |  |  |   Arg 1: 1
     |  |  |  FIB (# 4) return value = 1
     |  |  |  FIB reentry (# 4):
     |  |  |  |   Arg 1: 0
     |  |  |  FIB (# 4) return value = 0
     |  |  FIB (# 3) return value = 1
     |  |  FIB reentry (# 3):
     |  |  |   Arg 1: 1
     |  |  FIB (# 3) return value = 1
     |  FIB (# 2) return value = 2
     FIB return value = 5
     5
```

Defining the fibonacci numbers using tree recursion shows how fast the process can grow. A better way of defining the fibonacci function uses the linear iterative method.

```
(defun fib2 (x)
       (fibin 1 0 x))
⇒    FIB2

(defun fibin (previous second-previous count)
        (if (equal count 0) second-previous
            (fibin (+ previous second-previous) previous (- count 1)))))
⇒    FIBIN

(trace fib2)
⇒    (FIB2)

(trace fibin)
⇒    (FIBIN)

(fib2 5)
⇒    FIB2 entry:
     |  Arg 1: 5
     |  FIBIN entry:
     |  |  Arg 1: 1
     |  |  Arg 2: 0
     |  |  Arg 3: 5
     |  |  FIBIN reentry (# 2):
     |  |  |  Arg 1: 1
     |  |  |  Arg 2: 1
     |  |  |  Arg 3: 4
     |  |  |  FIBIN reentry (# 3):
     |  |  |  |  Arg 1: 2
     |  |  |  |  Arg 2: 1
     |  |  |  |  Arg 3: 3
     |  |  |  |  FIBIN reentry (# 4):
     |  |  |  |  |  Arg 1: 3
     |  |  |  |  |  Arg 2: 2
     |  |  |  |  |  Arg 3: 2
     |  |  |  |  |  FIBIN reentry (# 5):
     |  |  |  |  |  |  Arg 1: 5
     |  |  |  |  |  |  Arg 2: 3
     |  |  |  |  |  |  Arg 3: 1
     |  |  |  |  |  |  FIBIN reentry (# 6):
     |  |  |  |  |  |  |  Arg 1: 8
     |  |  |  |  |  |  |  Arg 2: 5
     |  |  |  |  |  |  |  Arg 3: 0
     |  |  |  |  |  |  FIBIN (# 6) return value = 5
     |  |  |  |  |  FIBIN (# 5) return value = 5
     |  |  |  |  FIBIN (# 4) return value = 5
     |  |  |  FIBIN (# 3) return value = 5
     |  |  FIBIN (# 2) return value = 5
     |  FIBIN return value = 5
     FIB2 return value = 5
     5
```

While there are better ways to define the fibonacci function, there are times when tree recursion is the best method of recursion available. This frequently occurs when looking at lists.

The `member` function looks at elements of a list and determines if an item is eq one of those elements.

```
(member 'a '(a b c))
⇒     (A B C)


(member 'a '(b (c a) d))
⇒     NIL
```

Because `member` does not look at the atoms of the list, it is possible that an item is somewhere in the lists substructure, but `member` won't see it.

You could use a tree recursion to look at every atom of the list.

**1.**  The stopping point is when the list is an atom.

**2.**  The operation is a test if the item is a member of the car of the list or a member of the cdr of the list.

**3.**  Because you are testing the car and cdr of the list, the entire list is not being passed to the function (i.e., the list is getting smaller).

Note that each element of the list is only looked at once. In this way, there is not the major problem of using large amounts of memory.

```
(defun rec-member (x a-list)
  (cond ((atom a-list) (equal x a-list))       ;; if atom, stop and return whether or
                                               ;;   not x is in the list.
        (t (or (rec-member x (car a-list))     ;; is x in the car of the list?
               (rec-member x (cdr a-list)))))) ;; is x in the cdr of the list?
⇒     REC-MEMBER

(rec-member 'a '(a b c))
⇒     T

(rec-member 'a '(b (c a) d))
⇒     T

(rec-member 'x '(b (c a) d))
⇒     NIL

(trace rec-member)
⇒     (REC-MEMBER)
```

```
(rec-member 'a '(b (c a) (d e) f g (h i)))
⇒    REC-MEMBER entry:

    |   Arg 1: A
    |   Arg 2: (B (C A) (D E) F G (H I))
    |   REC-MEMBER reentry (# 2):
    |   |   Arg 1: A
    |   |   Arg 2: B
    |   REC-MEMBER (# 2) return value = NIL
    |   REC-MEMBER reentry (# 2):
    |   |   Arg 1: A
    |   |   Arg 2: ((C A) (D E) F G (H I))
    |   |   REC-MEMBER reentry (# 3):
    |   |   |   Arg 1: A
    |   |   |   Arg 2: (C A)
    |   |   |   REC-MEMBER reentry (# 4):
    |   |   |   |   Arg 1: A
    |   |   |   |   Arg 2: C
    |   |   |   REC-MEMBER (# 4) return value = NIL
    |   |   |   REC-MEMBER reentry (# 4):
    |   |   |   |   Arg 1: A
    |   |   |   |   Arg 2: (A)
    |   |   |   |   REC-MEMBER reentry (# 5):
    |   |   |   |   |   Arg 1: A
    |   |   |   |   |   Arg 2: A
    |   |   |   |   REC-MEMBER (# 5) return value = T
    |   |   |   REC-MEMBER (# 4) return value = T
    |   |   REC-MEMBER (# 3) return value = T
    |   REC-MEMBER (# 2) return value = T
    REC-MEMBER return value = T
    T
```

The or macro evaluates its arguments until one of them returns a non-nil value. Thus, as soon as a match is found, the function exits. It does not bother to try matching all the elements.

---

**Exercise 9-3**

1. The length function returns the number of elements in a list. Write a recursive function that returns the number of atoms in a list.

2. Rewrite the rev-list function so that elements within a sublist are reversed. Given the list '(a (b c) d), the function should return '(d (c b) a). Using a calling function and subfunction as in linear iterative recursion, helps solve this problem.

---

## SUMMARY

Three methods of recursion were presented in this chapter.

| | |
|---|---|
| `linear recursive` | The operation is done after the recursion. |
| `linear iterative` | The operation is done as the recursion is in process. All information is passed to the function each time it is called. |
| `tree recursion` | Recursion is done on the car and the cdr of a list. Either linear recursive or linear iterative recursion is incorporated. |

Recursion does not depend on any set of predefined functions. Instead, recursion is a method of programming.

# PART 3
# Functions on Objects

## *10*

## *Lists*

Each chapter in Part 3 looks at one data type and the functions that operate on that type. Because some data types are subtypes of others, there may be functions in more than one chapter that operate on that data type. For instance, a string is a subtype of vector, array, and sequence. You will find functions in all four chapters that operate on strings.

At the beginning of Part 2, there is a discussion of the syntax used to describe functions, macros, and special forms. That same syntax is used throughout this part. In addition, many of the functions have lambda keywords. There are several keywords that are used frequently. These are described here. Examples and differences are shown where the keywords are used.

The keyword package contains a list of all the keywords used in system-defined functions. The following function lists all of the keywords in the keyword package. **Caution:** There are A LOT of keywords, several hundred. If you evaluate the following function, you may have to wait awhile for it to finish.

```
(do-symbols (x (find-package 'keyword))
           (print x))
```

:key                     The :key keyword requires a function as an argu-
                         ment. This can be the name of a function or a lambda
                         expression. The macro characters #' precede the

|  | function name. The function is applied to elements before other testing or comparison is done. The function should not change the element. In general, `#'identity` is the default value of `:key`. |
|---|---|
| `:start` | The `:start` keyword requires a form that returns a number as an argument. A function is applied to a subsequence beginning with the element specified by `:start`. The first element is element zero. This is the default value of `:start`. |
| `:end` | The `:end` keyword requires a form that returns a number as an argument. A function is applied to a subsequence ending with the element specified. `:end` is the exclusive end. The first element is element zero. The default value of `:end` is the length of the sequence plus 1. |
| `:test` | The `:test` keyword requires a function as an argument. The default value in many cases is `#'eql`. The argument function is used to test elements of a sequence. Sometimes the test is for equality. Othertimes the test is a different predicate. If the `:key` keyword is used, the `:key` argument function is applied before the `:test` argument function. |
| `:test-not` | This is similar to `:test`, except the function is looking for elements that fail the test. |
| `:from-end` | The `:from-end` keyword requires a nil or non-nil argument. If the argument is non-nil, the function is applied beginning with the last element in the sequence rather than the first element of the sequence. If the `:start` or `:end` keywords are used, the function is applied only to the subsequence either from the beginning of the subsequence or the end of the subsequence. |
| `:initial-element` | The `:initial-element` keyword requires an argument that is complementary to the function. (If you are creating a string, the argument must be a string character.) When many data types are created, all the elements take a default value unless this keyword is used. The default value can be nil, 0, or undefined. |

This chapter discusses how Lisp stores lists and the functions that operate only on lists. You should note that a list is a subtype of sequence. Chapter 14 also contains functions that operate on lists.

There are many functions presented in this chapters. You will learn how:

- To create a list

- To change the structure of a list

- To get an element from a list

- To build a list

- To modify a list

- To use a list like a stack

- To copy a list

- To use a list like a set

- To substitute elements in a list

- How a list can associate values

LISP is a list processing language. All the forms you have seen have been lists. Lisp takes the first element of a list as the name of a function and all other elements as arguments to that function. In order to have Lisp not evaluate a list, put that list within another list whose operator is `quote`.


## ATOMS AND LISTS

An atom is not a list. An *atom* in Lisp is like an atom in physics; there are individual letters to a Lisp name and that is as far as you can break it down. In physics, an atom is the smallest particle that makes up a substance with electrons, neutrons, and protons making up the name.

*Lists* are made up of atoms and other lists. (Molecules are made up of atoms and other molecules.)

These are lists:

```
(this is a list)
(another (inner list))
()
((((((a))))))
(one (two (three) four) five)
```

These are atoms:

```
atom
ATOM
1.2
some-name
NIL
```

A list contains zero or more atoms and zero or more lists. A list that has no atoms is called the empty list or *nil*.

```
()
```

nil is an atom. It is also a list. nil is the only symbol that is both an atom and a list.

```
() ≡ nil
```

There are two predicates that determine if an object is a list or an atom: listp and atom.

```
(listp '(a))
⇒    T

(listp 'a)
⇒    NIL

(listp '(a . b))
⇒    T

(listp '())
⇒    T

(atom '(a))
⇒    NIL

(atom 'a)
⇒    T

(atom '(a . b))
⇒    NIL

(atom ())
⇒    T
```

**cons**

The cons function builds a list. cons takes two arguments. The first argument becomes the first element in the list. This is called the *car* of the list. The second argument is the rest of the list. This is called the *cdr* of the list.

(cons *first-element rest-of-list*)

For example,

```
(cons 'a '(b))
⇒    (A B)

(cons 'a ())
⇒    (A)

(cons 4 '(1 2))
⇒    (4 1 2)
```

Just because the first argument is referred to as an element, that does not mean it must be an atom. It can also be a list.

```
(cons '(a) '(b))
⇒    ((A) B)

(cons '(1 2 3) '(4 5 6))
⇒    ((1 2 3) 4 5 6)

(cons '(1 (2 (3))) '(a))
⇒    ((1 (2 (3))) A)
```

Notice that when the first argument is a list, the first element of the new list is also a list.

Similarly, the *rest-of-list* does not have to be a list.

```
(cons 'a 'b)
⇒    (A . B)
```

```
(cons ' (a) 'b)
⇒     ((A) . B)

(cons () 'b)
⇒     (NIL . B)
```

When the *rest-of-list* is an atom, the resulting list is a *dotted pair*.

## Cons Cells

A list is represented as a chain of *cons cells*. A single cons cell has two parts: a car and a cdr. Cons cells are illustrated using box and pointer notation.

The box is divided into two sections: a car and a cdr, as shown in Fig. 10-1.

**Figure 10-1** Car and Cdr

If either the car or the cdr is a symbol (not a list), then a pointer comes from the section to point to the symbol. If either the car or the cdr is a list, then a pointer comes from the section to point to the car of another cons cell that illustrates that list.

Consider a list with only one element, B.

(B)

The car of this list is B. The cdr of the list is `nil`. In box and pointer notation, this list looks as shown in Fig. 10-2.

B

**Figure 10-2**  (B)

`nil` is a list. It specifies the empty list. When the cdr of a list is `nil`, the word nil is written outside the box. Not every list ends with nil.

The list (A . B) contains a single cons cell. The car is A and the cdr is B. This type of list is called a *dotted pair* and is shown in Fig. 10-3.

**Figure 10-3**  (A . B)

Most lists contain multiple elements. The following notation shows the list (A B C D). The car of the list is A. The cdr is (B C D). The car of (B C D) is B, and the cdr is (C D). See Fig. 10-4.

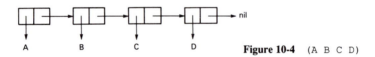

**Figure 10-4**  (A B C D)

Sometimes an element is a list itself. Consider ((A) B). The car of this list is (A). The cdr is (B). The notation for this list is shown in Fig. 10-5.

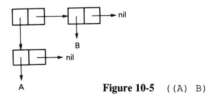

**Figure 10-5**  ((A) B)

In this illustration, the first cons cell contains two pointers. The first pointer points to the car list (A). The second pointer points to the cdr list (B). (A) is represented the same way as (B), except the car pointer points to a different symbol.

Each cons cell contains two sections: the car and the cdr. Both the car and the cdr contain a pointer that points to either a symbol or another cons cell. As you look at the next examples, consider what is the car and what is the cdr of each list.

     ((1 2 3) 4 5 6)

The car is (1 2 3). The cdr is (4 5 6). See Fig. 10-6.

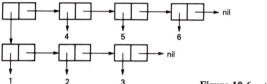

**Figure 10-6**   ((1  2  3)  4  5  6)

((A)  (B)  (C))

The car is (A). The cdr is ((B)  (C)). See Figs. 10-7–10-11 for more examples of box and pointer notation.

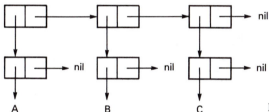

**Figure 10-7**   ((A)  (B)  (C))

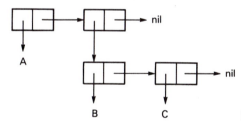

**Figure 10-8**   (A  (B  C))

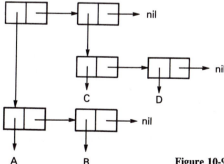

**Figure 10-9**   ((A  B)(C  D))

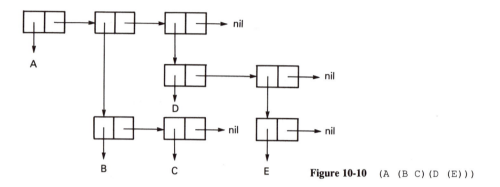

**Figure 10-10**   (A  (B  C) (D  (E)))

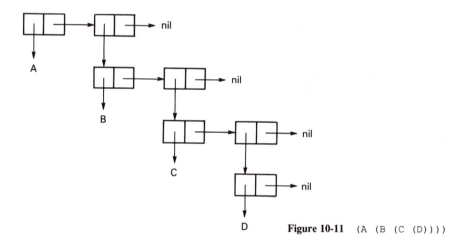

**Figure 10-11**   (A  (B  (C  (D))))

---

**Exercise 10-1**

Write the car and cdr of each of the following lists:

   **1.** (a  b  c)
   **2.** (a  .  b)
   **3.** (a  (b  c))
   **4.** ((a)  b  c)
   **5.** ((a  b) (c  d))

Write the car and cdr of each list and sublist in Exercises 6 and 7.  For example,

```
(a b c)
car of (a b c) = a
cdr of (a b c) = (b c)

car of (b c) = b
cdr of (b c) = (c)

car of (c) = c
cdr of (c) = nil
```

**6.** ((a b)(c d))

**7.** (a (b (c)))

Use the box and pointer notation for the following lists:

**8.** (a b c)

**9.** (a (b))

**10.** ((a) b)

**11.** ((a)(b))

**12.** (a (b (c)))

**13.** ((a (b))((d) e (f (g))))

**14.** (((1) 2) 3)

**15.** (a b . c)

---

## CAR AND CDR

Given a list, the `car` and `cdr` functions return the car and cdr of the list.

(car *list*)

(cdr *list*)

For example,

```
(car '(a b c))
⇒    A

(cdr '(a b c))
⇒    (B C)

(car '((a b)(c d)))
⇒    (A B)
```

```
(cdr '((a b)(c d)))
⇒   ((C D))

(car '((a (b)) c (d)))
⇒   (A (B))

(cdr '((a (b)) c (d)))
⇒   (C (D))
```

If you want to get the second element in a list, rather than the first, which car returns, you can nest the functions.

```
(cdr '(a b c))
⇒   (B C)

(car (cdr '(a b c)))
⇒   B
```

You can get the third, fourth, fifth, etc. element by applying the cdr functions as many times as necessary.

```
(car '(1 2 3 4 5 6 7 8 9 10))
⇒   1

(car (cdr '(1 2 3 4 5 6 7 8 9 10)))
⇒   2

(cdr '(1 2 3 4 5 6 7 8 9 10))
⇒   (2 3 4 5 6 7 8 9 10)

(cdr (cdr '(1 2 3 4 5 6 7 8  9 10)))
⇒   (3 4 5 6 7 8 9 10)

(car (cdr (cdr '(1 2 3 4 5 6 7 8 9 10))))
⇒   3

(car (cdr (cdr (cdr (cdr (cdr (cdr '(1 2 3 4 5 6 7 8 9 10)))))))))
⇒   7
```

Similarly, if the car of a list is a list and you want the car of the inner list, you can nest the cars.

```
(car '((a b)(c d)))
⇒   (A B)

(car (car '((a b)(c d))))
⇒   A
```

```
(car '(((((a) b) c) d) e))
⇒    ((((A) B) C) D)


(car (car (car (car '((((((a) b) c) c) e)))))
⇒    (A)
```

Actually, you can nest the `cars` and `cdrs` in any way you choose to get the element or sublist you want.

```
(setq fox '((the (quick) brown) fox (jumped (over the) lazy (dog))))
⇒    ((THE (QUICK) BROWN) FOX (JUMPED (OVER THE) LAZY (DOG)))


(car fox)
⇒    (THE (QUICK) BROWN)


(cdr fox)
⇒    (FOX (JUMPED (OVER THE) LAZY (DOG)))


(car (car fox))
⇒    THE


(car (car (cdr (car fox))))
⇒    QUICK


(car (cdr (cdr (car fox))))
⇒    BROWN


(car (cdr fox))
⇒    FOX
```

---

**Exercise 10-2**

Retrieve each word from the fox lists as was done for the first four words in the previous example.

---

## Shorthand

There is a shorthand for writing nested `cars` and `cdrs`. Both `car` and `cdr` begin with a `c` and end with an `r`. To combine the functions, use the middle letter, either `a` or `d`, between the `c` and `r`. You can combine up to four functions in any order.

```
(car (car '((a b))))
⇒    A


(caar '((a b)))
⇒    A


(cdr (car '((a b))))
⇒    (B)


(cdar '((a b)))
⇒    (B)


(car (cdr (car '((a b)))))
⇒    B


(cadar '((a b)))
⇒    B


caar   ≡ (car (car x))
cadr   ≡ (car (cdr x))
cdar   ≡ (cdr (car x))
cddr   ≡ (cdr (cdr x))
caaar  ≡ (car (car (car x)))
caadr  ≡ (car (car (cdr x)))
cadar  ≡ (car (cdr (car x)))
cdaar  ≡ (cdr (car (car x)))
caddr  ≡ (car (cdr (cdr x)))
cdadr  ≡ (cdr (car (cdr x)))
cddar  ≡ (cdr (cdr (car x)))
cdddr  ≡ (cdr (cdr (cdr x)))
caaaar ≡ (car (car (car (car x))))
caaadr ≡ (car (car (car (cdr x))))
caadar ≡ (car (car (cdr (car x))))
cadaar ≡ (car (cdr (car (car x))))
cdaaar ≡ (cdr (car (car (car x))))
caaddr ≡ (car (car (cdr (cdr x))))
caddar ≡ (car (cdr (cdr (car x))))
cddaar ≡ (cdr (cdr (car (car x))))
cadadr ≡ (car (cdr (car (cdr x))))
cdadar ≡ (cdr (car (cdr (car x))))
cdaadr ≡ (cdr (car (car (cdr x))))
cadddr ≡ (car (cdr (cdr (cdr x))))
cdaddr ≡ (cdr (car (cdr (cdr x))))
cddadr ≡ (cdr (cdr (car (cdr x))))
cdddar ≡ (cdr (cdr (cdr (car x))))
cddddr ≡ (cdr (cdr (cdr (cdr x))))
```

## CHANGING THE STRUCTURE OF A LIST

The cons cell has two halves: the car and the cdr. The `car` function returns the car, and the `cdr` function returns the cdr. Besides looking at the car and cdr, you can also change the car and cdr. The `rplaca` function replaces the car of a list. The `rplacd` function replaces the cdr of the list.

### rplaca

```
(rplaca list replacement)
```

For example,

```
(setq x '((a b)c d))
⇒    ((A B) C D)

(rplaca x 'm)
⇒    (M C D)

(rplaca x '(n o (e f)))
⇒    ((N O (E F)) C D)

(rplaca x 'p)
⇒    (P C D)
```

rplaca replaces the car of a list with whatever value you specify, as shown in Fig. 10-12. Because `rplaca` replaces the actual car, and not the value, you must be careful not to create circular lists. If you try this next example on your system, be sure that `*print-circle*` is `t`. This will stop the printer from trying to print a circular list. Instead, it shows that the list is circular. See Fig. 10-13.

```
(setq *print-circle* t)
⇒    T

(rplaca x x)
⇒    #0=(#0# (C D))
```

### rplacd

The `rplacd` function replaces the cdr of a list, as shown in Fig. 10-14.

```
(rplacd list replacement)
```

(setq x '((ab)cd))

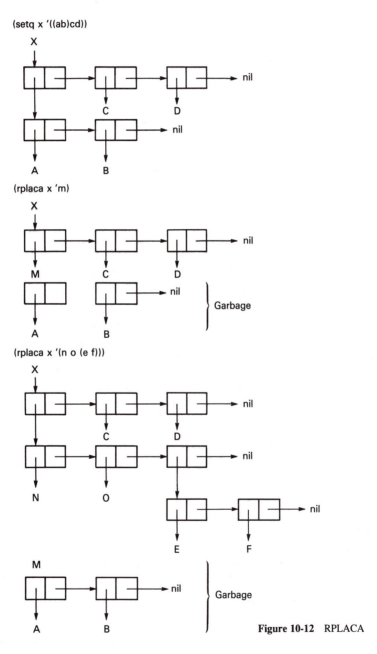

(rplaca x 'm)

(rplaca x '(n o (e f)))

**Figure 10-12**   RPLACA

(rplaca x 'p)

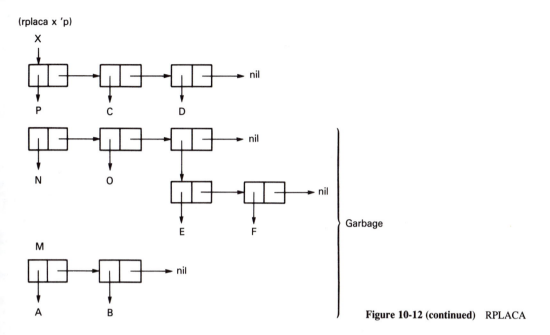

Figure 10-12 (continued)   RPLACA

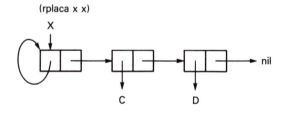

Figure 10-13   Circular RPLACA

For example,

```
(setq x '(a b c))
⇒    (A B C)

(rplacd x '(f))
⇒    (A F)

(rplacd x 'd)
⇒    (A . D)

(rplacd x '((m n)))
⇒    (A (M N))
```

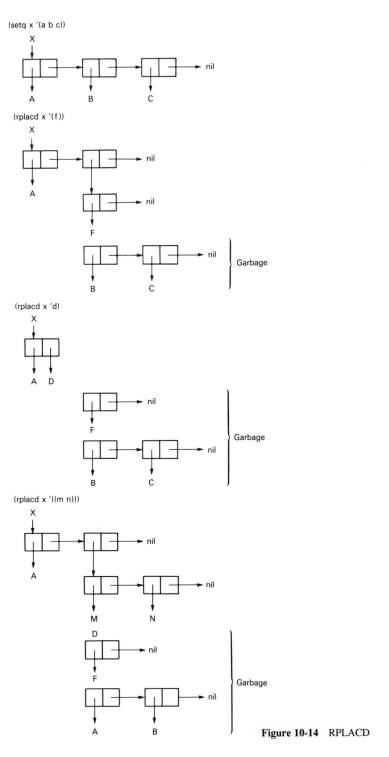

**Figure 10-14**   RPLACD

Similar to `rplaca`, `rplacd` can create a circular list by pointing to itself, as shown in Fig. 10-15.

```
(setq *print-circle* t)
⇒    T

(rplacd x x)
⇒    #0=(A . #0#)
```

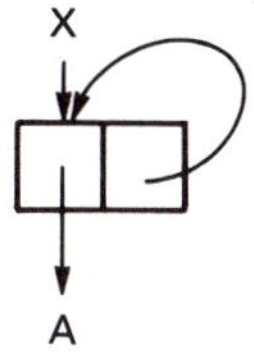

(rplacd x x)

**Figure 10-15**   Circular RPLACD

## Garbage

Every time you change the structure of a list, there may be parts of the list floating around that have no pointer directed to them. There is no way to access these parts. Every so often (time depends on implementation) Lisp collects all the garbage. If you are concerned with the time it takes to collect garbage, or the memory you are wasting, you should be aware of when you are creating a list, how often you create the same list, and methods for reducing consing.

If you evaluate the following, you create a list.

```
'(a b c)
```

There is no pointer to that list, so if you want a similar list, you have to create it again. By giving a symbol the value of the list, that same list is available at any time.

```
(setq x '(a b c))
```

Many of the functions in this chapter create a new list every time they are evaluated. Other functions modify their arguments rather than create a new list. If the function modifies its arguments, there is usually less memory used and less garbage left. However, destructive arguments can have side effects if more than one symbol points to the argument list. There are trade-offs for using destructive and nondestructive methods. At this point you should be aware of what the function does. Later, you can determine which method to use on particular problems.

## GETTING ELEMENTS FROM A LIST

In addition to car and cdr, there are several functions that return elements or sublists of the argument list.

### first through tenth

car returns the first element of a list. cadr returns the second element of a list. caddr returns the third element of a list. cadddr returns the fourth element of a list. Because you can only combine up to four functions by using car and cdr this way, there seems to be no easy way to get the fifth element of a list. Well, there is. The first, second, third, ..., or tenth function returns the first, second, third, ..., or tenth element of a list.

```
(setq numbers '(1 2 3 4 5 6 7 8 9 10))
⇒     (1 2 3 4 5 6 7 8 9 10)

(first numbers)
⇒     1

(third numbers)
⇒     3

(fifth numbers)
⇒     5

(seventh numbers)
⇒     7

(tenth numbers)
⇒     10
```

### nth

If you have more than ten elements in a list, you can still get a single element. The nth function returns the nth element of the list. Notice, however, that nth considers the first element to be the zeroth element.

```
(nth n list)
```

For example,

```
numbers
⇒     (1 2 3 4 5 6 7 8 9 10)

(nth 0 numbers)
⇒     1
```

```
(nth 1 numbers)
⇒    2

(nth 9 numbers)
⇒    10

(nth 10 numbers)
⇒    NIL
```

## nthcdr

You can also apply the `cdr` function several times without having to write it out.
`nthcdr` returns the nth cdr of the list. It applies `cdr` n times to the list and returns the
result.

    (nthcdr *n list*)

For example,

```
numbers
⇒    (1 2 3 4 5 6 7 8 9 10)

(nthcdr 0 numbers)
⇒    (1 2 3 4 5 6 7 8 9 10)

(nthcdr 5 numbers)
⇒    (6 7 8 9 10)

(nthcdr 9 numbers)
⇒    (10)

(nthcdr 10 numbers)
⇒    NIL
```

## rest

`cdr` can be described as returning the rest of the list. So there is a function `rest` that
is equivalent to `cdr`.

```
(cdr '((a b) c d))
⇒    (C D)

(rest '((a b) c d))
⇒    (C D)

(cdr (rest '((a b) c d)))
⇒    (D)

(rest (cdr '((a b) c d)))
⇒    (D)
```

## Butlast

There are times when you want the list without the last element, or without the last n
elements. For this, there is the function butlast.

```
(butlast list &optional n)

(butlast '(a b c d e))
⇒    (A B C D)

(butlast '((a b)(c d)(e f)))
⇒    ((A B) (C D))

(butlast '(a b c d e) 0)
⇒    (A B C D E)

(butlast '(a b c d e) 1)
⇒    (A B C D)

(butlast '(a b c d e) 3)
⇒    (A B)

(butlast '(a b c d e) 5)
⇒    NIL
```

## Returning an Object

While some functions return a copy of an element, or a copy of the list, other functions
return a pointer to that element, or list.

It is important to note which functions return copies and which return the actual
element. Of the functions you have seen so far, all return the actual element or sublist,
not a copy.

```
(setq p '(a b c))
⇒    (A B C)

(setf (cdr p) '(x y))
⇒    (X Y)

p
⇒    (A X Y)
```

When the list p is created, it becomes a list of three elements (A B C). The cdr
of p is the pointer from the first cons cell to the rest of the list. cdr returns the actual
pointer. You can change p with setf by changing the value of the cdr of p. See Fig.
10-16.

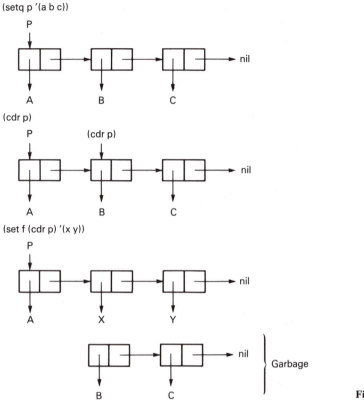

**Figure 10-16**   CDR

cons creates a list from its arguments.

```
(setq m '(a b))
⇒    (A B)

(setq n '(x y))
⇒    (X Y)

(setq o (cons m n))
⇒    ((A B) X Y)

m
⇒    (A B)

n
⇒    (X Y)

(setf (caar o) 'p)
⇒    P

m
⇒    (P B)
```

When cons creates list o, it uses lists m and n. Changing the value of an element in list o also changes the value of list m or n. See Fig. 10-17.

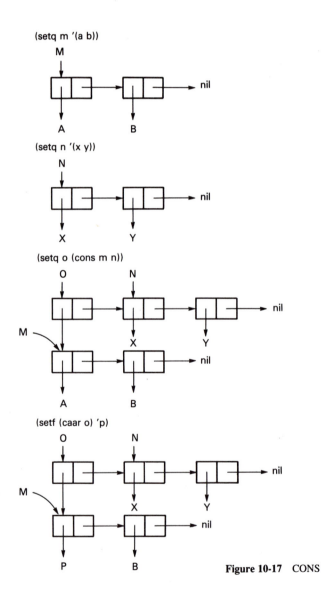

**Figure 10-17**   CONS

**Exercises 10-3**

Draw a cons cell showing the results of the following functions:

1. `(setq a '(1 2 3))`
2. `(setq b a)`
3. `(setq c (cons a b))`
4. `(setq x '(a b c))`
5. `(setq y (cdr x))`
6. `(setf (car y) 'z)`
7. Write a function that returns the eleventh element of a list.
8. If the telephone directory was in a list, each name, address, and phone number would be a sublist.

```
(setq directory '((john_smith 12345_Euclid 555-1212)
                  (sue_jones 1000_Chapman 555-1000)))
⇒     ((JOHN_SMITH \12345_EUCLID \555-1212)
       (SUE_JONES \1000_CHAPMAN \555-1000))
```

Write three functions (name, address, and phone) that take a single list and return one component of that list.

9. Why should these functions be created rather than using cars and cdrs to retrieve the components directly?

# BUILDING LISTS

`cons` is one way to construct a list. `cons` adds a new element to the front of an existing list. There are other functions that create, concatenate, and build lists from other lists.

## Make-List

The `make-list` function creates a lists.

```
(make-list size &key :initial-element)

(make-list 7)
⇒     (NIL NIL NIL NIL NIL NIL NIL)

(make-list 0)
⇒     NIL
```

**:initial-element.**   The syntax of the `make-list` function introduces the &key
parameters.  Recal in the discussions of `defun` and `lambda` that &key specifies that
the parameters that follow are keywords.  The keywords in most Lisp functions are
optional.  They have a default value.

When you use a keyword, type the keyword and then a value. `make-list` has
one keyword `:initial-element`.  If you specify the keyword and a value,
`make-list` creates a list with each element given the specified value.  The default
value for this keyword is `nil`.

```
(make-list 4 :initial-element 'a)
⇒    (A A A A)

(make-list 3 :initial-element '(a b))
⇒    ((A B) (A B) (A B))

(make-list 5)
⇒    (NIL NIL NIL NIL NIL)
```

## append

The `append` function concatenates lists into one list.  It creates a new list and does not
modify the argument lists.

```
(append &rest lists)

(append '(a b) '(c d))
⇒    (A B C D)

(append '((1 a)(2 b)) '((3 c)(4 d)))
⇒    ((1 A) (2 B) (3 C) (4 D))
```

`append` does not modify the argument lists.  It copies the top level of the arguments
except for the last argument.

```
(setq x '(a b (c d)))
⇒    (A B (C D))

(setq y '(e f))
⇒    (E F)

(setq z (append x y))
⇒    (A B (C D) E F)

(setf (car x) 'x)
⇒    X

x
⇒    (X B (C D))
```

```
z
⇒    (A B (C D) E F)

(setf (caaddr x) 'z)
⇒    Z

x
⇒    (X B (Z D))

z
⇒    (A B (Z D) E F)
```

This can be shown using box and pointer notation, as shown in Fig. 10-18.

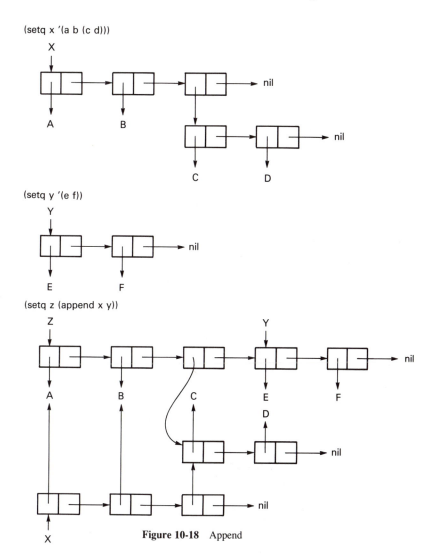

**Figure 10-18**   Append

## revappend

The `revappend` function concatenates the reverse of the first list with the second list.

```
(revappend first-list second-list)

(revappend '(1 2) '(3 4))
⇒    (2 1 3 4)

(revappend '((1 a)(2 b)) '(3 4))
⇒    ((2 B) (1 A) 3 4)
```

The top-level elements of the first list are reversed. Any elements within nested lists are not reversed.

```
(setq x '(a b))
⇒    (A B)

(setq y '(c d))
⇒    (C D)

(setq z (revappend x y))
⇒    (B A C D)
```

`revappend` does not change the argument lists. It creates a new list, as shown in Fig. 10-19.

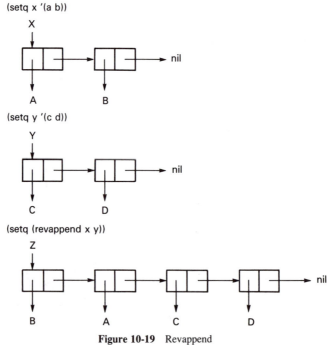

**Figure 10-19**   Revappend

## List

The `list` function constructs a list from its arguments.

```
(list &rest arguments)

(list 'a 'b '(c d))
⇒     (A B (C D))

(setq x '(a b))
⇒     (A B)

(setq y '(c d))
⇒     (C D)

(setq z (list x y '(x y) 'a))
⇒     ((A B) (C D) (X Y) A)
```

`list` constructs a list using all its arguments. If an argument is a list, that list is incorporated into the new list, as shown in Fig. 10-20.

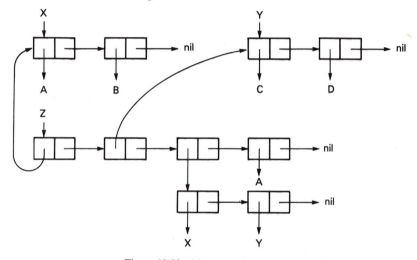

**Figure 10-20**   List

In Fig. 10-20 you can see that list x and list y have not been changed by the `list` function. However, since the `car` and `cadr` of z point to other lists, whenever list x or list y changes, so does the list z.

```
(setf (car x) 'x)
⇒     X


z
⇒     ((X B) (C D) (X Y) A)
```

You can also change list x or the list y by changing list z.

```
(setf (caar z) 'm)
⇒    M


z
⇒    ((M B) (C D) (X Y) A)


x
⇒    (M B)


(setf (caadr z) 'k)
⇒    K


z
⇒    ((M B) (K D) (X Y) A)


y
⇒    (K D)
```

## list*

The `list*` function is similar to `list` except that the last argument is used as the cdr of the new list.

```
(list* '(a b) '(c d))
⇒    ((A B) C D)

(list '(a b) '(c d))
⇒    ((A B) (C D))

(list* 'a 'b)
⇒    (A . B)

(setq x '(a b))
⇒    (A B)

(setq y '(c d))
⇒    (C D)

(setq z (list* x 'm y))
⇒    ((A B) M C D)
```

As with `list`, `list*` uses any argument lists as part of the constructed list. Changing values in one list changes the values in other lists that point to it, as shown in Fig. 10-21.

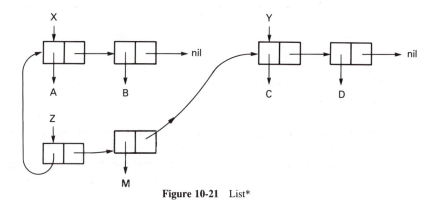

**Figure 10-21** List*

---

**Exercise 10-4**

Given:

```
(setq x '(a b c))
⇒    (A B C)


(setq y '(1 2 3))
⇒    (1 2 3)
```

what do the following functions return?

**1.** `(setq m (append x y))`

**2.** `(setf (car m) 'p)`
  `x`
  `(setf (fifth m) 5)`
  `y`

**3.** `(list 'x 'y)`

**4.** `(setq z (list x y))`

**5.** `(list* x y)`

**6.** `(setf (caar z) '(x y z))`
  `x`

## DESTRUCTIVE FUNCTIONS

There is a convention that if a function adds n to the beginning of its name, it is a *destructive function*. That is, it modifies its argument.

Some functions copy an argument before modifying it; others use the argument itself. It is important to note which functions modify their arguments and which do not. If you do not know this information, then, while you are building lists, you may be sharing structures without knowing and changing one list when you meant to change another list.

Why would you want to destroy the arguments? Consider the case where the arguments are supplied by another function and are not useful except as the arguments. Because the arguments are not referenced anywhere except within the function, when the function is done with them, they are collected in the next garbage collect. By using arguments and not copying them, you can save space. Additional cons are not created.

### nbutlast

The `nbutlast` function returns the original list with the last n elements removed, as shown in Fig. 10-22. This is different from `butlast`, which returns a new list and leaves the argument list unchanged.

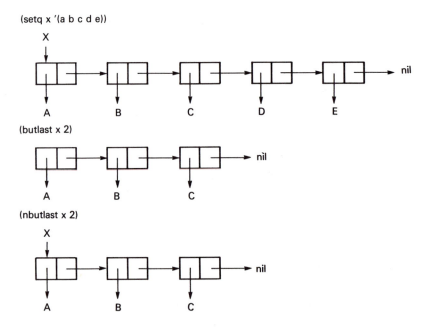

**Figure 10-22**   Butlast

```
(setq x '(a b c d e))
⇒    (A B C D E)

(butlast x 2)
⇒    (A B C)


x
⇒    (A B C D E)

(nbutlast x 2)
⇒    (A B C)


x
⇒    (A B C)
```

## nconc

The nconc function concatenates lists.  It uses the actual argument lists to construct a new list, as shown in Fig. 10-23.

```
(nconc &rest lists)

(setq x '(a b c))
⇒    (A B C)

(setq y '(d e f))
⇒    (D E F)

(setq z (nconc x y))
⇒    (A B C D E F)
```

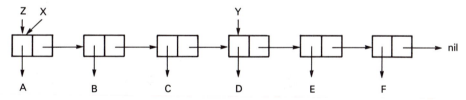

**Figure 10-23**   Nconc

```
(setf (car z) 'q)
⇒    Q


x
⇒    (Q B C D E F)

(setf (fourth z) 'w)
⇒    W
```

```
y
⇒     (W  E  F)


z
⇒     (Q  B  C  W  E  F)
```

## nreconc

The `nreconc` function concatenates the reverse of the first list with the second list.

(nreconc *first-list second-list*)

```
(setq  r  '(1  2  3))
⇒     (1  2  3)

(setq  s  '(4  5  6))
⇒     (4  5  6)

(setq  v  (nreconc  r  s))
⇒     (3  2  1  4  5  6)

r
⇒     (1  4  5  6)

s
⇒     (4  5  6)

(setf  (fourth  v)  9)
⇒     9

s
⇒     (9  5  6)

r
⇒     (1  9  5  6)
```

The `nreconc` function can modify its arguments, as shown in Fig. 10-24. When `nreconc` is applied to lists r and s, list r is modified. The value of list r is not the reverse of its original value. In this implementation, the value is its first element followed by the value of list s. When a function modifies its arguments, you cannot depend upon the values of those arguments. If a function uses its arguments, or constructs a result from its arguments, the values of the arguments remain the same from implementation to implementation. If the word "destructive" appears in the description of a function, the arguments may or may not change depending on implementation, and you should never depend on the changes. Appendix B contains the descriptions of all the functions, listing whether or not they are destructive.

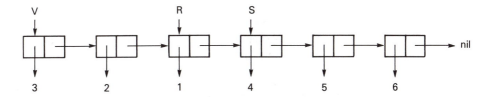

**Figure 10-24**   Nreconc

## LISTS AS STACKS

The `push` and `pop` macros put an element onto or take one off the front of a list. The element is returned and the list is modified. These macros use the list as if it were a stack.

### pop

The pop macro deletes the first element in the list and returns it.

```
(pop list)

(setq s '(a (b c) d e f))
⇒     (A (B C) D E F)

(pop s)
⇒     A

s
⇒     ((B C) D E F)

(pop s)
⇒     (B C)

s
⇒     (D E F)
```

### push

The push macro conses an item onto the front of a list.

```
(push item list)

(setq x '(a (b c)))
⇒     (A (B C))

(push 'a x)
⇒     (A A (B C))

(push '(e f) x)
⇒     ((E F) A A (B C))
```

### pushnew

The pushnew macro conses an item onto the front of a list if the item is not already in the list. pushnew returns the list.

```
(pushnew item list &key :test :test-not :key)

(setq x '(a (b c) d))
⇒     (A (B C) D)

(pushnew 'a x)
⇒     (A (B C) D)

(pushnew '(b c) x)
⇒     ((B C) A (B C) D)

(pushnew '(b c) x :test 'equal)
⇒     ((B C) A (B C) D)
```

## LENGTH

There are two functions that test the length of a list: endp and list-length. The endp function determines if a list is NIL.

```
(endp list)

(setq x '(a b))
⇒     (A B)

(endp x)
⇒     NIL

(pop x)
⇒     A

(endp x)
⇒     NIL

(pop x)
⇒     B

(endp x)
⇒     T

(pop x)
⇒     NIL
```

The `list-length` function returns the length of a list or `NIL` for a circular list.

```
(list-length list)

(setq x '(a (b c) d))
⇒    (A (B C) D)

(list-length x)
⇒    3

(pop x)
⇒    A

(list-length x)
⇒    2

(pop x)
⇒    (B C)

(list-length x)
⇒    1

(pop x)
⇒    D

(list-length x)
⇒    0

(setq *print-circle* t)
⇒    T

(setq y '(a b))
⇒    (A B)

(rplacd y y)
⇒    #0=(A . #0#)

(list-length y)
⇒    NIL
```

## COPYING LISTS

There are three functions that copy lists. These functions differ in the amount of the list that is copied compared with the amount of the list that is returned.

## copy-tree

copy-tree copies all conses recursively.  A non-cons is not copied: it is simply returned.  Circularities and sharing of substructures are not preserved.

```
(setq x '(a (b c) d))
⇒     (A (B C) D)

(setq y (copy-tree x))
⇒     (A (B C) D)
```

Notice that when an element of y is changed, nothing is changed in x.  This is shown in Fig. 10-25.

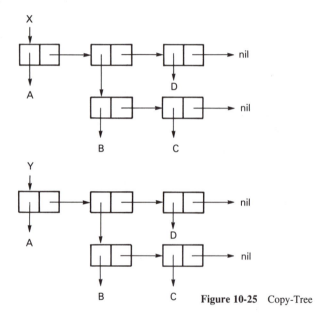

**Figure 10-25**  Copy-Tree

```
(setf (car y) 'w)
⇒     W

y
⇒     (W (B C) D)

x
⇒     (A (B C) D)

(setf (caadr y) 'm)
⇒     M
```

```
y
⇒    (W (M C) D)


x
⇒    (A (B C) D)
```

copy-tree can also be used on non-conses, such as vectors. For non-conses, copy-tree returns the original argument.

```
(setq x #(1 2 3))
⇒   #(1 2 3)

(setq y (copy-tree x))
⇒   #(1 2 3)

(eq x y)
⇒   T
```

## copy-list

copy-list copies only the top level; elements of the argument list that are conses are shared with the result list. See Figure 10-26. If the list is a dotted list, the result is also dotted.

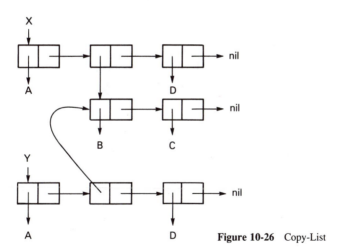

Figure 10-26  Copy-List

```
(setq x '(a (b c) d))
⇒   (A (B C) D)

(setq y (copy-list x))
⇒   (A (B C) D)
```

When an element of a sublist in x is changed, y is also changed.

```
(setf (caadr x) 'm)
⇒   M


x
⇒    (A (M C) D)


y
⇒    (A (M C) D)
```

When a top-level element of x is changed, y remains unchanged.

```
(setf (car x) 'w)
⇒   W


x
⇒    (W (M C) D) .


y
⇒    (A (M C) D)

(copy-list '(a . b))
⇒    (A . B)
```

## copy-alist

copy-alist copies the top level of the argument list and copies each element of the argument list that is a cons, as shown in Fig. 10-27.

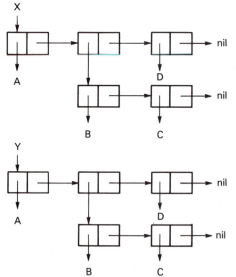

**Figure 10-27**   Copy-Alist

```
(setq x '(a (b c) d))
⇒   (A (B C) D)

(setq y (copy-alist x))
⇒   (A (B C) D)

(eq x y)
⇒   NIL

(equal x y)
⇒   T

(setf (caadr x) 'm)
⇒   M

x
⇒   (A (M C) D)

y
⇒   (A (B C) D)

(setf (car x) 'w)
⇒   W

x
⇒   (W (M C) D)

y
⇒   (A (B C) D)
```

## tree-equal

tree-equal determines if the two arguments are isomorphic trees with identical leaves. All three copy functions return trees that meet this criterion.

```
(setq x '(a (b c) d))
⇒   (A (B C) D)

(setq y (copy-tree x))
⇒   (A (B C) D)

(tree-equal x y)
⇒   T

(setq z (copy-list x))
⇒   (A (B C) D)
```

```
(tree-equal x z)
⇒    T

(setq a (copy-alist x))
⇒    (A (B C) D)

(tree-equal x a)
⇒    T
```

The arguments do not have to share structure.  If they "look" the same, the `tree-equal` function will return true.

```
(setq b '(a (b c) d))
⇒    (A (B C) D)

(tree-equal x b)
⇒    T
```

---

**Exercise 10-5**

Given:

```
(setq a '(1 2 (3 4 (5 6))))
⇒    (1 2 (3 4 (5 6)))

(setq b (copy-tree a))
⇒    (1 2 (3 4 (5 6)))

(setq c (copy-list a))
⇒    (1 2 (3 4 (5 6)))

(setq d (copy-alist a))
⇒    (1 2 (3 4 (5 6)))
```

what do the following functions return?

1. ```
   (setf (car b) 'q)
   a
   (setf (caddr b) 'z)
   a
   ```
2. ```
   (setf (car c) 'q)
   a
   (setf (caaddr c) 'w)
   a
   ```

**3.** `(setf (car d) 'r)`

`a`

`(setf (caadr (cdaddr d)) 't)`

`a`

---

## SUBLISTS

### tailp

The `tailp` function determines if a specified list is a sublist of another list. The sublist must share the tail (end) of the list for this function to return a true value. The structure must be shared. Even if the lists have equivalent elements, if the structure is not shared, one list cannot be the tail of the other.

```
(setq x '(a (b c) d))
⇒    (A (B C) D)

(setq y '(d))
⇒    (D)

(tailp y x)
⇒    NIL

(setq z (cdr x))
⇒    ((B C) D)

(tailp z x)
⇒    T

(setq w (cadr x))
⇒    (B C)

(tailp w x)
⇒    NIL
```

### ldiff

The `ldiff` function returns a copy of the elements of a list that appear before the specified sublist.

```
(ldiff list sublist)

(setq x '(a (b c) d))
⇒    (A (B C) D)
```

```
(setq y (cdr x))
⇒    ((B C) D)

(ldiff x y)
⇒    (A)

(setq a (cadr x))
⇒    (B C)

(ldiff x a)
⇒    (A (B C) D)

(setq b (cddr x))
⇒    (D)

(ldiff x b)
⇒    (A (B C))

(ldiff y b)
⇒    ((B C))
```

## LISTS AS SETS

There are several functions that look at lists as sets of elements. Set functions such as union, intersections, and difference are defined for lists.

### union

The union and nunion functions return a list that contains every element of the argument lists. nunion is destructive.

```
(union list1 list2 &key :test :test-not :key)
(nunion list1 list2 &key :test :test-not :key)

(setq class-one '(john betty carol tom sue))
⇒    (JOHN BETTY CAROL TOM SUE)

(setq class-two '(lisa richard chan bill sue john))
⇒    (LISA RICHARD CHAN BILL SUE JOHN)

(union class-one class-two)
⇒    (BILL CHAN RICHARD LISA JOHN BETTY CAROL TOM SUE)

(setq num1 '(1 2 3 4 5 6))
⇒    (1 2 3 4 5 6)
```

```
(setq num2 '(2 4 6 8 10 -2 -4 -6))
⇒    (2 4 6 8 10 -2 -4 -6)

(union num1 num2)
⇒    (-6 -4 -2 10 8 1 2 3 4 5 6)
```

The order of the results is implementation dependent.

**:test**  The `:test` keyword defaults to `eql`. This means that if two elements are `eql`, only one is placed in the result list. You can use any of the comparison functions that accept arguments that are the same type as the type of the elements in the lists. Because you are comparing two elements, the function must accept two arguments.

---

### Note

To indicate a function rather than a symbol, you must use the `function` special form. A shorthand notation for `function` is `#'`.

---

In the next example, each element in the second list is compared to each element in the first list. The comparison is <. Thus, if an element in the second list is greater than all the elements in the first list, it is included in the result list.

```
(union num1 num2 :test (function <))
⇒    (10 8 6 1 2 3 4 5 6)

(union num1 num2 :test #'<)
⇒    (10 8 6 1 2 3 4 5 6)
```

Step by step, this goes:

**1.** Each element in the first list is placed in the result list.

```
(1 2 3 4 5 6)
```

**2.** The first element in the second list is 2.

```
1 < 2    ⇒    T
2 < 2    ⇒    NIL
```

Go to the next element.

**3.** The next element in the second list is 4.

```
1 < 4  ⇒    T
2 < 4  ⇒    T
3 < 4  ⇒    T
4 < 4  ⇒    NIL
```

Go to the next element.

**4.** The next element is 6.

```
1 < 6  ⇒    T
2 < 6  ⇒    T
3 < 6  ⇒    T
4 < 6  ⇒    T
5 < 6  ⇒    T
6 < 6  ⇒    NIL
```

Go to the next element.

**5.** The next element is 8.

```
1 < 8  ⇒    T
2 < 8  ⇒    T
3 < 8  ⇒    T
4 < 8  ⇒    T
5 < 8  ⇒    T
6 < 8  ⇒    T
```

8 is greater than all the elements in the first list, so it is added to the result list.

**6.** The next element is 10.

```
1 < 10  ⇒    T
2 < 10  ⇒    T
3 < 10  ⇒    T
4 < 10  ⇒    T
5 < 10  ⇒    T
6 < 10  ⇒    T
```

10 is greater than all the elements in the first list, so it is added to the result list.

**7.** The next element is −2.

```
1 < −2  ⇒    NIL
```

Go to the next element.

**8.** The next element is –4.

```
1 < -4  ⇒    NIL
```

Go to the next element.

**9.** The next element is –6.

```
1 < -6  ⇒    NIL
```

The `eql` function, which is the default value of the `:test` keyword, is only one of several equal functions. When dealing with lists, numbers of different types, or strings you may find that `eql` is not the function you want to test for equality. Refer to Chapter 3, in the subsection on Predicates, for a list of all the equal functions.

```
(setq a '(a (b c) d))
⇒    (A (B C) D)

(setq b '(x (b c) d))
⇒    (X (B C) D)

(union a b)
⇒    ((B C) X A (B C) D)

(union a b :test #'equal)
⇒    (X A (B C) D)
```

`eql` considers character case (uppercase and lowercase letters) when comparing characters.

```
(setq str1 '(#\a #\b #\c #\f))
⇒    (#\a #\b #\c #\f)

(setq str2 '(#\A #\c #\d #\D #\F #\g))
⇒    (#\A #\c #\d #\D #\F #\g)

(union str1 str2)
⇒    (#\g #\F #\D #\d #\A #\a #\b #\c #\f)
```

The `char-equal` function ignores character case when comparing characters. Thus, only the first ''a'' is included in the result list. The ''a'' from the second list is not included.

```
(union str1 str2 :test# 'char-equal)
⇒    (#\g #\D #\d #\a #\b #\c #\f)
```

**:test-not.** The `:test-not` keyword specifies that if a pair of elements fail the test, the element is added to the result list.

```
(setq  a  '(1 3 5))
⇒     (1 3 5)

(setq b '(-1 2 6))
⇒     (-1 2 6)

(union a b)
⇒     (6 2 -1 1 3 5)

(union a b :test-not #'<)
⇒     (-1 1 3 5)
```

In this case, the elements of the first list are placed in the result list.

```
(1 3 5)
```

The elements of the second list are tested to see if they are greater than the elements of the first list. If they are, they are discarded. If they are not, they are added to the result list.

```
1 < -1  ⇒    NIL
3 < -1  ⇒    NIL
5 < -1  ⇒    NIL
```

Put −1 in the result list.

```
(-1 1 3 5)

1 < 2  ⇒    T
```

Go to next element.

```
1 < 3  ⇒    T
```

Go to next element.

```
1 < 5  ⇒    T
```

There are no more elements to test.

**:key.**    The third keyword is :key, which specifies a function that is applied to each element of both lists before the comparison test is done. The default value is identity. If the result value passes the test, the entire element is returned, not the result value.

Whereas the :key function is applied to both elements in union, there are other functions where the :key function is applied to elements of only one list. You should note which case is used when you see the :key keyword.

```
(setq set1 '((1 a)(2 b)(3 c)))
⇒    ((1 A) (2 B) (3 C))

(setq set2 '((1 b)(2 b)(3 d)))
⇒    ((1 B) (2 B) (3 D))

(union set1 set2 :test #'equal)
⇒    ((3 D) (1 B) (1 A) (2 B) (3 C))
```

The :test keyword was added because two lists are not eql unless they share structure.

```
(union set1 set2 :test #'equal :key #'car)
⇒    ((1 A) (2 B) (3 C))

(union set1 set2 :test #'equal :key #'cadr)
⇒    ((3 D) (1 A) (2 B) (3 C))
```

**1.** Each element of the first list is put in the result list.

```
((1 A) (2 B) (3 C))
```

**2.** Compare (1 B) against the elements in the first list.

```
(cadr '(1 A)) equal (cadr '(1 B))  ≡  'B equal 'A  ⇒    NIL
(cadr '(2 B)) equal (cadr '(1 B))  ≡  'B equal 'B  ⇒    T
```

Because B is already in the result list, it is not added.

**3.** Compare (2 B) against the elements in the first list.

```
(cadr '(1 A)) equal (cadr '(2 B))  ≡  'B equal 'A  ⇒    NIL
(cadr '(2 B)) equal (cadr '(2 B))  ≡  'B equal 'B  ⇒    T
```

Because B is already in the result list, it is not added.

**4.** Compare (3 D) against the elements in the first list.

```
(cadr '(1 A)) equal (cadr '(3 D))  ≡  'A equal 'D  ⇒    NIL
(cadr '(2 B)) equal (cadr '(3 D))  ≡  'B equal 'D  ⇒    NIL
(cadr '(3 C)) equal (cadr '(3 D))  ≡  'C equal 'D  ⇒    NIL
```

Because D is not in the first list, add it to the result list.

## intersection

The `intersection` and `nintersection` functions return a list that contains each element that appears in both argument lists.

```
(intersection list1 list2 &key :test :test-not :key)
(nintersection list1 list2 &key :test :test-not :key)
```

```
class-one
⇒      (JOHN BETTY CAROL TOM SUE)
```

```
class-two
⇒      (LISA RICHARD CHAN BILL SUE JOHN)
```

```
(intersection class-one class-two)
⇒      (SUE JOHN)
```

```
num1
⇒      (1 2 3 4 5 6)
```

```
num2
⇒      (2 4 6 8 10 -2 -4 -6)
```

```
(intersection num1 num2)
⇒      (6 4 2)
```

```
str1
⇒      ("a" "b" "c" "f")
```

```
str2
⇒      ("A" "c" "d" "D" "F" "g")
```

```
(intersection str1 str2)
⇒      NIL
```

```
(intersection str1 str2 :test #'string-equal)
⇒      ("f" "c" "a")
```

```
(intersection str1 str2 :test #'string=)
⇒      ("c")
```

```
set1
⇒      ((1 A) (2 B) (3 C))
```

```
set2
⇒      ((1 B) (2 B) (3 D))
```

```
(intersection set1 set2 :test-not #'equal)
⇒    ((3 C) (2 B) (1 A))


(intersection set1 set2 :test #'equal)
⇒    ((2 B))


(intersection set1 set2 :test #'equal :key #'car)
⇒    ((3 C) (2 B) (1 A))
```

## difference

The set-difference and nset-difference functions return a list of each element in the first list that is not in the second list.

```
(set-difference list1 list2 &key :test :test-not :key)
(nset-difference list1 list2 &key :test :test-not :key)


class-one
⇒    (JOHN BETTY CAROL TOM SUE)


class-two
⇒    (LISA RICHARD CHAN BILL SUE JOHN)


(set-difference class-one class-two)
⇒    (TOM CAROL BETTY)


num1
⇒    (1 2 3 4 5 6)


num2
⇒    (2 4 6 8 10 -2 -4 -6)


(set-difference num1 num2)
⇒    (5 3 1)


(setq num3 '(2 4 -5))
⇒    (2 4 -5)


(set-difference num1 num3)
⇒    (6 5 3 1)


(set-difference num1 num3 :key #'abs)
⇒    (6 3 1)
```

## Exclusive Or

The `set-exclusive-or` and `nset-exclusive-or` functions return a list that contains each element that appears in only one of the two argument lists.

```
(set-exclusive-or list1 list2 &key :test :test-not :key)
(nset-exclusive-or list1 list2 &key :test :test-not :key)


class-one
⇒     (JOHN BETTY CAROL TOM SUE)


class-two
⇒     (LISA RICHARD CHAN BILL SUE JOHN)


(set-exclusive-or class-one class-two)
⇒     (BILL CHAN RICHARD LISA TOM CAROL BETTY)


set1
⇒     ((1 A) (2 B) (3 C))


set2
⇒     ((1 B) (2 B) (3 D))


(set-exclusive-or set1 set2 :test #'equal)
⇒     ((3 D) (1 B) (3 C) (1 A))


(set-exclusive-or set1 set2 :test #'equal :key #'car)
⇒     NIL


(set-exclusive-or set1 set2 :test #'equal :key #'cadr)
⇒     ((3 D) (3 C) (1 A))
```

## subsetp

The `subsetp` function determines if every element of the first list appears in the second list. The order of the elements is not important.

```
(subsetp list1 list2 &key :test :test-not :key)

(setq a '(1 2 3))
⇒     (1 2 3)

(setq b '(2 4 5 1 9))
⇒     (2 4 5 1 9)

(subsetp a b)
⇒     NIL
```

```
(subsetp '(1 2) b)
⇒    T

(subsetp a b :test #'<)
⇒    T
```

## member

The member function determines if an element is a member of a list. The member-if and member-if-not functions determine if an element of the list satisfies (or not) a predicate.

```
(member item list &key :test :test-not :key)
(member-if predicate list &key :key)
(member-if-not predicate list &key :key)

class-one
⇒    (JOHN BETTY CAROL TOM SUE)

(member 'john class-one)
⇒    (JOHN BETTY CAROL TOM SUE)

(member 'sue class-one)
⇒    (SUE)

(member 'chan class-one)
⇒    NIL
```

member returns a sublist beginning with the matching element when it finds a match. It returns nil otherwise.

```
set1
⇒    ((1 A) (2 B) (3 C))

(member '(1 a) set1 :test #'equal)
⇒    ((1 A) (2 B) (3 C))

(member 'b set1 :key #'cadr)
⇒    ((2 B) (3 C))
```

The member-if and member-if-not functions test each element of the list to see if it satisfies a predicate function.

```
num2
⇒    (2 4 6 8 10 -2 -4 -6)
```

```
(member-if #'plusp num2)              ;; is there an element that is positive?
⇒    (2 4 6 8 10 -2 -4 -6)

(member-if #'minusp num2)             ;; is there an element that is negative?
⇒    (-2 -4 -6)

(member-if-not #'plusp num2)          ;; is there an element that is not positive?
⇒    (-2 -4 -6)

(member-if-not #'minusp num2)         ;; is there an element that is not negative?
⇒    (2 4 6 8 10 -2 -4 -6)

(member-if #'(lambda (x) (> x 4)) num2)      ;; is there an element that is
⇒    (6 8 10 -2 -4 -6)                        ;; greater than 4?

(member-if #'(lambda (x) (equal x -2)) num2) ;; is there an element that
⇒    (-2 -4 -6)                               ;; is equal -2?
```

Any function that takes a single argument of the type of the elements and returns a boolean value (nil or not-nil) can be used as the predicate. This can be a user-defined function, a lambda expression, or a predefined Lisp function.

## adjoin

The adjoin function adds an element to a set if the element is not already a member. adjoin only looks at the top level of the list.

```
(adjoin item list &key :test :test-not :key)

(setq x '(a (b c) d))
⇒    (A (B C) D)

(adjoin 'a x)
⇒    (A (B C) D)

(adjoin 'b x)
⇒    (B A (B C) D)

(adjoin '(c d) x)
⇒    ((C D) A (B C) D)

(adjoin '(b c) x)
⇒    ((B C) A (B C) D)

(adjoin '(b c) x :test #'equal)
⇒    (A (B C) D)
```

**Exercise 10-6**

1. Write your own adjoin function. Call it my-adjoin. It should produce the same results as `adjoin`.
2. Test your function to see that it returns the same list that `adjoin` returns. `adjoin` uses the argument list.
3. Modify your function so that it returns a new list with the item added, rather than adding the item to the list.

## SUBSTITUTION IN A TREE

The functions in this section look at a list as a tree, as shown in Fig. 10-28. The previous functions used only the top level of the lists to find elements. When the list is a tree, the entire list is an element and every sublist is an element. For example,

```
(setq tree '((a b) c (d (e f) g) h))
⇒    ((A B) C (D (E F) G) H)
```

This tree has the following "elements":

```
The entire tree: ((A B) C (D (E F) G) H)
The car of the tree: (A B)
    The car of the tree: A
    The cdr of the tree: (B)
        The car of the tree: B
        The cdr of the tree: nil
The cdr of the tree: (C (D (E F) G) H)
    The car of the tree: C
    The cdr of the tree: ((D (E F) G) H)
        The car of the tree: (D (E F) G)
            The car of the tree: D
            The cdr of the tree: ((E F) G)
                The car of the tree: (E F)
                    The car of the tree: E
                    The cdr of the tree: (F)
                        The car of the tree: F
                        The cdr of the tree: nil
                The cdr of the tree: (G)
                    The car of the tree: G
                    The cdr of the tree: nil
        The cdr of the tree: (H)
            The car of the tree: H
            The cdr of the tree: nil
```

'((a b) c (d (e f) g) h))

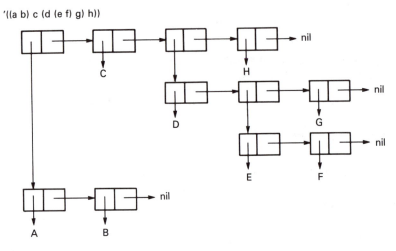

As a tree:

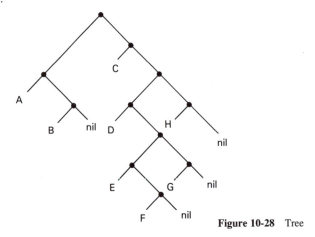

**Figure 10-28**   Tree

The car and cdr is taken repeatedly on every sublist of the list.

    The reason to note this difference is that the functions that test elements of the list must be able to take lists and atoms as their arguments.  If a function only takes atoms, it will cause an error when applied to a list.

## subst

The *substitute functions* substitute elements of a tree that satisfy (or not) a test.

```
(subst new old tree &key :test :test-not :key)
(subst-if new test tree &key :key)
(subst-if-not new test tree &key :key)

(nsubst new old tree &key :test :test-not :key)
(nsubst-if new test tree &key :key)
(nsubst-if-not new test tree &key :key)
```

For example,

```
(setq a '(() (a b) (c d () e) f))
⇒    (NIL (A B) (C D NIL E) F)

(subst '(x y) '() a :test #'equal)
⇒    ((X Y) (A B X Y) (C D (X Y) E X Y) F X Y)

(setq b '(() a . b))
⇒    (NIL A . B)

(subst '(x y) '() b :test #'equal)
⇒    ((X Y) A . B)
```

To change a sublist that has exactly two elements, you would have to write a lambda
expression that tested the sublist. The lambda expression must return a nil or non-nil
value that tells subst whether or not to do the substitution.

```
(setq x '(a (b c) e (f g h (z y)) ((q w) (t z))))
⇒    (A (B C) E (F G H (Z Y)) ((Q W) (T Z)))

(subst-if '(1 2) #'(lambda (y)
                     (cond ((equal y nil) nil)
                           ((atom y) nil)
                           ((equal (length y) 2) t)
                           (t nil)))
          x)
⇒    (A (1 2) E 1 2)

(subst-if '(1 2) #'(lambda (y)
                     (cond ((equal y nil) nil)
                           ((atom y) nil)
                           ((equal (length y) 2) t)
                           (t nil)))
          '(a b (c d) (e f (g h))))
⇒    (A B 1 2)
```

---

**Exercise 10-7**

Write a function that substitutes the symbol 'zero for each element that is equal to
zero. Because zero is a number, make sure that the function that tests the element
is given a number and not a list.

---

## ASSOCIATION LISTS

An *association list* is a list of dotted pairs. A dotted pair is a cons cell whose car is a symbol and whose cdr is a symbol, as shown in Fig. 10-29.

Symbol      Symbol     **Figure 10-29**   Dotted Pair

For example, the association list `((1 . a)(2 . b)(3 . c)(4 . d))` would be represented as shown in Fig. 10-30.

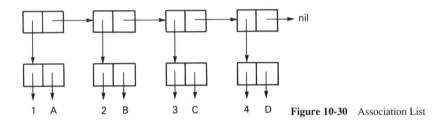

1   A        2   B        3   C        4   D     **Figure 10-30**   Association List

### Creating an Association List

You can create an association list with a `setq` or construct it with `acons` or `pairlis`.

```
(setq a '((1 . a)(2 . b)(3 . c)(4 . d)))
⇒    ((1 . A) (2 . B) (3 . C) (4 . D))
```

**acons.**   The `acons` function constructs a new association list by adding a new pair to the existing association list.

```
(acons key datum a-list)

(setq x (acons 0 'z a))
⇒    ((0 . Z) (1 . A) (2 . B) (3 . C) (4 . D))

a
⇒    ((1 . A) (2 . B) (3 . C) (4 . D))

(setf (car a) '(9 . z))
⇒    (9 . Z)

x
⇒    ((0 . Z) (9 . Z) (2 . B) (3 . C) (4 . D))
```

You can use `setq` to modify the value of the association list if you wish.

```
(setq a '((1 . a)(2 . b)(3 . c)(4 . d)))
⇒    ((1 . A) (2 . B) (3 . C) (4 . D))

(setq b (acons 0 'z a))
⇒    ((0 . Z) (1 . A) (2 . B) (3 . C) (4 . D))

(setq b (acons 9 'i b))
⇒    ((9 . I) (0 . Z) (1 . A) (2 . B) (3 . C) (4 . D))

b
⇒    ((9 . I) (0 . Z) (1 . A) (2 . B) (3 . C) (4 . D))
```

**pairlis.**   The `pairlis` function creates an association list by associating elements of the first list (the key) with corresponding elements of the second list (the data). The order of the resulting list is implementation dependent.

```
(pairlis key data &optional a-list)

(setq numbers '(0 1 2 3 4 5 6))
⇒    (0 1 2 3 4 5 6)

(setq letters '(a b c d e f g))
⇒    (A B C D E F G)

(setq pairs (pairlis numbers letters))
⇒    ((6 . G) (5 . F) (4 . E) (3 . D) (2 . C) (1 . B) (0 . A))
```

The resulting association list does not have the same order as the two argument lists. Instead, the association list is the reverse of the argument lists.

**copy-alist.**   The `copy-alist` function copies association lists. It copies the entire list.

```
(copy-alist list)

(setq num2 (copy-alist pairs))
⇒    ((6 . G) (5 . F) (4 . E) (3 . D) (2 . C) (1 . B) (0 . A))

(setf (car pairs) '(7 . h))
⇒    (7 . H)
```

```
pairs
⇒    ((7 . H) (5 . F) (4 . E) (3 . D) (2 . C) (1 . B) (0 . A))


num2
⇒    ((6 . G) (5 . F) (4 . E) (3 . D) (2 . C) (1 . B) (0 . A))
```

## Getting Values

Consider a telephone list that contains names and phone numbers. Each name is associated with a number. One way to represent this data is with an association list.

```
(setq phone '((andy . 5559876)
              (amy . 5551234)
              (betty . 5552345)
              (bob . 5557654)
              (carl . 5559999)
              (cindy . 5551111)))
```

The association list functions make it is easy to retrieve a number given a name or a name given a number.

```
(assoc item a-list &key :test :test-not :key)

(assoc-if test a-list &key :key)

(assoc-if-not test a-list &key :key)

(rassoc item a-list &key :test :test-not :key)

(rassoc-if test a-list &key :key)

(rassoc-if-not test a-list &key :key)
```

**assoc.**   The assoc function returns the first pair of an association list whose car satisfies the test. rassoc tests the cdr of the pair.

If you have the name of the person you want to call and are looking for the number, test the car of the pair.

```
(assoc 'amy phone)
⇒    (AMY . 5551234)

(assoc 'carl phone)
⇒    (CARL . 5559999)

(assoc 'cindy phone)
⇒    (CINDY . 5551111)
```

**rassoc.**    If you have a number and you want to find the matching name, test the cdr of the pair.

```
(rassoc '5551111 phone)
⇒    (CINDY . 5551111)

(rassoc '5557654 phone)
⇒    (BOB . 5557654)

(rassoc '5559999 phone)
⇒    (CARL . 5559999)

(rassoc '9991111 phone)
⇒    NIL
```

If there is no matching name or number, the function returns NIL.

## Substitutions

You can use an association list to substitute values in a tree. This is similar to doing subst on a list once for each pair in the association list. The key of the pair is compared with the element of the tree. If the comparison is true (or not), the datum of the pair is substituted for the element of the tree.

```
(sublis alist tree &key :test :test-not :key)
(nsublis alist tree &key :test :test-not :key)

(setq tree '(a b c d e))
⇒    (A B C D E)

(setq numbers '(0 1 2 3 4 5 6))
⇒    (0 1 2 3 4 5 6)

(setq letters '(a b c d e f g))
⇒    (A B C D E F G)

(setq pairs (pairlis letters numbers))
⇒    ((G . 6) (F . 5) (E . 4) (D . 3) (C . 2) (B . 1) (A . 0))

(sublis pairs tree)
⇒    (0 1 2 3 4)
```

As with subst, you must be sure that the function that compares the key and element can take lists and atoms, or you must test the element first.

```
(setq nums '(1 (2 3) 4))
⇒    (1 (2 3) 4)
```

```
(setq pairs '((1 . a)(2 . b)(3 . c)(4 . d)))
⇒    ((1 . A) (2 . B) (3 . C) (4 . D))

(sublis pairs nums)
⇒    (A (B C) D)
```

**Exercise 10-8**

1. Create three association lists. One associates numerals with ordinal numbers, one English with German, and one German with Spanish.

   Numerals are (1 2 3 4 5 6 7 8 9 10).

   Ordinal numbers are (one two three four five six seven eight nine ten).

   German numbers are (ein zwei drei vier funf sechs sieben acht neun zehn).

   Spanish numbers are (uno dos tres cuatro cinco seis siete ocho nueve diez).

   The association lists will look like

   ```
   ((1 . one)(2 . two))
   ((one . ein)(two . zwei))
   ((ein . uno)(zwei . dos))
   ```

2. Write three functions (get-english, get-german, and get-spanish) that take a number and return the name in the appropriate language.
3. Write a function that, given a numeral and a symbol, either 'English, 'German, or 'Spanish, returns the name of the number in the appropriate language.

   Given 1 and 'spanish, the function returns uno.
3. Write three functions that, given a name of a number in a language, returns the numeral for the name.

   Given drei, returns 3.
4. Write a function that, given the name of a number in one of the three languages and a symbol, returns the numeral.
5. Write a function that translates German numbers to Spanish.

## SUMMARY

While you have seen many list functions in this chapter, there are still more. A *list* is a subtype of sequence. Chapter 14 has more functions that also work on lists.

The following table shows the list functions.

**TABLE 10.1**  LIST FUNCTIONS

| | | **List Sets** | **List Tree** |
|---|---|---|---|
| list | copy-alist | difference | subst |
| car | copy list | ndifference | subst-if |
| cdr | copy tree | intersection | subst-if-not |
| cons | tree equal | nintersection | nsubst |
| atom | tailp | union | nsubst-if |
| listp | ldiff | nunion | nsubst-if-not |
| | | set-exclusive-or | |
| rplaca | first | | **Association List** |
| rplacd | second | nset-exclusive-or | acons |
| | third | substep | pairlis |
| make-list | fourth | member | assoc |
| append | fifth | member-if | assoc-if |
| revappend | sixth | member-if-not | assoc-if-not |
| list | seventh | adjoin | rassoc |
| list* | eighth | | rassoc-if |
| | ninth | | rassoc-if-not |
| nbutlast | tenth | | sublis |
| nconc | last | | nsublis |
| nreconc | rest | | |
| | nth | | |
| pop | nthcdr | | |
| push | butlast | | |
| push-new | | | |
| list-length | | | |

# *11*

# *Numbers*

Every computer language must handle numbers. So while Lisp's real forte is lists, it still has many functions that work with numbers. This chapter looks at the numeric functions. However, there is not a lot of information on how to use these functions. It is assumed that the reader has some mathematical knowledge. This chapter describes what functions and data types are defined in Lisp.

There are four types of numbers: integers, floating point, rationals, and complex. (There are four types floating-point numbers, but for most functions, they are considered the same type.)

In most of the examples, numbers are used as the arguments. You can also use variables that have a number value. Unless otherwise noted, the functions do not change the values of the variables.

## BASIC ARITHMETIC

The basic arithmetic functions are those that you learned in grade school: adding and subtracting and finding the absolute value, among others. These functions are shown in the following table.

**TABLE 11.1**   BASIC ARITHMETIC FUNCTIONS

| Function | Meaning |
| --- | --- |
| * | Returns the product of its arguments. |
| + | Returns the sum of its arguments. |
| – | Successively subtracts its arguments and returns the result. |
| / | Successively divides its arguments and returns the result. |
| 1+ | Adds 1 to its argument and returns the result. |
| 1– | Subtracts 1 from its argument and returns the result. |
| abs | Returns the absolute value of a number. |
| incf | Increments the argument and returns that value.  The argument must be a variable. |
| decf | Decrements the argument and returns that value.  The argument must be a variable. |
| max | Returns the largest number in the argument list. |
| min | Returns the smallest number in the argument list. |
| expt | Returns the base number raised to the specified power. |
| sqrt | Returns the square root of a number |
| isqrt | Returns the integer square root of an integer. |
| exp | Returns e raised to the specified power. |
| log | Returns the logarithm of a number in the specified base. |

(* &rest *numbers*)
(+ &rest *numbers*)
(– *number* &rest *numbers*)
(/ *number* &rest *numbers*)
(1+ *number*)
(1– *number*)
(abs *number*)
(incf *place*[*delta*])
(decf *place*[*delta*])
(max *number* &rest *numbers*)
(min *number* &rest *numbers*)
(expt *base power*)
(sqrt *number*)
(insqrt *integer*)
(exp *number*)
(log *number* &optional *base*)

As you look at the following examples, notice the type of the result. Integer arguments result in integer or ratio results.

(* 2 3)
⇒   6

```
(- 4 3 2)
⇒    -1

(/ 10 5 3)
⇒    2/3

(/ 10 5)
⇒    2

(+ 2 3)
⇒    5
```

A floating-point argument results in a floating point.  The precision of a result is implementation dependent.

```
(* 4 6.5)
⇒    26.0

(/ 10.0 5 3)
⇒    0.6666666666666666

(- 2 1.3)
⇒    0.7

(+ 4 5.6 7.8)
⇒    17.4
```

A ratio argument results in a ratio, unless there is also a floating-point number (in which case the result is floating-point), or results in an integer.

```
(* 5 3/2)
⇒    15/2

(* 3/2 6.5)
⇒    9.75

(+ 2 4.5 3/2)
⇒    8.0

(/ 5/6 7/9)
⇒    15/14

(- 12/10 2/10)
⇒    1
```

Multiplication or addition without an argument results in the identity of the operation.

```
(*)
⇒    1

(+)
⇒    0
```

In the following functions, the type of the result is the type of the single argument, except for complex arguments.

```
(abs -2.3)
⇒    2.3

(abs -3/4)
⇒    3/4

(abs 4)
⇒    4

(1+ 3)
⇒    4

(1- 5)
⇒    4

(1- 3.4)
⇒    2.4

(1- 3/4)
⇒    -1/4

(abs #c(8 3))
⇒    8.544003745317532

(abs #c(2.0 3.0))
⇒    3.6055512754639896

(abs #c(3.0 -4.0))
⇒    5.0
```

Complex numbers in the argument list result in complex numbers. The parts of the complex numbers (real and imaginary) follow the rules shown previously for non-complex numbers.

```
(* #c(4 2) #c(3 2))
⇒    #C(8 14)

(* #c(-2.0 1) #c(3 2))
⇒    #C(-8.0 -1.0)
```

```
(/ #c(3/4 -1) #c(1 1))
⇒    #C(-1/8 -7/8)

(+ 3 #c(2 3))
⇒    #C(5 3)

(- #c(4 6) 2.4)
⇒    #C(1.6 6.0)
```

Of course, you can have the result of one function as the argument to another function.

```
(+ 3 (- 4 5) (/ 3 (* 6 .2)))
⇒    4.5

(* 7 (+ 3 4 (/ 2 3 (- 6 4) -9)))
⇒    1316/27

(* 7.0 (+ 3 4 (/ 2 3 (- 6 4) -9)))
⇒    48.74074074074074
```

## Changing the Variable

The previous functions did not change the values of their arguments.

incf and decf add or subtract 1 from the argument. They change the value of their argument. 1+ and 1- do not change the value. For example,

```
(setq a 5)
⇒    5

(1+ a)
⇒    6

a
⇒    5

(incf a)
⇒    6

a
⇒    6
```

## Maximum and Minimum

The min and max functions find the smallest and largest numbers, respectively, in their argument list. Two numbers of different type that have the same value are considered equal.

```
(min 3 5 3/4 9.6)
⇒    3/4

(max 3 5 3/4 9.6)
⇒    9.6

(min 9 9.0)
⇒    9

(max 9.0   9)
⇒    9.0

(min 3/4 .75)
⇒    3/4

(min .75 3/4)
⇒    0.75
```

## Powers

These functions raise a number to a specified power.
     expt returns the base number raised to the specified power.

```
(expt 2 4)
⇒    16

(expt 2 1/2)
⇒    1.4142135623730951

(expt 1/2 2)
⇒    1/4

(expt 1/2 2.0)
⇒    0.25
```

The square-root functions return the result of raising their argument to the power
of one half.

```
(sqrt 2)
⇒    1.414213562373095

(isqrt 2)
⇒    1

(sqrt 34567)
⇒    185.92202666709505
```

```
(sqrt 3/4)
⇒    0.8660254037844386
```

```
(isqrt 98)
⇒    9
```

exp returns *e* raised to the specified power.  For example,

```
(exp 3)
⇒    20.085536923187668
```

```
(exp 10)
⇒    22026.465794806718
```

log returns the logarithm of a number in the specified base.  For example,

```
(log (exp 3))
⇒    3.0
```

```
(log 100 10)
⇒    2.0
```

```
(log 10 10)
⇒    1.0
```

---

**Exercise 11-1**

Given the equation $0 = ax^2 + bx + c$, the value of x is:

$$(-b \pm \sqrt{(b^2 - 4ac)}) / 2a$$

Write a function that, given the values of a, b, and c, returns a list of the possible values of x.

---

## TRIG

The trigonometric functions are defined in Lisp and are shown in the following table. Each function takes a single argument.  Lisp uses radians for all its trig functions.

**TABLE 11.2**  TRIGONOMETRIC FUNCTIONS IN LISP

| | |
|---|---|
| sin | Returns the sine of a number. |
| cos | Returns the cosine of a number. |
| tan | Returns the tangent of a number. |
| cis | Returns $e^{\wedge}i*radians$. |
| asin | Returns the arc sine of a number. |
| acos | Returns the arc cosine of a number. |
| atan | Returns the arc tangent of a number. |
| sinh | Returns the hyperbolic sine of a number. |
| cosh | Returns the hyperbolic cosine of a number. |
| tanh | Returns the hyperbolic tangent of a number. |
| asinh | Returns the hyperbolic arc sine of a number. |
| acosh | Returns the hyperbolic arc cosine of a number. |
| atanh | Returns the hyperbolic arc tangent of a number. |
| pi | The constant value approximation of $\pi$. |

```
(sin radians)
(cos radians)
(tan radians)
(cis radians)
(asin number)
(acos number)
(atan y &optional x)
(sinh number)
(cosh number)
(tanh number)
(asinh number)
(acosh number)
(atanh number)
pi
```

# DIVISION

In addition to simple division, there is integer division, finding the greatest common divisor, the least common multiple, remainders, and rounding.

## Divisors

gcd returns the greatest common divisor.

(gcd &rest *integers*)

lcm returns the least common multiple.

(lcd *integer* &rest *integers*)

(gcd 2 4 5)
⇒     1

(gcd 3 6 9)
⇒     3

(gcd 25 1265 35)
⇒     5

(lcm 34 6 19)
⇒     1938

(lcm 5 25)
⇒     25

## Rounding

There are eight rounding functions in Lisp as shown in the following table. Four functions deal with integers. The other four deal with floating-point numbers. Fig. 11-1 shows the relationship of the results of these functions.

**TABLE 11.3**  ROUNDING

| Integer Function | Floating-Point Function | Value |
| --- | --- | --- |
| ceiling | fceiling | The smallest integer not smaller than the argument |
| floor | ffloor | The largest integer not larger than the argument |
| round | fround | Rounds its argument to the nearest integer<br>    Numbers half way between two integers are rounded to the nearest even integer |
| truncate | ftruncate | Truncates its argument toward zero |

```
  -2......-1......0......1......2
   ↑ -1.6  ↑              ↑ 1.5 ↑
   floor  ceiling      floor  ceiling
     |       |           |       |
   round  truncate    truncate  round
```

**Figure 11-1**  Rounding

(floor -1.6)
⇒     -2
      0.4

(ffloor -1.6)
⇒     -2.0
      0.4

```
(truncate -1.6)
⇒     -1
      -0.6

(ceiling 5.1)
⇒      6
      -0.9

(round 5.1)
⇒      5
       0.1

(round 3.5)
⇒      4
      -0.5

(round 4.5)
⇒      4
       0.5
```

## Remainders

mod divides a number by a divisor and returns the difference between the largest integer not greater than the result and the result of the division.

> (mod *number divisor*)

rem divides a number by a divisor and returns the difference between the integer portion of the result and the result of the division.

> (rem *number divisor*)

For example,

```
(mod 5.2 3)
⇒     2.2

(rem 5.2 3)
⇒     2.2

(mod -3.4 1)
⇒      0.6

(rem -3.4 1)
⇒     -0.4
```

When the result of the division is a positive number, the results of rem and mod are the same. When the result of the division is a negative number, the results of these functions are different. Refer to Fig. 11-2 for a comparison of the results.

```
      mod    rem
      0.6   -.04
       |     |    |
.....-4.........-3......
         -3.4
```

**Figure 11-2**   Mod and Rem Values

−3.4 divided by 1 results in −3.4

The largest integer not greater than −3.4 is −4.  This is what mod uses.

The difference between −3.4 and −4 is 0.6.

The integer part of −3.4 is −3.  This is what rem uses.

The difference between −3.4 and −3 is −0.4.

## PREDICATES

The predicate functions determine characteristics of a number.

```
evenp
oddp
minusp
plusp
zerop
```

For example,

```
(zerop 0.0)
⇒    T


(zerop 0/3)
⇒    T


(zerop #c(0.0 0.0))
⇒    T


(plusp 0)
⇒    NIL


(minusp 0)
⇒    NIL


(plusp +0)
⇒    NIL
```

```
(minusp -0)
⇒    NIL

(oddp 0)
⇒    NIL

(evenp 0)
⇒    T
```

## COMPARISON

The comparison functions determine if the arguments are equal, not equal, or increasing or decreasing in the order they are presented.  Numbers of different type that have the same value are considered equal.

**TABLE 11.4**  COMPARISON

| Function | Meaning |
| --- | --- |
| /= | Not equal |
| < | Monotonically increasing |
| <= | Monotonically nondecreasing |
| = | Equal |
| > | Monotonically decreasing |
| >= | Monotonically nonincreasing |

The syntax is similar for all the predicates.

(*predicate number* &rest *numbers*)

```
(= 4 4.0)
⇒    T

(= 4.0 16/4)
⇒    T

(= #c(4 0) 4)
⇒    T

(/= 3 1 9)
⇒    T

(/= 4.0 12 4)
⇒    NIL
```

```
(> 3 4 5)
⇒    NIL

(< 3 4 5)
⇒    T

(< 3 3 4)
⇒    NIL

(<= 3 3 4)
⇒    T
```

## TYPE-SPECIFIC FUNCTIONS

Several function are related specifically to the type of data. You can determine the denominator of a rational number, the imaginary part of a complex number, and the radix of a floating-point number.

### Floats

There are four types of floating-point numbers: short, long, double, and single. The precision of these types varies with each implementation. Functions specific to floating-point numbers are shown in the following table.

**TABLE 11.5**  FLOATS

| Function | Meaning |
|---|---|
| float | Converts any noncomplex number to a floating point. |
| decode-float | Returns the significand, exponent, and sign. |
| float-radix | Returns the base of the number. |
| integer-decode-float | Returns the significand as an integer, exponent, and sign. |
| float-digits | Returns the number of digits used to represent the argument. |
| float-precision | Returns the number of significant digits in the argument. |
| float-size | Takes two arguments, returns a floating-point number with the same sign as the first argument and the same absolute value as the second argument. |
| scale-float | Returns (* f (expt (float b f) k)). |
| signum | Returns −1, 0, or +1, indicating the sign of the argument. |

**Float.**  The float function converts any noncomplex number into a floating-point number.

(float *number* &optional *format-number*)

If the optional argument is supplied, it must be a floating-point number, and the result of the float operation will be a floating-point number of the same type as the *format-number*. If the argument is not supplied, a single-float results.

```
(float 3/4)
⇒    0.75

(float 1)
⇒    1.0

(setq a (float 1 most-positive-double-float))
⇒    1.0

(typep a 'double-float)
⇒    T
```

In addition to float, coerce converts any noncomplex number to any type of floating-point number. (coerce also works on other objects and types.)

```
(coerce object result-type)

(coerce 1 'float)
⇒    1.0

(coerce 3/4 'short-float)
⇒    0.75

(coerce 2.3 'long-float)
⇒    2.3
```

**decode float.**    decode-float returns the significand, the exponent, and the sign of the argument.

```
(decode-float float)

(decode-float 12.56)
⇒    0.785
     4
     1.0

(decode-float 10.0)
⇒    0.625
     4
     1.0
```

The first value returned is the significand.  The value is the same type as the argument.
The number is between 1 (exclusive) and 1/b, where b is some base number (in many
cases 2).  (float-radix returns b.)

To reconstruct the floating-point number,

```
(* (expt b exponent) significand sign)

(decode-float 1.0)
⇒     0.5
      1
      1.0

(* (expt 2 1) 0.5 1.0)
⇒     1.0

(decode-float 4.5)
⇒     0.5625
      3
      1.0

(* (expt 2 3) 0.5625 1.0)
⇒     4.5
```

**float-radix.**    The float-radix function returns the base of the floating-
point number.  This is the *b* in the function.

```
(float-radix 1.0)
⇒     2

(float-radix 6.5)
⇒     2
```

The implementation on which these examples were produced uses a base of 2.  Other
implementations could use other bases.

**integer-decode-float.**    integer-decode-float returns the significand as
an integer, the exponent, and the sign of the argument.

```
(integer-decode-float 1.0)
⇒     4503599627370496
      −52
      1
```

```
(decode-float 1.0)
⇒    0.5
     1
     1.0

(decode-float 2.0)
⇒    0.5
     2
     1.0

(decode-float 3.0)
⇒    0.75
     2
     1.0

(decode-float 4.0)
⇒    0.5
     3
     1.0

(decode-float 8.0)
⇒    0.5
     4
     1.0

(decode-float 16.0)
⇒    0.5
     5
     1.0
```

**float-digits.**    float-digits returns an integer that is the number of digits used to represent the argument.

```
(float-digits 0.0)
⇒    53

(float-digits 2.654)
⇒    53

(float-digits -10.0)
⇒    53
```

**float-precision.**    float-precision returns an integer that is the number of significant digits present in the argument.

```
(float-precision 0.0)
⇒    0
```

```
(float-precision 2.654)
⇒    53
```

```
(float-precision -10.0)
⇒    53
```

**float-sign.**    float-sign returns a floating-point number with the same sign as the first argument and the same absolute value as the second argument.

```
(float-sign -1.0 12.987)
⇒    -12.987
```

```
(float-sign 0.0)
⇒    1.0
```

```
(float-sign -2.0)
⇒    -1.0
```

**scale-float**    scale-float takes a floating-point number f and an integer k and returns:

```
(* f (expt (float b f) k)
```

b is the value returned by float-radix.

```
(scale-float 10.0 2)
⇒    40.0
```

```
(scale-float 12.5 4)
⇒    200.0
```

**signum.**    signum returns −1, 0, or +1, indicating the sign of the argument.

```
(signum -3.4)
⇒    -1.0
```

```
(signum -0.0)
⇒    0.0
```

```
(signum 8.9)
⇒    1.0
```

## Rationals

There are two functions that convert noncomplex number to rational numbers: rational and rationalize. The denominator and numerator functions return the parts of a rational number. These functions are shown in the following table.

**TABLE 11.6**  RATIONALS

| Function | Meaning |
|---|---|
| rational | Converts a number into a rational number. It returns the precise value of the floating-point number. |
| rationalize | Returns an approximation of the floating-point number. It does not assume that the floating-point number is completely accurate. This result is usually simpler than the result of rational. |
| denominator | Returns the denominator of a rational number. |
| numerator | Returns the numerator of a rational number. |

```
(rationalize number)
(rational number)
(denominator rational)
(numerator rational)
```

Converting a floating-point number to a rational number, and then converting it back to a floating-point number results in the original number.

```
(float (rational x) x) ≡ x

(float (rationalize x) x) ≡ x

(rational 4.2)
⇒    4728779608739021/1125899906842624

(rationalize 4.2)
⇒    21/5

(rational .1)
⇒    3602879701896397/36028797018963968

(rationalize .1)
⇒    1/10

(float (rational 4.2) 4.2)
⇒    4.2

(float (rationalize .1) .1)
⇒    0.1
```

**denominator and numerator.**   The denominator and numerator functions return the denominator and numerator of a rational number.

```
(denominator 3/4)
⇒    4

(numerator 3/4)
⇒    3

(denominator 4)
⇒    1

(numerator 4)
⇒    4
```

The denominator is always a positive integer. The numerator can be positive or negative, depending on the sign of the rational.

```
(denominator -4/5)
⇒    5

(numerator -4/5)
⇒    -4
```

The rational number is reduced to its canonical (simplest) form before the functions are applied.

```
(denominator 2/4)
⇒    2

(numerator 2/4)
⇒    1
```

## Complex

Complex numbers have a real part and an imaginary part. There are three functions that make a complex number and take parts from the number: complex, imagpart, and realpart. The complex number functions are shown in the following table.

**TABLE 11.7**   COMPLEX NUMBERS

| Function | Meaning |
|----------|---------|
| complex | Returns a complex number. |
| imagpart | Returns the imaginary part of a number. |
| realpart | Returns the real part of a number. |
| phase | Returns the angle part of a number's polar representation in complex number format. |
| conjugate | Returns the complex conjugate of a number |

```
(complex 4 5)
⇒    #C(4 5)

(imagpart #C(4 5))
⇒    5

(realpart #C(4 5))
⇒    4
```

phase returns the angle part of a number's polar representation in complex number format.

```
(phase x) ≡ (atan (imagpart x)(realpart x))
```

For example,

```
(phase #c(12.9 −5))
⇒    −0.3697685347934171

(phase #c(10 2))
⇒    0.19739555984988078
```

phase also can take noncomplex arguments. phase of zero or of a positive noncomplex number is zero. phase of a negative noncomplex number is $\pi$.

```
(phase 0)
⇒    0.0

(phase 4.5)
⇒    0.0

(phase −8)
⇒    3.141592653589793
```

conjugate returns the complex conjugate of a number.

```
(conjugate x) ≡ (complex (realpart x) (- (imagpart x)))
```

For example,

```
(conjugate #c(4.5 −9.0))
⇒    #C(4.5 9.0)

(conjugate #c(−5.6 8))
⇒    #C(−5.6 −8.0)
```

## CONSTANTS

Lisp provides constants that represent large and small numbers in each of the floating-point types (short, long, single, and double), and in fixnum type. These values are the limits of the system in representing large and small numbers.

Epsilon comes in each of the four floating-point types and in positive and negative form.

```
double-float-epsilon
long-float-epsilon
short-float-epsilon
single-float-epsilon
double-float-negative-epsilon
long-float-negative-epsilon
short-float-negative-epsilon
single-float-negative-epsilon
```

Fixnum comes in most-positive and most-negative.
Floating point numbers come in large and small, positive and negative.

least-negative      Number closest in value to negative infinity provided.

least-positive      Number closest in value to zero provided.

most-negative       Negative number closest in value to infinity provided.

most-positive       Number closest in value to positive infinity provided.

Fig. 11-3 shows the relationship of the constant values.

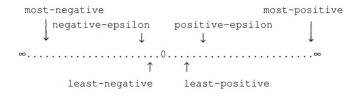

**Figure 11-3**   Constants

```
most-negative-double-float
⇒    -1.7976931348623149E+308

least-positive-single-float
⇒    2.2250738585072027E-308
```

```
most-positive-fixnum
⇒    268435455
```

```
short-float-negative-epsilon
⇒    5.551115123125784E-17
```

## BINARY FUNCTIONS

These functions are not functions of two arguments. Rather, they operate on the binary representation of a number.

### Logical Functions

Logical functions look at an integer as a bit vector. The integer 4, for example, is `#*100`. The integer 3 is `#*011`. If you were to take the logical or of 4 and 3, the or function is applied to each bit, and the result is `#*111`.

```
(logior 4 3)
⇒  7
```

There are two methods of applying a logical operator to the arguments. The `boole` function takes a constant value as the operator. The logical functions are themselves the operator. The `boole` function lends itself to the situation where you are passing the operator as an argument to a function. Most of the logical operations can be done with either a `boole` or a logical function. For example,

```
(boole boole-and x y) ≡ (logand x y)
```

All boole functions require two arguments.

```
(boole boole-and 2 4)
⇒    0
```

```
(defun test (fun arg1 arg2)
  (boole fun arg1 arg2))
⇒    TEST
```

```
(test boole-xor 2 4)
⇒    6
```

```
(test boole-and 2 4)
⇒    0
```

The following table shows the `boole` functions, the logical functions, and their meanings.

**TABLE 11.8**  BOOLE AND LOGICAL FUNCTIONS

| Boole Function | Logical Function | Meaning |
|---|---|---|
| boole-1 | --- | Returns the first argument in the `boole` function. |
| boole-2 | --- | Returns the second argument in the `boole` function. |
| boole-and | logand | Logical and operation. |
| boole-andc1 | logandc1 | Logical and operation of the complement of the first integer argument with the second argument. |
| boole-andc2 | logandc2 | Logical and operation on the first integer argument with the complement of the second argument. |
| --- | logbitp | Determines if the specified bit in the integer argument is set. |
| boole-c1 | --- | Returns the logical complement of the first argument. |
| boole-c2 | --- | Returns the logical complement of the second argument. |
| boole-clr | --- | Returns the logical clear operation. |
| --- | logcount | Returns the number of 1 bits in the argument. |
| boole-eqv | logeqv | Logical equivalence (exclusive nor) operation. |
| boole-ior | logior | Logical inclusive or operation. |
| boole-nand | lognand | Logical not and operation. |
| boole-nor | lognor | Logical not or operation. |
| --- | lognot | Returns the logical not of its arguments. |
| boole-orc1 | logorc1 | Logical or operation on the complement of the first argument with the second argument. |
| boole-orc2 | logorc2 | Logical or operation on the first argument with the complement of the second argument. |
| boole-set | --- | Set. |
| --- | logtest | Determines if the bits set in the first argument are set in the second argument. |
| boole-xor | logxor | Exclusive or. |

The log functions take one or more, two, or one argument. `logior`, `logxor`, `logand`, and `logeqv` take one or more arguments. `longnand`, `lognor`, `logandc1`, `logandc2`, `logorc1`, `logorc2`, `logtest`, and `logbitp` take exactly two arguments. `lognot` and `logcount` take one argument.

```
(logand 2 4)
⇒    0


(logior 2)
⇒    2
```

```
(logxor 2 3)
⇒   1


(logcount 2)
⇒   1


(logcount 3)
⇒   2
```

`logbitp` takes two arguments: an index into an integer and the integer.

```
(logbitp 0 2)
⇒   NIL


(logbitp 1 2)
⇒   T
```

## Bits and Bytes

There are many functions that look at the binary representation of an integer. They can return a byte, change a byte, rotate the digits and perform other operations. These functions are shown in the following table.

**TABLE 11.9** BITS AND BYTES

| Function | Meaning |
|---|---|
| byte | Returns a byte specifier. |
| byte-position | Returns the first location in the byte specifier. |
| byte-size | Returns the length of the byte specifier. |
| ldb | Loads a byte. Returns the specified byte. |
| ldb-test | Determines if a byte is nonzero. |
| dpb | Returns the result of replacing a byte of an integer with the right-most byte from a different number. |
| deposit-field | Returns the result of replacing a byte of an integer with the same byte from a different number. |
| integer-length | Returns the number of bits required to represent an integer. |
| ash | Arithmetically moves all of the bits of the integer to the left or right. |
| mask-field | Returns the specified byte of the integer argument in the same position as in the integer with zeros in all other bit positions. |

**Byte.** A *bit* is one position in a binary number. A *byte* is a contiguous set of bits. The length of a byte is not fixed. Neither does the set of bits have to begin at some fixed position. Instead, a byte can be of any length and can be in any location within a number.

The `byte` function returns a *byte specifier*, which is used in byte-manipulation functions.

(byte *size position*)

The *size* is the number of bits in the byte. The *position* specifies the right-most bit to begin the byte. Zero is the first bit.

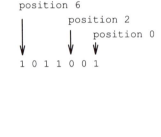

```
(byte 3 0)
⇒     (3 0)

(byte 5 4)
⇒     (5 4)
```

This implementation returns a list of two numbers that indicate the size and position. Other implementations can return other values. If you use the `byte` function to construct the *byte specifier*, you won't have to modify procedures when you change implementations.

`byte-position` returns the first location of the byte specifier.

(byte-position *byte-spec*)

`byte-size` returns the size of the byte specifier.

(byte-size *byte-spec*)

```
(byte-size (byte 4 2))
⇒     4

(byte-position (byte 4 2))
⇒     2

(byte-size (byte x y))        ≡ x
(byte-position (byte x y))    ≡ y
```

`byte-specifier` extracts a byte from an integer or replaces a byte in an integer.

**load-byte.**   ldb extracts a byte from an integer.   ldb stands for load byte.

(ldb *byte-spec integer*)

The binary representation is translated back into decimal representation before it is printed. When the byte is one bit long, the result is either 0 or 1.

```
(ldb (byte 1 0) 2)     2 ≡ #b10   (byte 1 0) is bit zero, one bit long.
⇒    0                      ↑

(ldb (byte 1 1) 2)     2 ≡ #b10  (byte 1 1) is bit one, one bit long.
⇒    1                      ↑

(ldb (byte 1 0) 3)     3 ≡ #b011  (byte 1 0) is bit zero, one bit long.
⇒    1                        ↑

(ldb (byte 1 1) 3)     3 ≡ #b011  (byte 1 1) is bit one, one bit long.
⇒    1                       ↑

(ldb (byte 1 2) 3)     3 ≡ #b011  (byte 1 2) is bit two, one bit long.
⇒    0                      ↑
```

When the byte is longer, the result can be any integer.

```
(ldb (byte 2 0) 10)    10 ≡ #b1010 (byte 2 0) is bit zero, two bits long.
⇒    2                       ↑↑

(ldb (byte 3 1) 10)    10 ≡ #b1010 (byte 3 1) is bit one, three bits long.
⇒    5                      ↑↑↑
```

ldb-test determines if a byte is nonzero.

```
(ldb-test (byte 1 1) 2)
⇒    T

(ldb-test (byte 0 1) 2)
⇒    NIL
```

**deposit-byte.**   dpb returns the result of replacing a byte of an integer with the right-most byte from a different number.

(dpb *newbyte byte-specifier integer*)

```
(dpb 4 (byte 1 2) 8)    4 ≡ #b100    8 ≡ #b1000
⇒    8                          ↑              ↑
```

```
(dpb 7 (byte 1 2) 8)        7 ≡ #b111    8 ≡ #b1000
⇒    12                              ↑              ↑
```

**deposit-field.**   deposit-field returns the result of replacing a byte of an integer with the same byte from a different number.

```
(deposit-field newbyte byte-specifier integer)

(deposit-field 4 (byte 1 2) 8)      4 ≡ #b100   8 ≡ #b1000
⇒    12                                   ↑            ↑↑

                                    12 ≡ #b1100
```

**integer-length.**   integer-length returns the number of bits required to represent an integer.

```
(integer-length integer)

(integer-length 2)          2 ≡ #b10
⇒    2

(integer-length 3)          3 ≡ #b11
⇒    2

(integer-length 4)          4 ≡ #b100
⇒    3

(integer-length 10)        10 ≡ #b1010
⇒    4
```

**ash.**   ash arithmetically moves all bits of the integer to the left or right.

```
(ash integer count)

(ash 2 2)                   2 ≡ #b0010   (ash #b0010 2)  ⇒    #b1000
⇒    8

(ash 3 1)                   3 ≡ #b0011   (ash #b0011 1)  ⇒    #b0110
⇒    6

(ash 10 −1)                10 ≡ #b1010   (ash #b1010 −1) ⇒    #b0101
⇒    5
```

**mask-field.**   mask-field returns the specified byte of the integer argument to the same position as in the integer with zeros in all other bit positions.

```
(mask-field byte-specifier integer)
```

```
(mask-field (byte 2 2) 11)      11 ≡ #b1011     mask-field ⇒    #b1000
⇒    8                                  ↑↑
                                        save
```

```
(mask-field (byte 3 1) 11)      11 ≡ #b1011     mask-field ⇒    #b1010
⇒    10                                ↑↑↑
                                       save
```

## RANDOM

There are four functions that deal with random numbers. Those are shown in the following table.

**TABLE 11.10**   FOUR RANDOM NUMBER FUNCTIONS

| Function | Meaning |
|---|---|
| make-random-state | Returns a new object of type random-state. |
| random | Returns a pseudo-random number. |
| *random-state* | Holds a random-state object used by random. |
| random-state-p | Determines if an object is of type random-state. |

```
(make-random-state &optional state)
(random number &optional state)
*random-state*
(random-state-p object)
```

The random function returns a number between zero and the argument number. The returned number is the same type as the argument number, which may be a nonnegative integer or floating-point number.

```
(random 3)
⇒    0
```

```
(random 3)
⇒    2
```

```
(random 3)
⇒    0
```

```
(random 3)
⇒    1

(random 3.4)
⇒    1.9899834359025965
```

The *state* argument in random specifies the random-state object to use to determine the random number. The default value is *random-state*. The value of the
random state object is changed as side effect of random.

```
(random 3 (make-random-state t))
⇒    1

(setq a (make-random-state))
⇒    #.(random-state 164744276845669)

(random 3 a)
⇒    0

a
⇒    #.(random-state 240537155779854)

(random 3 a)
⇒    2

a
⇒    #.(random-state 194463953064707)
```

---

**Exercise 11-2**

1. Write a function that picks a random number between 1 and 10 inclusively.
2. Write a function that picks a random number between two given numbers.

---

## SUMMARY

There are nearly 150 functions and constants dealing with numbers. They were
presented briefly in this chapter.

| | |
|---|---|
| Arithmetic | All the arithmetic functions are present in Lisp. |
| Trigonometric | Trig functions take radian arguments or return radian results. |
| Division | Besides simple division, there are several functions that return remainders or modulos of numbers. |

Predicates        The predicate functions determine the type of a number.

Comparison        You can compare numbers of different type.

Type specific     Some functions are type specific. They only operate on float-
                  ing-point or complex numbers, for example.

Constants         Lisp provides constants that give the largest and smallest
                  numbers it can store.

Bits              There are several functions that look at the binary representa-
                  tion of an integer.

Random            Random-number functions provide a method of obtaining
                  pseudorandom numbers.

# 12

## *Arrays*

This chapter looks at the data type array and the functions that operate on arrays.

- How do you create an array?
- What are the differences between an array, a vector, and a string?
- What is a simple array?
- How can an array share its structure with another array?
- How can you find the size of an array?
- How do you change data in an array?

## WHAT IS AN ARRAY?

An *array* is a collection of individual pieces of data, called elements, that are arranged according to a coordinate system. The array can have zero, one, two, or more dimensions. A zero-dimensional array has exactly one element. A one-dimensional array is called a *vector*. A two-dimensional array is called a *matrix*.

Arrays are grouped according to the number of dimensions and the type of elements they contain.

## Vectors

A *vector* is a one-dimensional array. Vector is a subtype of array. Vector is also a subtype of sequence. (Sequence functions are described in Chapter 14.)
Vector notation is

# ( *elements of vector*)

A vector can contain any element type. The types can be mixed.

## Strings

A *string* is a one-dimensional array whose elements are characters.
Strings have different notation.

```
"abc"
""
"ace1234"
```

In addition to array functions, there are specific string functions. These functions are discussed in Chapter 15. Because strings are a subtype of vectors, they are also a subtype of sequence.

## Bit-Vectors

A *bit-vector* is a vector whose elements are 0s and 1s.

```
#*1011
#*0000
#*1110
```

## General Multidimensional Arrays

An array can contain any element type and can be multidimensional.

```
#2A((1 2 3)(4 5 6))
#3A(((1 2 3 4) (5 6 7 8) (9 0 1 2)) ((3 4 5 6) (7 8 9 0) (1 2 3 4)))
#(1 2 3)
#*0000
"abcd"
```

Each of the above examples shows a different array.

#2A means a two-dimensional array.
#3A means a three-dimensional array.

#    means a one-dimensional array, also called a vector.

#*   means a one-dimensional array, a vector, whose elements can only be 0s or 1s.

"    means a one-dimensional array, a vector, whose elements can only be string characters.  This is a string.

---

**Exercise 12-1**

Specify the type of array for each of the following:

```
#2A((a) (b) (c))

#((1 2)(2 3)(4 5))

"abc123"

#*10010

#1A(#\a #\b #\c)

#1A(#*1111 #*0000 a b c (a b c) "abc" "123")
```

---

## MAKING AN ARRAY

The make-array function creates an array.

```
(make-array dimensions &key :element-type :initial-element
                            :initial-contents :adjustable :fill-pointer
                            :displaced-to :displaced-index-offset)
```

The simpliest form of make-array creates an array with undefined elements. You only specify the size of the array.

```
(make-array 4)
⇒    #(LISP::*UNDEFINED* LISP::*UNDEFINED* LISP::*UNDEFINED*
        LISP::*UNDEFINED*)

(make-array 2)
⇒    #(LISP::*UNDEFINED* LISP::*UNDEFINED*)

(make-array '(1 2))
⇒    #2A((LISP::*UNDEFINED* LISP::*UNDEFINED*))
```

```
(make-array '(2 2))
⇒    #2A((LISP::*UNDEFINED* LISP::*UNDEFINED*)
         (LISP::*UNDEFINED* LISP::*UNDEFINED*))
```

## :initial-element

To initialize every element of an array to a single value, use the keyword :initial-element.

```
(make-array '(1 2 3) :initial-element 3)
⇒    #3A(((3 3 3) (3 3 3)))

(make-array '(2 3 4) :initial-element 0)
⇒    #3A(((0 0 0 0) (0 0 0 0) (0 0 0 0)) ((0 0 0 0) (0 0 0 0) (0 0 0 0)))

(make-array 7 :initial-element 'a)
⇒    #(A A A A A A A)

(make-array 10 :initial-element #\a)
⇒    #(#\a #\a #\a #\a #\a #\a #\a #\a #\a #\a)
```

## :initial-contents

To specify values for each element in an array, use :initial-contents. When you use :initial-contents, you cannot specify :initial-element.

```
(make-array 5 :initial-contents '(1 2 3 4 5))
⇒    #2A(1 2 3 4 5)

(make-array 4 :initial-contents '(#\a 4 k (1 2 3)))
⇒    #(#\a 4 K (1 2 3))
```

When you specify the contents for a one-dimensional array, put the elements in a list. Each element of the list specifies one element of the array. Thus, the list

```
'(1 2 3 4 5)
```

gives the first element of the array the value of 1, the second element of the array the value of 2, and so forth.

The list

```
'(#\a 4 k (1 2 3))
```

gives the first element of the array the value of #\a, the second element the value of 4, the third element the value of k, and the fourth element the value of the list (1 2 3).

```
(make-array '(2 3) :initial-contents '((1 0 1)(0 0 1)))
⇒    #2A((1 0 1) (0 0 1))


(make-array '(2 3 4) :initial-contents '(((1 2 3 4)(5 6 7 8)(9 0 1 2))
                                         ((3 4 5 6)(7 8 9 0)(1 2 3 4))))
⇒    #3A(((1 2 3 4) (5 6 7 8) (9 0 1 2)) ((3 4 5 6) (7 8 9 0) (1 2 3 4)))
```

When specifying the contents for a multidimensional array, nest the lists. The number of elements in the innermost list corresponds to the last dimension specified in the *dimensions* list.

A two-by-three array would have three elements in each inner list and would have two inner lists. For example,

```
'((1 0 1)(0 0 1))
```

A two-by-three-by-four array would have four elements in each inner list and would have three inner lists within two outer lists. For example,

```
'(((1 2 3 4)(5 6 7 8)(9 0 1 2))
  ((3 4 5 6)(7 8 9 0)(1 2 3 4)))
```

A 7-by-8 array would have eight elements within seven lists. A 5-by-3-by-8-by-2 array would have two elements within eight lists, within three lists, and within five lists.

```
                                              2 lists
                                     ┌─────────────────────┐
                                       6 elements
                                     ┌──────────┐
(make-array '(3 4 2 6) :initial-contents '((((1 2 3 4 5 6)(1 2 3 4 5 6))⎤
                        ((1 2 3 4 5 6)(1 2 3 4 5 6))    ⎬ 4 lists
                        ((1 2 3 4 5 6)(1 2 3 4 5 6))
                        ((1 2 3 4 5 6)(1 2 3 4 5 6)))⎦
                       (((1 2 3 4 5 6)(1 2 3 4 5 6))
                        ((1 2 3 4 5 6)(1 2 3 4 5 6))
                        ((1 2 3 4 5 6)(1 2 3 4 5 6))    ⎬ 3 lists
                        ((1 2 3 4 5 6)(1 2 3 4 5 6)))
                       (((1 2 3 4 5 6)(1 2 3 4 5 6))
                        ((1 2 3 4 5 6)(1 2 3 4 5 6))
                        ((1 2 3 4 5 6)(1 2 3 4 5 6))
                        ((1 2 3 4 5 6)(1 2 3 4 5 6))
                        ((1 2 3 4 5 6)(1 2 3 4 5 6)))))))
```

There are six elements in the innermost lists. There are two innermost lists that are the elements of the next list. There are four of these lists that are elements of the outermost three lists.

If you consider the array a list, which it is internally, and look at the box and pointer notation for the array, you will see how the dimensions are organized. This is shown in Fig. 12-1.

```
(make-array '(2 3 4) :initial-contents '(((a b c d)(e f g h)(i j k l))
                                         ((m n o p)(q r s t)(u v w x))))
```

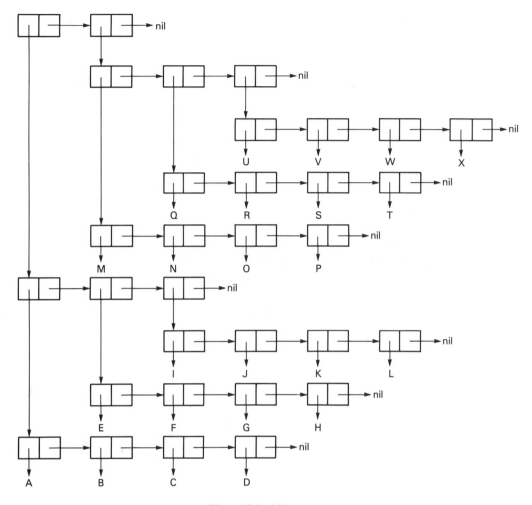

**Figure 12-1**   Make-array

## :element-type

A few of the previous examples created an array with elements of 1s and 0s, which should be bit arrays. Yet, the results did not show the bit-vector format. The reason is that you could change the value of an element to something other than a 1 or 0. If you want to create an array where the elements must be a particular type, use :element-type.

```
(make-array 4 :element-type 'bit)
=>    #*0000

(make-array 4 :element-type 'string-char)
=>    "    "
```

```
(make-array 9 :element-type 'string-char :initial-element #\a)
⇒    "aaaaaaaaa"


(make-array 2 :element-type 'bit :initial-contents '(1 0))
⇒    #*10


(make-array 4 :element-type 'integer :initial-element 4)
⇒    #(4 4 4 4)


(make-array '(2 2) :element-type 'symbol :initial-element 'a)
⇒    #2A((A A) (A A))
```

## :fill-pointer

The :fill-pointer keyword indicates whether or not a vector has a *fill pointer*. A fill pointer is an indicator that specifies where elements are added or deleted from a vector. It can also specify the current length of a vector.

If you set :fill-pointer to t, then it is set to the allocated length of the vector. You can also specify an integer in the range zero to the allocated length of the vector.

The fill-pointer function returns the value of a vector's fill pointer.

```
(setq a (make-array 4 :fill-pointer t))
⇒    #(LISP::*UNDEFINED* LISP::*UNDEFINED* LISP::*UNDEFINED* LISP::*UNDEFINED*)


(fill-pointer a)
⇒    4


(setq b (make-array 7 :fill-pointer 0))
⇒    ()


(fill-pointer b)
⇒    0
```

## :adjustable

The :adjustable keyword specifies whether or not the array size can be changed. If the array is adjustable, you can change its size, shape, or displacement with the adjust-array function. When elements are added to a vector, the vector-push-extend function adds an element even if the allocated size of the vector has been exceeded.

```
(make-array '(2 4 7) :initial-element 1 :adjustable t)
⇒    #3A(((1 1 1 1 1 1 1) (1 1 1 1 1 1 1) (1 1 1 1 1 1 1) (1 1 1 1 1 1 1))
         ((1 1 1 1 1 1 1) (1 1 1 1 1 1 1) (1 1 1 1 1 1 1) (1 1 1 1 1 1 1)))

(make-array 7 :fill-pointer 0 :adjustable t)
⇒    #()
```

## :displaced

The :displaced-to and :displaced-index-offset keywords specify that the array being created will share the elements of another array.

```
(setq a (make-array 7 :initial-contents '(a b c d e f g)))
⇒    #(A B C D E F G)

(setq b (make-array 4 :displaced-to a :displaced-index-offset 2))
⇒    #(C D E F)
```

Whenever an element in either array is changed, the corresponding element in the other array is also changed. (aref returns an element of an array.)

```
(setf (aref a 3) 'changed)
⇒    CHANGED

a
⇒    #(A B C CHANGED E F G)

b
⇒    #(C CHANGED E F)

(setf (aref b 0) 'other)
⇒    OTHER

b
⇒    #(OTHER CHANGED E F)

a
⇒    #(A B OTHER CHANGED E F G)
```

## Vectors and Strings

In addition to make-array, there are two other functions that create arrays: vector and make-string. As their names imply, respectively, they create a one-dimensional array and a one-dimensional array of type string.

vector creates a one-dimensional array that can contain any type of elements.

```
(vector &rest objects)
```

For example,

```
(make-array 9 :initial-element 7)
⇒    #(7 7 7 7 7 7 7 7 7)

(vector 7 7 7 7 7 7 7 7 7)
⇒   #(7 7 7 7 7 7 7 7 7)

(vector 'a 'b 'c 'd 'e)
⇒    #(A B C D E)

(vector #\x #\y #\z)
⇒    #(#\x #\y #\z)

(vector 1 0 1 0 1 1)
⇒    #(1 0 1 0 1 1)
```

make-string creates a one dimensional array that can contain elements of type string-char.

```
(make-string size &key :initial-element)
```

For example,

```
(make-string 7)
⇒    "       "

(make-array 10 :initial-element #\a :element-type 'string-char)
⇒    "aaaaaaaaaa"

(make-string 10 :initial-element #\a)
⇒    "aaaaaaaaaa"
```

---

**Exercise 12-2**

1. Create a two-by-five array. Add some contents to the array.
2. Create a string array that has five elements.
3. Create a string array that has a fill pointer. The array can have up to ten elements. Initially there are no elements.
4. Create a bit vector that has five elements, all of which are zero.
5. Create a vector of eight characters. The element-type is anything.

## PREDICATES ON ARRAYS

To change the values of the elements of arrays, it is necessary to know the type of array with that you are dealing. There are several predicates which determine if an object is a particular type of array.

```
adjustable-array-p
arrayp
bit-vector-p
simple-bit-vector-p
simple-string-p
simple-vector-p
stringp
vectorp
```

### arrayp

The `arrayp` function determines if an object is an array.

```
(setq z 12)
⇒    12

(arrayp z)
⇒    NIL

(setq a (make-array '(2 2)))
⇒    #2A((LISP::*UNDEFINED* LISP::*UNDEFINED*)
          (LISP::*UNDEFINED* LISP::*UNDEFINED*))

(arrayp a)
⇒    T
```

`arrayp` returns true for any type or subtype of array.

```
(setq v (vector 1 2 3 4))
⇒    #(1 2 3 4)

(arrayp v)
⇒    T

(setq bv #*10010)
⇒    #*10010

(arrayp bv)
⇒    T
```

```
(setq s "abcde")
⇒    "abcde"

(arrayp s)
⇒    T
```

## vectorp

The `vectorp` function determines if an object is a vector. To be a vector, the object must be a one-dimensional array. A vector can contain any type of element.

```
(setq a (make-array '(2 2)))
⇒    #2A((LISP::*UNDEFINED* LISP::*UNDEFINED*)
           (LISP::*UNDEFINED* LISP::*UNDEFINED*))

(vectorp a)
⇒    NIL

(setq v (vector 1 2 3 4))
⇒    #(1 2 3 4)

(vectorp v)
⇒    T

(setq bv #*10010)
⇒    #*10010

(vectorp bv)
⇒    T

(setq s "abcde")
⇒    "abcde"

(vectorp s)
⇒    T
```

## stringp

The `stringp` function determines if an object is a string. A string is a one-dimensional array that contains elements of type `string-char`.

```
(setq a (make-array '(2 2)))
⇒    #2A((LISP::*UNDEFINED* LISP::*UNDEFINED*)
           (LISP::*UNDEFINED* LISP::*UNDEFINED*))
```

```
(stringp a)
⇒    NIL

(setq s "abcde")
⇒    "abcde"

(stringp s)
⇒    T
```

In order for an array to be a string, the type must be specified. It is not enough to make the array with the initial contents of type string.

```
(stringp (make-array 3 :initial-contents "abc"))
⇒    NIL

(stringp (make-array 3 :initial-contents "abc" :element-type 'string-char))
⇒    T
```

## bit-vector-p

The `bit-vector-p` function determines if an object is a bit vector. A *bit vector* is a one-dimensional array with elements of type bit.

```
(setq bv #*10010)
⇒    #*10010

(bit-vector-p bv)
⇒    T

(bit-vector-p "101")
⇒    NIL

(bit-vector-p #*1010)
⇒    T

(bit-vector-p (make-array 3 :initial-element 1))
⇒    NIL

(bit-vector-p (make-array 3 :initial-element 1 :element-type 'bit))
⇒    T
```

## adjustable-array-p

The `adjustable-array-p` function determines if the array is adjustable.

```
(setq c (make-array '(4 5) :initial-element 'a :adjustable t))
⇒   #2A((A A A A A) (A A A A A) (A A A A A) (A A A A A))

(adjustable-array-p c)
⇒   T

(adjustable-array-p (vector 123))
⇒   NIL

(adjustable-array-p "abc")
⇒   NIL

(adjustable-array-p (make-array 3 :initial-element #\a
                                :adjustable t :element-type 'string-char))
⇒   T
```

## Simple

There are three predicates that test for simplicity: `simple-vector-p`, `simple-bit-vector-p`, and `simple-string-p`.

A vector is simple if it can take any type of elements. Thus, bit vectors and strings are not subtypes of a simple vector.

```
(simple-bit-vector-p #*111)
⇒   T

(simple-vector-p #*111)
⇒   NIL

(simple-string-p "abc")
⇒   T

(simple-vector-p "abc")
⇒   NIL
```

A vector is simple if is not adjustable and does not have a fill pointer.

```
(setq a (make-array 3))
⇒   T

(simple-vector-p a)
⇒   T

(simple-vector-p '#(123))
⇒   T
```

```
(setq a (make-array 3 :fill-pointer 0))
⇒    #()

(simple-vector-p a)
⇒    NIL
```

## Element Type

The `array-element-type` function returns the type of elements the array can hold.

```
(array-element-type "abc")
⇒    STRING-CHAR

(array-element-type #*00)
⇒    BIT

(array-element-type '#(a b c))
⇒    T

(array-element-type (make-array 3 :element-type 'float))
⇒    FLOAT
```

## Fill Pointer

The `array-has-fill-pointer-p` function determines if an array has a fill pointer.

```
(array-has-fill-pointer-p "abc")
⇒    NIL

(array-has-fill-pointer-p (make-array 3 :fill-pointer t))
⇒    T
```

The only way a vector can get a fill pointer is through the `:fill-pointer` keyword.

---

**Exercise 12-3**

Write the function `simple-array-p` that determines if an object is a simple array. A *simple array* is an array that has no fill pointer, is not adjustable, and is not displaced.

---

## SIZE OF AN ARRAY

There are several functions that return the size of an array, which are defined in the table.

**TABLE 12.1**  SIZE OF AN ARRAY

| Function | Meaning |
| --- | --- |
| array-dimension | Returns the length of the specified dimension. |
| array-dimensions | Returns a list of the dimensions. |
| array-rank | Returns the number of dimensions. |
| array-total-size | Returns the number of elements. |
| array-row-major-index | Returns an index that identifies a single element. |

```
(setq arr (make-array '(2 3) :initial-contents '((1 2 3)(4 5 6))))
⇒    #2A((1 2 3) (4 5 6))


(array-dimension arr 0)
⇒    2


(array-dimension arr 1)
⇒    3


(array-dimensions arr)
⇒    (2 3)


(array-rank arr)
⇒    2


(array-total-size arr)
⇒    6


(array-row-major-index arr 1 0)
⇒    3                         ;; a pointer, not the element value
```

The maximum size of these results is implementation dependent. There are constants that give the system's limits, as shown in the table.

**TABLE 12.2**   SYSTEM LIMITS FOR CONSTANTS

| Constant | Value |
|---|---|
| array-dimension-limit | Upper exclusive bound on the size of each dimension. |
| array-rank-limit | Upper exclusive bound on the rank. |
| array-total-size-limit | Upper exclusive bound on the number of elements. |

```
array-dimension-limit
⇒    16777216

array-rank-limit
⇒    16777211

array-total-size-limit
⇒    16777216
```

## DATA IN AN ARRAY

Once you have created an array, you need to be able to look at individual elements and change the values of elements, as can be done with the functions in the table.

**TABLE 12.3**   FUNCTIONS FOR CHANGING THE VALUES OF ELEMENTS

| Function | Meaning |
|---|---|
| aref | Returns an element of an array. |
| bit | Returns an element in a bit array. |
| sbit | Returns an element in a simple bit vector. |
| svref | Returns an element in a simple vector. |
| vector-pop | Removes and returns the first element in a vector. |
| vector-push | Adds an element to the end of a vector and returns the fill-pointer value. |
| vector-push-extend | Adds an element to the end of a vector. If the vector is already full, the vector is extended. |
| fill-pointer | Returns the value of the fill pointer. |
| adjust-array | Changes the size, shape, elements, or displacement of an array. |

### aref

The aref function looks at a single element of any type of array.

```
(aref array &rest subscripts)
```

The number of *subscripts* must match the number of dimensions in the array.

```
(setq a (make-array '(4 2) :initial-contents '((1 2)(3 4)(5 6)(7 8))))
⇒    #2A((1 2) (3 4) (5 6) (7 8))

(aref a 0 0)
⇒    1

(aref a 1 1)
⇒    4

(aref a 4 2)
⇒    Error
```

Note that 0  0 is the first element of this array and 3  1 is the last element of this array. Whenever you access an array, the base for each dimension is 0.

```
(setq v (vector 1 2 3 4 5 6 7))
⇒    #(1 2 3 4 5 6 7)

(aref v 0)
⇒    1

(aref v 6)
⇒    7

(setq bv #*110010)
⇒    #*110010

(aref bv 0)
⇒    1

(aref bv 2)
⇒    0

(setq s "abcde")
⇒    "abcde"

(aref s 1)
⇒    #\b

(aref s 4)
⇒    #\e
```

When you use `aref` with `setf`, you can change the value of elements of the array.

```
(setq a (make-array '(4 2) :initial-contents '((1 2)(3 4)(5 6)(7 8))))
⇒    #2A((1 2) (3 4) (5 6) (7 8))


(aref a 1 0)
⇒    3

(setf (aref a 1 0) 'changed)
⇒    CHANGED


a
⇒    #2A((1 2) (CHANGED 4) (5 6) (7 8))

(setq s "abcdef")
⇒    "abcdef"


(setf (aref s 3) #\z)
⇒    #\z


s
⇒    "abczef"

(setf bv #*1111111)
⇒    #*1111111


(setf (aref bv 2) 0)
⇒    0


bv
⇒    #*1101111
```

You must be careful to use the correct type of value whenever you give an element a value. In a general array, one in which no type was specified, you can change the values to anything you wish. In an array that has a specified type, only that type of value can be used.

In addition to `aref`, there are three other functions that look at elements of the arrays: `bit`, `sbit`, and `svref`. These functions are dependent on the type of array.

## bit

`bit` looks at a bit or element of an array of type bit.

```
(bit bit-array &rest subscripts)

(setq x (make-array '(2 3) :initial-contents '((1 0 1)(0 1 0))
                          :element-type 'bit)
⇒    #2A((1 0 1) (0 1 0))
```

```
(bit x 1 1)
⇒    1

(bit x 0 0)
⇒    1

(bit x 0 1)
⇒    0

(setq z #*10110)
⇒    #*10110

(bit z 0)
⇒    1

(bit z 1)
⇒    0
```

Using setf with bit changes the value of an element.

```
(setf (bit x 0 0) 0)
⇒    0

x
⇒    #2A((0 0 1) (0 1 0))

(setf (bit x 1 0) 1)
⇒    1

x
⇒    #2A((0 0 1) (1 1 0))

(setf (bit x 0 2) 0)
⇒    0

x
⇒    #2A((0 0 0) (1 1 0))

z
⇒    #*10110

(setf (bit z 0) 0)
⇒    0

z
⇒    #*00110
```

## Sbit

`sbit` looks at a bit of a simple array of type bit.

```
(sbit simple-bit-array &rest subscripts)

(setq sb (make-array '(1 2 3) :initial-contents '(((1 1 1)(0 0 0)))
                              :element-type 'bit))
⇒    #3A(((1 1 1) (0 0 0)))

(sbit sb 0 1 1)
⇒    0

(setf (sbit sb 0 0 0) 0)
⇒    0

sb
⇒    #3A(((0 1 1) (0 0 0)))

(setf (sbit sb 0 1 1) 1)
⇒    1

sb
⇒    #3A(((0 1 1) (0 1 0)))

z
⇒    #*00110

(setf (sbit z 2) 0)
⇒    0

z
⇒    #*00010
```

## svref

`svref` looks at an element of a simple vector.

```
(svref simple-vector index)

(setq sv (make-array 7 :initial-contents '(a b c d e f g)))
⇒    #(A B C D E F G)

(svref sv 0)
⇒    A
```

```
(setf (svref sv 3) 'modified)
⇒    MODIFIED

sv
⇒    #(A B C MODIFIED E F G)
```

## Elements in a Vector

In addition to the previous functions that return an element, there are three functions that change the elements in a vector. These functions use the vector like a stack. The `vector-pop` function takes an element off the front of the vector and returns it. The `vector-push` function puts an element onto the end of the vector and returns the index value to its location. The `vector-push-extend` function works like `vector-push` except that if the vector is full and adjustable, the vector is lengthened and the element is added.

```
(setq vec (make-array 0 :fill-pointer t :adjustable t))
⇒    #()

(vector-push-extend 'a vec)
⇒    0

vec
⇒    #(A)

(vector-push-extend 'b vec)
⇒    1

vec
⇒    #(A B)

(vector-pop vec)
⇒    B

vec
⇒    #(A)
```

When `vector-push-extend` lengthens the vector, it can add an implementation-dependent length to the vector. This is usually some factor times the current length of the vector (such as 1.25 or 1.5). You can also specify the minimum number of elements to add.

```
(vector-push-extend 'a vec 10)
⇒    3

vec
⇒    #(A A)
```

The `vector-push` function does not extend the vector. It returns nil if the vector is full.

```
(setq vec2 (make-array 1 :fill-pointer 0 :adjustable t))
⇒    # ()


(vector-push 'a vec2)
⇒    0


vec2
⇒    # (A)


(vector-push 'b vec2)
⇒    NIL
```

**fill-pointer.** The `fill-pointer` function returns the current position in a vector. This is the location where an element is put by `vector-push` or `vector-push-extend`.

```
(setq vec (make-array 3 :fill-pointer 0 :adjustable t))
⇒    # ()


(fill-pointer vec)
⇒    0


(vector-push 'a vec)
⇒    0


vec
⇒    # (A)


(fill-pointer vec)
⇒    1


(setf (fill-pointer vec) (array-total-size vec))
⇒    3


vec
⇒    # (A LISP::*UNDEFINED* LISP::*UNDEFINED*)
```

# Adjust

The `adjust-array` function can change the size, shape, elements, and displacement of an adjustable array.

```
(adjust-array array new-dimensions &key :element-type :initial-element
                                        :initial-contents :fill-pointer
                                        :displaced-to :displaced-index-offset)

(setq a-array (make-array '(2 2) :initial-contents '((1 2)(3 4)) :adjustable t))
⇒    #2A((1 2) (3 4))

(adjust-array a-array '(2 3))
⇒    #2A((1 2 LISP::*UNDEFINED*) (3 4 LISP::*UNDEFINED*))

(adjust-array a-array '(3 3) :initial-element 'new)
⇒    #2A((1 2 LISP::*UNDEFINED*) (3 4 LISP::*UNDEFINED*) (NEW NEW NEW))

(adjust-array a-array '(3 4) :initial-contents '((a b c d)(e f g h)(i j k l)))
⇒    #2A((A B C D) (E F G H) (I J K L))
```

The :initial-element keyword specifies the value of the elements that were not part of the array. The :initial-contents keyword gives values to all elements regardless of whether or not they had values in the previous array.

When arrays are displaced, you obtain interesting results.

```
(setq array-1 (make-array '(2 2) :initial-contents '((a b)(c d)) :adjustable t))
⇒    #2A((A B) (C D))

(setq array-2 (make-array 3 :displaced-to array-1 :adjustable t))
⇒    #(A B C)

(adjust-array array-1 '(2 3) :initial-element 'z)
⇒    #2A((A B Z) (C D Z))

array-2
⇒    #(A B Z)

(adjust-array array-2 4)
⇒    #(A B Z LISP::*UNDEFINED*)
```

When the array being displaced to (array-1) is adjusted, it will change the value of the arrays displacing to it (array-2). When you specify that an array is to displace to another array, they share the same structure.

If a displaced array is adjusted but the :displaced-to keyword is not specified, then the result is a new array. The structure is no longer shared.

```
(setf (aref array-2 1) 'z)
⇒    Z

array-2
⇒    #(A Z Z LISP::*UNDEFINED*)

array-1
⇒    #2A((A B Z) (C D Z))
```

**Exercise 12-4**

Given the following array, answer the questions that follow.

```
(setq a (make-array '(4 2 3) :initial-contents '(((1 2 3)(4 5 6))
                                                  ((7 8 9)(a b c))
                                                  ((d e f)(g h i))
                                                  ((j k l)(m n o)))
                                  :adjustable t))
⇒    #3A(((1 2 3) (4 5 6)) ((7 8 9) (A B C))
         ((D E F) (G H I)) ((J K L) (M N O)))
```

**1.** What subscripts identify the element a?

**2.** What subscripts identify the element k?

**3.** What does the following function return?

```
(setq b (make-array '(3 2) :displaced-to a :displaced-index-offset 5))
```

**4.** If you adjust the array a as follows, what is the result?

```
(adjust-array a '(4 2 4) :initial-element 0)
```

**5.** What is the new value of b?

Given:

```
(setq vec (make-array 5 :initial-contents '(1 2 3 4 5) :fill-pointer t))
⇒    #(1 2 3 4 5)
```

answer the following questions:

**6.** What is the value of the fill pointer?

**7.** After the following steps are done, what is the value of vec?

```
(vector-pop vec)
(vector-pop vec)
(vector-push 'z vec)
```

**8.** What is the value of the fill pointer?

## BIT ARRAYS

As with numbers, you can apply a logical function to bit arrays. These functions, which apply the function to each bit in the array and return an array, are shown in the table.

**TABLE 12.4**  BIT ARRAYS

| Function | Meaning |
|---|---|
| bit-and | Returns the result of anding the bits of the first with the bits of the second array. |
| bit-andc1 | Returns the result of anding the complement of the first array with the second array. |
| bit-andc2 | Returns the result of anding the first array with the complement of the second array. |
| bit-eqv | Returns the result of exclusively noring the first array with the second array. |
| bit-ior | Returns the result of inclusively oring the first array with the second array. |
| bit-nand | Returns the result of not anding the first array with the second array. |
| bit-nor | Returns the result of not oring the first array with the second array. |
| bit-not | Returns the result of noting the bits of the argument array. |
| bit-orc1 | Returns the result of oring the complement of the first array with the second array. |
| bit-orc2 | Returns the result of oring the first array with the complement of the second array. |
| bit-xor | Returns the result of exclusively oring the first array with the second array. |

For example,

```
(bit-ior #*1111 #*0000)
⇒    #*1111


(bit-xor #*1111 #*1001)
⇒    #*0110


(bit-and #*1111 #*1001)
⇒    #*1001


(bit-eqv #*1111 #*1001)
⇒    #*1001
```

## SUMMARY

An *array* is a structure that stores data using a coordinate system. You can use one of the functions to make an array or you can type the array structure using macro characters to indicate the type of array. Either way, you can specify the array's size, shape, and elements.

Using `make-array`, you can also specify a fill pointer for a vector, whether or not the array is adjustable, and whether the array shares its structure with another array.

There are several functions that determine the size of the array and its type. Knowing this information is important when you want to get data from the array or put data into the array.

# 13

## Characters

This chapter describes characters—what they are, how to create them, and the functions that operate on them.

- What is the character syntax?
- What are the parts of a character coding?
- How do you build a character?
- How do you compare characters?
- What is a macro character?

## CHARACTER OBJECTS

A character object has its own syntax: #\a, #\space, #\x, #\control-d, etc.

A character object has integer encoding. This encoding includes a standard code (such as ASCII); bits determining if the character is a meta, hyper, super, or control character; and bits determining the font of the character. (Not all systems support fonts.) For example, the character #\control-a has a coding of 16777281. The character #\a has a coding of 97. The coding can be different on each implementation.

## MAKING A CHARACTER

To make a character, you can type the character using the #\ syntax. Or you can begin with a symbol and change the symbol to a character.

### Character

```
(character object)
```

If the object is a single character symbol, or a string of a single character, the character that corresponds to that symbol is returned. For example,

```
(character 'a)
⇒   #\A

(character '\a)
⇒   #\a

(character '\5)
⇒   #\5

(character "a")
⇒   #\a

(character "A")
⇒   #\A
```

If the object is a nonnegative integer, the character that is encoded by that integer is returned. The largest integer that returns a character is implementation dependent. For example,

```
(character 97)
⇒   #\a

(character 100)
⇒   #\d

(character 400)
⇒   NIL
```

### Make Character

The make-char function constructs a new character from its arguments.

```
(make-char character &optional bits fonts)
```

The *bits* and *fonts* arguments are integers that specify those attributes. For example,

```
(make-char #\a 2 0)
⇒   #\META-\a

(make-char #\control-a 0 0)
⇒   #\A
```

More information on the values of *bits* and *fonts* is given later in this chapter.

## CHARACTER ENCODING

Character coding has three parts: the code, the bits, and the fonts. How these are arranged is implementation dependent. On the author's system, the character is encoded as shown in Fig. 13-1. The functions that return information on the character coding are shown in Table 13.1.

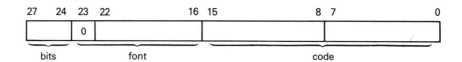

**Figure 13-1**  Character encoding

## CHARACTER CODE

The character code is a coding that can be ASCII, EBCDIC, or some other code. The code does not include bits and fonts.

The `char-code` function returns the character code.

```
(char-code character)
```

The `code-char` function returns the character for the specified code.

```
(code-char code &optional bits font)
```

`char-code-limit` specifies the maximum code for any character.

**TABLE 13.1**  CHARACTER CODING

| Function | Meaning |
|---|---|
| char-code | Returns the character code. |
| code-char | Returns the character for the specified character code. |
| char-code-limit | Returns the maximum character code allowed. |
| char-control-bit | Returns the weight of the control bit. |
| char-meta-bit | Returns the weight of the meta bit. |
| char-hyper-bit | Returns the weight of the hyper bit. |
| char-super-bit | Returns the weight of the super bit. |
| char-bit | Determines if the bit is set for a character. |
| set-char-bit | Sets the bit for the specified character. |
| char-bits | Returns the bits attribute for a character. |
| char-bit-limit | Returns the maximum value that can be returned by char-bits. |
| char-font | Returns the font attribute for a character. |
| char-font-limit | Returns the maximum value that can be returned by char-font. |
| char-int | Returns the integer encoding of a character. |
| int-char | Returns the character encoded by the integer. |

For example,

```
char-code-limit
⇒    256


(char-code #\a)
⇒    97


(code-char 97)
⇒    #\a


(char-code #\space)
⇒    32


(char-code #\A)
⇒    65


(code-char 1)
⇒    #\Soh
```

The fonts and bits attributes can be specified in code-char. These attributes are described in the next sections.

## CHARACTER BITS

There are four bits that can be set: control, meta, super, and hyper. Each bit has a
weight (or value). The constants `char-control-bit`, `char-meta-bit`, `char-super-bit`, and `char-hyper-bit` return the weight of the specified bit. For
example,

```
char-control-bit
⇒    1
```

```
char-meta-bit
⇒    2
```

```
char-super-bit
⇒    4
```

```
char-hyper-bit
⇒    8
```

When you create a character using `code-char`, you can specify the bit attribute.

```
(code-char 97)
⇒    #\a
```

```
(code-char 97 1)
⇒    #\CONTROL-\a
```

```
(code-char 97 8)
⇒    #\HYPER-\a
```

```
(code-char 97 3)
⇒    #\CONTROL-META-\a
```

The `char-bit` function determines if the named bit is set for the specified character.

```
(char-bit character character-bit)
```

```
(char-bit #\control-a :control)
⇒    T
```

```
(char-bit #\control-a :hyper)
⇒    NIL
```

The `char-bits` function returns the bits attribute of the character object.

```
(char-bits character)

(char-bits #\control-a)
⇒    1

(char-bits #\a)
⇒    0

(char-bits #\control-meta-a)
⇒    3
```

The `char-bits-limit` constant is the upper exclusive bound of the values produced by `char-bits`.

```
char-bits-limit
⇒    16

(code-char 97 15)
⇒    #\CONTROL-META-HYPER-SUPER-\a

(code-char 97 16)
⇒    NIL
```

The `set-char-bit` function sets the named bit for the specified character.

```
(set-char-bit character character-bit new-value)

(set-char-bit #\a :control t)
⇒    #\CONTROL-\a

(set-char-bit #\hyper-a :hyper nil)
⇒    #\A
```

When you are using the bits attributes, you need to watch for uppercase and lowercase letters. As you can see in the previous example, #\hyper-a is read as #\hyper-A. If you want lowercase, you must use the escape character \.

```
#\hyper-a
⇒    #\HYPER-A

#\control-\a
⇒    #\CONTROL-\a
```

When you are not using the bits attributes, the character is already escaped.

```
#\a
⇒    #\a


#\A
⇒    #\A
```

## CHARACTER FONTS

Fonts specify how a character is printed. Not all implementations support fonts; however, the following function and constant are supported.

char-font returns the font attribute of the character object.

```
(char-font character)
```

char-font-limit is the upper exclusive bound of the values produced by char-font.

For example,

```
char-font-limit
⇒    128

(char-font #\a)
⇒    0

(char-font (code-char 97 0 5))
⇒    5
```

The font attribute is shown as an integer between the # and \. For cxamplc,

```
#2\a
#8\K
```

**Integer Encoding**   In addition to obtaining the values of the code, bits, and fonts, you can obtain the entire encoding of the character with char-int and you can create a character object by specifying an integer in int-char.

```
(char-int character)
```

```
(int-char integer)
```

For example,

```
(char-int #\control-\a)
⇒    16777313


(int-char 16777313)
⇒    #\CONTROL-\a


(char-int #\a)
⇒    97


(int-char 97)
⇒    #\a
```

Not all integers map to a character. If no character exists, nil is returned.

```
(int-char 300)
⇒    NIL
```

---

**Exercise 13-1**

**1.** Use `code-char` to create the following characters:

```
#\meta-\a
#\control-meta-A
#\control-meta-super-hyper-\z
```

**2.** Use `make-char` to create the following characters:

```
#2\hyper-\a
#\A
#3\control-meta-c
```

**3.** What is the integer encoding of the following characters?

```
#\a
#3\a
#3\control-\a
```

---

## PREDICATES

There are several predicates that determine the type of a character. That is, they determine if it is an alphabetic character, an alphanumeric character, a digit character, a graphics character, or a string character. The predicates are defined in the table.
For example,

```
(alpha-char-p #\a)
⇒    T

(alpha-char-p #\1)
⇒    NIL

(alpha-char-p #\control-a)
⇒    NIL

(alphanumericp #\control-a)
⇒    NIL

(alphanumericp #\1)
⇒    T

(alphanumericp #\cr)
⇒    NIL

(graphic-char-p #\cr)
⇒    NIL

(graphic-char-p #\space)
⇒    T

(graphic-char-p #\control-a)
⇒    NIL

(string-char-p #\cr)
⇒    T

(string-char-p #\tab)
⇒    T

(string-char-p #\control-a)
⇒    NIL
```

**TABLE 13.2**  PREDICATES

| Function | Meaning |
|---|---|
| alpha-char-p | Determines if a character object is an alphabetic character. |
| alphanumericp | Determines if a character object is an alphanumeric character. |
| digit-char-p | Determines if a character object represents a digit. |
| graphic-char-p | Determines if a character object is a graphic (printing) character. |
| string-char-p | Determines if a character object can be stored in a string. |

## CHARACTER CASE

The letters a through z and A through Z have character case. The letters a through z are lowercase letters and A through Z are uppercase letters. You can test a character to see if it has an uppercase or lowercase equivalent. You can also change the case of a character. The functions for character case are shown in the following table.

**TABLE 13.3**  PREDICATES

| Function | Meaning |
|----------|---------|
| lower-case-p | Determines if the character is a lowercase character. |
| upper-case-p | Determines if the character is an uppercase character. |
| both-case-p | Determines if the character has an uppercase and lowercase equivalent. |
| char-upcase | Returns the uppercase equivalent of the character. |
| char-downcase | Returns the lowercase equivalent of the character. |

For example,

```
(lower-case-p #\a)
⇒    T


(upper-case-p #\Z)
⇒    T


(lower-case-p #\1)
⇒    NIL


(upper-case-p #\3)
⇒    NIL
```

The both-case-p determines if a character has a lowercase equivalent if it is uppercase or has an uppercase equivalent if it is lowercase.

```
(both-case-p #\a)
⇒    T


(both-case-p #\A)
⇒    T


(both-case-p #\control-a)
⇒    NIL


(both-case-p #\8)
⇒    NIL
```

The char-upcase and char-downcase functions change the character case.

```
(char-upcase #\a)
⇒    #\A
```

```
(char-upcase #\control-\a)
⇒    #\CONTROL-\a

(char-downcase #\a)
⇒    #\a

(char-downcase #\A)
⇒    #\a

(char-downcase #\$)
⇒    #\$
```

## COMPARISONS

When comparing characters, you can use the entire encoding, which includes bits and character case, or you can ignore bits and character case. Table 13.4 shows the character-comparison functions. The functions `char=`, `char>`, etc. use the entire encoding of the character. The functions `char-equal`, `char-greaterp`, etc. ignore bits and case.

**TABLE 13.4**   CHARACTER-COMPARISON FUNCTIONS

| Uses Bits and Case | Ignores Bits and Case | Meaning |
|---|---|---|
| char= | char-equal | Characters are equal. |
| char/= | char-not-equal | Characters are distinct. |
| char< | char-greaterp | Characters are monotonically increasing. |
| char<= | char-not-greaterp | Characters are monotonically nondecreasing (less than or equal). |
| char> | char-lessp | Characters are monotonically decreasing. |
| char>= | char-not-lessp | Characters are monotonically nonincreasing (greater than or equal). |

Each function takes one or more characters.
For example,

```
(char= #\a #\A)
⇒    NIL

(char-equal #\a #\A)
⇒    T

(char-equal #\control-a #\a)
⇒    T

(char> #\a #\A)
⇒    T
```

```
(char< #\a #\c #\f #\z)
⇒    T


(char-lessp #\A #\a)
⇒    NIL


(char-lessp #\A #\b #\c)
⇒    T
```

## CHARACTER NAME

Some characters have names. Characters such as #\a or #\Z do not necessarily have names. Characters that have zero fonts, zero bits, and are nongraphic always have names.

The char-name function returns a string that represents the character name.

```
(char-name character)
```

For example,

```
(char-name #\a)
⇒    NIL

(char-name #\space)
⇒    "Space"

(char-name #\sp)
⇒    "Space"

(char-name #\cr)
⇒    "Return"
```

The name-char function returns the character represented by the string argument.

```
(name-char name)
```

For example,

```
(name-char "return")
⇒    #\Return
```

```
(name-char "a")
⇒    NIL


(name-char "space")
⇒    #\Space
```

## MACRO CHARACTERS

A *macro character* is a character that expands into some function. For example, the (
character tells the reader that the objects following are part of a list. The ) character
tells the reader that the list has ended. The table shows the macro characters and their
meanings.

**TABLE 13.5**  MACRO CHARACTERS

| Char | Meaning |
| --- | --- |
| ( | Begins reading a list. Continues reading until a matching right parenthesis is read. |
| ) | Ends reading a list. |
| ' | The accent acute is an abbreviation for the symbol `quote`. |
| ; | The semicolon stops the reader from reading anything further on the current line. Comments are preceded by the semicolon. |
| " | Begins reading a string. Continues until a second double quote is read, which ends the string. |
| ` | The accent grave, or backquote, is used for constructing complex data structures. |
| , | The comma is used within a backquoted list. |
| @ | The commercial ''at'' is used within a backquoted list. |

### Backquote

The backquote, ` , macro character has a meaning similar to quote. The form that fol-
lows the backquote is not evaluated, except for certain items. These items have a
comma preceding them.

The backquote is equivalent to quote when a form follows the character.

```
'a
⇒    A

`a
⇒    A
```

```
(setq a '(1 2 3))
⇒    (1 2 3)


(setq b `(1 2 3))
⇒    (1 2 3)
```

When a comma appears before an object, that object is evaluated.

```
`(,a b c)
⇒    ((1 2 3) B C)

`(a ,b c)
⇒    (A (1 2 3) C)

`,a
⇒    (1 2 3)
```

When a comma and a commercial "at" sign appear before an object, that object is evaluated and expanded in the list.

```
`(,@a b c)
⇒    (1 2 3 B C)


`(,@a ,@b c)
⇒    (1 2 3 1 2 3 C)
```

The comma followed by a period is similar to a comma followed by a commercial "at." The same result is produced; however, the expanded list may be destroyed.

```
a
⇒    (1 2 3)

`(,.a b c)
⇒    (1 2 3 B C)

a
⇒    (1 2 3 B C)
```

## The Dispatching Macro Character

The # character is a *dispatching macro character*. This character tells the reader that the characters that follow have a macro function. The characters can not have a function if the # character does not precede them. For example, O is a symbol unless # precedes it; then it specifies that the number that follows is in octal form. The table shows and defines the # macro characters.

**TABLE 13.6**  MACRO CHARACTERS

| Char | Meaning |
|------|---------|
| #'   | Abbrevation for function |
| # (  | Simple vector |
| #*   | Bit vector |
| #\   | Character object |
| #\|  | Balanced comment |
| #a  #A | Array |
| #b  #B | Binary rational |
| #c  #C | Complex number |
| #o  #O | Octal rational |
| #r  #R | Radix-n rational |
| #s  #S | Structure |
| #x  #X | Hexadecimal rational |
| ##   | Reference to  #= label |
| #,   | Load time evaluation |
| #:   | Uninterned symbol |
| #=   | Label following object |
| #+   | Read time conditional |
| #-   | Read time conditional |
| #.   | Read time evaluation |

The macros  #0,  #1, ...,  #9  are used for macros that use a numerical argument, such as arrays and radix.

Some macros are specifically reserved for the user. They are #!, #?, #[, #], #{, and #}.

---

**Exercise 13-2**

**1.** What is the meaning of the following objects?

```
(a b c)
#(1 2 3)
'(a b c)
'(,a b c)
'(,@a b c)
```

**2.** Given the following,

```
(setq a '(1 2 3))
⇒    (1 2 3)

(setq b '(a b (d)))
⇒    (A B (D))

(setq c '(a b))
⇒    (A B)
```

what do the following lists return?

```
'(a b c)
`(a b c)
`(a ,b 'c)
`(a b ,(eval 'c))
`(a ,@b c)
`(a ,.b c)
```

---

## SUMMARY

A character has three parts: code, bits, and fonts. In any implementation, only the code must be included. This code is usually a standard character code such as ASCII.

Characters can be compared either ignoring or using the letter case and bits attribute of the character.

Macro characters have a definition beyond their character code. The definition can be an abbrevation for a function or be a function itself. The dispatching macro character tells the reader to look at several more characters as macro characters rather than simple characters.

# *14*

# *Sequences*

A *sequence* is an object that is a vector, a list, or a subtype of either. This chapter looks at the functions that operate on both lists and vectors. Chapters 10, 12, and 15 describe functions that operate on specific types of sequences.

## MAKING A SEQUENCE

The `make-sequence` function creates a sequence. You specify the type, size, and initial element of the sequence.

```
(make-sequence type size &key :initial-element)
```

For example,

```
(make-sequence 'list 5 :initial-element 'a)
⇒   (A A A A A)

(make-sequence 'list 5)
⇒   (NIL NIL NIL NIL NIL)
```

```
(make-sequence 'string 3 :initial-element #\a)
⇒    "aaa"

(make-sequence '(vector integer) 7 :initial-element 0))
⇒    #(0 0 0 0 0 0 0)
```

In addition, `list`, `vector`, `make-array`, and other functions also make objects that are sequences.

```
(setq a (list 'a 'b 'b))
⇒    (A B B)

(typep a 'sequence)
⇒    T

(typep '#(1 2 3) 'sequence)
⇒    T

(typep '#((1 2)(3 4)) 'sequence)
⇒    T

(typep '#2A((1 2)(3 4)) 'sequence)
⇒    NIL

(typep "abc" 'sequence)
⇒    T
```

---

**Exercise 14-1**

There is no function `sequencep` defined in Lisp. As an exercise, write this function. `sequencep` is true if the argument is a list or a vector. It returns nil for all other data types.

---

## COPIES

There are two functions that return copies of a sequence: `copy-seq` and `subseq`. `copy-seq` returns a copy of a full sequence whereas `subseq` returns a copy of a subsequence.

(`copy-seq` *sequence*)

(`subseq` *sequence start* &optional *end*)

The first element in a sequence is element zero. The *end* argument specifies the exclusive end of the sequence.

For example,

```
(setq seq '(a b c))
⇒     (A B C)

(setq seq2 (copy-seq seq))
⇒     (A B C)

(setq seq (cons seq '(1 2 3)))
⇒     ((A B C) 1 2 3)

seq2
⇒     (A B C)

(setq seq3 (subseq seq2 2))
⇒     (C)

(subseq seq2 0)
⇒     (A B C)

(subseq seq2 0 2)
⇒     (A B)
```

## COMBINING SEQUENCES

When you have several sequences and want one, you can use the concatenate function. This function returns a new sequence. It does not modify the argument
sequences.

> (concatenate *result-type* &rest *sequences*)

For example,

```
(concatenate 'string "abc" '#(#\1 #\2 #\3))
⇒     "abc123"

(concatenate 'list '#(a b c) '((1 2)(3 4)) "xyz")
⇒     (A B C (1 2) (3 4) #\x #\y #\z)

(concatenate 'list '#(a b c))
⇒     (A B C)

(setq a "abc")
⇒     "abc"
```

```
(setq b "123")
⇒     "123"

(concatenate 'string a b)
⇒     "abc123"


a
⇒     "abc"


b
⇒     "123"
```

The elements of the argument sequences must fit the type specified.  That is, if the type is string, the elements of all the sequences must be characters.

```
(concatenate 'string '(1 2))
⇒     !!!!! Error: The argument 1 is not of type STRING-CHAR.

(concatenate 'string '(#\1 #\2))
⇒     "12"
```

---

**Exercise 14-2**

**1.** What do the following functions return?

```
(concatenate 'bit-vector '#(1 0 1) #*000)

(concatenate 'list "abc" #*11 '(a b c))

(concatenate 'vector '(a b c) "123")
```

**2.** Using `concatenate`, you can change the type of a sequence.  What must be true to change a list to a vector?

**3.** What must be true to change a vector to a string?

**4.** What must be true to change a string to a bit vector?

---

## LENGTH OF A SEQUENCE

The `length` function returns the length of a sequence.  It returns the number of elements in a list.  If an element is a list, the elements within the sublist are not counted.  If the sequence is a vector, the active length of the vector is returned.

```
(setq list-seq '(a (b c) d))
⇒    (A (B C) D)


(length list-seq)
⇒    3


(setq vec-seq (make-array 5 :fill-pointer 1 :adjustable t :initial-element
⇒    #(T)


(length vec-seq)
⇒    1


(setf (fill-pointer vec-seq) 5)
⇒    5


vec-seq
⇒    #(T T T T T)


(length vec-seq)
⇒    5


(length "abc")
⇒    3


(length "")
⇒    0
```

---

**Exercise 14-3**

There is no Lisp function that traverses a tree and returns a count of all atoms in a list. Write this function. This function can be done recursively. If the element is an atom, count 1. If the element is a list, pass the element to the function and count all of the sublist's atoms.

---

## SINGLE ELEMENTS

You need to be able to look at single elements of a sequence. If you know where the element is, use elt to retrieve it. If you want to find an element, use find. If you want to know where an element is located, use position. You can also compare two sequences and determine where one sequence matches the other by using search, or where they diverge by using mismatch. These functions are shown in the following table.

**TABLE 14.1**   SINGLE ELEMENTS

| Function | Meaning |
|----------|---------|
| elt | Returns the element in the sequence specified by the index. |
| find | Returns an element that satisfies a test. |
| find-if | Returns an element that satisfies a test. |
| find-if-not | Returns an element that fails the test. |
| position | Finds an element that satisfies a test and returns the index. |
| position-if | Finds an element that satisfies a test and returns the index. |
| position-if-not | Finds an element that fails the test and returns the index. |
| search | Returns an index in a sequence specifying where a match of a subsequence occurs. |
| mismatch | Returns an index in a sequence specifying where a mismatch of a subsequence occurs. |

## Getting an Element

When looking at the elements of a list, you can use `nth` to get one element. For any sequence, you can use `elt` to get one element.

(elt *sequence index*)

For example,

```
(nth 0 '(a b c))
⇒    A

(elt '(a b c) 0)
⇒    A

(elt '#(a b c) 2)
⇒    C

(elt "01234567" 6)
⇒    #\6

(elt '(a (b c) d) 1)
⇒    (B C)
```

**Exercise 14-4**

1. Write the function `vec-length` that returns the number of atoms in a vector if the vector contains lists. If the element is a list, call `all-atoms` on that list. If the element is not a list, count 1. As with `all-atoms`, you can recursively call the function to look at each element.

2. Write the function `total` that returns the total number of atoms of any sequence.

## Returning an Element

There are times when you do not want the nth element, instead, you want an element that satisfies a test. The `find` function looks at a sequence and returns this element.

```
(find item sequence &key :from-end :test :test-not :start :end :key)
```

There are also matching `find-if` and `find-if-not` functions.

```
(find-if test sequence &key :from-end :start :end :key)
```

```
(find-if-not test sequence &key :from-end :start :end :key)
```

For example,

```
(find 'a '#(s z (a b) a d))
⇒    A

(find 'a '#((s z) (a b) (a c)) :key #'car)
⇒    (A B)

(find #\m "admnp" :test 'char-lessp)
⇒    #\n

(find-if #'listp '(a (b c) d))
⇒    (B C)

(find-if-not #'atom '(a (b c) k (d e) f) :start 2)
⇒    (D E)
```

## Finding an Element by Index

While `find` returns the element that satisfies the test, it does not tell you where the element came from. Thus, you would have to use `find` each time you wanted the element, rather than using `elt` or another function. The `position` function looks for an element that satisfies a test; however, `position` returns an index into the sequence that specifies where the element is rather than returning the element directly.

```
(position item sequence &key :from-end :test :test-not :start :end :key)
```

```
(position-if test sequence &key :from-end :start :end :key)
```

```
(position-if-not test sequence &key :from-end :start :end :key)
```

When you specify a subsequence to search (using the `:start` or `:end` keywords), the index refers to the original sequence, not the subsequence. For example,

```
(position 'a '(a b d a k f) :start 2)
⇒    3

(position-if #'zerop '#(0 5 3 0 9) :from-end t)
⇒    3

(position-if #'zerop '#(0 5 3 0 9))
⇒    0
```

There are two other functions that return an index into the sequence. search looks for a match of two sequences. mismatch looks for the first element that does not match.

```
(search sequence1 sequence2 &key :from-end :test :test-not
                            :key :start1 :start2 :end1 :end2)

(mismatch sequence1 sequence2 &key :from-end :test :test-not
                            :key :start1 :start2 :end1 :end2)
```

For example,

```
(search '(a b c) '(1 2 a b c 3 4))
⇒    2

(search '(a (b) c) '(a b (a (b) c) d))
⇒    NIL

(search '((a (b) c)) '(a b (a (b) c) d) :test #'equal)
⇒    2

(mismatch '#(a b c d e) '(a b))
⇒    2

(mismatch '(1 2 3) '(a 1 2 3))
⇒    0
```

---

**Exercise 14-5**

1. Can you search for a string sequence within a vector sequence? Why?

2. The find function looks for an element in a sequence. If the element is a list, find does not recursively look at the elements in the list. Write a recursive find function that does this.

    **a.** Write the function ignoring the keywords. The default test is eql.

**b.** This exercise uses some programming techniques you may not have used in a while. Without the keywords, a simple linear recursive function could be written. When you add the keywords, a linear iterative recursive function solves the problem better. Here, however, you will be passing functions as variables. When you use a variable as a function, you must apply the function `funcall` to the variable to get the function definition.

There are two functions that can be specified: test and key functions. The test function is used to compare the item and sequence. The key function is applied to the element of the sequence (not the item) before the test function.

## COUNT

The previous functions tell you what element satisfies a test and where this element is in the sequence. You might also want to know how many elements satisfy the test.

The `count` function counts the number of elements in the sequence that satisfy the test. There are also `count-if` and `count-if-not` functions.

```
(count item sequence &key :from-end :test :test-not :start :end :key)

(count-if test sequence &key :from-end :start :end :key)

(count-if-not test sequence &key :from-end :start :end :key)
```

For example,

```
(count 'a '(a b c (a b) a))
⇒    2

(count 10 '(1 2 5 12 15) :test #'<)
⇒    2

(count-if #'listp '#(a (b c) d))
⇒    1

(count-if-not #'listp '#(a (b c) d))
⇒    2
```

## PREDICATES

A predicate returns a nil or non-nil value. There are four functions that test all the elements of a sequence against a predicate, as shown in the table.

**TABLE 14.2**  PREDICATES

| Function | Meaning |
|----------|---------|
| every | Tests each element of a sequence until it reaches an element that fails the test, in which case it returns nil, or until it reaches the end of the sequence, in which case it returns a non-nil value. |
| notany | Tests each element of a sequence until it reaches an element that satisfies the test, in which case it returns nil, or until it reaches the end of the sequence, in which case it returns a non-nil value. |
| notevery | Tests each element of a sequence until one elements fails the test, in which case it returns a non-nil value, or until it reaches the end of the sequence, in which case it returns nil. |
| some | Tests each element of a sequence until one element satisfies the test, in which case it returns a non-nil value, or until it reaches the end of the sequence, in which case it returns nil. |

(every *predicate sequence* &rest *more-sequences*)

(notany *predicate sequence* &rest *more-sequences*)

(notevery *predicate sequence* &rest *more-sequences*)

(some *predicate sequence* &rest *more-sequences*)

These functions construct sequences that are applied to the predicate. The predicate must be able to take as many arguments as there are sequences. For example,

```
(every #'< '(1 2 3) '(2 3 4))
⇒    T
```

This is equivalent to:

```
(and (< 1 2)(< 2 3)(< 3 4))
⇒    T

(some #'char-equal "abc" "Abcd" "ABCD")
⇒    T
```

This is equivalent to:

```
(or (char-equal #\a #\A #\A)
    (char-equal #\b #\b #\B)
    (char-equal #\c #\c #\C))
⇒    T
```

The  d character is not used in the last example. Because the shortest sequence is three elements long, only the first three elements of all the sequences are tested.

The functions do not necessarily test all the elements. Once the condition is met, the function returns a value.

The following function tests the first three elements and then returns nil:

```
(notany #'evenp '#(3 5 6 5))
⇒    NIL
```

The following function tests the first element and then returns true:

```
(notevery #'evenp '#(3 5 6 5))
⇒    T
```

---

**Exercise 14-6**

1. Write a function that `concatenates` a vector to a string. Test all elements of the vector to make sure they are all string characters. Return an appropriate error message if they are not.

2. A sequence can be made into a bit vector if each element is either 1 or 0. Write a function that tests all elements to see if they meet this requirement.

---

## MODIFYING A SEQUENCE

You can delete elements from a sequence, delete duplicate elements, substitute one element for another, and replace a subsequence with another subsequence. These modifications can be done to the argument sequence or you can get a new sequence with no change to the argument sequence. These functions are shown in the following table.

**TABLE 14.3**  MODIFICATIONS TO A SEQUENCE

| Function | Meaning |
| --- | --- |
| delete | Deletes elements from the argument sequence. |
| remove | Returns a new sequence with the specified elements removed. |
| delete-duplicates | Returns the argument sequence with duplicate elements deleted. |
| remove-duplicates | Returns a new sequence with duplicate elements removed. |
| substitute | Returns a new sequence with elements satisfying a test replaced by a specified item. |
| nsubstitute | Returns the argument sequence with elements satisfying a test replaced by a specified item. |
| fill | Returns the argument sequence with a specified subsequence replaced by an item. |
| replace | Returns the argument sequence with a specified subsequence replaced by a subsequence of another sequence. |

## Deleting and Removing Elements

`delete` and `remove` find an element in the sequence and delete it. If the `:count` keyword is specified, that number of elements is deleted. `delete` returns the argument sequence. `remove` returns a new sequence.

> (delete *item sequence* &key :from-end :test :test-not :start :end :count :key)

> (delete-if *test sequence* &key :from-end :start :end :count :key)

> (delete-if-not *test sequence* &key :from-end :start :end :count :key)

> (remove *item sequence* &key :from-end :test :test-not :start :end :count :key)

> (remove-if *test sequence* &key :from-end :start :end :count :key)

> (remove-if-not *test sequence* &key :from-end :start :end :count :key)

For example,

```
(delete #\a "abcdalkja;;;")
⇒   "bcdlkj;;;"

(delete #\a "abcdalkja;;;" :count 1)
⇒   "bcdalkja;;;"

(delete #\a "abcdalkja;;;" :from-end t :count 1)
⇒   "abcdalkj;;;"

(remove-if #'zerop '#(1 2 0 4 0 2))
⇒   #(1 2 4 2)

(remove-if #'zerop '#(1 2 0 4 0 2) :from-end t :count 1)
⇒   #(1 2 0 4 2)

(remove-if #'zerop '#(1 2 0 4 0 2) :start 3)
⇒   #(1 2 0 4 2)
```

## Duplicate Elements

Again, `delete-duplicates` returns the argument sequence and `remove-duplicates` returns a new sequence. These functions delete elements that match previous elements.

```
(delete-duplicates sequence &key :from-end :test :test-not :start :end :key)

(remove-duplicates sequence &key :from-end :test :test-not :start :end :key)
```

For example,

```
(setq a '(a b c d a a b k l p c))
⇒    (A B C D A A B K L P C)

(remove-duplicates a)
⇒    (D A B K L P C)

(remove-duplicates a :from-end t)
⇒    (A B C D K L P)

a
⇒    (A B C D A A B K L P C)

(delete-duplicates a :start 3 :end 7)
⇒    (A B C D A B K L P C)

a
⇒    (A B C D A B K L P C)
```

## Substitution

In substitution, an element of the sequence is replaced by a new item. The replaced element can be a single element or one that satisfies a test. The :count keyword allows you to specify the maximum number of replacements that can be done.

```
(substitute newitem olditem sequence &key :from-end :test :test-not
                                     :start :end :count :key)

(substitute-if newitem test sequence &key :from-end :start :end :count :key)

(substitute-if-not newitem test sequence &key :from-end :start :end :count :key)
```

There are also nsubstitute, nsubstitute-if, and nsubstitute-if-not functions that change the argument sequence rather than returning a new sequence. For example,

```
(substitute 'a 'b '(a b c d a b c d))
⇒    (A A C D A A C D)

(substitute-if nil 'characterp '#(0 b #\a d 8 #\2))
⇒    #(0 B NIL D 8 NIL)
```

## Filling

All elements within the specified subsequence are replaced. The sequence is modified.

```
(fill sequence item &key :start :end)
```
For example,
```
(fill "012345" #\a :start 3)
⇒    "012aaa"

(fill "abcde" #\space)
⇒    "     "
```

## Replace

All elements in the specified subsequence of sequence1 are replaced by the elements in the specified subsequence of sequence2. The length of the shorter subsequence is used.

```
(replace sequence1 sequence2 &key :start1 :end1 :start2 :end2)
```
For example,
```
(replace "abcdef" "01234567" :start1 0 :end1 3 :start2 5)
⇒    "567def"

(replace '(john 555-1212) '(john 555-0012)  :start1 1 :start2 1)
⇒    (JOHN \555-0012)
```

---

**Exercise 14-7**

Given a sequence of names and numbers, write a function that looks up a name and changes the number. The function should take two arguments: the sequence of names and numbers and a sequence containing two elements, the name and number to be changed.

---

## ORDERING THE SEQUENCE

The functions which order sequences are shown in the following table.

**TABLE 14.4**   ORDERING THE SEQUENCE

| Function | Meaning |
|---|---|
| sort | Returns the argument in a sorted order. |
| stable-sort | Returns the argument in a sorted order. Elements that were in order before the function was called remain in the same order. |
| merge | Merges two sorted sequences. |
| reverse | Returns a sequence in the reverse order of the argument sequence. |
| nreverse | Returns an argument sequence in the reverse order. |

## Sorting

The functions `sort` and `stable-sort` put the elements of a sequence into an order that satisfies a predicate, for example, in an increasing numeric order or in a decreasing alphabetic order. These functions modify the argument sequence.

```
(sort sequence predicate &key :key)
```

```
(stable-sort sequence predicate &key :key)
```

The `merge` function takes two sorted sequences and merges them into one sequence. The argument sequences can be modified.

```
(merge result-type sequence1 sequence2 predicate &key :key)
```

For example,

```
(sort "akebdslkabc" #'char<)
⇒    "aabbcdekkls"

(sort '#(5 3 9 0 1 4) #'>)
⇒    #(9 5 4 3 1 0)

(merge 'list (sort "ytesgly" #'char<)
             (sort '#(#\a #\k #\m #\a #\b) #'char<) #'char<)
⇒    (#\a #\a #\b #\e #\g #\k #\l #\m #\s #\t #\y #\y)
```

## Reversing

The `reverse` function reverses the order of the elements in the sequence. `reverse` returns a new sequence. `nreverse` modifies the argument sequence.

```
(reverse sequence)
```

```
(nreverse sequence)
```

For example,

```
(reverse "012345")
⇒    "543210"

(reverse '#(a (b c) (d e)))
⇒    #((D E) (B C) A)
```

**Exercise 14-8**

Write a function that takes the sequence of names and numbers and returns the sequence alphabetized by name.

## SUMMARY

The data type sequence is made up of lists and vectors. In addition to the functions found in this chapter, list, array, and string functions can be applied to sequences.

The sequence functions include ways to make, copy, and combine sequences. You can look at single elements of a sequence, count elements in a sequence, and modify either single elements of entire subsequences of a sequence. You can also sort a sequence or reverse its order.

# 15

## Strings

A *string* is a vector with elements of type character. Because strings are a subtype of vectors, arrays, and sequences, functions that operate on these types also work on strings. Because a string is a sequence of characters, any function that operates on characters also operates on the elements of strings. Also, there are functions that are specific to strings. You can create a string, gets a single character from the string, compare strings, change the character case, and trim characters from a string.

## CREATING STRINGS

The `make-string` function returns a string of a specified length and initial character.

```
(make-string length &key :initial-element)
```

For example,

```
(make-string 5)
⇒    "     "

(make-string 5 :initial-element #\c)
⇒    "ccccc"
```

The same string could be made with the `make-array` function.

```
(make-array 5 :initial-element #\c :element-type 'string-char)
⇒    "ccccc"
```

Another function that returns a string is `string`. This function take an argument and coerces it to a string. The argument must be a string, symbol, or string-character.

```
(string #\5)
⇒    "5"

(string 'abc)
⇒    "ABC"

(string "abc")
⇒    "abc"
```

---

**Exercise 15-1**

1. Show all the ways you can make a string with the result string "abc".
2. Create a string of three characters.
3. What results if you try to use `vector` to create a string?

---

## RETRIEVING A CHARACTER

There are several functions that can retrieve a single character from a string. `char` only works on strings. `aref` and `elt` also work on strings.

(char *string index*)

(aref *array* &rest *subscripts*)

(elt *sequence index*)

For example,

```
(char "abc" 0)
⇒    #\a

(aref "abc" 1)
⇒    #\b

(elt "abc" 2)
⇒    #\c
```

**Exercise 15-2**

This exercise deals with a string that contains a person's name. The format is "first middle-initial last".

1. Write a function that determines if a middle initial was included in the argument string.

2. Write a function that returns the last name.

3. Write a function that returns the first name and middle initial.

4. Write a function that returns the name as "last, first mi".

## CHARACTER CASE

The character case of the string can be all uppercase letters, all lowercase letters, or initial uppercase letters (capitalized). You can change the string itself or return a new string. The functions that change the character case are:

```
nstring-capitalize
nstring-downcase
nstring-upcase
string-capitalize
string-downcase
string-upcase
```

For example,

```
(string-capitalize "abc ONE/two")
⇒    "Abc One/Two"

(string-upcase "abc one/two")
⇒    "ABC ONE/TWO"

(string-downcase "abC oNE/Two")
⇒    "abc one/two"
```

**Exercise 15-3**

Continuing with the name string:

1. Write the last name in uppercase.

2. Capitalize the first name and middle initial.

3. Rewrite the `rev-name` function so that it returns the name as "LAST, First MI".

## COMPARISONS

There are many string-comparison functions. These functions compare the characters within the strings for lexical position, that is #\a < #\b < #\c, etc.

There are two sets of functions. The first set uses symbols to show the comparison. For example, string= and string<. These functions use character case when determining the results. #\a > #\A.

The second set uses words to show the comparison, for example, string-equal and string-lessp. These functions ignore character case when determining the results. #\a = #\A.

The functions that determine equality return t or nil. All other functions return the first character position that satisfies the condition. The string comparison functions are shown in the following table.

**TABLE 15.1**   STRING COMPARISONS

| Case Important | Ignore Case | Meaning |
|---|---|---|
| string= | string-equal | Equal |
| string/= | string-not-equal | Not equal |
| string< | string-lessp | Less than |
| string>= | string-not-lessp | Not less than (greater than or equal) |
| string> | string-greaterp | Greater than |
| string<= | string-not-greaterp | Not greater than (less than or equal) |

```
(string= "abc" "ABC")
⇒    NIL

(string-equal "abc" "ABC")
⇒    T

(string< "ABC" "abc")
⇒    0

(string-lessp "ABC" "abc")
⇒    NIL
```

---

**Exercise 15-4**

1. Write a function that determines if the name is in the desired format, "LAST, First MI".

2. Write a function that changes the format of the name if it is needed.

3. Write a function that returns true if two names are given in alphabetic order and nil if they are not.

---

## TRIMMING

When looking at strings, it is sometimes desirable to remove certain characters from the front or end of the strings. For example, you might want to remove any space characters from an input item. There are three functions that remove characters: `string-trim`, `string-left-trim`, and `string-right-trim`. These functions remove characters from both the front and back of the string, from the left (front), and from the right (end). They return a substring. They do not modify the argument string.

```
(setq a "  *  start  *  ")
⇒    "  *  start  *  "

(string-trim " " a)
⇒    "*  start  *"

(string-right-trim " *" a)
⇒    "  *  start"

(string-left-trim " *" a)
⇒    "start  *  "

(string-trim "t* " a)
⇒    "star"
```

---

**Exercise 15-5**

1. Write a function that removes blanks from the beginning and end of a string.
2. Given a list of names, write a function that sorts them. The function should take each name, make it into the standard form, uppercase the last name, remove any blanks, and then return the sorted list of names.

---

## SUMMARY

Strings are vectors that can only contain characters.
- You create strings using `make-string`, `string`, or `make-array`.
- You can get elements from a string using `char`, `aref`, or `elt`.
- The character case of the elements can be changed to uppercase, lowercase, or initial capital.
- Comparison can be done either using character case or ignoring it.
- Characters can be trimmed from the ends of a string.
- Also, array, sequence, and vector functions can be used on strings.

# 16

# *Symbols*

# *and Property Lists*

*Symbols* are used as names of functions and names of variables. They name declarations and types. In addition, they can also have a property list associated with them.

Each symbol has several components associated with it. You have already seen several of these components. The rest are described in this chapter.

- The value of a symbol is the value assigned using `setq` or `setf`.
- The function of a symbol is the function definition given the symbol in a `defun`.
- The print name is the printed representation of the symbol.
- The property list is a list of properties and values associated with the symbol.
- The package cell contains the package where the symbol was defined.

## NAME AND VALUE

There are functions that return the name, value, function, and package of a symbol. These are shown in the following examples.

```
(symbol-name 'a)
⇒    "A"

(setq a 5)
⇒    5
```

```
(symbol-value 'a)
⇒    5

(defun a ()
  "a is a function")
⇒    A

(symbol-function 'a)
⇒    #<FUNCTION  Max Args= 0  Lambda Name= A  Interpreted>

(symbol-package 'a)
⇒    #<Package USER>
```

## PROPERTIES AND VALUES

A property list consists of a property and a value. The value can be any type. For example, the symbol book can have a property title with a value Common Lisp, a property date with a value 1988, a property author with a value Milner, and a property readers with a value John, Sue, Mary, Mark. The property list would look as follows:

```
(TITLE "Common Lisp" DATE 1988 AUTHOR MILNER READER (JOHN SUE MARY MARK))
```

To give properties to a symbol, use setf and get.

```
(setf {place newvalue}*)
```

where *place* is the property returned by get.

```
(get symbol indicator &optional default)
```

For example, to create the property list for book:

```
(setf (get 'book 'readers) '(john sue mary mark))
⇒    (JOHN SUE MARY MARK)

(setf (get 'book 'author) 'milner)
⇒    MILNER

(setf (get 'book 'date) 1988)
⇒    1988

(setf (get 'book 'title) "Common Lisp")
⇒    "Common Lisp"
```

The get function returns the value associated with a property. If the property does not exist, get returns NIL. setf modifies the value of the property.

You can look at each property value without changing the value.

```
(get 'book 'title)
⇒    "Common Lisp"

(get 'book 'author)
⇒    MILNER

(get 'book 'readers)
⇒    (JOHN SUE MARY MARK)

(get 'book 'page-count)
⇒    NIL                 ; there is no property called page-count
```

To tell the difference between a value that is NIL and a property that does not exist, use the *default* argument in get.

```
(get 'book 'page-count 'does-not-exist)
⇒    DOES-NOT-EXIST
```

The symbol-plist function returns the entire property list of a symbol.

```
(symbol-plist symbol)

(symbol-plist 'book)
⇒    (TITLE "Common Lisp" DATE 1988 AUTHOR MILNER READERS
             (JOHN SUE MARY MARK))
```

If the symbol has no property list, symbol-plist returns NIL.

```
(symbol-plist 'empty)
⇒    NIL
```

The remprop function removes a property and value from the property list.

```
(remprop symbol indicator)
```

On successfully removing a property and value, remprop returns T. If it could not remove the property and value, remprop returns NIL.

```
(remprop 'book 'date)
⇒    T

(symbol-plist 'book)
⇒    (TITLE "Common Lisp" AUTHOR MILNER READERS (JOHN SUE MARY MARK))

(remprop 'empty 'time)
⇒    NIL
```

Using setf and get, you can modify the value of a property.

```
(setf (get 'book 'readers) (cons 'tim (get 'book 'readers)))
⇒    (TIM JOHN SUE MARY MARK)

(setf (get 'book 'author) 'wendy-milner)
⇒    WENDY-MILNER
```

---

**Exercise 16-1**

This exercise creates a library catalog system. There is a title catalog and an author catalog.

```
author-catalog (authors (author1 author2 ...))

title-catalog (titles (title1 title2 ...))
```

Each author has a property list that consists of a list of titles by that author. Each title has a property list that consists of information about the book.

```
author (titles (title1 title2 ...))

title (publisher name date year author name)
```

1. Write a function that adds a title to the title catalog. Add the following four titles to the catalog:

```
lisp
lisp-a-gentle-introduction
common-lisp-a-tutorial
common-lisp-the-language
```

2. Write a function that creates a property list for a title. The function should take the title, publisher, date, and author as arguments. Add the following entries:

```
lisp (publisher addison-wesley date 1984 author winston)

lisp-a-gentle-introduction (publisher harper&row date 1984 author touretzky)

common-lisp-a-tutorial (publisher prentice-hall date 1988 author milner)

common-lisp-the-language (publisher digital-press date 1984 author steele)
```

3. Write a function that returns the author of a book.
4. Write a function that creates an author catalog using the titles in the title catalog. The author catalog contains a list of author names.

5. Write a function that adds an author to the author catalog if the author is not already in the catalog.
6. Write a function that adds a title to the author property list if the title does already exist in the list.
7. Write a function that adds a book to both catalogs and makes appropriate entries for title and author symbols.

## SUMMARY

The functions dealing with symbols and property lists are shown in the following table.

**TABLE 16.1** SYMBOLS AND PROPERTY LISTS

| Function | Meaning |
| --- | --- |
| get | Returns a property value. |
| symbol-plist | Returns the entire property list. |
| remprop | Removes a property value from a list. |
| symbol-name | Returns the name of the symbol. |
| symbol-value | Returns the value of the symbol. |
| symbol-function | Returns the function associated with the symbol. |
| symbol-package | Returns the package in which the function was created. |

defun create-author ( title)
(setf (get 'author-catalog author (get 'title 'authors)

# 17

## *Structures*

A *structure* is a data type that you define. It has a name and named parts (referred to as slots). In Chapter 16, you saw how a symbol could have a property list. A structure's parts are similar. However, unlike symbols, once you have defined a structure:

- You cannot add or delete parts to a defined structure.
- The structure is an outline for other objects.
- One structure can inherit another structure.
- There are new functions defined for each new structure.

For example, an auto has a make, model, year, and color. You define the structure to be auto.

```
(defstruct auto
          make
          model
          year
          color)
⇒    AUTO
```

Once the structure is defined, you can make objects of the type auto.

```
(setq johns-car (make-auto :make 'dodge :model 'truck :year 1986
                           :color 'red))
⇒     #S(AUTO MAKE DODGE MODEL TRUCK YEAR 1986 COLOR RED)


(setq sues-car (make-auto :make 'chevy :model 'camero :year 1985
                          :color 'silver))
⇒     #S(AUTO MAKE CHEVY MODEL CAMARO YEAR 1985 COLOR SILVER)
```

When you have objects of the specified type, you can retrieve individual elements from the structure.

```
(auto-model johns-car)
⇒     TRUCK


(auto-make sues-car)
⇒     CHEVY
```

The type of the structure is the name of the structure.

```
(type-of sues-car)
⇒     AUTO


(typep johns-car 'auto)
⇒     T
```

## defstruct

You create a new structure with the defstruct macro. You must have a name for the structure and one or more slots.

```
(defstruct {structure-name| (structure-name {options}*) }
           [doc-string]
           {slot-name| (slot-name[default-initial-value]{slot-option slot-option-value}*) }+)
```

## Slot Values

You can have default values for any of the slots. Then when an object is created of this type, it is not necessary to include a value for each slot. For example,

```
(defstruct grades
        (homework 0)
        (quizzes 0)
        (final 0))
⇒     GRADES
```

When you make objects of type grades, you do not have to give the values of the slots.

```
(setq tim (make-grades))
⇒    #S(GRADES HOMEWORK 0 QUIZZES 0 FINAL 0)
```

There are two options you can set for each slot: the data type of the slot and whether or not the slot is read only.

```
(defstruct grades
          (homework (make-array 0 :adjustable t :fill-pointer t)
                    :type vector)
          (quizzes  (make-array 0 :adjustable t :fill-pointer t)    ▪
                    :type vector)
          (final 0 :type number))
⇒    GRADES

(setq tim (make-grades))
⇒    #S(GRADES HOMEWORK #() QUIZZES #() FINAL 0)

(grades-homework tim)
⇒    #()

(vector-push-extend 100 (grades-homework tim))
⇒    0

(grades-homework tim)
⇒    #(100)

(grades-quizzes tim)
⇒    #()
```

In this example, it is not desirable to make any of the slots read only. If you did, once you made an object, you would never be able to change value. For purposes of illustration,

```
(defstruct any
          (some 'thing :read-only t))
⇒    ANY
```

In order to use either type or read-only, you must have a default value for the slot.

## Structure Options

There are several functions associated with structures. You make objects, access individual slot values, determine the type name of the structure, and print the structure. When creating a structure, you can include another structure, specify the type of data structure in which to store the structure, and specify an offset within the storing structure.

## Constructor

To make an object, use make-*structname*. This is what the previous examples have done.

```
(setq mine (make-grades))
⇒    #S(GRADES HOMEWORK #() QUIZZES #() FINAL 0)
```

make-grades *constructs* an object of type grades.

```
(type-of mine)
⇒    GRADES
```

The :constructor keyword allows you to change the name of the function that creates an *instance* of the structure. In the following example, the name of the :constructor is changed from make-grade to new-student.

```
(defstruct (grades
          (:constructor new-student))  ;; instead of make-grades
          (homework (make-array 0 :adjustable t :fill-pointer t) :type vector)
          (quizzes  (make-array 0 :adjustable t :fill-pointer t) :type vector)
          (final 0 :type number))
⇒    GRADES
```

The :constructor keyword also allows you to change the way in which the initial values are input. Currently, you use the name of the slot followed by a value.

```
(setq bob (new-student))
⇒    #S(GRADES HOMEWORK #() QUIZZES #() FINAL 0)

(setq jim (new-student :homework #(50) :final 0 :quizzes #(10 10)))
⇒    #S(GRADES HOMEWORK #(50) QUIZZES #(10 10) FINAL 0)
```

You can change this using a lambda expression in the :constructor expression.

```
(defstruct (grades
          (:constructor new-student     ;; instead of make-grades
                        (&optional homework quizzes final)))
          (homework (make-array 0 :adjustable t :fill-pointer t)
                    :type vector)
          (quizzes  (make-array 0 :adjustable t :fill-pointer t)
                    :type vector)
          (final 0 :type number))
⇒    GRADES
```

Now, if you construct the new object and include values for the slots, the values must be input in order and you do not use keywords.

```
(setq isabel (new-student #() #(10) 0))
⇒    #S(GRADES HOMEWORK #() QUIZZES #(10) FINAL 0)
```

## Access Functions

When you want to look at the value of a slot, you can use *structname-slotname*.

```
(grades-quizzes isabel)
⇒    #(10)
```

You can change the prefix name of this access function with :conc-name.

```
(defstruct (grades
             (:constructor new-student    ;; instead of make-grades
                          (&optional homework quizzes final))
             (:conc-name total-))         ;; instead of grades-
            (homework (make-array 0 :adjustable t :fill-pointer t)
                      :type vector)
            (quizzes  (make-array 0 :adjustable t :fill-pointer t)
                      :type vector)
            (final 0 :type number))
⇒    GRADES


(setq raymond (new-student '#(100)))
⇒    #S(GRADES HOMEWORK #(100) QUIZZES #() FINAL 0)


(total-homework raymond)
⇒    #(100)
```

## Predicate Name

You can ask for the type of the structure using the type-of function. In addition, you can ask if the structure is of a particular type with *structurename*-p.

```
(type-of raymond)
⇒    GRADES


(grades-p raymond)
⇒    T
```

There are three keywords that interact to determine the names of type and function predicate: :predicate, :named, and :type.

:predicate specifies the name used in the *structurename*-p function. If :named is not used and :type is used, then you should not specify :predicate. Otherwise, you can specify any predicate name you wish.

```
                  (defstruct (grades
                             (:constructor new-student     ;; instead of make-grades
                                        (&optional homework quizzes final))
                             (:conc-name total-)           ;; instead of grades-
                             (:predicate cs101-p))         ;; instead of grades-p
                         (homework (make-array 0 :adjustable t :fill-pointer t)
                                   :type vector)
                         (quizzes  (make-array 0 :adjustable t :fill-pointer t)
                                   :type vector)
                         (final 0 :type number))
             ⇒    GRADES


             (setq harriet (new-student))
             ⇒    #S(GRADES HOMEWORK #() QUIZZES #() FINAL 0)


             (cs101-p harriet)
             ⇒    T
```

There are two types that can be returned by `type-of`: the name of the structure
or the data type in which the structure is stored.

If the structure is unnamed, the data type is returned. You do not have to do anything to name the structure; that is, all the previous structures have been named. To
unname the structure, the type must be specified and the name not specified.

```
(type-of harriet)
⇒    GRADES


(defstruct (grades
           (:constructor new-student     ;; instead of make-grades
                      (&optional homework quizzes final))
           (:conc-name total-)           ;; instead of grades-
;comment out  (:predicate cs101-p)       ;; instead of grades-p
           (:type vector))               ;; the structure is stored in a vector
                                         ;;  no name is specified.
         (homework (make-array 0 :adjustable t :fill-pointer t)
                           :type vector)
         (quizzes  (make-array 0 :adjustable t :fill-pointer t)
                           :type vector)
         (final 0 :type number))
⇒    GRADES


(setq norton (new-student))
⇒    #(#() #() 0)


(type-of norton)
⇒    (SIMPLE-VECTOR 3)
```

To name the structure when you use the `:type` keyword, include `:named` in the
options list.

```
(defstruct (grades
              (:constructor new-student  ;; instead of make-grades
                            (&optional homework quizzes final))
              (:conc-name total-)           ;; instead of grades-
              (:predicate cs101-p)          ;; instead of grades-p
              (:type vector)                ;; the structure is stored in a vector
              :named)                       ;; the structure is named
              (homework (make-array 0 :adjustable t :fill-pointer t)
                                :type vector)
              (quizzes  (make-array 0 :adjustable t :fill-pointer t)
                                :type vector)
              (final 0 :type number))
⇒     GRADES


(setq samantha (new-student))
⇒     #S(GRADES HOMEWORK #() QUIZZES #() FINAL 0)


(type-of samantha)
⇒     GRADES
```

## Storage of Structure

As you saw, :type specifies the data type in which the structure is stored.

The type of the structure can be a vector, a vector with a specified element type, or a list. If you specify an element type, every element must meet that type. In the grades example, this is not the case. The name of the structure is a symbol, two slots are vectors, and one slot is a number. You could change this to

```
(defstruct (grades
              (:constructor new-student  ;; instead of make-grades
                            (&optional homework quizzes final))
              (:conc-name total-)           ;; instead of grades-
              (:type (vector vector)))     ;; the structure is stored in a vector,
                                            ;; each element is a vector
                                            ;; no name.
              homework
              quizzes
              final)

⇒     GRADES

(setq zack (new-student))
⇒     #(NIL NIL NIL)

(setq olga (new-student '#(0) '#(10)))
⇒     #(#(0) #(10) NIL)
```

If you specify a list, you cannot specify element type.

```
(defstruct (grades
              (:constructor new-student  ;; instead of make-grades
                          (&optional homework quizzes final))
              (:conc-name total-)         ;; instead of grades-
              (:predicate cs101-p)        ;; instead of grades-p
              (:type list )               ;; the structure is stored in a list
              :named)                     ;; the structure is named
              (homework (make-array 0 :adjustable t :fill-pointer t)
                                        :type vector)
              (quizzes  (make-array 0 :adjustable t :fill-pointer t)
                                        :type vector)
              (final 0 :type number))
⇒   GRADES


(setq mona (new-student))
⇒    (GRADES #() #() 0)
```

When you specify :type, you can also include an initial offset. This causes the first slot to be allocated after the number of the offset.

```
(defstruct (grades
              (:constructor new-student  ;; instead of make-grades
                          (&optional homework quizzes final))
              (:conc-name total-)         ;; instead of grades-
              (:predicate cs101-p)        ;; instead of grades-p
              (:type list )               ;; the structure is stored in a list
              :named                      ;; the structure is named
              (:initial-offset 2))        ;; reserve two slots
              (homework (make-array 0 :adjustable t :fill-pointer t)
                                          :type vector)
              (quizzes  (make-array 0 :adjustable t :fill-pointer t)
                                          :type vector)
              (final 0 :type number))
⇒    GRADES


(setq joshua (new-student '#(100)))
⇒    (GRADES NIL NIL #(100) #() 0)
```

## Including Another Structure

Suppose you wanted to create a structure very similar to grades. However, the name of the class is bs200 and there are midterms in addition to quizzes and the final. You don't have to start from scratch. You can begin with the grades structure.

```
(defstruct (bs200
            (:include grades)
            (:type list)          ;; the types must be the same
            :named)
           (midterms (make-array 0 :adjustable t :fill-pointer t)
                               :type vector))
⇒     BS200


(setq keith (make-bs200))
⇒     (BS200 #() #() 0 #())
```

The slots and their descriptions are copied from grades to bs200. You could also modify one or more of the slot descriptions from grades.

```
(defstruct (bs200
            (:include grades
                      (homework 0))
            (:type list)
            :named)
            (midterms (make-array 0 :adjustable t :fill-pointer t)
                                :type vector))
⇒     BS200


(setq jennifer (make-bs200))
⇒     (BS200 0 #() 0 #())
```

The structure options (such as `:constructor`) are not inherited from grades. Only the slots are inherited.

## Copy

The object constructed can be copied to another object.

```
(setq karl (copy-grades joshua))
⇒     (GRADES NIL NIL #(100) #() 0)


joshua
⇒     (GRADES NIL NIL #(100) #() 0)
```

If you used `setq`, the object is not copied. You would have two symbols pointing at the same object, and when one value was changed, it would change for both symbols (i.e., changing a grade for karl would change the same grade for joshua).

```
(setq trouble joshua)
⇒     (GRADES NIL NIL #(100) #() 0)


(setf (total-final joshua) 54)
⇒     54


trouble
⇒     (GRADES NIL NIL #(100) #() 54)
```

The copy-*structurename* function can be given another name.

```
(defstruct (grades
            (:constructor new-student  ;; instead of make-grades
                      (&optional homework quizzes final))
            (:conc-name total-)        ;; instead of grades-
            (:predicate cs101-p)       ;; instead of grades-p
            (:type vector)             ;; the structure is stored in a vector
            :named                     ;; the structure is named
            (:copier same-as))         ;; instead of copy-grades
            (homework (make-array 0 :adjustable t :fill-pointer t)
                                   :type vector)
            (quizzes  (make-array 0 :adjustable t :fill-pointer t)
                                   :type vector)
            (final 0 :type number))
⇒    GRADES


(setq nancy (make-grades))
⇒    #S(GRADES HOMEWORK #() QUIZZES #() FINAL 0)


(setq ned (same-as nancy))
⇒    #S(GRADES HOMEWORK #() QUIZZES #() FINAL 0)


(setf (total-final nancy) 99)
⇒    99


nancy
⇒    #S(GRADES HOMEWORK #() QUIZZES #() FINAL 99)


ned
⇒    #S(GRADES HOMEWORK #() QUIZZES #() FINAL 0)
```

## Printing the Structure

The default method of printing the structure is simply to print the object as has been
done in all the previous examples. You can also specify a function that will print the
structure object.

```
(defun print-grades (struct &optional (stream t) (depth t))
      (format stream "Homework ~a~%" (total-homework struct))
      (format stream "Quizzes ~a~%" (total-quizzes struct))
      (format stream "Final ~a~%" (total-final struct)))
⇒    PRINT-GRADES
```

The print function must accept three arguments: the structure, a stream, and a depth. The *stream* specifies where the printing is done, and the *depth* specifies how much of the structure is printed. These arguments are described in Chapters 19 and 20. The format function prints its arguments based on the control string. In the above case, the word homework, quizzes, or final is printed, followed by an ASCII object, followed by a new line. format is described fully in Chapter 20.

```
(defstruct (grades
          (:constructor new-student   ;; instead of make-grades
                        (&optional homework quizzes final))
          (:conc-name total-)         ;; instead of grades-
          (:predicate cs101-p)        ;; instead of grades-p
;no type may be specified
;          (:type vector)             ;; the structure is stored in a vector
;           :named                    ;; the structure is named
          (:copier same-as)           ;; instead of copy-grades
          (:print-function print-grades))
          (homework (make-array 0 :adjustable t :fill-pointer t)
                             :type vector)
          (quizzes  (make-array 0 :adjustable t :fill-pointer t)
                             :type vector)
          (final 0 :type number))
⇒    GRADES

(setq hester (new-student '#(100 100) '#(10 10) 100))
⇒    Homework #(100 100)
     Quizzes #(10 10)
     Final 100
```

Now whenever a grade structure object is printed, the function print-grades is used. You can also call print-grades directly.

```
(print-grades hester)
⇒    Homework #(100 100)
     Quizzes #(10 10)
     Final 100
     NIL
```

---

### Exercise 17-1

Now that you have been overloaded with all the possible options available in defstruct, you should try them on your own.

```
(defstruct auto
          make
          model
          year
          color)
```

Using the auto structure as a beginning point, modify it as follows:

1. The make of the auto can only be one of the following: chevy, dodge, ford or am (American Motors). Write a function that determines if the car is an American auto. Use this function in the definition of auto as the type of the make.

2. The year must be a number.

3. Change the way you create a new object. Instead of make-auto, use new-car.

4. Rather than use keywords to enter the slot values, put them in a lambda list.

5. When accessing a value, use the term car instead of auto.

6. Write a function that takes four arguments, the four slot values. The function returns a structure. Create several owners for these autos.

7. Write a function that, given a slot name and owner name, returns the value for that slot.

8. Write a function that, given an owner name, a slot, and a value, returns nil if the owner's car does not match the value and returns non-nil if the owner's car does match.

9. Write a function that takes a list of owner names, a slot name, and a value. The function returns the names of the owners who own a car with the specified value.

---

## SUMMARY

The `defstruct` macro defines a structure. This structure forms an "outline" for making objects. Objects following this outline have the type defined by the structure. This type is either the name of the structure or the type of object that contains the structure.

Several functions are automatically defined for the structure:

- `make-`*structurename* creates an object.
- `copy-`*structurename* copies an object created by `make-`*structurename*.
- *structurename*-`p` determines if an object's type is that of a structure.
- *structurename-slotname* returns the value of an object's slot.

# 18

## Packages

In Chapter 4, packages are introduced as a way to avoid name conflicts. If two people are using the same machine, they can each use a different package to avoid using each other's functions and variables. In addition, when several people are writing one large program, each person can create their own package and write their code in that package. When the large program is put together, only the names of the functions that the programmers want to share are visible to the other functions in the program.

While a package may appear to be a separate environment, it is really a data structure that establishes a mapping from print names to symbols.

### BUILT-IN PACKAGES

There are four built-in packages: lisp, user, keyword, and system. They are defined in Table 18.1.

**TABLE 18.1** BUILT-IN PACKAGES

| Package | Meaning |
|---------|---------|
| lisp | Contains the Common Lisp system. All functions and global variables are external symbols to this package. |
| user | This is the current package when Lisp starts up. The user package uses the lisp package. |
| keyword | All the keywords used by system- and user-defined functions are contained in this package. This package is unique in that each time a new keyword symbol is used, it is automatically placed in this package and also exported from the package. |
| system | This package contains the implementation's functions. The system package uses the lisp package. It has a nickname, sys. |

## USING PACKAGES

There are two cases where you will use packages:

1. Your program needs to be in a different package to avoid internal symbol usage.
2. Your program uses symbols defined in packages other than the user, lisp, and keyword packages.

### Building a Package

When you are writing a portion of a large program, you might want your internal symbols to be invisible to the rest of the program. There may be the case where only one or two symbols need to be seen by other portions of the program. In this case, you want to build a package in which your code resides.

The provide function announces the module name. There can be more than one package in a module, but, typically, only one package exists in each module.

```
(provide module-name)
```

The in-package function establishes the package.

```
(in-package package-name &key :nicknames :use)
```

The export function specifies the symbols that can be seen by functions outside the package.

```
(export symbols &optional package)
```

For example,

```
;;;;;;;;;;;
;; This program is a package.  The entire file is one
;; package, and one module.
```

```
(provide 'extend)
(in-package 'extend :nicknames '(ext mine))

;; There are two symbols that I want to be seen by other
;; packages.

(export '(tyco io))

;; Now comes the code.
```

---

**Exercise 18-1**

1. Set the value of the symbol a to 100.
2. Create a package named `test`.
3. Evaluate the symbol a.
4. Set the value of b to "abc".
5. Return to the user package.
6. Evalute the symbol b.

---

## Using a Package

There are three functions that give you access to the symbols in another package. They are `require`, `use-package`, and `import`. These functions are placed at the start of the program. The order in which they appear is important.

The `require` function loads a module (a subsystem of one or more files). The symbols in these packages become available to your program. You must use the package prefix when using these symbols unless you first execute the `use-package` or `import` functions.

    (require *module-name* &optional *pathname*)

The `use-package` function adds the specified packages to the use-list. All the symbols of those packages become available to your program. You do not have to use the package prefix when using these symbols.

    (use-package *packages-to-use* &optional *package*)

The `import` function adds the specified symbols from the specified package. You do not have to use the package prefix when using these symbols.

    (import *symbols* &optional *package*)

For example,

```
;;;;
;; This program is in the solar module and package.
;;

(provide 'solar)
(in-package 'solar)
(export '(tyco io))


;; After these three functions, you can require, use-package
;; and import other packages and symbols.  Note that since the package
;; named by in-package has been established before you require other
;; packages, the required packages can use the exported symbols of this
;; new package.


;; This program needs symbols from three packages.
;; All the external symbols in the Math package are used.

(require 'math)
(use-package 'math)


;; A few of the external symbols in the Computer package are used.

(require 'computer)
(import '(patch relocation optimization))


;; A few of the external symbols in the Dictionary package are used.
;; These symbol names might interfere with the use of internal
;; symbols, so none of the symbols are imported.


(require 'dictionary)


;;     Next is the program code.
```

---

**Exercise 18-2**

1. Return to the test package and evaluate the symbol a again by using the package prefix.
2. Because a is an internal symbol, you must specify a double colon between the package and the symbol.

**3.** Make the symbol b external to the package test.

**4.** Return to the user package and evaluate the necessary commands so that you can get the value of b without specifying a package.

---

## Shadowing

There may be cases where the internal symbol names of the new package conflict with the names of symbols you are importing. The shadow function specifies that the internal symbols of the specified names are used rather than the imported symbols.

```
(shadow symbols &optional package)
```

```
;;;;;;;
;; This program contains internal symbol names that conflict
;; with some names from a required package.

(provide 'solar)
(in-package 'solar)

;; I want three names to refer to symbols in this package.

(shadow '(sun moon star))

;; Now require the other package.  If I need the three
;; symbols from the other package, I'll put the package qualifier
;; in the name.

(require 'extend)
(use-package 'extend)

;; Next is the code.
```

There may be cases where the external symbols of two packages you want to use have name conflicts, that is, the symbols have the same name. In these cases, you must either require the package but not use use-package or import, or you tell the system which name to use.

The shadowing-import function specifies how to resolve name conflicts.

```
(shadowing-import symbols &optional package)
```

For example,

```
;; There are two packages that will be used, there are some
;; name conflicts.

(require 'package1)
(require 'package2)

;; The following symbols are defined in both packages:
;; alpha, beta, and gamma.  I want the alpha symbol from
;; package1 and the beta and gamma symbols from package2.

(shadowing-import '(package1:alpha package2:beta package2:gamma))

;; Now I can use both packages without worry of name conflicts.

(use-package '(package1 package2))
```

## PACKAGE NAMES

When referring to a package name, you can use a symbol or a string. In the previous examples, a symbol was used. As with symbol names, lowercase letters are translated to uppercase. If you specify a package using a string, make sure you use uppercase letters. If you specify a symbol, its print name is used.

Some package functions require a package object rather than the name of the package. The find-package function returns the package that is referred to by a name or nickname.

```
(find-package name)
```

For example,

```
(find-package 'system)
⇒    #<Package SYSTEM>
```

A list of all packages available is returned by list-all-packages. The list of packages returned by your system will be different from the author's system. Execute this function to see which packages you have.

```
(list-all-packages)
⇒    (#<Package HP-UX_3G> #<Package TUTOR> #<Package LAN>
     #<Package HP-UX_2> #<Package TERMINAL> #<Package HP-UX_3W>
     #<Package Non-Lisp Identifiers> #<Package NMODE>
     #<Package INTERPRETER> #<Package COMPILER> #<Package EXTN>
     #<Package ERROR> #<Package DEBUG> #<Package PREPROCESSOR>
     #<Package PRIM> #<Package USER> #<Package SYSTEM> #<Package LISP>
     #<Package IMPL> #<Package KEYWORD>)
```

The *package* variable contains the current package. The *current* package is
initially set to be user. When you do a load, or in-package, the value of this
variable changes. If you deliberately set this variable, the value must be a package, not
a package name.

```
*package*
⇒    #<Package USER>
```

A package can have nicknames as well as a given name. When you create the
package, you can specify the nicknames using the :nicknames keyword.

```
(in-package 'solar :nicknames '(mine))
⇒    #<Package SOLAR>
```

The package-nicknames function returns all of a package's nicknames.

```
(package-nicknames (find-package 'solar))
⇒    ("MINE")
```

```
(package-nicknames (find-package 'system))
⇒    ("SYS")
```

The package-name function returns the name of a package.

```
(package-name (find-package 'user))
⇒    "USER"
```

Finally, the rename-package function renames a function.

```
(rename-package package new-name &optional new-nicknames)
```

```
(rename-package (find-package 'solar) 'sun '(astro))
⇒    #<Package SUN>
```

## USE LIST

There are two functions that determine which packages use which packages. These are `package-use-list` (what packages are used by the specified package) and `package-used-by-list` (what packages use the specified package). Both functions require a package object.

```
(package-use-list (find-package 'user))
⇒   (#<Package LISP>)


(package-used-by-list (find-package 'lisp))
⇒   (#<Package TUTOR> #<Package LAN> #<Package TERMINAL>
     #<Package HP-UX_3W> #<Package PRIM> #<Package INTERPRETER>
     #<Package COMPILER> #<Package EXTN> #<Package DEBUG>
     #<Package PREPROCESSOR> #<Package USER> #<Package SYSTEM>)
```

## SYMBOLS

The purpose of packages is to hide symbols from use by other programs. Many of the symbols you use in writing programs are only of use within the program. These are *internal symbols*. There are only a few symbols that you want the rest of the world to know about. These are *external symbols*. There is a specific manner in which the system looks for symbols.

### Referring to Symbols

When you use a symbol, the system looks for that symbol in the current package. If the symbol is not found, the system looks for the symbol in any *inherited* packages (any package that has been required). If the name is found, the symbol is returned. If the name is not found, the symbol is created and placed in the current package.

To refer to a symbol in another package that has been required but not imported, place the package name in front of the symbol, for example, `package:symbol`.

To refer to an internal symbol, use double colons, for example, `package::symbol`. You should be careful in doing this because if the orginator of the package really wanted you to use that symbol, the symbol would be external to the package.

Because keywords are used frequently, you are not required to specify their package. Instead, you simply place a colon in front of them, for example, `:keyword`. Lisp looks up the symbol in the keyword package and returns its value.

Table 18.2 describes some of the terms used when referring to symbols and packages.

**TABLE 18.2**  PACKAGE TERMS

| Term | Meaning |
|------|---------|
| Import | Takes an external symbol and adds it to the current package as an internal symbol. It is not automatically exported from the current package. If the symbol is already present in the current package, a continual error is reported. Import does not let one symbol shadow another. |
| Shadowing | If symbol a would be accessible by inheritance if not for the presence of symbol b, a would be shadowed by b. If you want to import a symbol without the possiblity of a shadowing error, use shadowing-import. The symbol in the current package is uninterned, then the new symbol is added to the package's shadowing-import list. Consistency rules may fail when using shadowing. |
| Use-package | Inherits all of the external symbols of the other package. These symbols are not passed to any package that uses this current package. Use-package does not cause symbols to be present in the current package; it only makes them accessible. It checks carefully for name conflicts. |
| Unuse-package | Removes the named packages from the use-list. |
| Export | Takes a symbol that is accessible either directly or by inheritance and makes it an external symbol of that package. If the symbol is internal, it is changed to an external symbol. If the symbol is accessible as internal through use-package, the symbol is first imported into the package, then exported. The symbol is then present in the current package even if the original package is no longer used by the current package. |
| Unexport | Undos calls to export. |
| External and Internal | Symbols can be either *external* or *internal* to the package. The symbol defined in the package can either be seen (external) or not seen (internal) by another package. *External* symbols are the package's public interface to other packages. *Internal* symbols are hidden from other packages and are intended for internal use only. Most symbols are internal. They become external through the use of the export function. |
| Interned | The symbol table contains a cell called the *package cell*. This contains a pointer to the *home* package for the symbol. *Interned* symbols are owned by some package; they have a home package. *Uninterned* symbols are not owned by any package. The package cell of an uninterned symbols contains the value nil. |

## Symbol Functions

The find-all-symbols function searches all the packages for the symbol that has a specified name. It returns a list of the symbols.

```
(find-all-symbols string-or-symbol)

(find-all-symbols 'c)
⇒    (IMPL:C LISP::C C EXTN::C)

(find-all-symbols 'print)
⇒    (:PRINT IMPL:PRINT PRINT)
```

The `package-shadowing-symbols` function returns a list of all the symbols that have been declared shadowing symbols by `shadow` or `shadowing-import`.

```
(package-shadowing-symbols package)

(package-shadowing-symbols (find-package 'lisp))
⇒    (DEBUG:INSPECT-TOP DEBUG:INSPECT-UP DEBUG:INSPECT-SOURCE
     DEBUG:INSPECT-MODIFY DEBUG:INSPECT-INSPECT DEBUG:INSPECT-DESCRIBE
     DEBUG:INSPECT-? DEBUG::WITH-STACK-ITEMS SYSTEM:*EXIT-LISTENER-ON-EOF*
     SYSTEM:*LISTENER-BANNER* SYSTEM:*LISTENER-MODE* SYSTEM:*LISTENER-NAME*
     SYSTEM:*LISTENER-PRINT* SYSTEM:*LISTENER-EVAL* SYSTEM:*LISTENER-READ*
     SYSTEM:LISTENER-CONTINUE SYSTEM:LISTENER-QUIT SYSTEM:LISTENER-ABORT
     SYSTEM:LISTENER)
```

There are three functions that perform an iteration over all symbols found in a package. *Iteration* is the process of repeating a series of functions a number of times. This is fully described in Chapter 8.

```
(do-symbols  (var [package [result-form]])  {declaration}*
             {tag | statement}*)

(do-external-symbols  (var [package [result]])  {declaration}*
                      {tag | statement}*)

(do-all-symbols  (var [result-form])  {declaration}*
                 {tag | statement}*)
```

The body of the function (the tags and statements) is iterated once for each symbol found.  `do-symbols` finds all the symbols (internal, external, and inherited) in the specified package.  `do-external-symbols` finds all the external symbols in the specified package.  `do-all-symbols` finds all symbols in all packages. (This can be a very long list of symbols, and many symbols may be found in more than one package.)

```
(do-external-symbols (variable (find-package 'test) '**done**)
                     (print variable))
⇒    TEST:B
     **DONE**
```

---

### Exercise 18-3

**1.** How many external symbols would you expect to find in the user package?

**2.** How many external symbols would you expect to find in the lisp package?

**3.** Prove this by printing the symbols.

4. When might you be interested in the external symbols of a package?

5. Write a function that determines if a particular symbol is an external symbol of a package. Two functions that will help you are `symbol-name`, which returns the name of a symbol as a string, and `string-equal`, which determines if two strings are equal.

## SUMMARY

Packages map print names to symbols. The same names can appear in several packages with no misunderstanding of what symbols are being used. Packages are established with the functions shown in Table 18.3 The functions are shown in the order that they must be used.

**TABLE 18.3**  PACKAGE FUNCTIONS

| Function | Meaning |
| --- | --- |
| provide | Announces the name of the module. |
| in-package | Establishes the package. |
| shadow | Establishes local symbols that will shadow otherwise inherited symbols. |
| export | Establishes all external symbols in the current package. |
| require | Loads other modules that the current package might want to use. |
| shadowing-import | Specifies how to resolve name conflicts in inherited symbols. |
| use-package | Establishes all symbols in a package to be made available to the current package. |
| import | Makes available individual symbols from other packages to the current package. |

# PART 4
## I/O Functions and Streams

# 19

# Streams

Three chapters that are dependent on one another, and which should be read in order, open this part. In addition, a chapter entitled ''Miscellaneous'' closes the part. Because all input and output is done through streams, streams are presented first in Chapter 19. Chapter 20 describes I/O functions, and Chapter 21 deals with I/O files.

If you are reading this part before Parts 2 or 3, go back to the Part pages describing the syntax used to describe functions. You may find that some functions and programming constructs used in the following chapters are unfamiliar to you. These are fully described in the appropriate chapters earlier in the book.

---

This chapter discusses streams in general, streams that the system creates, streams that you can create, types of streams, and closing streams. In Chapters 20 and 21, *Input/Output* and *Files*, you will be using these streams. Some functions that are not fully defined in this chapter are used in the examples. Because the only way to show streams is through the use of input/output operations this was unavoidable. You will find the definitions of the functions in the next chapters.

A *stream* is a data object that you use as an interface to or from an I/O device. The device can be a keyboard, a display screen, a file, or a program. In Lisp, the only way to do I/O is through streams. You create a stream and connect it to a device. Then you send data to the stream and the data goes through the stream to the device. Similarly, you ask for data from a stream and the data comes from the device through the stream to you.

## SYSTEM-DEFINED STREAMS

There are seven streams created by the system, as is shown in Table 19.1. Several of the I/O functions use these streams as their default streams.

**TABLE 19.1**   SYSTEM-DEFINED STREAMS

| Variable | Meaning |
|---|---|
| *debug-io* | The default stream used by interactive debugging. |
| *error-output* | The default output stream used for reporting error messages. |
| *query-io* | The default stream for queries to the operator. |
| *standard-input* | The default stream for many input functions. |
| *standard-output* | The default stream for many output functions. |
| *terminal-io* | The default stream used to interface with a terminal. |
| *trace-output* | The default stream to which the trace function prints its output. |

Notice the use of input, output, and io in the names of these streams. A stream has direction. It can be an input, output, or a bidirectional (io) stream. You read from an input stream and write to an output stream. You can do either operation to a bidirectional stream.

## STRING STREAMS

A *string stream* uses a string as the source or destination of the data. When you write to an output string stream, all the data written is collected into a string. Data goes into an input string stream as a string. This data can be read as a complete string or character by character. The stream functions are shown in the following table.

**TABLE 19.2**   STRING STREAM FUNCTIONS

| Function | Meaning |
|---|---|
| make-string-output-stream | Creates an output string stream. |
| get-output-stream-string | Returns the data in an output string stream. |
| close | Closes a stream. |
| make-string-input-stream | Creates an input string stream. |
| with-output-to-string | Creates a dynamic output string stream. |
| with-input-from-string | Creates a dynamic input string stream. |

## Output String Stream

You create an output string stream using `make-string-output-stream`, and you
get the data from this stream with `get-output-stream-string`. You can write
to the stream using any output function, such as `print` or `write`.

```
(make-string-output-stream)

(get-output-stream-string string-output-string)

(setq out-stream (make-string-output-stream))
⇒    #<String-Output Stream>

(print 'abcd out-stream)
⇒    ABCD

(print 9876 out-stream)
⇒    9876
```

The `print` function outputs a carriage-return line-feed followed by the object;
thus, the output stream also contains the carriage-return line-feed and the object.

The `get-output-stream-string` function returns all data in the string
since the last time this function was executed on that stream.

```
(get-output-stream-string out-stream)
⇒    "
    ABCD
    9876 "
```

The `write` function only outputs the object. It does not output extra white space
such as spaces, tabs, or carriage-return-like feeds. Thus, the objects sent to the stream
may become crowded. More information on `write` is contained in Chapter 20.

```
(write 'symbol :stream out-stream)
⇒    SYMBOL

(write '(a b c) :stream out-stream)
⇒    (A B C)

(get-output-stream-string out-stream)
⇒    "SYMBOL(A B C)"
```

When you are done with a stream, you should close it.

```
(close out-stream)
⇒    T
```

## Input from a String Stream

While the previous string described appears to be an I/O stream, it is in fact only an output stream. The only way to get data from that stream is through the get-output-stream-string. Standard read functions cannot get the data from the stream. An input string stream gets its data from a string when it is created. Then you can use read to get the data from the stream.

```
(make-string-input-stream string &optional start end)

(setq st (make-string-input-stream "abcdef"))
⇒    #<String-Input Stream>

(read st)
⇒    ABCDEF
```

You specify a substring of a string through two arguments. The first argument specifies the beginning of the substring. Zero is the first element of the string. The second argument specifies the exclusive end of the substring.

```
(setq sst (make-string-input-stream "0123456" 2 5))
⇒    #<String-Input Stream>

(read sst)
⇒    234
```

After the data has been read, the stream is at end-of-file. Further attempts to read from the stream will cause an error.

```
(setq sst (make-string-input-stream "qwerty"))
⇒    #<String-Input Stream>

(read-char sst)
⇒    #\q

(read-char sst)
⇒    #\w

(read sst)
⇒    ERTY

(read sst)
⇒    !!!!! Error: Unexpected end-of-file encountered.
```

More information on read and read-char is contained in Chapter 20.

## Dynamic String Streams

There are two string stream macros that create string streams of dynamic extent. The macros create the stream, execute a body of forms, then close the stream.

`with-output-to-string` executes a sequence of forms with a specified variable bound to an output stream and saves outputs to the stream in a string. The string is optional. If it is not supplied, the result of the macro is the output string. If it is supplied, the result of the macro is nil, and the string contains the output written to it.

```
(with-output-to-string (variable [string])
                       {declaration}* {form}*)
```

`with-input-from-sting` executes a sequence of forms with a specified variable bound to an input stream that supplies successive characters from a specified string.

```
(with-input-from-string (variable string {keyword value}*)
                        {declaration}* {form})
```

The following example shows how these macros can be used to pass input and output from one function to another. To begin with, the `caller` function, which is shown next, passes the string stream variable to the `fun-1` function. `fun-1` then outputs information to this stream. The stream then passes the data to the string. The string can be shown within the `caller` function and outside the function.

```
(defun caller (out-st)
  (with-output-to-string (out-stream out-st)
    (fun-1 out-stream)
    out-string))
⇒    CALLER

(defun fun-1 (out)
  (print 'fun-1 out)
  (print 'more out))
⇒    FUN-1

(setq out-string (make-array 1 :element-type 'string-char
                               :fill-pointer 0 :adjustable t))
⇒    #()

(caller out-string)
⇒    #(#\Linefeed #\F #\U #\N #\- #\1 #\Space #\Linefeed #\M #\O #\R
      #\E #\Space)

out-string
⇒    #(#\Linefeed #\F #\U #\N #\- #\1 #\Space #\Linefeed #\M #\O #\R
      #\E #\Space)
```

The above example shows how one function passes a stream to another function and how the second function can write to that stream and change the value of the associated string. In the next example, a simple string is passed. Although the second function tries to change the value of the string, the value reverts to its original value on exit from the second function.

```
(defun test (x)
  (setq x 'abc)
  (test2 x)
  (print "from test")
  x)
⇒    TEST

(defun test2 (y)
  (print "from test2")
  (print y)
  (setq y '123))
⇒    TEST2

(setq b 'xyz)
⇒    XYZ

(test b)
⇒    "from test2"
     ABC
     "from test"
     ABC
```

The next example has two streams. `with-output-to-string` creates an output stream. The output becomes the input to the input stream created by `with-input-from-stream`. This input stream can also be passed to another function. Remember, if you do not include a string variable in `with-output-to-string`, the result of the macro is the string.

```
(defun caller1 ()
  (with-input-from-string (in-stream
                              (with-output-to-string (out-stream)
                                            (fun-1 out-stream)))
                 (fun-2 in-stream)))
⇒    CALLER1

(defun fun-1 (out)
  (print 'fun-1 out)
  (print 'more out))
⇒    FUN-1

(defun fun-2 (in)
  (print "what is read")
  (print (read-line in))
  (print (read-line in))
  (read-line in))
⇒    FUN-2
```

```
(caller1)
⇒    "what is read"
     ""
     "FUN-1 "
     "MORE "
     "MORE "
```

This simple example shows how output from one function can become input to another function through the use of string streams.

The `with-input-from-string` macro allows three keywords: `:index`, `:start`, and `:end`. The `:index` keyword gives its generalized variable the value of the index of the next character to be read. `:start` and `:end` specify the beginning and exclusive end of the string to be used as input.

```
(with-input-from-string (in "0123456789" :index p :start 2 :end 7)
                        (read in))
⇒    23456


p
⇒    7
```

The value of the index variable is updated at the end of the reading; it is not incrementally updated.

```
(with-input-from-string (in "0123
4567
890 "                            :index axb)
                        (print (read-line in))
                        (print axb)
                        (print (read-line in))
                        (print (read-line in))
                        xb)
⇒    "0123"
     !!!!! Error: The symbol AXB has no value.

(with-input-from-string (in "0123
4567
890 "
                          :index axb)
                        (print (read-line in))
                        (print (read-line in))
                        (print (read-line in))
                        xb)
⇒    "0123"
     "4567"
     "890 "
     14


xb
⇒    14
```

## CREATING NEW STREAMS

In addition to streams connected to strings, you can create streams that are connected to files or other devices. The functions that do this are shown in Table 19.3.

**TABLE 19.3**  CREATING NEW STREAMS

| Function | Meaning |
|----------|---------|
| make-two-way-stream | Creates and returns a bidirectional stream that gets input from specified input stream and send its output to the specified output stream. |
| make-broadcast-stream | Creates and returns an output stream that sends output to all listed output streams. |
| make-concatenated-stream | Creates and returns an input stream that takes input from each of the listed input streams and concatenates that input. |
| make-echo-stream | Creates and returns a bidirectional stream that gets input from the specified input stream and send its output to the specified output stream. All input is echoed to the output stream. |
| make-synonym-stream | Creates and returns a synonym stream. |

The streams created by these functions take other streams as their parameters.

### Broadcast Stream

make-broadcast-stream creates a stream that outputs everything written to it to all the output streams specified.

```
(setq a-stream (make-string-output-stream))
⇒    #<String-Output Stream>

(setq m-stream (make-string-output-stream))
⇒    #<String-Output Stream>

(setq b-stream (make-broadcast-stream a-stream m-stream))
⇒    #<Broadcast Stream, Streams =
        (#<String-Output Stream> #<String-Output Stream>)>

(write-line "abcd" b-stream)
⇒    "abcd"

(get-output-stream-string a-stream)
⇒    "abcd
     "
(get-output-stream-string m-stream)
⇒    "abcd
     "
```

## Concatenated Stream

`make-concatenated-stream` creates an input stream that takes the data from other input streams.

```
(setq a-s (make-string-input-stream "abcd"))
⇒    #<String-Input Stream>

(setq b-s (make-string-input-stream "1234"))
⇒    #<String-Input Stream>

(setq c-s (make-string-input-stream "xyz"))
⇒    #<String-Input Stream>

(setq c-stream (make-concatenated-stream a-s b-s c-s))
⇒    #<Concatenated Stream, Streams = (#<String-Input Stream>
                      #<String-Input Stream> #<String-Input Stream>)>

(read c-stream)
⇒    ABCD1234XYZ
```

## Bidirectional Streams

There are two functions that create bidirectional streams: `make-two-way-stream` and `make-echo-stream`. They are similar in that they get input from an input stream and send output to an output stream. `make-echo-stream`, in addition, echoes its input to the output stream.

```
(setq in-stream (make-string-input-stream "asdfghjkl"))
⇒    #<String-Input Stream>

(setq out-stream (make-string-output-stream))
⇒    #<String-Output Stream>

(setq two-stream (make-two-way-stream in-stream out-stream))
⇒    #<Two-Way Stream, Input = #<String-Input Stream>,
                      Output = #<String-Output Stream>>

(write-line "output" two-stream)
⇒    "output"

(get-output-stream-string out-stream)
⇒    "output
     "
```

When you read from the `two-stream`, you are actually getting data from `in-stream`.

```
(read two-stream)
⇒    ASDFGHJKL
```

Nothing is sent to out-stream.

```
(get-output-stream-string out-stream)
⇒    ""
```

When you create an echo string, all input is echoed to the output stream.

```
(setq in (make-string-input-stream "123445566"))
⇒    #<String-Input Stream>

(setq out (make-string-output-stream))
⇒    #<String-Output Stream>

(setq echo (make-echo-stream in out))
⇒    #<Echo Stream, Input = #<String-Input Stream>,
                       Output = #<String-Output Stream>>

(write-line "abcdef" echo)
⇒    "abcdef"

(get-output-stream-string out)
⇒    "abcdef
     "
(read echo)
⇒    123445566

(get-output-stream-string out)
⇒    "123445566"
```

## Synonym Stream

The make-string-synonym-stream function creates a stream that is associated
with a symbol that is in turn associated with a stream; and that associated stream can
change, as shown in the following example:

```
(setq a-stream (make-string-output-stream))
⇒    #<String-Output Stream>

(setq b-stream (make-string-input-stream "Once upon a time,"))
⇒    #<String-Input Stream>

(setq dynamic-stream (make-synonym-stream 'dynamic))
⇒    #<Synonym Stream to DYNAMIC>
```

```
(setq dynamic a-stream)
⇒    #<String-Output Stream>

(write-line "in the land of kings" dynamic-stream)
⇒    "in the land of kings"

(get-output-stream-string a-stream)
⇒    "in the land of kings
     "
(setq dynamic b-stream)
⇒    #<String-Input Stream>

(read dynamic-stream)
⇒    ONCE

(read dynamic-stream)
⇒    UPON

(read-line dynamic-stream)
⇒    "a time,"
     T
```

## File Streams

The open and with-open-file functions create a stream associated with a file.
Only open is shown in the following example. More information on these functions is
contained in Chapter 21. They are mentioned here because they create streams.

```
(setq file-stream (open "/users/wendy/temp/example1" :direction :output
                        :if-exists :overwrite :if-does-not-exist :create))
⇒    #<File Stream /users/wendy/temp/example1>

(write-line "first line" file-stream)
⇒    "first line"

(write-line "second line" file-stream)
⇒    "second line"

(close file-stream)
⇒    T

(setq in-file (open "/users/wendy/temp/example1" :direction :input
                                                 :if-does-not-exist nil))
⇒    #<File Stream /users/wendy/temp/example1>

(read-line in-file)
⇒    "first line"
     NIL
```

```
(read-line in-file)
⇒    "second line"
     NIL


(close in-file)
⇒    T
```

## DYNAMIC STREAM OBJECTS

The stream object can be passed as a parameter to a function.  The function can write to the stream or read from the stream.  On return from that function, the data left in the stream can be read.

```
(defun local ()
  (setq x (make-string-output-stream))
  (next-fun x)
  (print (get-output-stream-string x))
  (close x))
⇒    LOCAL

(defun next-fun (k)
  (print 'inside k))
⇒    NEXT-FUN

(local)
⇒    "
     INSIDE"
     T
```

If you do not close the stream, then it remains open after you leave the function. Thus, you could still read and write to the stream. To ensure that the stream is closed, use `with-open-stream`. This macro opens a stream, executes forms, and then closes the stream.

```
(defun dynamic ()
  (with-open-stream (st (make-string-output-stream))
                    (next-fun st)
                    (get-output-stream-string st)))
⇒    DYNAMIC

(defun next-fun (k)
  (print 'inside k))
⇒    NEXT-FUN

(dynamic)
⇒    "
     INSIDE"
```

The complete syntax for `with-open-stream` is

```
(with-open-stream (variable stream) {declaration}* {form}*)
```

The *variable* is bound to the object produced by the *stream* form, which must be a stream. The forms are executed as an implicit `progn`. The value of the last form is returned as the value of `with-open-stream`. Whether the exit is normal or not, the stream is closed on exit of the `with-open-stream` macro.

## PREDICATES ON STREAMS

Several tests can be made of the stream. First, an object can be tested to see if it is a stream. Then, its direction can be tested. Finally, the type of data it handles can be determined.

```
(streamp out-stream)
⇒    T

(output-stream-p out-stream)
⇒    T

(input-stream-p out-stream)
⇒    NIL

(stream-element-type out-stream)
⇒    STRING-CHAR
```

When you are finished with a stream, you `close` it. Although you cannot read or write to the stream, the stream object still exists.

```
(close out-stream)
⇒    T

(streamp out-stream)
⇒    T

(print 'abc out-stream)
⇒    !!!!! Error: #<String-Output Stream> is closed.
```

## SUMMARY

Streams are used to perform input and output operations. A stream data object has direction. The type of data that can be passed through a stream can also be specified.

The direction of a stream can be input, output, or bidirectional.

The types of data in a stream can be string characters or bytes. Other data types can be specified, but usually are not.

# 20

## Input/Output

This chapter discusses input and output. *I/O* is the process where data is passed between functions, programs, and devices. The data is passed through streams; you should read Chapter 19 before reading further.

This chapter answers the following questions:

- How do you go about displaying the intermediate results of a function?
- How do you get input from an operator?
- How do you change the way that numbers are output?
- How do you avoid printing circular lists?

### PRINT

The `print` function outputs a new line followed by the printed representation of an object.

The syntax of the `print` function is:

(`print` *object* &optional *stream*)

The following examples show the results of `print`.

```
(print "Hello")
⇒    "Hello"        ;; printed result
     "Hello"        ;; value returned

(setq a '(1 3 a b))
⇒    (1 3 A B)

(print a)
⇒    (1 3 A B)
     (1 3 A B)

(print 'b)
⇒    B
     B

(setq c "abc DEF")
⇒    "abc DEF"

(print c)
⇒    "abc DEF"
     "abc DEF"
```

When used within another function, the `print` function still outputs the same value; however, `print` returns the object to the enclosing function and this value may or may not be output.

```
(defun print-it ()
  (print "hello")
  (setq a '(a b c))
  (print a)
  (setq b "a b c d e")
  (print b))
⇒    PRINT-IT

(print-it)
⇒    "hello"         ;; printed result
     (A B C)         ;; printed result
     "a b c d e"     ;; printed result
     "a b c d e"     ;; value returned
```

In the above example, there are three `print` functions in the `print-it` definition. When `print-it` is evaluated, the first `print` outputs "hello", the second `print` outputs (A B C), and the third `print` outputs "a b c d e". The `print-it` function then returns the value of the last form, which is the returned value of the last `print`.

Look at another example,

```
(defun new-print (a)
  (print a)
  t)
⇒    NEW-PRINT

(new-print '(1 2 3))
⇒    (1 2 3)          ;; printed result
     T                ;; value returned
```

In `new-print`, the value of the last form is `t`, so this is the value output.

## Output Streams

As you know, all output is done through an output stream; however, in the above examples, no output stream was specified. In a `print` function, when you do not specify an output stream, `*standard-output*` is used.

```
(print a)  ≡  (print a *standard-output*)
           ≡  (print a NIL)
```

A frequently used stream is `*terminal-io*`. You can specify this stream by the value `t`.

```
(print a t)   ≡   (print a *terminal-io*)
```

You can also specify any other character output stream.

```
(print "Entering print loop" *debug-io*)
(print a *trace-output*)
(print '(1 2 3) my-stream)
```

## Other Print Functions

There are several "print" functions, as shown in the Table 20.1. The first four functions take an object and, optionally, a stream. The object is output to the stream in a specified format. The last two functions do not have an optional stream variable. Output goes to `*standard-output*`.

**TABLE 20.1**  PRINT FUNCTIONS

| Function | Meaning |
|----------|---------|
| prin1 | Outputs the printed representation of the object using escape characters where necessary. Output from prin1 is acceptable as input to read. |
| print | Outputs a new line, the object printed as in prin1, followed by a space. |
| pprint | Outputs the object as in print, except the trailing blank is not printed. It outputs the object with *print-pretty* flag non-nil.  pprint does not return a value. (pprint is unique in returning no value.) |
| princ | Outputs the printed representation of the object without using escape characters. |
| prin1-to-string | Outputs the object as prin1 does, but first makes it a string. |
| princ-to-string | Outputs the object as princ does, but first makes it a string. |

## New Lines Output

In addition to the print functions outputting a new line, there are two functions that just output a new line.

fresh-line outputs a new line if the stream is not currently at a new line. It returns t if a new line is output and nil if a new line is not output.

terpri always outputs a new line.

```
(setq a (make-string-output-stream))
⇒    #<String-Output Stream>

(prin1 "string" a)
⇒    "string"

(print "string" a)
⇒    "string"

(pprint "string" a)
⇒                    ;; no return value

(princ "string" a)
⇒    "string"

(get-output-stream-string a)
⇒    "\"string\"           ;prin1
     \"string\" \"string\"  ;print pprint
     string"               ;princ

(pprint "string" a)
⇒
```

```
(fresh-line a)
⇒    NIL


(pprint "next" a)
⇒


(get-output-stream-string a)
⇒    "\"string\"
      \"next\"
      "


(print "string" a)
⇒    "string"


(terpri a)
⇒    NIL


(pprint "next" a)
⇒


(get-output-stream-string a)
⇒    "
    \"string\"
    \"next\" "
```

## FORMAT

The print function can output only a single object. format can output multiple objects. In addition, format allows you to "format" the output: you can add spaces and blank lines, output in columns, and implement many other features.

> (format *destination control-string* &rest *arguments*)

Before you look at some of the more exotic features of format, here are some simple examples:

```
(format t "abc")
⇒    abc
     NIL


(format t "~a" 'x)
⇒    X
     NIL
```

```
(format t "~a" '(a b c))
⇒    (A B C)
     NIL

(format t "~f" (sin 3))
⇒    0.1411200080598672
     NIL

(format t "Hello ~a" (setq name "Wendy"))
⇒    Hello Wendy
     NIL

(format nil "abc")
⇒    "abc"

(format nil "~a" 'x)
⇒    "X"

(format nil "~a" '(a b c))
⇒    "(A B C)"
```

## Destination

Unlike `print`, in a `format` function, you must specify a destination.

If you specify `t` as a destination, the output is sent to `*standard-output*` and `format` returns `nil`. If you specify `nil` as a destination, `format` returns a string; nothing is output. To see the difference in using `nil` and `t`, look at the following examples:

```
(setq x (format t "Hello"))
⇒    Hello                  ;; format output
     NIL                    ;; returned by setq

x
⇒    NIL                    ;; x has the value returned by format.

(setq y (format nil "Hello"))
⇒    "Hello"                ;; returned by setq

y
⇒    "Hello"                ;; y has the value returned by format.
```

You can also specify a string output stream as a destination. The output is added to the end of the stream.

```
(setq n (make-string-output-stream))
⇒    #<String-Output Stream>
```

```
(format n "Hello")
⇒    NIL


(get-output-stream-string n)
⇒    "Hello"


(format n "Next")
⇒    NIL


(format n " words")
⇒    NIL


(get-output-stream-string n)
⇒    "Next words"
```

You can also send the formatted output to a string.

```
(setq st (make-array 1 :adjustable t :element-type 'string-char
                       :fill-pointer 0))
⇒    #()


(format st "hello")
⇒    NIL


st
⇒    #(#\h #\e #\l #\l #\o)


(format st " next")
⇒    NIL


st
⇒    #(#\h #\e #\l #\l #\o #\Space #\n #\e #\x #\t)
```

And, of course, you can specify any character output stream.

```
(format *terminal-io* "Message")
(format *debug-io* "Error in Handling routine")
(format my-stream "Hello")
```

## Formatted Output

format uses a control string to produce its output. In the above examples, the only control directive used was ~a.  A, ASCII, directs format to output an argument without escape characters.  There are many more directives, each with options of their own.

```
(format t "~r cat~:p" 3)
⇒    three cats
     NIL


(format t "~r tr~:@p" 3)
⇒    three tries
     NIL


(format t "~:r tr~:@p" 1)
⇒    first try
     NIL


(format t "try ~@r" 4)
⇒    try IV
     NIL


(format t "binary ~2r" 7)
⇒    binary 111
     NIL
```

A directive consists of a tilde, ~, and a directive character. The directive character can have options preceding it. The option characters can be a colon, :, a commercial at sign, @, or a number (not a symbol with a numeric value). The options have different meanings for each directive. In most cases, more than one option can be used.

In the previous examples, the ~R directive was used. ~R specifies the radix to use when outputting the argument. The number before the character R specifies the radix. When no options are used, a cardinal number is output. @ specifies output as a Roman numeral. : specifies output as an ordinal number.

The ~P directive specifies that the preceding word can be plural. If the argument is not 1, an s is output. : specifies that the preceding argument is used. @ specifies that an ies is output if the argument is not 1 and a y is output if the argument is 1.

## Summary of Format Directives

There are many format directives. Some are used frequently, whereas others are not. In Table 20.2, an uppercase character is used for the directives. In a `format` function, you can use either uppercase or lowercase.

Scan the table so that you are familiar with what can be done with `format`. Format examples of some of the directives are given to show you how to use the directives. There are also exercises so that you can try the various directives.

**TABLE 20.2** FORMAT DIRECTIVES

| Directive | Meaning and Arguments |
|---|---|
| V | Uses the argument as a variable for any directive that accepts a prefix number. |
| # | Returns the number of remaining arguments. Used by any directive that accepts a prefix number. |
| ~A | ASCII; argument printed without escape characters.<br> *~column-width,column-incr,minimum-padding,padding-character*A<br>Default values for the above arguments are ~0,0,1,#\space. |
| ~@A | Padding added to left. |
| ~:A | NIL is printed as () except in list structure. |
| ~S | Symbolic expression; argument is printed with escape characters, and same options as ~A. |
| ~C | Character argument. |
| ~:C | Name of character. |
| ~:@C | Name of character and shift keys, if any. |
| ~@C | Character is output so reader can understand it; #\ format. |
| ~P | Plural; numeric argument. |
| ~:P | Previous argument is used. |
| ~@P | ies or y is output. |
| ~~ | Tilde is output. |
| ~ (*string*~) | Case conversion. |
| ~: (*string*~) | Capitalize all words. |
| ~@ (*string*~) | Capitalize first word and lowercase all other words. |
| ~:@ (*string*~) | Uppercase all letters. |
| ~D | Decimal.<br>*~column-width,padding-char,comma-char*D |
| ~:D | Output comma character. |
| ~@D | Output number sign. |
| ~B | Binary; same options as ~D. |
| ~O | Octal; same options as ~D. |
| ~X | Hexadecimal; same options as ~D. |
| ~R | Radix; argument is output as an integer of the specified radix or as a non-number. |
| ~$n$R | Radix of n. |
| ~R | Cardinal number: one, two, three, etc. |
| ~:R | Ordinal number: first, second, third, etc. |
| ~@R | Roman numeral: I, II, III, IV, V, etc. |
| ~:@R | Old Roman numeral, I, II, III, IIII, etc. |

**TABLE 20.2**  FORMAT DIRECTIVES (Continued)

| Directive | Meaning and Arguments |
|---|---|
| ~F | Fixed-format floating-point. |
| | *~field-width,digits-after,scale,overflow-char,pad-char*F |
| | As many characters as necessary are printed as default. |
| ~@F | Always outputs the sign. |
| ~E | Exponential floating point. |
| | *~width,dig-after,dig-in-expt,scale,overflow-char,pad-char,expt-char*E |
| ~@E | Always outputs the sign. |
| ~G | General floating point, fixed, or exponential is used depending on argument; same options as ~E. |
| ~$ | Dollar floating point. |
| | *~digits-after,digits-before,width,padding-char*$ |
| | Default values for the arguments are ~2,1,0,#\space. |
| ~@$ | Always outputs the sign. |
| ~:$ | Outputs the sign before padding the characters. |
| ~<newline> | Continue on the next line. |
| ~: | Ignore a new line, but not white space. |
| ~@ | Ignore white space, but not a new line. |
| ~% | Newline is output. |
| ~& | Freshline; newline is output if it is not currently at the beginning of a line. |
| ~\| | Page is output. |
| ~T | Tabulate; move cursor to the next tab. |
| | *~column-number,column-increment*T |
| ~@T | Relative tab. |
| ~* | Ignore the argument. |
| *~n*\* | Ignore n arguments. |
| ~:* | Back up the arguments. |
| *~n*@\* | Move to the nth argument in the list. |
| ~? | Indirection; the next argument is a format-control-string; |
| | the following argument is a list of arguments passed to the string. |
| ~@? | Only the format-control-string is needed. |
| ~[*s0*~;*s1*~;...~;*sn*~] | Conditional expression; the integer argument selects which string is output. |
| ~[*s0*~;...~;*sn*~:;*else*~] | Outputs else if no other string is selected. |
| ~:[*false*~;*true*~] | Outputs false if the argument is NIL. Outputs true if the argument is non-nil; the argument is used again in the next directive. |
| ~@[*true*~] | If the argument is NIL, true-string is not output and the argument is not re-used. |
| ~#[*s0*~;*s1*~;...~;*sn*~] | Counts the number of arguments and processes the corresponding string. |

**TABLE 20.2**   FORMAT DIRECTIVES (Continued)

| Directive | Meaning and Arguments |
|---|---|
| ~{*string*~} | Iteration; the argument is a list; the string is repeated for each element. |
| ~n{*string*~} | At most, n iterations are done; n can appear before any other option. |
| ~:{*string*~} | The argument is a list of sublists. |
| ~@{*string*~} | Uses all remaining arguments as the argument list. |
| ~:@{*string*~} | Uses all remaining arguments; the arguments must be lists. |
| ~:} | Ending the directive with  :} causes the directive to be used at least once. |
| ~<*string*~> | Justification. |
| | ~*width,width-increment,minimum-padding,padding-char*<*string*~> |
| ~@<*string*~> | Adds spacing after the last segment. |
| ~:<*string*~> | Adds spacing before the first segment. |
| ~@:<*string*~> | Adds spacing before the first and after last segment. |
| ~<*s*~:;*s2*~;...*s*~> | If all strings except the first can be output on the current line, they are and the first string is thrown away; otherwise the first string is output, which should contain a new line, followed by the other strings. |
| ~<*s*~n,*wdth*:;*s2*~;...~> | String and n characters must fit on the line. |
| ~^ | Up and out; terminate a  ~{ or  ~<.  If there are no constructs, terminate formatting. |
| ~n^ | Terminate if n is zero. |
| ~a,b^ | Terminate if  a equals  b. |
| ~a,b,c^ | Terminate if  a <= b <= c.   a, b or c can be a number, a variable that takes the next argument, or  # that returns the number of remaining arguments. |
| ~<~s;~^s2~;~^s3~...~> | No more segments are processed before justification. |
| ~:{~^*string*~} | Terminate the current iteration step. |
| ~:{~:^*string*~} | Terminate the entire iteration. |
| ~? | Within an indirection,  ~^ terminates the construct or the indirection. |
| ~[  ~( | Within a  ~[ or  ~(, ~^ terminates the construct processing. |

## Format Examples

Now here are a couple of examples.  Each step shows you the effect of the various directives.

### Example 20-1

Take each argument and output it in decimal, binary, octal, and hexadecimal format.  Put each number in a column.  Put each argument on a separate line.

**1.** The ~d, ~b, ~o, and ~x directives output numbers in decimal, binary, octal, and hexadecimal, respectively.

```
(format t "~d ~b ~o ~x" 25 25 25 25)
⇒    25 11001 31 19
     NIL
```

**2.** You want to use the same argument for each number format. ~:* backs up one argument.

```
(format t "~d ~:* ~b ~:* ~o ~:* ~x" 25)
⇒    25  11001  31  19
     NIL
```

**3.** You want to repeat the string for each argument. ~@{...~} uses the arguments as a list and repeats the string for each argument.

```
(format t "~@{~d ~:* ~b ~:* ~o ~:* ~x~}" 1 5 7 9 12 25)
⇒   1   1   1   15   101   5   57   111   7   79   1001   11   912
    1100  14   C25  11001   31   19
    NIL
```

**4.** Each argument should be on a new line. ~% outputs a new line.

```
(format t "~@{~d ~:* ~b ~:* ~o ~:* ~x ~%~}" 1 5 7 9 12 25)
⇒   1   1   1   1
    5   101   5   5
    7   111   7   7
    9   1001   11   9
    12  1100   14   C
    25  11001   31   19
    NIL
```

**5.** And each number should be in a column. ~column,widthT outputs spaces to put the next argument in a column.

```
(format t "~@{~1,10t ~d ~:* ~2,10t ~b ~:* ~3,10t ~o ~:*
            ~4,10t ~x ~%~}"
         1 5 7 9 12 25)
⇒      1              1          1              1
       5              101        5              5
       7              111        7              7
       9              1001       11             9
       12             1100       14             C
       25             11001      31             19
       NIL
```

---

**Example 20-2**

Write a function that accepts up to three arguments. The arguments represent the numbers of cautions, warnings, and errors that have occurred in a program. Format the numbers and their meanings.

**1.** Output the number of cautions, warnings, and errors.

```
(defun warns (&optional (cautions 0)(warnings 0)(errors 0))
  (format t "Done. ~d cautions ~d warnings ~d errors" cautions warnings errors))
⇒    WARNS


(warns 1 2 3)
⇒    Done. 1 cautions 2 warnings 3 errors
     NIL
```

**2.** If the number is not 1, output the plurals of the words.

```
(defun warns (&optional (cautions 0)(warnings 0)(errors 0))
  (format t "Done. ~d caution~:p ~d warning~:p ~d error~:p"
    cautions warnings errors))
⇒    WARNS

(warns 1 2 1)
⇒    Done. 1 caution 2 warnings 1 error
     NIL
```

**3.** If the argument is 0, it should not be output. Remember to reuse the argument.

```
(defun warns (&optional (cautions 0)(warnings 0)(errors 0))
  (format t "Done. ~v^ ~:* ~d caution~:p ~v^ ~:* ~d warning~:p
    ~v^ ~:* ~d error~:p" cautions warnings errors))
⇒    WARNS

(warns 1 2 0)
⇒    Done.   1 caution   2 warnings
     NIL

(warns 1 0 2)
⇒    Done.   1 caution
     NIL
```

**4.** Notice that all processing stops at the first zero argument. Three `format` functions can be used.

```
(defun warns (&optional (cautions 0)(warnings 0)(errors 0))
  (format t "Done. ~v^ ~:* ~d caution~:p" cautions)
  (format t "~v^ ~:* ~d warning~:p" warnings)
  (format t "~v^ ~:* ~d error~:p" errors))
⇒    WARNS
```

```
(warns 1 0 2)
⇒   Done.   1 caution  2 errors
    NIL


(warns 0 0 1)
⇒   Done.   1 error
    NIL


(warns 0 0 0)
⇒   Done.
    NIL


(warns 1 5 99)
⇒   Done.   1 caution  5 warnings  99 errors
    NIL
```

---

**Exercise 20-1**

1. Given a list of numbers, output them in fields of not more than 10 characters.

2. Given a list of objects, output them two at a time. Left justify the first, and right justify the second. Do not assume there is an even number of objects.

---

## OUTPUT VARIABLES

There are several variables that affect the way objects are output. Symbols can be output in uppercase or lowercase. Numbers may appear in any base. When lists are output, these variables specify the number of levels and the length of the list to be printed. One variable determines if an array is output in full or just partially. These variables are:

```
*print-array*
*print-base*
*print-case*
*print-circle*
*print-length*
*print-level*
*print-radix*
```

## Numbers

The two variables that affect the output of numbers are `*print-base*` and `*print-radix*`.

**\*print-base\*.**  The `*print-base*` variable specifies the number base in which numbers are output.  The default is decimal.

```
100
⇒    100

(setq *print-base* 16)
⇒    10
```

Note that the output value is 10.  Remember the read-eval-print loop?  After `*print-base*` is set to 16, the printer outputs the value, now, in base 16.

```
100
⇒    64

12
⇒    C

15
⇒    F

(setq *print-base* 2)
⇒    10

100
⇒    1100100

(setq *print-base* 10)
⇒    10

100
⇒    100
```

**\*print-radix\*.**  In the previous examples, you cannot tell what base is being output from what is printed.  To output the radix, set `*print-radix*` to t.

```
(setq *print-radix* t)
⇒    T

(setq *print-base* 16)
⇒    #x10
```

```
100
⇒    #x64

(setq *print-base* 2)
⇒    #b10

100
⇒    #b1100100

(setq *print-base* 12)
⇒    #12r10

100
⇒    #12r84

(setq *print-base* 10)
⇒    10.

100
⇒    100.
```

Notice the decimal point following the number. When *print-radix* is T, the decimal point is output for all numbers, not just floating-point numbers. When *print-radix* is NIL, the decimal point is not output for integers.

```
(setq *print-radix* nil)
⇒    NIL

100
⇒    100
```

## Symbols

The *print-case* variable determines the character case in which symbols are output.

```
'word-one
⇒    WORD-ONE

(setq *print-case* :downcase)
⇒    :downcase

⇒    word-one
```

When *print-case* is :downcase, all lowercase characters are used to output symbols.

```
(setq *print-case* :capitalize)
⇒     :Capitalize

'word-one
⇒     Word-One
```

When *print-case* is :capitalize, the first character of the symbol is output in uppercase and all other characters are lowercase. Words are separated by blanks, hyphens, and other nonalphanumeric characters.

```
'word2one
⇒     Word2one

'word.one
⇒     Word.One

'word*one
⇒     Word*One
```

When *print-case* is :upcase, all characters are output in uppercase.

```
(setq *print-case* :upcase)
⇒     :UPCASE

'word-one
⇒     WORD-ONE
```

## Lists

There are three variables that affect the length of lists output, the number of levels output, and whether or not circular lists are output.

**\*print-length\*.**  *print-length* affects the number of elements at each level of a list that is output.

```
(setq x '(1 2 3 4 5 6 7 8 9 0))
⇒     (1 2 3 4 5 6 7 8 9 0)

(setq y '(1 2  (1 2 (1 2 3 4 5 6 7) 3 4 5)))
⇒     (1 2 (1 2 (1 2 3 4 5 6 7) 3 4 5))

x
⇒     (1 2 3 4 5 6 7 8 9 0)

(setq *print-length* 8)
⇒     8
```

```
x
⇒    (1 2 3 4 5 6 7 8 ...)

(setq *print-length* 5)
⇒    5

y
⇒    (1 2 (1 2 (1 2 3 4 5 ...) 3 4 ...))

(setq *print-length* 2)
⇒    2

x
⇒    (1 2 ...)
```

To reset *print-length* to the default value, no limit on the length, setq it to NIL.

```
(setq *print-length* nil)
⇒    NIL

x
⇒    (1 2 3 4 5 6 7 8 9 0)
```

**\*print-level\*.**   The *print-level* variable affects the number of levels that are output.

```
(setq x '(1 1 (2 2 (3 3 (4 4 (5 5))))))
⇒    (1 1 (2 2 (3 3 (4 4 (5 5))))))

x
⇒    (1 1 (2 2 (3 3 (4 4 (5 5))))))

(setq *print-level* 4)
⇒    4

x
⇒    (1 1 (2 2 (3 3 (4 4 #))))

(setq *print-level* 2)
⇒    2

x
⇒    (1 1 (2 2 #))
```

To reset the value of *print-level* to the default value, no limit on the number of levels output, setq it to NIL.

```
(setq *print-level* nil)
⇒    NIL


x
⇒    (1 1 (2 2 (3 3 (4 4 (5 5)))))
```

**\*print-circle\*.**  The value of \*print-circle\* determines whether or not the printer checks for circular lists.

```
(setq x '(a))
⇒    (A)

(setf (cdr x) x)
⇒    (A A A A A A A A A A A A A A A .....
```

You will have to break from this example because the list is circular and won't stop until you run out of memory.

```
(setq *print-circle* T)
⇒    T

(setq x '(a))
⇒    (A)

(setf (cdr x) x)
⇒    #0=(A . #0#)

(setq x '(A))
⇒    (A)
```

The default value of \*print-circle\* is NIL, that is, the printer does not check for circular structures.  When you set \*print-circle\* to T, the printer checks for circular structures and does not print them.  It does not stop you, however, from creating circular structures.

**Numbers and Symbols.**  Of course, the variables that affect the output of numbers and symbols are also in effect when the numbers and symbols are in lists.

```
(setq x '(2 4 6 8 10 12 14 16))
⇒    (2 4 6 8 10 12 14 16)

(setq *print-base* 2)
⇒    10


x
⇒    (10 100 110 1000 1010 1100 1110 10000)
```

```
(setq *print-radix* t)
⇒    T


x
⇒    (#b10 #b100 #b110 #b1000 #b1010 #b1100 #b1110 #b10000)


(setq *print-radix* nil)
⇒    NIL


(setq *print-base* 10)
⇒    10


(setq *print-case* :capitalize)
⇒    :Capitalize


(setq x '(abc def ghi jkl))
⇒    (Abc Def Ghi Jkl)


(setq *print-case* :downcase)
⇒    :downcase


x
⇒    (abc def ghi jkl)


(setq *print-case* :upcase)
⇒    :UPCASE


x
⇒    (ABC DEF GHI JKL)
```

## Arrays

**\*print-array\*.**   The `*print-array*` variable determines how much of an array is output.

```
(setq a (make-array '(2 3) :initial-contents '((a b c)(d e f))))
⇒    #2((A B C) (D E F))


(setq *print-array* nil)
⇒    NIL


a
⇒    #<Array, rank=2 #x746F00>


(setq b (make-array '(4 5 6)))
⇒    #<Array, rank=3 #x74EAA8>
```

```
(setq *print-array* t)
⇒    T
```

When `*print-array*` is NIL, enough information about the array is output to identify the array. The elements of the array are not output.

**Length and Level.**  The `*print-length*` and `*print-level*` variables also affect the output of an array.

```
(setq *print-length* 2)
⇒    2

a
⇒    #2A((A B ...) (D E ...))

(setq *print-level* 2)
⇒    2

a
⇒    #2A((# # ...) (# # ...))

(setq *print-length* nil)
⇒    NIL

a
⇒    #2A((# # #) (# # #))

(setq *print-level*  nil)
⇒    NIL

a
⇒    #2A((A B C) (D E F))
```

**Numbers and Symbols.**  The variables that affect numbers and symbols also affect arrays when those numbers and symbols are the elements of the array.

```
(setq a (make-array '(2 3) :initial-contents '((2 4 6)(8 10 12))))
⇒    #2A((2 4 6) (8 10 12))

(setq b (make-array '(2 3) :initial-contents
                    '((one two three)(four five six))))
⇒    #2A((ONE TWO THREE) (FOUR FIVE SIX))

(setq *print-base* 2)
⇒    10
```

```
a
⇒     #10A((10 100 110) (1000 1010 1100))

(setq *print-radix* t)
⇒     T

a
⇒     ##b10A((#b10 #b100 #b110) (#b1000 #b1010 #b1100))

(setq *print-base* 10)
⇒     10.

(setq *print-radix* nil)
⇒     NIL

(setq *print-case* :capitalize)
⇒     :Capitalize

b
⇒     #2A((One Two Three) (Four Five Six))

(setq *print-case* :downcase)
⇒     :downcase

b
⇒     #2A((one two three) (four five six))
       nil

(setq *print-case* :upcase)
⇒     :UPCASE
```

## INPUT VARIABLES

The `*read-base*` and `*read-default-float-format*` determine how a number is read.

`*read-base*` determines the base of the numbers read.

`*read-default-float-format*` determines the floating-point format (single, short, double, or long) of floating-points numbers that are read and do not have an exponent marker.

```
*read-base*
⇒     10

12
⇒     12
```

```
(setq *read-base* 2)
⇒     2


11
⇒     3


(setq *read-base* 10000)
⇒     16


aaa
⇒     2730


(setq *read-base* a)
⇒     10
```

Notice the last function in the previous example.  The base is set to a.  This is because all numbers are read in base 16 (from the previous call).  Thus, to reset the base to 10, the letter-number a is used.


## WRITE/READ

Reading and writing is the method most associated with I/O.  Notice in the following list that for every write there is a corresponding read.  In general, if you use the write function to output an object, the corresponding read function can read the object.

```
write             read
write-byte        read-byte
write-char        read-char
write-string      read-from-string
```

### write

The write function outputs the printed representation of an object.  The function provides keywords that correlate to the output variables in the previous section.

```
(write object &key :stream :escape :radix :base :circle :pretty
                   :level :length :case :gensym :array)
```

For example,

```
(write 'symbol)
⇒     SYMBOL
      SYMBOL
```

```
(write "string" :escape t)
⇒     "string"
      "string"

(write "string" :escape nil)
⇒     string
      "string"
```

The default stream for write is `*standard-output*`. You can specify any open stream. If the stream is open to a file, the object is written to the file.

```
(setq stream (make-string-output-stream))
⇒     #<String-Output Stream>

(write "this is an example" :stream stream)
⇒     "this is an example"

(write "
      test" :stream stream)
⇒     "
      test"

(get-output-stream-string stream)
⇒     "\"this is an example\"\"
      test\""

(write "test" :stream stream :escape nil)
⇒     "test"

(get-output-stream-string stream)
⇒     "test"

(write 'symbol :stream stream)
⇒     SYMBOL

(get-output-stream-string stream)
⇒     "SYMBOL"

(write 'symbol :stream stream :escape nil)
⇒     SYMBOL

(get-output-stream-string stream)
⇒     "SYMBOL"

(close stream)
⇒     T
```

**read**

The read equivalent to write is read.

> (read &optional *input-stream eof-error-p eof-value recursive-p*)

To read keyboarded input, execute (read), type characters, and press [ENTER] (which may be the same as executing a function).

```
(read)
abcde
⇒    ABCDE

(read)
"abcde"
⇒    "abcde"
```

In order for read to input the same object output by write, write must have :escape set to t. (The open function connects a stream with a file.)

```
(setq stream (open "/users/wendy/temp/io" :direction :output
                 :if-exists :supersede))
⇒    #<File Stream /users/wendy/temp/io>

(write "string" :stream stream :escape nil)
⇒    "string"

(close stream)
⇒    T

(setq stream (open "/users/wendy/temp/io" :direction :input
                 :if-does-not-exist :error))
⇒    #<File Stream /users/wendy/temp/io>

(read stream)
⇒    STRING

(close stream)
⇒    T

(setq stream (open "/users/wendy/temp/io" :direction :output
                 :if-exists :supersede))
⇒    #<File Stream /users/wendy/temp/io>

(write "string" :stream stream :escape t)
⇒    "string"
```

```
(close stream)
⇒    T

(setq stream (open "/users/wendy/temp/io" :direction :input
                 :if-does-not-exist :error))
⇒    #<File Stream /users/wendy/temp/io>

(read stream)
⇒    "string"

(close stream)
⇒    T
```

**End-of-File.**   There are two arguments, *eof-error-p* and *eof-value*, that determine what to do should read come to an end-of-file between objects.  If *eof-error-p* is
nil, no error is reported.  Instead, the value of *eof-value* is returned.  If *eof-error-p* is t,
an error is reported.

```
(setq stream (open "/users/wendy/temp/io" :direction :output
                 :if-exists :supersede))
⇒    #<File Stream /users/wendy/temp/io>

(write "first line" :stream stream :escape t)
⇒    "first line"

(write "second line" :stream stream :escape t)
⇒    "second line"

(close stream)
⇒    T

(setq stream (open "/users/wendy/temp/io" :direction :input
                 :if-does-not-exist :error))
⇒    #<File Stream /users/wendy/temp/io>

(read stream nil 'eof)
⇒    "first line"

(read stream nil 'eof)
⇒    "second line"

(read stream nil 'eof)
⇒    EOF
```

If read comes to an end-of-file while reading an object, it will still report an
error.  This situation might occur while reading lines of Lisp code that do not have
matching parentheses.

```
(setq stream (open "/users/wendy/temp/io" :direction :output
                   :if-exists :supersede))
⇒   #<File Stream /users/wendy/temp/io>


(write "first line" :stream stream :escape t)
⇒   "first line"


(write "(fun1 (x)" :stream stream :escape nil)
                            ;; non-match () inside the string.
                            ;; escape nil so that the string is
                            ;; read as a symbol.
⇒   "(fun1 (x)"


(close stream)
⇒   T


(setq stream (open "/users/wendy/temp/io" :direction :input
                   :if-does-not-exist :error))
⇒   #<File Stream /users/wendy/temp/io>


(read stream)
⇒   "first line"


(read stream nil 'eof)
⇒   !!!!! Error: Unexpected end-of-file encountered.


(close stream)
⇒   T
```

The read function reads an object from a stream. If the object is a string, it looks for matching quote marks. If the object is a list, it looks for matching parentheses. And if the object is a symbol, it looks for spaces. The quote marks, parentheses, and spaces are delimiters.

```
(setq a (open "/users/wendy/temp/reading" :direction :output
              :if-exists :supersede))
⇒   #<File Stream /users/wendy/temp/reading>


(write "(a b c) one two \"string\" " :stream a :escape nil)
⇒   "(a b c) one two \"string\" "


(close a)
⇒   T


(setq a (open "/users/wendy/temp/reading" :direction :input
              :if-does-not-exist :error))
⇒   #<File Stream /users/wendy/temp/reading>
```

```
(read a)
⇒    (A  B  C)

(read a)
⇒    ONE

(read a)
⇒    TWO

(read a)
⇒    "string"

(close a)
⇒    T
```

## write-byte

The `write-byte` function writes a byte.

```
(write-byte integer binary-output-stream)
```

*integer* is the byte that is output. It must be the same type as that specified in `:element-type` when the stream was opened. The only stream opened with this keyword is one that is connected to a file.

```
(setq binary (open "/users/wendy/temp/bin" :direction :output
                   :element-type 'bit :if-exists :supersede))
⇒    #<File Stream /users/wendy/temp/bin>

(write-byte 0 binary)
⇒    0

(write-byte 1 binary)
⇒    1

(close binary)
⇒    T
```

With `:element-type` set to `bit`, only 0 and 1 can be written to the file.

```
(setq binary (open "/users/wendy/temp/bin" :direction :output
                   :element-type '(mod 10) :if-exists :supersede))
⇒    #<File Stream /users/wendy/temp/bin>

(write-byte 9 binary)
⇒    9
```

```
(write-byte 4 binary)
⇒    4


(close binary)
⇒    T
```

With :element-type set to '(mod 10), numbers 0,...,9 can be output.

```
(setq binary (open "/users/wendy/temp/bin" :direction :output
                   :element-type 'signed-byte :if-exists :supersede))
⇒    #<File Stream /users/wendy/temp/bin>


(write-byte 12 binary)
⇒    12


(write-byte -99 binary)
⇒    -99


(close binary)
⇒    T
```

With :element-type set to 'signed-byte, integers can be output. The maximum number is determined by the system.

## read-byte

read-byte reads the file in the same format that write-byte wrote to the file.

```
(read-byte binary-input-stream &optional eof-error-p eof-value)

(setq binary (open "/users/wendy/temp/bin" :direction :input
                   :element-type 'signed-byte :if-does-not-exist :error))
⇒    #<File Stream /users/wendy/temp/bin>


(read-byte binary nil 'eof)
⇒    12


(read-byte binary nil 'eof)
⇒    -99


(close binary)
⇒    T
```

Notice what happens if you try to change the :element-type after the file has been written.

```
(setq binary (open "/users/wendy/temp/bin" :direction :input
                   :element-type 'bit :if-does-not-exist :error))
⇒    #<File Stream /users/wendy/temp/bin>

(read-byte binary nil 'eof)
⇒    !!!!! Error: 12 out of range in READ-BYTE in
        #<File Stream /users/wendy/temp/bin> with element-type BIT

(close binary)
⇒    T
```

## write-char

The `write-char` function outputs characters to the stream.

write-char *character* &optional *output-stream*)

```
(setq char-stream (open "/users/wendy/temp/char" :direction :output
                       :if-exists :supersede))
⇒    #<File Stream /users/wendy/temp/char>

(write-char #\a char-stream)
⇒    #\a

(write-char #\LF char-stream)
⇒    #\Linefeed

(write-char #\e char-stream)
⇒    #\e

(write-char #\n char-stream)
⇒    #\n

(write-char #\d char-stream)
⇒    #\d

(write "next line" :stream char-stream)
⇒    "next line"

(close char-stream)
⇒     T
```

## read-char

`read-char` reads the characters output by `write-char`. It can also read characters output by `write`. Similarly, `read` can read what is written by `write-char`.

```
(setq char-stream (open "/users/wendy/temp/char" :direction :input
                        :if-does-not-exist :error))
⇒    #<File Stream /users/wendy/temp/char>

(read-char char-stream nil 'eof)
⇒    #\a

(read-char char-stream nil 'eof)
⇒    #\Linefeed

(read char-stream nil 'eof)
⇒    END

(read-char char-stream nil 'eof)
⇒    #\"

(read-char char-stream nil 'eof)
⇒    #\n

(read-char char-stream nil 'eof)
⇒    #\e

(read-char char-stream nil 'eof)
⇒    #\x

(read-char char-stream nil 'eof)
⇒    #\t

(read char-stream nil 'eof)
⇒    LINE
```

**read-char-no-hang.**   When characters are read from a file, there is seldom the chance that you will have to wait for the input. However, when asking for characters from an interactive device, such as a keyboard, the program might have to wait. read-char-no-hang looks at a stream and if there is a character available, gets that character. If no character is available, read-char-no-hang immediately returns nil.

```
(read-char-no-hang &optional input-stream eof-error-p eof-value recursive-p)

(read-char-no-hang)
a            ;type this character before evaluating the function.
⇒    #\a

(read-char-no-hang)
⇒    NIL
```

```
(read-char-no-hang (make-string-input-stream "ab"))
⇒    #\a
```

```
(read-char-no-hang  (make-string-input-stream "") nil 'eof)
⇒    EOF
```

**listen.**   The `listen` function also looks to see if there is a character in a stream. However, it does not get the character. It also does not distinguish the difference between an end-of-file and no character.

(listen &optional *input-stream*)

```
(listen (make-string-input-stream ""))
⇒    NIL
```

```
(listen)
⇒    NIL
```

```
(listen)
⇒    NIL
```

**unread-char.**   The `unread-char` writes a character to the beginning of the input stream. The character must be the same character that was last read.

(unread-char *character* &optional *input-stream*)

```
(setq a (make-string-input-stream "abcde"))
⇒    #<String-Input Stream>
```

```
(read-char a)
⇒    #\a
```

```
(read-char a)
⇒    #\b
```

```
(unread-char #\b a)
⇒    NIL
```

```
(read-char a)
⇒    #\b
```

You can put back one character in the input stream. You cannot undo more than one character at a time. That is, for every `unread-char`, there must be a preceding `read-char`.

**peek-char.**    The `peek-char` function looks at the next character in the input stream. It can return the next character without removing the character from the stream, it can skip over white space before looking at the character, or it can look for a specific character.

> (peek-char &optional *peek-type input-stream eof-error-p eof-value recursive-p*)

*peek-type* can be `nil`, `t`, or a character object. When `nil`, `peek-char` looks at the next character. This is the default. When `t`, `peek-char` returns the first character that is not white space. It updates the pointer in the stream to this character. When *peek-type* is a character object, `peek-char` looks for that character, updates the stream pointer, and returns the character.

```
(setq a (make-string-input-stream "a b cdef"))
⇒    #<String-Input Stream>

(peek-char nil a)
⇒    #\a

(read-char a)
⇒    #\a

(peek-char nil a)
⇒    #\Space

(read a)
⇒    B

(peek-char t a)
⇒    #\c

(peek-char #\f a)
⇒    #\f

(read-char a)
⇒    #\f

(close a)
⇒    T
```

## write-string

The `write-string` function outputs a string to a stream.

> (write-string *string* &optional *output-stream* &key `:start` `:end`)

:start and :end specify the substring to output. The first character in a string is element zero. :end specifies the exclusive end of the substring.

```
(write-string "012345"  t :start 2 :end 5)
⇒    234
     "012345"

(write-string "once upon a time")
⇒    once upon a time
     "once upon a time"
```

write-string always returns the entire string, not just the substring that it outputs.

```
(setq a (make-string-output-stream))
⇒    #<String-Output Stream>

(write-string "string" a)
⇒    "string"

(get-output-stream-string a)
⇒    "string"
```

**write-to-string.**    If you have an object that is not a string, but which you want to output using write-string, you can use write-to-string. The write-to-string function returns the object as a string.

```
(write-to-string object)

(write-to-string 'abc)
⇒    "ABC"

(write-to-string "abc")
⇒    "\"abc\""

(write-string (write-to-string 'abc))
⇒    ABC
     "ABC"
```

## read-from-string

The read-from-string function takes input from a string. It reads each character until an object is built. The :preserve-whitespace keyword determines if blanks and other "white space" are thrown away.

Two values are returned: the object read and the index of the next character to be read.

```
(read-from-string string &optional eof-error-p eof-value
                       &key :start :end :preserve-whitespace)

(read-from-string "a b c"  nil 'eof :preserve-whitespace t)
⇒   A
    1

(read-from-string "a b c" nil 'eof :preserve-whitespace nil)
⇒   A
    2

(read-from-string "abc" nil 'eof)
⇒   ABC
    3

(read-from-string "(a b c)")
⇒   (A B C)
    7
```

---

**Exercise 20-2**

1. Write a function that asks for input from the operator and then retrieves that input.
2. Write a function that opens a file and asks the operator for data to be put in the file. Read until the operator inputs some end value.
3. Write a function that reads each line of a file and prints the results.

---

## STREAM FUNCTIONS

There are four functions that "clear" a stream, as shown in Table 20.3. If the output is buffered before it is sent to an output stream, there are times when you want to force this output to be sent to the stream before you continue. If an error occurs, you may want to halt the output operation. Similarly, if input is buffered, as in a type-ahead buffer, you would want to clear this buffer if an error occurred and the input was no longer valid.

**TABLE 20.3** CLEARING FUNCTIONS

| Function | Meaning |
|----------|---------|
| clear-input | Clears the input buffer. |
| clear-output | Aborts the output operation, thus allowing as little output as possible to go through the stream. |
| finish-output | Causes execution to pause until the output is finished. |
| force-output | Begins emptying the output buffer and returns nil without waiting for the operation to complete. |

```
(clear-input *standard-input*)
⇒    NIL

(clear-output *standard-output*)
⇒    NIL

(force-output out-stream)
⇒    NIL

(finish-output other-stream)
⇒    NIL
```

## SUMMARY

- How do you display the intermediate results of a function?

  Using print, format, or any of the write functions, you can display results.

- How do you get input from an operator?

  Using the output commands, you can prompt the operator for information. Using the read commands, you can get the information.

- How do you change the way in which numbers are output?

  There are several variables that determine the format in which numbers and other objects are output. *print-base* and *print-radix* are the variables associated with numbers.

- How do you avoid printing circular lists?

  Another variable, *print-circle*, determines if a list is checked for circularity before it is printed.

# 21

## Files

This chapter describes the Lisp interface to files. Because each machine on which Lisp runs can have different file structures, the exact nature of your file names can be different from the names shown in the examples that follow. The author's system uses a hicrarchical file structure, which is reflected in the examples.

*Files* are a special type of I/O device. You can read the same data from a file several times. You can write to a file and later write to it again without erasing the first set of data. The file exists even after the program stops. You create files and delete them when they are of no further use. Several programs can access the same file. A file is not bound to a physical device. You can transfer a file from a disc to a tape to another disc.

Reading and writing to a file is done with the same functions described in the previous chapter. In addition, there are some functions that only deal with files. A file must be opened before you can access it. When you are done with a file, it should be closed.

This chapter will look at several topics: pathnames, namestrings, file I/O, operations on files, and loading program files.

## PATHNAMES

A file has a unique name. The name includes the directory in which the file is located, the device on which the file resides, the name of the host machine, and the version and type of the file. And the actual "name" of the file. The entire name is called a pathname. *pathname* is a data object that identifies the file.

The `make-pathname` function constructs a pathname from components.

```
(make-pathname &key :host :device :directory
                    :name :type :version :defaults)
```

Not all the keywords need to be used. If the file does not have a type or version, you do not have to specify that component. If there is only one host machine or device, that component may be left off. If your file system does not have directories, that component is not needed. The only component that is almost essential in identifying a file is its name. However, a pathname does not need any one component. A pathname by itself does not connect to a file. The pathname can identify a single file, no file, or multiple files.

```
(setq first-dir (make-pathname :directory "/users/wendy/"))
⇒   #.(make-pathname :host NIL :device NIL
                     :directory '("" "users" "wendy")
                     :name NIL :type NIL :version NIL)


(setq second-file (make-pathname :directory "/users/wendy/"
                        :name "temp" :type "l" :version :newest))
⇒   #.(make-pathname :host NIL :device NIL
                     :directory '("" "users" "wendy")
                     :name "temp" :type "l" :version :NEWEST)
```

`:version` can have a value of `:oldest`, `:newest`, `:previous`, or `:installed`. Some implementations can have numbers that equate to these values.

### pathname

Another way to create a pathname is through the `pathname` function.

```
(pathname pathname)
```

*pathname* can be a string, stream, symbol, or pathname.

```
(setq new-path (pathname "/users/wendy/temp"))
⇒   #.(make-pathname :host NIL :device NIL
                     :directory '("" "users" "wendy")
                     :name "temp" :type NIL :version NIL)


(setq path2 (pathname 'a-file.b))
⇒   #.(make-pathname :host NIL :device NIL :directory NIL
                     :name "A-FILE" :type B :version NIL)
```

### pathnamep

The `pathnamep` function determines if an object is a pathname.

```
(pathnamep "/users/wendy/temp")
⇒    NIL

(pathnamep (pathname "/users/wendy/temp"))
⇒    T
```

## Pathname Components

The different components of a pathname can be retrieved from the pathname object.
You should note that the component supported by any system is implementation dependent.

```
(pathname-device (make-pathname :device "S320"))
⇒    "S320"

(pathname-host (make-pathname :host "HP-UX" :name "temp"))
⇒    "HP-UX"

(pathname-version (make-pathname :version :newest))
⇒    :NEWEST

(pathname-directory (pathname "/users/wendy/temp"))
⇒    ("" "users" "wendy")

(pathname-name (pathname "/users/wendy/temp.b"))
⇒    "temp"

(pathname-type (pathname "/users/wendy/temp.l"))
⇒    "l"
```

## Default Values

In the above examples, when a component is not supplied, its value becomes `nil`. If
you do not want to supply all the components, but do not want a value of `nil`, you can
set the variable `*default-pathname-defaults*` to a pathname with the desired
components set to the desired default values.

```
(setq *default-pathname-defaults*
   (make-pathname :host "HP-UX" :device "S320"))
⇒    #.(make-pathname :host "HP-UX" :device "S320" :directory NIL
                      :name NIL :type NIL :version NIL)
```

Note in the following examples how the default values are given to the components.

```
(pathname "/users/wendy/temp")
⇒    #.(make-pathname :host "HP-UX" :device "S320"
                        :directory '("" "users" "wendy") :name "temp"
                        :type NIL :version NIL)


(make-pathname :name "temp")
⇒    #.(make-pathname :host "HP-UX" :device "S320" :directory NIL
                        :name "temp" :type NIL :version NIL)


(setq home (make-pathname :directory "/users/wendy/"))
⇒    #.(make-pathname :host "HP-UX" :device "S320"
                        :directory '("" "users" "wendy")
                        :name NIL :type NIL :version NIL)
```

Another way to specify default values is through `merge-pathnames`.

> (merge-pathnames *pathname* &optional *defaults default-version*)

*pathname* is a pathname, string, stream, or symbol. *defaults* is a pathname. Any missing components in *pathname* use values from the `defaults` pathname.

```
(merge-pathnames "/users/wendy/" "file.type" :newest)
⇒    #.(make-pathname :host "HP-UX" :device "S320"
                        :directory '("" "users" "wendy") :name "file"
                        :type "type" :version :NEWEST)
```

`merge-pathnames` returns a new pathname object. It does not alter an existing pathname.

```
(setq path (pathname "/users/wendy/temp"))
⇒    #.(make-pathname :host "HP-UX" :device "S320"
                        :directory '("" "users" "wendy") :name "temp"
                        :type NIL :version NIL)


(merge-pathnames path "test.b")
⇒    #.(make-pathname :host "HP-UX" :device "S320"
                        :directory '("" "users" "wendy") :name "temp"
                        :type "b" :version NIL)


path
⇒    #.(make-pathname :host "HP-UX" :device "S320"
                        :directory '("" "users" "wendy") :name "temp"
                        :type NIL :version NIL)
```

The `user-homedir-pathname` returns a pathname that specifies the user's home directory.

```
(user-homedir-pathname)
⇒   #.(make-pathname :host NIL :device NIL
                    :directory '("" "users" "wendy")
                    :name NIL :type NIL :version NIL)


(merge-pathnames (user-homedir-pathname) "test2")
⇒   #.(make-pathname :host NIL :device NIL
                    :directory '("" "users" "wendy") :name "test2"
                    :type NIL :version NIL)
```

---

**Exercise 21-1**

1. Set the default components of a pathname to be your home directory, your host, and device type.

2. Create a pathname that has file name test and all other components nil.

---

## NAMESTRINGS

A *namestring* is a string representation of the pathname.  `namestring` returns the string representation of the full pathname.

```
(namestring (make-pathname :host "HP-UX" :device "S320" :directory "/users/"
                           :name "temp" :version :oldest :type "b"))
⇒   "/users/temp.b"
```

As with the "pathname" functions, you can retrieve components of the pathname with "namestring" functions, as shown in Table 21.2. The result is a string representing the component value.

**TABLE 21.1**  NAMESTRINGS

| Function | Meaning |
|---|---|
| directory-namestring | Returns a string representing the directory name component of the pathname. |
| file-namestring | Returns a string representing the name, type and version components of the pathname. |
| host-namestring | Returns a string representing the host component of the pathname. |

```
(setq example (pathname "/users/wendy/test.l"))
⇒    #.(make-pathname :host "HP-UX" :device "S320"
                      :directory '("" "users" "wendy") :name "test"
                      :type "l" :version NIL)

(directory-namestring example)
⇒    "/users/wendy/"

(file-namestring example)
⇒    "test.l"

(host-namestring example)
⇒    "HP-UX"

(namestring example)
⇒    "/users/wendy/test.l"
```

namestring returns the full pathname. enough-namestring returns an abbreviated namestring that is sufficient to identify the file named by the pathname. Remember, pathnames do not always identify a file. enough-namestring is concerned with files. How much of the pathname is needed depends on the individual system.

```
(enough-namestring example)
⇒    "/users/wendy/test.l"
```

## FILES

Pathnames and namestrings are two ways to identify a file or set of files. Each of the functions in this section asks for a pathname to identify the file upon which the function operates. The pathname can be a pathname object, string, symbol, or stream. Whichever type of object you use, it must identify a unique file.

### Open a File

When working with a file, you must open it before you can read from it or write to it. open returns a stream that is connected to a specific file. It is through this stream that you read and write to the file.

```
(open filename &key :direction :element-type :if-exists :if-does-not-exist)
```

The *filename* can be a string, pathname, or stream. If it is a stream, the stream provides a file name for the opening of a new stream. The provided stream is not altered.

```
(setq ex-stream (open "/users/wendy/temp/example1.s"))
⇒    #<File Stream /users/wendy/temp/example1.s>

(setq ex (make-pathname :directory "/users/wendy/temp/" :name "test1.l"))
⇒       #.(make-pathname :host "HP-UX" :device "S320"
                          :directory '("" "users" "wendy" "temp")
                          :name "test1.l" :type NIL :version NIL)

(setq ex-stream2 (open ex))
⇒    #<File Stream /users/wendy/temp/test1.l>
```

**direction.**    The `:direction` keyword in `open` provide a means to determine
if the stream is an input, output, or nondirectional stream.  The values of the keyword
can be `:input`, `:output`, `:io`, or `:probe`.   `:input` is the default value.

```
(setq ex-stream (open "/users/wendy/temp/example1.s" :direction :input))
⇒    #<File Stream /users/wendy/temp/example1.s>

(input-stream-p ex-stream)
⇒    T

(output-stream-p ex-stream)
⇒    NIL
```

You can now read from ex-stream because it is an input stream.  You cannot
write to it.  If you want to write to it, you must close the stream (which closes the file)
and then open it in the output direction.  Or, when you originally open the file, use the
`:io` direction.

The `:probe` direction creates a stream and then closes the stream.  The purpose
for this is to test if the file exists.

```
(setq ex-stream (open "/users/wendy/temp/example1.s" :direction :probe))
⇒    #<File Stream /users/wendy/temp/example1.s>

(setq non-file (open "/users/wendy/temp/nothing" :direction :probe))
⇒    NIL
```

If you try to open a file that does not exist, `:probe` returns NIL.  However, if you try
to open a file that does not exist with any other direction, you get an error message.

**element-type.**    The `:element-type` keyword specifies the type of unit of
transaction.  This can be any subtype of character or integer.  The default is string-char.
It can also be bit, unsigned-byte, etc.

```
(setq ex-stream (open "/users/wendy/temp/example1.s" :direction :input
                      :element-type 'string-char))
⇒    #<File Stream /users/wendy/temp/example1.s>
```

**if-exists.**   The :if-exists keyword specifies what to do if the file already exists and the direction is :output or :io. The value of :if-exists can be

- :error signals an error if the file exists. If the version component of the file name is not :newest, :error is the default.

- :new-version creates a new file with the same file name. The version number is larger. If the version component of the filename is :newest, :new-version is the default.

- :rename renames the existing file. It creates a new file with the specified file name.

- :rename-and-delete renames the existing file and then deletes it. It creates a new file with the specified filename.

- :overwrite uses the existing file and destructively modifies the file with any output operation. The file pointer is placed at the beginning of the file; however, the file is not truncated.

- :append uses the existing file and destructively modifies the file with any output operation. The file pointer is placed at the end of the file.

- :supersede creates a file with the same name as the existing file. The existing file is not deleted until the new file is successfully closed.

- nil returns nil without creating either a stream or a file.

**:if-does-not-exist.**   The :if-does-not-exist keyword specifies what to do if the file does not exist.

- :error signals an error. If the direction is :input or if the :if-exists argument is :overwrite or :append, :error is the default.

- :create creates an empty file. If the direction is :output or :io and the :if-exists argument is anything except :overwrite or :append, :create is the default.

- nil returns nil without creating a stream or file. If the direction is :probe, nil is the default.

**Examples.**   Now that you have multiple options to choose from, here are a few examples.

```
(setq first (open "/users/wendy/temp/ex1" :direction :output
            :if-does-not-exist :create))
⇒    #<File Stream /users/wendy/temp/ex1>

(write-line "this is the first line" first)
⇒    "this is the first line"
```

```
(write-line "this is the second line" first)
⇒    "this is the second line"

(write-line "hello" first)
⇒    "hello"

(close first)
⇒    T
```

Now that the information is in the file, you can open the file and read the data.

```
(setq first (open "/users/wendy/temp/ex1" :direction :input))
⇒    #<File Stream /users/wendy/temp/ex1>

(read-line first)
⇒    "this is the first line"
     NIL

(read-line first)
⇒    "this is the second line"
     NIL

(read-line first)
⇒    "hello"
     NIL

(read-line first)
⇒    !!!!! Error: Unexpected end-of-file encountered.
```

As with streams, you need to look for the end-of-file. Use the arguments in read-line to do this.

```
(read-line first nil 'eof)
⇒    EOF
```

## Create a File

The open function provides the only way to create a file from Lisp. Using the :create option to :if-does-not-exist, Lisp creates a file if a file by the specified name does not already exist. If you are inputting data from a file, this is probably not the option to use. Creating a file is often used when outputting to a file.

```
(defun create-file (directory name)
   (setq temp (open (make-pathname :directory directory :name name)
                                 :direction :output
                                 :if-does-not-exist :create
                                 :if-exists :supersede))
   (close temp))
⇒    CREATE-FILE

(create-file "/users/wendy/temp/" "testa")
⇒    T
```

### Delete a File

The function `delete-file` removes the specified file.

```
(delete-file "/users/wendy/temp/testa")
⇒    T


(delete-file "/users/wendy/temp/ex1")
⇒    T
```

`delete-file` returns a non-nil value if it succeeds in deleting the file. If the file does not exist, the implementation determines the value to return. If the file cannot be deleted, an error message is returned.

```
(delete-file "/users")
⇒    !!! Error: Unable to delete file "users"
```

---

**Exercise 21-2**

1. Create a file named "test."
2. Probe the file to see if it exists.
3. Open the file and write three lines of data to it.
4. Write a function that reads all the lines in the file and writes them to the display.

---

## with-open-file

The `with-open-file` macro opens a file, binds a stream to the file, executes a body of forms, and then closes the stream. Whenever the body is exited, the stream is always closed. If a new output file was created and there is an abnormal exit from the body, `with-open-file` closes the file in such a way that it appears that the file was never opened. This is limited by implementation.

```
(with-open-file (stream filename {options}*) {declarations}* {forms}*)
```

*stream* is the stream bound to the file named by *filename*. *options* are the `open` option keywords.

The following example reads lines from the standard input stream (such as a keyboard) and writes the line to the output file. When an empty string is returned (i.e., a carriage return on a blank line), the function exits.

```
(defun read-from-keyboard (file)
  (catch 'end
    (with-open-file (out-stream file :direction :output
                                    :if-exists :supersede
                                    :if-does-not-exist :create)
            (loop
             (setq line (read-line))
             (if (string= line "") (throw 'end "end of input"))
             (write-line line out-stream)))))
⇒    READ-FROM-KEYBOARD
```

Once the function is executed, the only thing it returns is "end of input", which is the result of the throw.

```
(read-from-keyboard "/users/wendy/temp/out-file")
a
b
next-line
⇒    "end of input"
```

The output file now contains three lines of data: a, b, and next-line.

```
(defun write-to-screen (file)
  (catch 'end
    (with-open-file (in-stream file :direction :input
                                   :if-does-not-exist :error)
            (loop
             (setq line (read-line in-stream nil 'eof))
             (if (equal line 'eof) (throw 'end "end of file"))
             (write-line line)))))
⇒    WRITE-TO-SCREEN

(write-to-screen "/users/wendy/temp/out-file")
⇒    a
      b
      next-line
      "end of file"
```

with-open-files can be nested so that more than one file at a time can be opened within the function. The following function takes input from one file, modifies the data, and outputs to another file.

```
(defun trim-blanks (in-file out-file)
  (catch 'eof
    (with-open-file (in-stream in-file :direction :input
                               :if-does-not-exist :error)
        (with-open-file (out-stream out-file :direction :output
                                             :if-does-not-exist :create
                                             :if-exists :supersede)
            (loop
             (setq line (read-line in-stream nil 'eof))
             (if (equal line 'eof) (throw 'eof "end of file"))
             (setq line (string-trim " " line))
             (if (not (string-equal line ""))
                 (write-line line out-stream)))))))
  'end-of-file)
⇒    TRIM-BLANKS
```

Using `read-from-keyboard` to output data to a file, you can put in lines that have blanks at the beginning and end and some lines that consist entirely of blanks.

```
(read-from-keyboard "/users/wendy/temp/out-file")
    abcde
line two

line four
    line five


⇒    "end of input"
```

Now, using the string function `trim-blanks`, you can remove the blanks and place the data in another file.

```
(trim-blanks "/users/wendy/temp/out-file" "/users/wendy/temp/newfile")
⇒    END-OF-FILE
```

Using the `write-to-screen` function, you can see the difference in the original and modified files.

```
(write-to-screen "/users/wendy/temp/out-file")
⇒          abcde
    line two

    line four
        line five


    "end of file"

(write-to-screen "/users/wendy/temp/newfile")
⇒    abcde
    line two
    line four
    line five
    "end of file"
```

## FILE OPERATIONS

In addition to creating a file, writing to and reading from a file, and deleting a file, there are several operations you can use on files.

### File Data

The first set of functions deals with the file itself, not the data within the file. These functions return information on who created the file, when it was created, its length, and where the file pointer is located within the file.

- `file-author` returns the name of the author of the file.
- `file-length` returns the length of the file.
- `file-position` returns or sets the current position within a random-access file.
- `file-write-date` returns the time at which the file was created or last written to.

#### file-author

```
(file-author "/users/wendy/temp/newfile")
⇒    "wendy"

(file-author "/tmp")
⇒    "root"

(file-author "/lib")
⇒    "bin"
```

**file-write-date.** The write-date is returned in universal time format. To change this format to a legible format, use `decode-universal-time`. This format returns the second, minute, hour, date, month, year, day-of-week, daylight-savings-time-p, and time-zone.

```
(file-write-date "/tmp")
⇒    2737219636

(decode-universal-time (file-write-date "/lib"))
⇒    47 39 15 2  5 1986 4 T 7
```

**file-length.** The `file-length` function returns the length of a file. The unit of measure is determined by the `:element-type` specified when a file was opened. The file must be opened and the stream specified in the function.

```
(setq file (open "/users/wendy/temp/newfile"))
⇒    #<File Stream /users/wendy/temp/newfile>
```

```
(file-length file)
⇒    35


(close file)
⇒    T
```

The default :element-type is string-char. Thus, there are 35 characters in this file.

**file-position.**    The file-position function has an optional argument. If the position is specified, the file position is set. If the position is not specified, the current value is returned.

```
(file-position file-stream &optional position)

(with-open-file (file "/users/wendy/temp/newfile" :direction :input
                      :if-does-not-exist :error)
    (pprint (file-position file))
    (write-line (read-line file))
    (pprint (file-position file))
    (write-line (read-line file))
    (file-position file 0)    ;; reset pointer to beginning of file
    (write-line (read-line file))
    "end")
⇒    0
     abcde
     6
     line two
     abcde
     "end"
```

*position* can be set as :start, :end, or an integer to indicate the new position in the file. The integer cannot be larger than the value returned by file-length.

## Directories and File Names

The name of a file can be changed with rename-file.

```
(rename-file "/users/wendy/temp/newfile" "/users/wendy/temp/oldfile")
⇒    #.(make-pathname :host NIL :device NIL
                      :directory '("" "users" "wendy" "temp")
                      :name "oldfile" :type NIL :version NIL)
     #.(make-pathname :host NIL :device NIL
                      :directory '("" "users" "wendy" "temp")
                      :name "newfile" :type NIL :version NIL)
     #.(make-pathname :host NIL :device NIL
                      :directory '("" "users" "wendy" "temp")
                      :name "oldfile" :type NIL :version NIL)
```

`probe-file` determines if there is a file with a specified name.

```
(probe-file "/users/wendy/temp/newfile")
⇒    NIL


(probe-file "/users/wendy/temp/oldfile")
⇒    #.(make-pathname :host NIL :device NIL
                      :directory '("" "users" "wendy" "temp")
                      :name "oldfile" :type NIL :version NIL)
```

The `directory` function returns a list of all the files that match the given pathname. In the following example, a directory is specified as the pathname. All files in
the directory are listed.

```
(directory "/users/wendy/temp/")
⇒    (#.(make-pathname :host NIL :device NIL
                       :directory '("" "users" "wendy" "temp" NIL)
                       :name "." :type NIL :version NIL)
     #.(make-pathname :host NIL :device NIL
                      :directory '("" "users" "wendy" "temp" NIL)
                      :name "." :type "" :version NIL)
     #.(make-pathname :host NIL :device NIL
                      :directory '("" "users" "wendy" "temp" NIL)
                      :name "newout" :type "text" :version NIL)
     #.(make-pathname :host NIL :device NIL
                      :directory '("" "users" "wendy" "temp" NIL)
                      :name "test1" :type "l" :version NIL)
     #.(make-pathname :host NIL :device NIL
                      :directory '("" "users" "wendy" "temp" NIL)
                      :name "test2" :type "text" :version NIL)
     #.(make-pathname :host NIL :device NIL
                      :directory '("" "users" "wendy" "temp" NIL)
                      :name "example1" :type "s" :version NIL)
     #.(make-pathname :host NIL :device NIL
                      :directory '("" "users" "wendy" "temp" NIL)
                      :name "file1" :type "text" :version NIL)
     #.(make-pathname :host NIL :device NIL
                      :directory '("" "users" "wendy" "temp" NIL)
                      :name "out-file" :type NIL :version NIL)
     #.(make-pathname :host NIL :device NIL
                      :directory '("" "users" "wendy" "temp" NIL)
                      :name "oldfile" :type NIL :version NIL))
```

The function could also take a pathname where the components were specified, for
example, the directory and type.

```
(directory
 (make-pathname :directory "/users/wendy/temp/" :name "*"
                :type "text"))
```

## LOADING A FILE

Loading a file consists of reading the file and evaluating all the forms in the file.

```
(load filename &key :verbose :print :if-does-not-exist)
```

Place the following function in a file.

```
(defun load-ex (test)
  (print test))

(load "/users/wendy/temp/test-load" :verbose t :print t
                                    :if-does-not-exist t)
⇒   ; Loading /users/wendy/temp/test-load.
    #| Input:        (DEFUN LOAD-EX (TEST) (PRINT TEST)) |#
    LOAD-EX
    ; Finished loading /users/wendy/temp/test-load.
    "/users/wendy/temp/test-load"
```

Now that the function is loaded and evaluated, it can be used. Notice that the `defun` was not evaluated before the `load`. The function was simply put into a file.

```
(load-ex 'abc)
⇒   ABC
    ABC
```

The following examples load the same file using different defaults.

```
(load "/users/wendy/temp/test-load" :verbose nil :print t)
⇒   LOAD-EX
    "/users/wendy/temp/test-load"

(load "/users/wendy/temp/test-load" :verbose t :print nil)
⇒   ; Loading /users/wendy/temp/test-load.
    #| Input:        (DEFUN LOAD-EX (TEST) (PRINT TEST)) |#
    #| Result:       LOAD-EX |#
    ; Finished loading /users/wendy/temp/test-load.
    "/users/wendy/temp/test-load"
```

The `:if-does-not-exist` keyword specifies whether `nil` or an error is output if a file does not exist. If the value is `nil`, no error is reported.

`:verbose` outputs information about the load process and what is being done. In this short example, very little is output. In more complex files, many items could be output.

`:print` prints the input and results of evaluating the forms in the file.

The default for these keywords is `:if-does-not-exist t`, `:verbose` the value of `*load-verbose*`, and `:print nil`.

```
(load "/users/wendy/temp/test-load")
⇒    "/users/wendy/temp/test-load"
```

You can set the `*load-verbose*` variable to `t` or `nil`. This value is used by the `:verbose` keyword to specify the amount of information output during the loading of files.


## SUMMARY

Several topics on files are presented in this chapter:

- Pathnames
- Namestrings
- File I/O
- File operations
- Loading files

The exact format for files and directories is implementation dependent. However, the majority of the Lisp functions do not use the actual name or description of a file. Instead, once a file is identified, in whatever format the system uses, all functions use a symbol to identify the file. The symbol can be a pathname or a stream, depending on the operation. If you write programs that are independent of actual file names and descriptions, then your programs are more portable.

# *22*

# *Miscellaneous*

As usual, there are several functions that, for want of a better place, are presented together under Miscellaneous. Do not discount them because they do not have their own chapters. You may find a few of them quite useful in your programming.

## TIMINGS

The time of day has many uses beside providing a running clock on your screen. Some programs begin running at particular times. The time it takes to run a section of code can be important. And some programs stop for a specific length of time to let other programs run.

### The Time of Day

Rarely does a computer keep the time of day in a format that everyone understands, such as 10:45 a.m. Instead, time is kept in a universal format. It is usually the number of seconds past a particular point in history. In Common Lisp, this is 1 January 1900. There are two functions that return the time of day.

```
(get-decoded-time)
(get-universal-time)
```

`get-decoded-time` returns the time in a format that specifies the second, minute, hour, date, month, year, day-of-week, daylight-savings-time-p and time-zone.

```
(get-decoded-time)
⇒     18
      15
      15
      25
      4
      1986
      4
      NIL
      7
```

This function was executed at 15:15:18 (3:15:18 p.m.), 25 April 1986, on a Friday, not daylight savings time, in time zone 7.

The day of the week begins on Monday and has a value of zero.  The last day of the week is Sunday and has a value of 6.

Time zones are the number of hours west from Greenwich Mean Time (GMT).

The universal time is the number of seconds past 1 January 1900, GMT.

```
(get-universal-time)
⇒     2723829354
```

## Decoding Time

In order to decode universal time, you must figure the date, add the number of hours west from GMT, and determine if daylight savings time is in effect.  Or you can use the `decode-universal-time` function.

```
(decode-universal-time universal-time &optional time-zone)

(decode-universal-time get-universal-time))
⇒     12
      16
      12
      25
      4
      1986
      4
      NIL
      7
```

You can also encode time to the universal time format with `encode-universal-time`.

```
(encode-universal-time second minute hour date month year &optional time-zone)

(encode-universal-time 0 20 17 25 4 1986)
⇒    2723847600

(encode-universal-time 0 20 17 25 4 1986 0)
⇒    2723822400
```

## Internal Time

Internal time is a measure of time that is dependent on the hardware. While decoded time and universal time are accurate to the second, internal time is accurate to a measure of time based on hardware ability. It is usually more accurate than to a second; tenth of second or a microsecond, for example.

The `get-internal-real-time` function returns the current internal time.

```
(get-internal-real-time)
⇒    21561495
```

The `internal-time-units-per-second` constant contains the accuracy of the internal time. It is the number of time units within a second.

```
internal-time-units-per-second
⇒    50
```

The `time` function evaluates a form and outputs timing information.

```
(time (sqrt 55555555))
⇒    Real time:    0.14 s
     Run time:     0.00 s
     7453.559887731499
```

The `sleep` function causes evaluation to wait for a specified number of seconds.

```
(sleep 5)
⇒    NIL
```

You might use this function while waiting for an I/O operation to complete.

## COMPILING

There are two functions that compile: `compile` compiles a definition and `compile-file` compiles the contents of a file.

```
(compile name &optional definition)
(compile-file input-pathname &key :output-file)
```

For example,

```
(defun foo (x)
  (print x))
⇒    FOO


(compile 'foo)
⇒    FOO


(compile 'bar '(lambda (x)(+ (sin x)(cos x))))
⇒    BAR
```

## HARDWARE AND SOFTWARE

There are several functions that identify the hardware and software upon which your
version of Lisp is running and the location of that hardware. Some of the functions
may return an empty string. And unless you are running on the same software and
hardware as this writer, all the functions will return different values from the ones
shown here.

```
(lisp-implementation-type)
⇒    "Hewlett-Packard Common Lisp"

(lisp-implementation-version)
⇒    "1.0   860419 23:25"

(long-site-name)
⇒    "Hewlett-Packard Fort Collins"

(short-site-name)
⇒    "HPFC"

(machine-instance)
⇒     ""

(machine-type)
⇒    "Hewlett-Packard Series 300"

(machine-version)
⇒     ""

(software-type)
⇒    "HP-UX"

(software-version)
⇒    "5.1"
```

The information on hardware and software can be used in two ways. For security purposes, the program can check that it is running on a legitimate system. The program can also check the type of hardware and software and make changes to its routines based on that information. For example, Hewlett-Packard Common Lisp has extensions that allow calls to non-Lisp code. If a program is run on an HP system, it could call non-Lisp programs; however, if the same program is run on a non-HP system, these calls could not be made.

## DEBUGGING

No one writes error-free code the first time, every time. Therefore, debugging becomes an important part of programming. Lisp provides several functions that can help you in debugging. The information reported and the method of reporting is implementation dependent.

### Trace

The `trace` and `untrace` macros allow you to look at the values passed to a function and the values returned by this function. The output varies with implementation. (Refer to Chapter 9 for examples of output.)

```
(trace {function}⁺ {options}*)
(untrace {function}⁺ {options}*)
```

*function* is the name of the function to be traced.
*options* specify when predicates or forms should be evaluated.

| | |
|---|---|
| `:breakb` [*predicate*] | *predicate* is evaluated before calling the traced function. If true, `break` is called. |
| `:breaka` [*predicate*] | *predicate* is evaluated after returning from the traced function. If true, `break` is called. |
| `:break` [*predicate*] | *predicate* is evaluated both before and after the traced function. If true, `break` is called. |
| `:before` *form* | *form* is evaluated before calling the traced function. |
| `:after` *form* | *form* is evaluated after returning from the traced function. |
| `:both` *form* | *form* is evaluated both before and after the traced function. |

### Step

The `step` macro gives you control over the execution of a function. Again, the implementation of this macro is dependent on the system.

```
(step form)
```

Each step that is evaluated is output. You can have options to step slowly, fast, and stop. Most systems understand ''?'' and give a list of acceptable commands that can be executed during the step.

## Describe

The describe function outputs information about an object.

```
(describe 'describe)
⇒    #<ITEM: #x900905A8> : SYMBOL
     Package      : "LISP"
     Name         : "DESCRIBE"
     Value        : "Unbound"
     Function     : #<FUNCTION  Max Args= 1  Lambda Name= DESCRIBE
                    Compiled #x2744A0>
                    " (describe object)    [25.3]

                    The DESCRIBE function prints to the *STANDARD-OUTPUT*
                    stream information about an object. "
     Properties   : (LISP::FUN-DOCUMENTATION LISP::PROCLAIM-FTYPE)

(setq a 4)
⇒    4

(describe 'a)
⇒    #<ITEM: #x9042EED8> : SYMBOL
     Package          : "USER"
     Name             : "A"
     Value            : 4
```

## Documentation

The documentation function returns the documentation string of a function.

```
(documentation symbol doc-type)
```

The *doc-type* depends on how the symbol was defined. Function, variable, type, structure, and setf are the acceptable values.

```
(defun test ()
  "this is a doc string")
⇒    TEST

(documentation 'test 'function)
⇒    "this is a doc string"
```

## MISCELLANEOUS

### The Editor

The ed function invokes the editor if your system provides one. The editor is highly implementation dependent. The type of editor and what it does when invoked is dependent on each system. Common Lisp provides the means to invoke the editor. Your system may have other methods.

```
(ed {pathname|symbol})
```

You can specify a pathname that causes the editor to get a file for editing.

If you do not specify a pathname, the editor uses the current file. It places you at the same location at which you left the editor.

Specifying a symbol causes the editor to look for a function named by that symbol and then lets you edit the text.

### Room

The room function provides information on the internal storage and its management. Once again, the information provided is implementation dependent.

```
(room)
⇒    Dynamic Heap: 3,103,020 bytes total
                   2,890,392 bytes used
                   212,628 bytes free   7% free
      Static Heap: 732,832 bytes free
```

### Features

The features of the system are returned by the *features* variable.

```
*features*
⇒    (T HP)
```

# Appendix A

## Exercises

**CHAPTER 3**

**Exercise 3-1**

1. What is the most specific data type for the following?

```
"abc"          (simple-string 3)
'(1 2 3)       list
1/2            ratio
10             fixnum
:start         keyword
'a             symbol
```

2. Name all the types in which the following are members:

```
"abc"          (simple-string 3)
               string
               vector
               sequence
               array
               common
               t
```

```
'(1 2 3)        list
                sequence
                common
                t

5.43            short floating point
                floating point
                number
                common
                t

3               (mod n) where n is greater than 3
                fixnum
                integer
                rational
                number
                common
                t

'a              symbol
                common
                t

nil             everything in the list
```

## Exercise 3-2

**1.** Translate the following numbers into base ten.

```
#b110           6
#8r11           9
#o14           12
#xf            15
#10r25         25
```

**2.** Translate the following integers from base ten to the indicated radix:

```
Radix 2: 2, 4, 8                    #b10, #b100, #b1000
Radix 8: 1, 8, 10, 64               #o1, #o10, #o12, #o100
Radix 16: 1, 16, 12, 256, 4096      #x1, #x10, #xc, #x100, #x1000
```

**3.** Use the computer to translate the following integers to base ten:

```
10              10
#2r10            2
#xadfb       44539
#9r158         134
#o7777        4095
#3r122211      481
```

**4.** For the curious, find a way for the computer to translate from decimal to octal.

```
(setq *print-radix* t)
(setq *print-base* 8)
```

To get back to printing in base ten:

```
(setq *print-base* 10)
(setq *print-radix* nil)
```

## Exercise 3-3

Which of the following ratios are legal and which are not?

```
1/2            legal
1.2/3.4        illegal
7/-2           illegal
#b100/110      legal
100/#b110      illegal
-5/100         legal
#x1/c          legal
```

## Exercise 3-4

Create the function `make-float` that forces the result of any math operation to return a floating-point value. Note that the value returned from a math operation is always a number.

```
(defun make-float (x)
   (+ 0.0 x))
⇒    MAKE-FLOAT
```

## Exercise 3-5

Which of the following are characters?

```
#\a            character
'a             symbol
(#\a)          a list with a single element, the character #\a
#\tab          character
#\control      not a character
#\meta-A       character
'meta-a        symbol
```

## Exercise 3-6

What symbol is specified by the following?

| abc |          abc
'abc            ABC
| #\a |          #\a
#\a             character #\a
555-1212        555-1212
555             number 555
(ab)            list with element AB
| (ab) |         (ab)

## Exercise 3-7

Which of the following are lists, atoms, or neither?

```
a           atom.
nil         atom, list.
(a b)       list, a and b are atoms.
(a (b c))   list, a is an atom, (b c) is a list, b and c are atoms.
()          the empty list.
((((A))))   list, a is an atom.
(#\a)       list, the character #\a is an atom.
(a (b)      neither, there is an unbalanced number of parentheses.
(1 2 a b)   list, 1, 2, a, and b are atoms.
```

## Exercise 3-8

**1.** Write a function that determines if an object is a number or a character.

```
(defun num-char (x)
  (or (numberp x)
      (characterp x)))

(num-char 'a)
⇒    NIL

(num-char 4)
⇒    T

(num-char #\c)
⇒    T
```

**2.** If the number is zero, the function should return the symbol 'zero.

```
(defun num-char (x)
  (or (and (numberp x) (zerop x) 'zero)
      (numberp x)
      (characterp x)))
⇒    NUM-CHAR
```

```
(num-char 0)
⇒    ZERO


(num-char 4)
⇒    T


(num-char #\a)
⇒    T
```

**3.** If the argument is a character, return that character.

```
(defun num-char (x)
  (or (and (numberp x) (zerop x) 'zero)
      (numberp x)
      (and (characterp x) x)))
⇒    NUM-CHAR


(num-char #\a)
⇒    #\a


(num-char 8)
⇒    T


(num-char #\0)
⇒    #\0
```

**4.** If the argument is not a number or a character, return a message that says so.

```
(defun num-char (x)
  (or (and (numberp x) (zerop x) 'zero)
      (numberp x)
      (and (characterp x) x)
      'the-argument-is-not-a-number-or-character))
⇒    NUM-CHAR


(num-char #\a)
⇒    #\a


(num-char 'a)
⇒    THE-ARGUMENT-IS-NOT-A-NUMBER-OR-CHARACTER


(num-char 0)
⇒    ZERO
```

# CHAPTER 4

**Exercise 4-1**

Which of the following are legal names for variables?

```
a99          symbol
open         symbol
#\a          character
99           fixnum
a-5          symbol
12s5         short floating point number
start-time   symbol
| 99 |       symbol
&other       symbol
H*@$         symbol
```

**Exercise 4-2**

What do the following lambda expressions return?

1. ```
   ((lambda (x &optional y &rest z &key a)
      (list x y z a))
      1 2 :a 3)
   ⇒    (1 2 (:A 3) 3)
   ```

2. ```
   ((lambda (&optional (a 1) &key r)
      (list a r))
      :r 'r)
   ⇒    !!!!! Error: No value for keyword R
   ```

3. ```
   ((lambda (&optional (a 1) &key r)
      (list a r))
      12 :r 'r)
   ⇒    (12 R)
   ```

4. ```
   ((lambda (&rest a &key (m 'def x) ((:q n)))
      (list a m x n))
      :m 12 :q 5)
   ⇒    ((:M 12 :Q 5) 12 T 5)
   ```

5. ```
   ((lambda (&rest a &key (m 'def x) ((:q n)))
      (list a m x n)))
   ⇒    (NIL DEF NIL NIL)
   ```
   ```

**6.** ((lambda (&optional a (b 'c) (d 1 r))
   (list a b d r)))
 ⇒   (NIL C 1 NIL)


**7.** ((lambda (&optional a (b 'c) (d 1 r))
   (list a b d r))
   1 2)
 ⇒   (1 2 1 NIL)


**8.** ((lambda (&optional a (b 'c) (d 1 r))
   (list a b d r))
   'a 'b 'c)
 ⇒   (A B C T)


Write a lambda list that takes the following arguments and prints them.

**9.** Three arguments are required.  One additional argument can be supplied.

```
((lambda (a b c &optional d)
   (list a b c d)))
```

**10.** One argument is required.  The keyword test is optional; its value is held by the variable x.

```
((lambda (a &key ((:test x)))
   (list a x)))
```

**11.** The variable x holds a list of all arguments passed.  Three keywords can be supplied. Their default values are 1, 2, and 3.

```
((lambda (&rest x &key (a 1)(b 2)(c 3))
   (list x a b c)))
```

**Exercise 4-3**

Use the following functions to answer the questions.

```
(setq a 1 b 2 c 3)
⇒    3

(defun ex1 ()
  (print b)
  (ex3))
⇒    EX1
```

```
(defun ex2 (b)
  (declare (special b))
  (ex1)
  (ex3)
  (print b))
⇒    EX2


(defun ex3 ()
  (print c))
⇒    EX3
```

**1.** Given the functions above, what are the printed values?

```
(ex3)
⇒    3          ; printed by ex3
     3          ; returned by ex3


(ex2 a)
⇒    1          ; printed by ex1
     3          ; printed by ex3
     3          ; printed by ex3
     1          ; printed by ex2
     1          ; returned by ex2


(ex1)
⇒    2          ; printed by ex1
     3          ; printed by ex3
     3          ; returned by ex1
```

**2.** In ex3, what does c refer to?

c is value set by setq.

**3.** In ex1, what does b refer to?

b is either the value set by setq, or the value sent to ex2.

**4.** If ex1 is changed,

```
(defun ex1 ()
  (print b)
  (setq b 5)
  (ex3))
⇒    EX1
```

what is the printed result of the following?

```
(ex2 a)
⇒    1              ; printed by ex1
     3              ; printed by ex3
     3              ; printed by ex3
     5              ; printed by ex2
     5              ; returned by ex2
```

**5.** What is the value of b outside the functions?

```
b
⇒    2
```

**6.** Why?

The setq function in ex1 only changes the special value of b. It changes the value of b in ex1, and ex2. As soon as ex2 has completed execution, the value of b is returned to its previously held value.


# CHAPTER 6

### Exercise 6-1

Write a function that takes two arguments, a number, and a list.

**1.** If the number argument was not passed a number value, exit the function with an appropriate message.
**2.** Within a block, cons the square of the number to the list.
**3.** If the cdr of the list is not a list, exit from the block and return the list.
**4.** Add the length of the list to the front of the list and return the list.

```
(defun blocking (a-num a-list)
  (if (not (subtypep (type-of a-num) 'number))
      (return-from two "not a number"))
  (block sub-two
    (setq a-list (cons (* a-num a-num) a-list))
    (if (not (listp (cdr a-list))) (return-from sub-two a-list))
    (cons (length a-list) a-list)))
⇒    BLOCKING

(two 1 nil)
⇒    (1 1)

(two 3 '(a b c))
⇒    (4 9 A B C)

(two 'a 'b)
⇒    "not a number"
```

```
(two 5 'b)
⇒    (25 . B)
```

## Exercise 6-2

```
(defun throwing (flag)
  (if flag (throw global-value "end of throw"))
  (print "exiting the throw"))
⇒    THROWING


(defun catching (flag-1)
  (print "where am i")
  (catch global-value
    (print "catch the global-value")
    (catch 'symbol
      (print "catch the symbol")
      (throwing flag-1)
      (print "exit symbol"))
    (print "exit global"))
  (print "leaving it all behind"))
⇒    CATCHING


(setq global-value 'name)
⇒    NAME
```

**1.** Using the above functions, what are the results of the following?

```
(catching t)
⇒    "where am i"
      "catch the global-value"
      "catch the symbol"
      "leaving it all behind"
      "leaving it all behind"


(catching nil)
⇒    "where am i"
      "catch the global-value"
      "catch the symbol"
      "exiting the throw"
      "exit symbol"
      "exit global"
      "leaving it all behind"
      "leaving it all behind"
```

```
(catching 'symbol)
⇒    "where am i"
     "catch the global-value"
     "catch the symbol"
     "leaving it all behind"
     "leaving it all behind"
```

**2.** If you change the value of `global-value` to `symbol`, does it change the results? Why?
The result changes because the throw now throws to the first catch it finds with a tag
of `'symbol`.

```
(setq global-value 'symbol)
⇒    SYMBOL

(catching t)
⇒    "where am i"
     "catch the global-value"
     "catch the symbol"
     "exit global"                        ; this is the change.
     "leaving it all behind"
     "leaving it all behind"

(catching nil)
⇒    "where am i"
     "catch the global-value"
     "catch the symbol"
     "exiting the throw"
     "exit symbol"
     "exit global"
     "leaving it all behind"
     "leaving it all behind"
```

## Exercise 6-3

Write a function that takes two numeric arguments. If the first argument is 1, return the
second argument. If the first argument is 2, return the square of the second argument. If
the first argument is 3, return the cube of the argument. If the first argument is not 1, 2, or
3, return an error message.

```
(defun multiply (ex arg)
  (tagbody
    (if (eq ex 1) (go 1))
    (if (eq ex 2) (go 2))
    (if (eq ex 3) (go 3)
        (return-from multiply "first argument is not 1, 2 or 3"))
  1
    (return-from multiply arg)
```

```
        2
          (return-from multiply (* arg arg))
        3
          (return-from multiply (* arg arg arg)))))
⇒       MULTIPLY

(multiply 1 2)
⇒       2

(multiply 2 2)
⇒       4

(multiply 3 2)
⇒       8

(multiply 4 2)
⇒       "first argument is not 1, 2 or 3"
```

# CHAPTER 7

**Exercise 7-1**

1. Create three lists: class1, class2, and class3.  Each class has students.  Some students are in one class, some are in two classes and some are in three classes.

```
(setq class1 '(larry moe curley sue))
⇒       (LARRY MOE CURLEY SUE)

(setq class2 '(sue mary jane))
⇒       (SUE MARY JANE)

(setq class3 '(tom jerry karen sue curley mary))
⇒       (TOM JERRY KAREN SUE CURLEY MARY)
```

2. Create a function that determines if a student is in all three classes.

```
(defun three-class (name)
  (and (member name class1)
       (member name class2)
       (member name class2)))
⇒       THREE-CLASS

(three-class 'sue)
⇒       (SUE MARY JANE)
```

```
(three-class 'tom)
⇒    NIL

(three-class 'me)
⇒    NIL
```

**3.** Create a function that determines if a student is in exactly two classes.

```
(defun two-class (name)
  (and (not (three-class name))
       (or (and (member name class1)
                (member name class2))
           (and (member name class2)
                (member name class3))
           (and (member name class3)
                (member name class1)))))
⇒    TWO-CLASS

(two-class 'mary)
⇒    (MARY)

(two-class 'sue)
⇒    NIL

(two-class 'curley)
⇒    (CURLEY SUE)

(two-class 'me)
⇒    NIL
```

**4.** Create a function that determines if a student is in exactly one class.

```
(defun one-class (name)
  (and (not (two-class name))
       (not (three-class name))
       (or (member name class1)
           (member name class2)
           (member name class3))))
⇒    ONE-CLASS

(one-class 'sue)
⇒    NIL

(one-class 'tom)
⇒    (TOM JERRY KAREN SUE CURLEY MARY)
```

```
(one-class 'mary)
⇒    NIL


(one-class 'me)
⇒    NIL
```

**5.** Create a function that determines if a student is in no class.

```
(defun no-class (name)
  (not (or (member name class1)
           (member name class2)
           (member name class3))))
⇒    NO-CLASS

(no-class 'me)
⇒    T


(no-class 'mary)
⇒    NIL
```

### Exercise 7-2

Create a function that when given a name returns the number of classes in which the student appears.

```
(defun num-classes (name)
  (if (no-class name) (list name 'is 'in 'no 'classes)
    (if (one-class name) (list name 'is 'in 'one 'class)
      (if (two-class name) (list name 'is 'in 'two 'classes)
        (if (three-class name) (list name 'is 'in 'three 'classes))))))
⇒    NUM-CLASSES

(num-classes 'mary)
⇒    (MARY IS IN TWO CLASSES)

(num-classes 'sue)
⇒    (SUE IS IN THREE CLASSES)

(num-classes 'tom)
⇒    (TOM IS IN ONE CLASS)

(num-classes 'me)
⇒    (ME IS IN NO CLASSES)
```

### Exercise 7-3

Use cond to rewrite the num-classes function.

```
(defun num-cl (name)
  (cond ((no-class name) (list name 'has 'no 'classes))
        ((one-class name) (list name 'has 'one 'class))
        ((two-class name) (list name 'has 'two 'classes))
        (t (list name 'has 'three 'classes))))
⇒    NUM-CL


(num-cl 'sue)
⇒    (SUE HAS THREE CLASSES)


(num-cl 'mary)
⇒    (MARY HAS TWO CLASSES)


(num-cl 'tom)
⇒    (TOM HAS ONE CLASS)


(num-cl 'me)
⇒    (ME HAS NO CLASSES)
```

### Exercise 7-4

Write a function of one argument. The argument is the name of a class. The function returns a list of all the students in that class.

```
(defun students (class-name)
  (case class-name
    (class1 (list class1))
    (class2 (list class2))
    (class3 (list class3))
    (otherwise 'not-a-class)))
⇒    STUDENTS


(students 'class1)
⇒    ((LARRY MOE CURLEY SUE))


(students 'class3)
⇒    ((TOM JERRY KAREN SUE CURLEY MARY))


(students 'hello)
⇒    NOT-A-CLASS
```

### Exercise 7-5

The following function sends a form letter to students:

```
(defun form1 (name reason)
  (cond ((equal reason 'register)
           (format t "Dear ~a, ~% It has come to our attention that
             you have not registered for classes.~%" name))
          ((equal reason 'too-many)
           (format t "Dear ~a, ~% You are registered for too many
             classes.  Please get the dean's signature." name))))
```

**1.** If a student is in no class, write the student a letter. Tell the student that he or she must register for a class. Use when to test for this case.

```
(defun letters (name)
    (when (equal 'no (third (num-classes name)))
    (form1 name 'register)))
⇒   LETTERS
```

**2.** If a student is in more than two classes, write the student a letter. Tell the student they must get the dean's signature for having too many classes. Use unless for this.

```
(defun letters (name)
  (when (equal 'no (third (num-cl name)))
    (form1 name 'register))
  (unless (not (equal 'three (third (num-cl name))))
    (form1 name 'too-many)))
⇒    LETTERS
```

```
(letters 'larry)
⇒    NIL
```

```
(letters 'me)
⇒    Dear ME,
     It has come to our attention that
            you have not registered for classes.
     NIL
```

```
(letters 'sue)
⇒    Dear SUE,
     You are registered for too many
            classes.  Please get the dean's signature.
     NIL
```

# CHAPTER 8

### Exercise 8-1

Write a function that prints each element of a list.

```
(defun print-list (a-list)
  (loop
   (print (car a-list))
   (setq a-list (cdr a-list))
   (if (not a-list) (return a-list))))
⇒    PRINT-LIST

(print-list '(a b c))
⇒    A
     B
     C
     NIL

(print-list '(a (b c)))
⇒    A
     (B C)
     NIL
```

## Exercise 8-2

**1.** Write a function using do that builds a list. The function takes one argument, which specifies the number of x's to put in the list.

```
(defun build1 (how-many)
  (do ((count 1 (1+ count)) (a-list nil (cons 'x a-list)))
    ((> count how-many) a-list)))
⇒    BUILD1

(build1 3)
⇒    (X X X)

(build1 1)
⇒    X)

(build1 0)
⇒    NIL
```

**2.** Write the same function using dotimes.

```
(defun build2 (how-many)
  (let ((a-list nil))
    (dotimes (count how-many a-list)
      (setq a-list (cons 'x a-list)))))
⇒    BUILD2

(build2 3)
⇒    (X X X)
```

```
(build2 1)
⇒    (X)


(build2 0)
⇒    NIL
```

**3.** Write a function that takes a list of numbers. Each number specifies the number of x's in an element of the list being built. For example,

```
(build-it '(1 2 3))
⇒    ((x)(x x)(x x x))
```

Use `dolist` to create this function.

```
(defun round3 (x)
  (let ((result '()))
    (dotimes (n (length x) result)
      (setq result (cons (car (nthcdr n x)) result)))))
⇒    ROUND3


(defun build-it (arg-list)
  (let ((result '()))
    (dolist (a (round3 arg-list) result)
      (setq result (cons (build1 a) result)))))
⇒    BUILD-IT


(build-it '(1 2 3))
⇒    ((X) (X X) (X X X))


(build-it '(4 1))
⇒    ((X X X X) (X))


(build-it '(1))
⇒    ((X))


(build-it '(0))
⇒    (NIL)
```

## Exercise 8-3

**1.** Write a function that `applys` the minus function (−) to every element in a list of numbers.

```
(defun minus (a-list)
  (apply #'- a-list))
⇒    MINUS
```

```
(minus '(1 2 3))
⇒    -4
```

**2.** Write a function that returns a list where the minus function (−) has been applied to each element. Use `mapcar`.

```
(defun minus-list (a-list)
  (mapcar #'- a-list))
⇒    MINUS-LIST

(minus-list '(1 2 3))
⇒    (-1 -2 -3)
```

**3.** Write a function that returns a list where every number in the list is negative. Use `mapcar`.

```
(defun all-negative (a-list)
  (mapcar #'(lambda (x)
              (if (plusp x) (- x) x)) a-list))
⇒    ALL-NEGATIVE

(all-negative '(1 0 -3))
⇒    (-1 0 -3)
```

**4.** Use `maplist` to rewrite the round function. This function will reverse the elements in a list.

```
(defun round-4 (a-list)
  (let ((result nil))
    (car (last (maplist #'(lambda (x)
                (setq result (cons (car x) result)))
            a-list)))))
⇒    ROUND-4

(round-4 '(a b c))
⇒    (C B A)

(round-4 '(a (b c) d e))
⇒    (E D (B C) A)
```

**5.** Write a function that, given a list of numbers, returns their average.

```
(defun average (a-list)
  (/ (apply #'+ a-list) (length a-list)))
⇒    AVERAGE
```

```
(average '(2 4 6))
⇒    4

(average '(7 5 3 1))
⇒    4

(average '(2.3 8.1 0))
⇒    3.4666666666666663
```

# CHAPTER 9

### Exercise 9-1

1. Write a recursive countdown function. Given the value 5, the function should print:

```
5
4
3
2
1
"lift off"

(defun count-down (x)
  (cond ((zerop x) "lift off")
        (t (print x)
           (count-down (- x 1)))))
⇒    COUNT-DOWN

(count-down 5)
⇒    5
      4
      3
      2
      1
      "lift off"
```

2. Write a function that puts the numbers into a list rather than printing them.

```
(defun count-list (x)
  (cond ((zerop x) '(0))
        (t (cons x (count-list (- x 1))))))
⇒    COUNT-LIST

(count-list 5)
⇒    (5 4 3 2 1 0)
```

**Exercise 9-2**

**1.** Rewrite the count-list program using the linear-iterative method.

```
(defun count-list (x)
  (cl x nil 0))
⇒    COUNT-LIST

(defun cl (x c-list counter)
  (cond ((equal counter x) (cons counter c-list))
        (t (cl x (cons counter  c-list) (+ counter 1)))))
⇒    CL

(count-list 4)
⇒    .(4 3 2 1 0)
```

**2.** Write a function that reverses the order of elements in a list.

```
(defun rev-list (a-list)
  (rev-round a-list nil))
⇒    REV-LIST

(defun rev-round (a-list result-list)
  (cond ((null a-list) result-list)
        (t (rev-round (cdr a-list)(cons (car a-list) result-list)))))
⇒    REV-ROUND

(rev-list '(a b c))
⇒    (C B A)

(rev-list '(a (b c) d))
⇒    (D (B C) A)
```

**Exercise 9-3**

**1.** The `length` function returns the number of elements in a list.  Write a recursive function that returns the number of atoms in a list.

```
(defun counter (a-list)
  (cond ((null a-list) 0)
        ((atom a-list) 1)
        (t (+ (counter (car a-list))
              (counter (cdr a-list))))))
⇒    COUNTER

(counter '(a b c))
⇒    3
```

```
(counter '(a (b c) d))
⇒    4
```

**2.** Rewrite the rev-list function so that elements within a sublist are reversed. Given the list ' (a (b c) d), the function should return ' (d (c b) a). Using a calling function and subfunction, as in linear-iterative recursion, helps you solve this problem.

```
(defun rev-list (a-list)
  (rev-round a-list nil))
⇒    REV-LIST
```

```
(defun rev-round (a-list result-list)
  (cond ((null a-list) result-list)
        (t (rev-round (cdr a-list)
                      (cons (if (atom (car a-list)) (car a-list)
                                (rev-round (car a-list) '()))
                            result-list)))))
⇒    REV-ROUND
```

```
(rev-list '(a b c))
⇒    (C B A)
```

```
(rev-list '(a (b c) d))
⇒    (D (C B) A)
```

```
(rev-list '(a (b (c d) e)(f g (h i))))
⇒    (((I H) G F) (E (D C) B) A)
```

# CHAPTER 10

## Exercise 10-1

Write the car and cdr of each of the following lists:

**1.** (a b c)

```
car = a
cdr = (b c)
```

**2.** (a . b)

```
car = a
cdr = b
```

**3.** (a  (b  c))

```
car = a
cdr = ((b  c))
```

**4.** ((a)  b  c)

```
car = (a)
cdr = (b  c)
```

**5.** ((a  b) (c  d))

```
car = (a  b)
cdr = ((c  d))
```

Write the car and cdr of each list and sublist.  For example,

```
(a  b  c)

car of (a  b  c) = a
cdr of (a  b  c) = (b  c)

car of (b  c) = b
cdr of (b  c) = (c)

car of (c) = c
cdr of (c) = nil
```

**6.** ((a  b) (c  d))

```
car of ((a  b) (c  d)) = (a  b)
cdr of ((a  b) (c  d)) = (c  d)

car of (a  b) = a
cdr of (a  b) = (b)

car of (b) = b
cdr of (b) = nil

car of (c  d) = c
cdr of (c  d) = (d)

car of (d) = d
cdr of (d) = nil
```

**7.** (a  (b  (c)))

```
car of (a (b (c))) = a
cdr of (a (b (c))) = ((b (c)))

car of ((b (c))) = (b (c))
cdr of ((b (c))) = nil

car of (b (c)) = b
cdr of (b (c)) = ((c))

car of ((c)) = (c)
cdr of ((c)) = nil

car of (c) = c
cdr of (c) = nil
```

Use the box and pointer notation for the following lists.

**8.** (a b c)

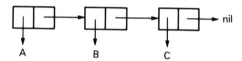

**9.** (a (b))

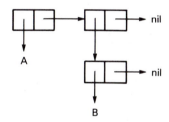

**10.** ((a) b)

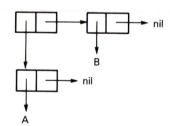

**11.** ((a)(b))

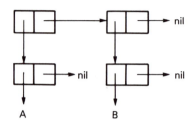

**12.** (a (b (c)))

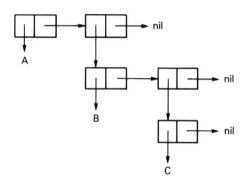

**13.** ((a (b))((d) e (f (g))))

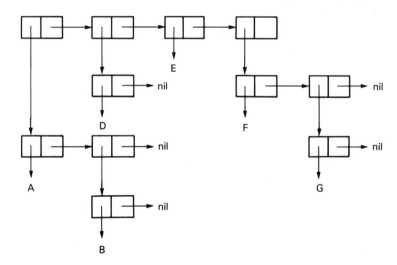

**14.** ( ( (1) 2) 3)

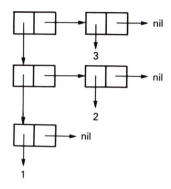

**15.** (a b . c)

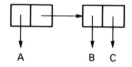

### Exercise 10-2

Retrieve each word from the fox lists as was done for the first four words in the previous text example.

```
(car (car (cdr (cdr fox))))
⇒    JUMPED

(car (car (cdr (car (cdr (cdr fox))))))
⇒    OVER

(car (cdr (car (cdr (car (cdr (cdr fox)))))))
⇒    THE

(car (cdr (cdr (car (cdr (cdr fox))))))
⇒    LAZY

(car (car (cdr (cdr (cdr (car (cdr (cdr fox)))))))))
⇒    DOG
```

### Exercise 10-3

Draw a cons cell showing the results of the following functions.

**1.** `(setq a '(1 2 3))`

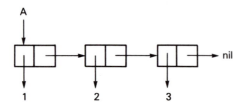

**2.** `(setq b a)`

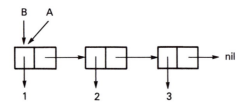

**3.** `(setq c (cons a b))`

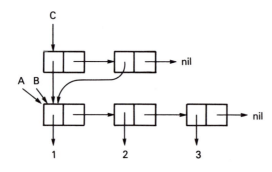

**4.** `(setq x '(a b c))`

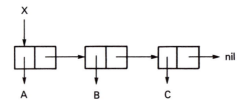

**5.** `(setq y (cdr x))`

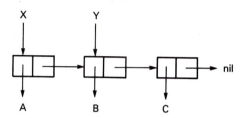

**6.** `(setf (car y) 'z)`

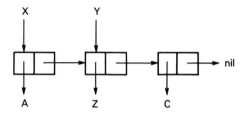

**7.** Write a function that returns the eleventh element of a list.

```
(defun eleventh (a-list)
  (car (nthcdr 10 a-list)))
⇒    ELEVENTH

(eleventh '(1 2 3 4 5 6 7 8 9 10 11 12 13))
⇒    11
```

**8.** If a telephone directory were in a list, each name, address, and phone number would be a sublist.

```
(setq directory '((john_smith 12345_Euclid 555-1212)
                  (sue_jones 1000_Chapman 555-1000)))
⇒    ((JOHN_SMITH \12345_EUCLID \555-1212)
       (SUE_JONES \1000_CHAPMAN \555-1000))
```

Write three functions (name, address, and phone) that take a single list and return one component of that list.

```
(defun name (a-list)
  (car a-list))
⇒    NAME
```

```
(defun address (a-list)
  (cadr a-list))
⇒    ADDRESS

(defun phone (a-list)
  (caddr a-list))
⇒    PHONE

(name (car directory))
⇒    JOHN_SMITH

(phone (car directory))
⇒    \555-1212
```

9. Why should these functions be created rather than using cars and cdrs to retrieve the components directly?

   Using indirection in this way allows other functions to not care how the list structure is built. These functions can call name or phone. They do not have to know that the name is the first element of a list and the phone is the third. At a later time, if the list structure is changed, only the small functions (name, address, and phone) have to change. All the functions that use these three functions do not have to change just because the data structure changed.

**Exercise 10-4**

Given:

```
(setq x '(a b c))
⇒    (A B C)

(setq y '(1 2 3))
⇒    (1 2 3)
```

what do the following functions return?

1. ```
   (setq m (append x y))
   ⇒    (A B C 1 2 3)
   ```

2. ```
   (setf (car m) 'p)
   ⇒    P

   x
   ⇒    (A B C)

   (setf (fifth m) 5)
   ⇒    5
   ```

```
  y
  ⇒    (1 5 3)
```

**3.** `(list 'x 'y)`
   ⇒    `(X Y)`

**4.** `(setq z (list x y))`
   ⇒    `((A B C) (1 5 3))`

**5.** `(list* x y)`
   ⇒    `((A B C) 1 5 3)`

**6.** `(setf (caar z) '(x y z))`
   ⇒    `(X Y Z)`

```
  x
  ⇒    ((X Y Z) B C)
```

## Exercise 10-5

Given:

```
(setq a '(1 2 (3 4 (5 6))))
⇒    (1 2 (3 4 (5 6)))

(setq b (copy-tree a))
⇒    (1 2 (3 4 (5 6)))

(setq c (copy-list a))
⇒    (1 2 (3 4 (5 6)))

(setq d (copy-alist a))
⇒    (1 2 (3 4 (5 6)))
```

what do the following functions return?

**1.** `(setf (car b) 'q)`
   ⇒    `Q`

```
a
⇒    (Q 2 (3 4 (5 6)))

(setf (caddr b) 'z)
⇒    Z

a
⇒    (1 2 (3 4 (5 6)))
```

**2.** `(setf (car c) 'q)`
   ⇒    `Q`

```
a
⇒    (1 2 (3 4 (5 6)))


(setf (caaddr c) 'w)
⇒    W


a
⇒    (1 2 (W 4 (5 6)))
```

**3.** (setf (car d) 'r)
```
⇒    R


a
⇒    (1 2 (W 4 (5 6)))


(setf (caadr (cdaddr d)) 't)
⇒    T


a
⇒    (1 2 (W 4 (T 6)))
```

### Exercise 10-6

**1.** Write your own adjoin function. Call it my-adjoin. It should produce
the same results as adjoin.

```
(defun my-adjoin (item a-list &key (test #'eql t-flag)
                                   (test-not nil n-flag)
                                   (key #'identity k-flag))
     (cond (n-flag (if (member item a-list :test-not test-not
                                          :key key)
                     (return-from my-adjoin a-list)
                     (return-from my-adjoin (cons item a-list))))
           (t (if (member item a-list :test test :key key)
                (return-from my-adjoin a-list)
                (return-from my-adjoin (cons item a-list)))))))
⇒    MY-ADJOIN

(my-adjoin 'a '(b c))
⇒    (A B C)

(my-adjoin 'a '(a b c))
⇒    (A B C)

(my-adjoin 'a '(a a a) :test-not #'equal)
⇒    (A A A A)

(my-adjoin '(a b) '((b c)(d e)) :key #'car)
⇒    ((A B) (B C) (D E))
```

**2.** Test your function to see that it returns the same list that `adjoin` returns. `adjoin` uses the argument list.

```
(setq a '(x y z))
⇒    (X Y Z)

(setq b (adjoin 'q a))
⇒    (Q X Y Z)

(setf (cadr b) 'r)
⇒    R

a
⇒    (R Y Z)

(setq a '(x y z))
⇒    (X Y Z)

(setq b (my-adjoin 'q a))
⇒    (Q X Y Z)

(setf (cadr b) 'r)
⇒    R

a
⇒    (R Y Z)
```

**3.** Modify your function so that it returns a new list with the item added, rather than adding the item to the list.

```
(defun my-adjoin2 (item a-list &key (test #'eql t-flag)
                                    (test-not nil n-flag)
                                    (key #'identity k-flag))
  (cond (n-flag (if (member item a-list :test-not test-not
                                        :key key)
                    (return-from my-adjoin2 (copy-tree a-list))
                    (return-from my-adjoin2
                      (cons item (copy-tree a-list)))))
        (t (if (member item a-list :test test :key key)
               (return-from my-adjoin2 (copy-tree a-list))
               (return-from my-adjoin2
                 (cons item (copy-tree a-list)))))))
⇒    MY-ADJOIN2

(setq a '(x y z))
⇒    (X Y Z)

(setq b (my-adjoin2 'q a))
⇒    (Q X Y Z)
```

```
(setf (cadr b) 'r)
⇒    R


a
⇒    (X Y Z)
```

## Exercise 10-7

Write a function that substitutes the symbol 'zero for each element that is equal to zero. Because zero is a number, make sure that the function that tests the element is given a number and not a list.

```
(defun nil-for-zero (a-list)
  (subst-if '(zero) '(lambda (x) (when (numberp x) (zerop x)))
           a-list
            :key '(lambda (x) (if (atom x) x (car x))))))
⇒    NIL-FOR-ZERO

(nil-for-zero '(1 s (5 0) k 0))
⇒    (1 S (5 ZERO) K ZERO)
```

## Exercise 10-8

**1.** Create three association lists. One associates numerals with ordinal numbers, one English with German, and one German with Spanish.

Numerals are (1 2 3 4 5 6 7 8 9 10).
Ordinal numbers are (one two three four five six seven eight nine ten).
German numbers are (ein zwei drei vier funf sechs sieben acht neun zehn).
Spanish numbers are (uno dos tres cuatro cinco seis siete ocho nueve diez).

The association lists will look like

```
((1 . one)(2 . two))
((one . ein)(two . zwei))
((ein . uno)(zwei . dos))

(setq numerals '(1 2 3 4 5 6 7 8 9 10))
⇒    (1 2 3 4 5 6 7 8 9 10)

(setq ordinals '(one two three four five six seven eight nine ten))
⇒    (ONE TWO THREE FOUR FIVE SIX SEVEN EIGHT NINE TEN)

(setq german '(ein zwei drei vier funf sechs sieben acht neun zehn))
⇒    (EIN ZWEI DREI VIER FUNF SECHS SIEBEN ACHT NEUN ZEHN)
```

```
(setq spanish '(uno dos tres cuatro cinco seis siete ocho nueve diez))
⇒    (UNO DOS TRES CUATRO CINCO SEIS SIETE OCHO NUEVE DIEZ)

(setq num-ord (pairlis numerals ordinals))
⇒    ((10 . TEN) (9 . NINE) (8 . EIGHT) (7 . SEVEN) (6 . SIX)
      (5 . FIVE) (4 . FOUR) (3 . THREE) (2 . TWO) (1 . ONE))

(setq ord-ger (pairlis ordinals german))
⇒    ((TEN . ZEHN) (NINE . NEUN) (EIGHT . ACHT) (SEVEN . SIEBEN)
      (SIX . SECHS) (FIVE . FUNF) (FOUR . VIER) (THREE . DREI)
      (TWO . ZWEI) (ONE . EIN))

(setq ger-span (pairlis german spanish))
⇒    ((ZEHN . DIEZ) (NEUN . NUEVE) (ACHT . OCHO) (SIEBEN . SIETE)
      (SECHS . SEIS) (FUNF . CINCO) (VIER . CUATRO) (DREI . TRES)
      (ZWEI . DOS) (EIN . UNO))
```

**2.** Write three functions (get-english, get-german, and get-spanish) that take a number and return the name in the appropriate language.

```
(defun get-english (number)
  (cdr (assoc number num-ord)))
⇒    GET-ENGLISH

(get-english 3)
⇒    THREE

(defun get-german (number)
  (cdr (assoc (get-english number) ord-ger)))
⇒    GET-GERMAN

(get-german 3)
⇒    DREI

(defun get-spanish (number)
  (cdr (assoc (get-german number) ger-span)))
⇒    GET-SPANISH

(get-spanish 3)
⇒    TRES
```

**3.** Write a function that, given a numeral and a symbol, either 'English, 'German, or 'Spanish, returns the name of the number in the appropriate language.

Given 1 and 'spanish, the function returns uno.

```
(defun get-value (number language)
  (cond ((equal language 'english) (get-english number))
        ((equal language 'german) (get-german number))
        ((equal language 'spanish) (get-spanish number))
        (t 'error)))
⇒    GET-VALUE

(get-value 3 'german)
⇒    DREI

(get-value 1 'english)
⇒    ONE

(get-value 10 'spanish)
⇒    DIEZ

(get-value 11 'french)
⇒    ERROR
```

**4.** Write three functions that, given a name of a number in a language, return the numeral for the name.

Given drei, returns 3.

```
(defun return-english (number)
  (car (rassoc number num-ord)))
⇒   RETURN-ENGLISH

(return-english 'four)
⇒   4

(defun return-german (number)
  (return-english (car (rassoc number ord-ger))))
⇒   RETURN-GERMAN

(return-german 'ein)
⇒   1

(defun return-spanish (number)
  (return-german (car (rassoc number ger-span))))
⇒   RETURN-SPANISH

(return-spanish 'uno)
⇒   1
```

**5.** Write a function that, given the name of a number in one of the three languages and a symbol, returns the numeral.

```
(defun get-number (number language)
  (cond ((equal language 'english) (return-english number))
        ((equal language 'german) (return-german number)
        ((equal language 'spanish) (return-spanish number)))))
⇒    GET-NUMBER

(get-number 'uno 'spanish)
⇒    1
```

**6.** Write a function that translates German numbers to Spanish.

```
(defun german-to-spanish (number)
  (cdr (assoc number ger-span)))
⇒    GERMAN-TO-SPANISH

(german-to-spanish 'ein)
⇒    UNO
```

# CHAPTER 11

### Exercise 11-1

Given the equation $0 = ax^2 + bx + c$, the value of x is
$$(-b \pm \sqrt{(b^2 - 4ac)}) / 2a$$
Write a function that, given the values of a, b, and c, returns a list of the possible values of x.

```
(defun quadratic (a b c)
  (if (not (zerop a))
    (list (/ (+ (- b) (sqrt (- (* b b) (* 4 a c)))) (* 2 a))
          (/ (- (- b) (sqrt (- (* b b) (* 4 a c)))) (* 2 a)))
    (if (not (zerop b))
      (list (/ (- c) b))
      (list c))))
⇒    QUADRATIC

(quadratic 1 -5 5)
⇒    (3.618033988749895 1.3819660112501053)

(quadratic 1 -9/2 2)
⇒    (4.0 0.5)
```

### Exercise 11-2

**1.** Write a function that picks a random number between 1 and 10 inclusively.

```
(defun 1-to-10 ()
  (1+ (random 10)))
⇒   \1-TO-10

(1-to-10)
⇒   6

(1-to-10)
⇒   4

(1-to-10)
⇒   1

(1-to-10)
⇒   2

(1-to-10)
⇒   7

(1-to-10)
⇒   2

(1-to-10)
⇒   10
```

**2.** Write a function that picks a random number between two given numbers.

```
(defun a-to-b (a b)
  (+ a (random (- b a))))

(a-to-b 0 1)
⇒   0

(a-to-b 3 6)
⇒   3

(a-to-b 3 6)
⇒   5
```

# CHAPTER 12

### Exercise 12-1

Specify the type of array for each of the following:

**1.** `#2A((a) (b) (c))`
A two-dimensional array with elements of symbols.

**2.** `#((1 2)(2 3)(4 5))`
A vector with lists as elements.

**3.** `"abc123"`
A string.

**4.** `#*10010`
A bit vector.

**5.** `#1A(#\a #\b #\c)`
A one-dimensional array with elements of characters.

**6.** `#1A(#*1111 #*0000 a b c (a b c) "abc" "123")`
A one-dimensional array with elements of vectors, symbols, lists, and strings.

## Exercise 12-2

**1.** Create a two-by-five array. Add some contents to the array.

```
(make-array '(2 5) :initial-contents '((1 2 3 4 5)(1 2 3 4 5)))
⇒    #2A((1 2 3 4 5) (1 2 3 4 5))
```

**2.** Create a string array that has five elements.

```
(make-array 5 :element-type 'string-char :initial-element #\space)
⇒    "     "

(string "abcde")
⇒    "abcde"
```

**3.** Create a string array that has a fill pointer. The array can have up to 10 elements. Initially, there are no elements.

```
(make-array 10 :fill-pointer 0 :element-type 'string-char)
⇒    #()
```

**4.** Create a bit vector that has five elements, all of which are zero.

```
(make-array 5 :element-type 'bit :initial-element 0)
⇒    #*00000
```

**5.** Create a vector of eight characters. The element-type is anything.

```
(make-array 8 :initial-contents '(#\a #\b #\c #\d #\e #\f #\g #\h))
⇒    #(#\a #\b #\c #\d #\e #\f #\g #\h)
```

## Exercise 12-3

Write the function `simple-array-p` that determines if an object is a simple array. A *simple array* is one that has no fill pointer, is not adjustable, and is not displaced.

```
(defun simple-array-p (obj)
  (and (typep obj 'simple-array)
       (not (array-has-fill-pointer-p obj))
       (not (adjustable-array-p obj))
       (equal (array-element-type obj) t)))
⇒    SIMPLE-ARRAY-P


(setq a '#2A((1 2 3)(4 5 6)))
⇒    #2A((1 2 3) (4 5 6))


(simple-array-p a)
⇒    T


(simple-array-p "abc")
⇒    NIL


(simple-array-p 5)
⇒    NIL


(simple-array-p (make-array 2))
⇒    T


(simple-array-p '#(1 2 3))
⇒    T
```

### Exercise 12-4

Given the following array, answer the questions that follow.

```
(setq a (make-array '(4 2 3) :initial-contents '(((1 2 3)(4 5 6))
                                                  ((7 8 9)(a b c))
                                                  ((d e f)(g h i))
                                                  ((j k l)(m n o)))
                   :adjustable t))
⇒    #3A(((1 2 3) (4 5 6)) ((7 8 9) (A B C))
          ((D E F) (G H I)) ((J K L) (M N O)))
```

**1.** What subscripts identify the element a?

```
(aref a '1 1 0)
⇒    A
```

**2.** What subscripts identify the element k?

```
(aref a 3 0 1)
⇒    K
```

**3.** What does the following function return?

```
(setq b (make-array '(3 2) :displaced-to a
                           :displaced-index-offset 5))
⇒    #2A((6 7) (8 9) (A B))
```

**4.** If you adjust the array a as follows, what is the result?

```
(adjust-array a '(4 2 4) :initial-element 0)
⇒    #3A(((1 2 0 0) (0 0 0 0)) ((3 4 0 0) (0 0 0 0))
           ((5 6 0 0) (0 0 0 0)) ((7 8 0 0) (0 0 0 0)))
```

**5.** What is the new value of b?

```
b
⇒    #2A((0 0) (0 3) (4 0))
```

Given:

```
(setq vec (make-array 5 :initial-contents '(1 2 3 4 5)
                        :fill-pointer t))
⇒    #(1 2 3 4 5)
```

answer the following questions:

**6.** What is the value of the fill pointer?

```
(fill-pointer vec)
⇒    5
```

**7.** After the following steps are done, what is the value of vec?

```
(vector-pop vec)
(vector-pop vec)
(vector-push 'z vec)

vec
⇒    #(1 2 3 Z)
```

**8.** What is the value of the fill pointer?

```
(fill-pointer vec)
⇒    4
```

## CHAPTER 13

**Exercise 13-1**

1. Use `code-char` to create the following characters:

```
#\meta-\a
#\control-meta-A
#\control-meta-super-hyper-\z

(code-char 97 2)
⇒    #\META-\a

(code-char (char-code #\A) (+ char-control-bit char-meta-bit))
⇒    #\CONTROL-META-A

(code-char 122 (+ 1 2 4 8))
⇒    #\CONTROL-META-HYPER-SUPER-\z
```

2. Use `make-char` to create the following characters:

```
#2\hyper-\a
#\A
#3\control-meta-c

(make-char #\a char-hyper-bit 2)
⇒    #2\HYPER-\a

(make-char #\A)
⇒    #\A

(make-char #\c (+ char-meta-bit char-control-bit) 3)
⇒    #3\CONTROL-META-\c
```

3. What is the integer encoding of the following characters?

```
#\a
#3\a
#3\control-\a

(char-int #\a)
⇒    97

(char-int #3\a)
⇒    196705
```

```
(char-int #3\control-\a)
⇒     16973921
```

## Exercise 13-2

**1.** What is the meaning of the following objects?

| | |
|---|---|
| (a b c) | A list containing three objects. |
| #(1 2 3) | A vector containing three objects. |
| `(a b c) | A list containing three objects. |
| `(,a b c) | A list containing three objects. A will be evaluated. |
| `(,@a b c) | A list containing three objects. A will be expanded. The resulting list may be longer. |

**2.** Given the following,

```
(setq a '(1 2 3))
⇒     (1 2 3)

(setq b '(a b (d)))
⇒     (A B (D))

(setq c '(a b))
⇒     (A B)
```

what do the following lists return?

```
'(a b c)
⇒     (A B C)

`(a b c)
⇒     (A B C)

`(a ,b 'c)
⇒     (A (A B (D)) (QUOTE C))

`(a b ,(eval 'c))
⇒     (A B (A B))

`(a ,@b c)
⇒     (A A B (D) C)

`(a ,.b c)
⇒     (A A B (D) C)
```

# CHAPTER 14

### Exercise 14-1

There is no function `sequencep` defined in Lisp. As an exercise, write this function. `sequencep` is true if the argument is a list or a vector. It returns nil for all other data types.

```
(defun my-sequencep (seq)
  (cond ((listp seq) t)
        ((vectorp seq) t)
        (t nil)))
⇒    MY-SEQUENCEP

(my-sequencep 'a)
⇒    NIL

(my-sequencep "abc")
⇒    T

(my-sequencep '#(a b c))
⇒    T

(my-sequencep '((a b)(c d)))
⇒    T
```

### Exercise 14-2

1. What do the following functions return?

```
(concatenate 'bit-vector '#(1 0 1) #*000)
⇒    #*101000

(concatenate 'list "abc" #*11 '(a b c))
⇒    (#\a #\b #\c 1 1 A B C)

(concatenate 'vector '(a b c) "123")
⇒    #(A B C #\1 #\2 #\3)
```

2. Using `concatenate`, you can change the type of a sequence. What must be true to change a list to a vector?

   A vector can accept any elements that a list can accept.

3. What must be true to change a vector to a string?

   All elements in the vector must be string characters.

4. What must be true to change a string to a bit vector?

   Even if the characters in the string are characters 1 and 0, they are still characters, and a bit vector cannot have character elements. A string cannot be changed to a bit vector.

**Exercise 14-3**

There is no Lisp function that traverses a tree and returns a count of all atoms in a list. Write this function. This function can be done recursively. If the element is an atom, count 1. If the element is a list, pass the element to the function and count all of the sublist's atoms.

```
(defun all-atoms (list-seq)
  (cond ((null list-seq) 0)
        ((atom list-seq) 1)
        ((listp list-seq) (+ (all-atoms (car list-seq))
                             (all-atoms (cdr list-seq)))))))
⇒    ALL-ATOMS

(all-atoms '(a (b c) d))
⇒    4

(all-atoms '())
⇒    0

(all-atoms '(a b))
⇒    2

(all-atoms '(a (b c) (d (e f))))
⇒    6
```

**Exercise 14-4**

**1.** Write the function `vec-length` that returns the number of atoms in a vector if the vector contains lists. If the element is a list, call `all-atoms` on that list. If the element is not a list, count 1. As with `all-atoms`, you can recursively call the function to look at each element.

```
(defun vec-length (vect)
  (cond ((equal (length vect) 0) 0)
        (t (+ (cond ((listp (elt vect 0)) (all-atoms (elt vect 0)))
                    (t 1))
              (vec-length (subseq vect 1)))))))
⇒    VEC-LENGTH

(vec-length '#(a b c))
⇒    3

(vec-length '#((a b)(c d) e f))
⇒    6
```

**2.** Write the function `total` that returns the total number of atoms of any sequence.

```
(defun total (seq)
  (cond ((listp seq) (all-atoms seq))
        ((vectorp seq) (vec-length seq)))))
⇒    TOTAL


(total '(a b (c d) e))
⇒    5


(total "abc")
⇒    3


(total '#(a (b c) d))
⇒    4
```

**Exercise 14-5**

**1.** Can you search for a string sequence within a vector sequence? Why?

Because `search` looks at elements in a sequence, a sequence of string characters can appear in a vector or a list as well as within a string.

**2.** The `find` function looks for an element in a sequence. If the element is a list, `find` does not recursively look at the elements in the list. Write a recursive find function that does this.

**a.** Write the function ignoring the keywords. The default test is `eql`.

```
(defun rec-find (item seq)
  (cond ((equal (length seq) 0) nil)
        ((eql (elt seq 0) item)(elt seq 0))
        ((atom (elt seq 0))(rec-find item (subseq seq 1)))
        (t (rec-find item (elt seq 0))))))
```

**b.** This exercise uses some programming techniques that you may not have used in a while. Without the keywords, a simple linear-recursive function could be written. When you add the keywords, a linear-iterative recursive function solves the problem better. Here, however, you will be passing functions as variables. When you use a variable as a function, you must apply the function `funcall` to the variable to get the function definition.

There are two functions that can be specified: the test and key functions. The test function is used to compare the item and sequence. The key function is applied to the element of the sequence (not the item) before the test function.

```
(defun i-find (item seq &key (test #'eql)(test-not nil)
                            (start 0 s-flag)(end nil)
                            (key #'identity)(from-end nil))
   (if s-flag (setq seq (subseq seq start)))
   (if end (setq seq (subseq seq 0 end)))
   (if from-end (setq seq (reverse seq)))
   (if test-not (setq test #'(lambda (x y)
                                (not (funcall test-not x y)))))
   (rec-find item seq test key))
⇒   I-FIND


(defun rec-find (item seq test key)
   (cond ((equal (length seq) 0) nil)
         ((funcall test (funcall key (elt seq 0)). item) (elt seq 0))
         ((atom (elt seq 0)) (rec-find item (subseq seq 1) test key))
         (t (rec-find item (elt seq 0) test key))))
⇒   REC-FIND


(i-find 'a '(b c d))
⇒   NIL


(i-find 'a '(b a c))
⇒   A


(i-find 'a '(b (c a) d))
⇒   A


(i-find #\a "bca")
⇒   #\a


(i-find #\a "BAC" :test #'char-equal)
⇒   #\A


(i-find 'a '((a b)(c d)) :key #'car)
⇒   (A B)


(i-find 3 '(3 3 4 3) :test-not #'eql)
⇒   4
```

## Exercise 14-6

1. Write a function that concatenates a vector to a string. Test all elements of the vector
   to make sure they are all string characters. Return an appropriate error message if they are
   not.

```
(defun vec-to-string (seq)
  (if (every #'(lambda (x) (if (typep x 'string-char) t nil)) seq)
          (concatenate 'string seq)
          "elements are not of type 'string-char"))
⇒    VEC-TO-STRING


(vec-to-string '#(#\a #\5))
⇒    "a5"


(vec-to-string '#(a b))
⇒    "elements are not of type 'string-char"
```

**2.** A sequence can be made into a bit vector if each element is either 1 or 0.  Write a function
that tests all elements to see if they meet this requirement.

```
(defun to-bit-vector (seq)
  (if (every #'(lambda (x) (if (or (equal x 0)
                                    (equal x 1)) t nil)) seq)
            (concatenate 'bit-vector seq)
            "elements are not of type 'one or zero"))
⇒    TO-BIT-VECTOR


(to-bit-vector '(0 0 1))
⇒    #*001


(to-bit-vector "000")
⇒    "elements are not of type 'one or zero"
```

## Exercise 14-7

Given a sequence of names and numbers, write a function that looks up a name and
changes the number. The function should take two arguments: the sequence of names and
numbers, and a sequence containing two elements, the name and number to be changed.

```
(defun change-number (name-num seq)
  (let ((index (position (car (elt name-num 0)) seq :key #'car)))
    (if index (replace seq name-num :start1 index :end1 (1+ index))
        "name is not in sequence")))
⇒    CHANGE-NUMBER

(setq name-nums '((mary 555-1111)(joe 555-1234)
                  (john 555-0000)(sue 555-9999)))
⇒    ((MARY \555-1111) (JOE \555-1234)
      (JOHN \555-0000) (SUE \555-9999))
```

```
(change-number '((john 555-1212)) name-nums)
⇒    ((MARY) (\555-1111) (JOE) (\555-1234)
      (JOHN) (\555-1212) (SUE) (\555-9999))

(change-number '((larry 111-5555)) name-nums)
⇒    "name is not in sequence"
```

### Exercise 14-8

Write a function that takes the sequence of names and numbers and returns the sequence alphabetized by name.

```
(setq name-nums '((mary 555-1111)(joe 555-1234)
                    (john 555-0000)(sue 555-9999)))
⇒    ((MARY \555-1111) (JOE \555-1234)
      (JOHN \555-0000) (SUE \555-9999))

(defun alpha (seq)
  (sort seq #'string-lessp :key #'(lambda (x) (string (car x)))))
⇒    ALPHA

(alpha name-nums)
⇒    ((JOE \555-1234) (JOHN \555-0000)
      (MARY \555-1111) (SUE \555-9999))
```

# CHAPTER 15

### Exercise 15-1

**1.** Show all the ways you can make a string with the result string "abc".

```
(string 'abc)
⇒    "ABC"

(string "abc")
⇒    "abc"

"abc"
⇒    "abc"

(coerce '#(#\a #\b #\c) 'string)
⇒    "abc"

(make-array 3 :element-type 'string-char :initial-contents "abc")
⇒    "abc"
```

**2.** Create a string of three characters.

```
(make-string 3)
⇒    "   "

(make-array 3 :element-type 'string-char)
⇒    "   "

(string "   ")
⇒    "   "
```

**3.** What results if you try to use `vector` to create a string?

`vector` creates a simple vector. While you can place string characters into a vector, it will never become a string.

```
(vector #\a #\b #\c)
⇒    #(#\a #\b #\c)
```

## Exercise 15-2

This exercise deals with a string that contains a person's name. The format is "first middle-initial last".

**1.** Write a function that determines if a middle initial was included in the argument string.

```
(defun find-second-space (name)
  (position #\space name :start (+ 1 (position #\space name))))
⇒    FIND-SECOND-SPACE

(defun test-middle (name)
  (if (find-second-space name) t nil))
⇒    TEST-MIDDLE

(test-middle "Wendy L. Milner")
⇒    T

(test-middle "Wendy Milner")
⇒    NIL
```

**2.** Write a function that returns the last name.

```
(defun last-name (name)
  (if (test-middle name)
                 (subseq name (+ 1 (find-second-space name)))
                 (subseq name (+ 1 (position #\space name)))))
⇒    LAST-NAME

(last-name "Wendy L. Milner")
⇒    "Milner"
```

```
(last-name "Wendy Milner")
⇒    "Milner"
```

**3.** Write a function that returns the first name and middle initial.

```
(defun first-name (name)
  (if (test-middle name) (subseq name 0 (find-second-space name))
                         (subseq name 0 (position #\space name))))
⇒    FIRST-NAME

(first-name "Wendy L. Milner")
⇒    "Wendy L."

(first-name "Wendy Milner")
⇒    "Wendy"
```

**4.** Write a function that returns the name as "last, first mi".

```
(defun rev-name (name)
  (concatenate 'string (last-name name) ", " (first-name name)))
⇒    REV-NAME

(rev-name "Wendy L. Milner")
⇒    "Milner, Wendy L."

(rev-name "Wendy Milner")
⇒    "Milner, Wendy"
```

## Exercise 15-3

Continuing with the name string:

**1.** Write the last name in uppercase.

```
(defun upper-last (name)
  (string-upcase (last-name name)))

(upper-last "Wendy L. Milner")
⇒    "MILNER"
```

**2.** Capitalize the first name and middle initial.

```
(defun cap-first (name)
  (string-capitalize (first-name name)))
⇒    CAP-FIRST
```

```
(cap-first "wendY l. milner")
⇒     "Wendy L."
```

**3.** Rewrite the `rev-name` function so that it returns the name as "LAST, First MI".

```
(defun rev-name (name)
  (concatenate 'string (upper-last name) ", " (cap-first name)))
⇒     REV-NAME
```

```
(rev-name "wendy l. milner")
⇒     "MILNER, Wendy L."
```

**Exercise 15-4**

**1.** Write a function that determines if the name is in the desired format, "LAST, First MI".

```
(defun name-format-p (name)
  (position #\, name))
⇒     NAME-FORMAT-P
```

```
(name-format-p "wendy l. milner")
⇒     NIL
```

```
(name-format-p (rev-name "wendy l. milner"))
⇒     6
```

**2.** Write a function that changes the format of the name if it is needed.

```
(defun change-name (name)
  (if (name-format-p name) name (rev-name name)))
⇒     CHANGE-NAME
```

```
(change-name "wendy l. milner")
⇒     "MILNER, Wendy L."
```

```
(change-name "MILNER, Wendy L.")
⇒     "MILNER, Wendy L."
```

**3.** Write a function that returns true if two names are given in alphabetic order and nil if they are not.

```
(defun alpha-p (name1 name2)
  (if (string> name1 name2) nil t))
⇒     ALPHA-P
```

```
(alpha-p "MORGAN, J. P." "GETTY, J. P.")
⇒     NIL
```

```
(alpha-p "DOE, John" "DOE, Mary")
⇒    T
```

## Exercise 15-5

**1.** Write a function that removes blanks from the beginning and end of a string.

```
(defun remove-blanks (name)
  (string-trim " " name))
⇒    REMOVE-BLANKS


(remove-blanks " Harrison Clark  ")
⇒    "Harrison Clark"
```

**2.** Given a list of names, write a function that sorts them. The function should take each name, make it into the standard form, uppercase the last name, remove any blanks, and then return the sorted list of names.

```
(setq names '("wendy l. milner" "john d. milner" "susan j. miller"
              "robert m. dale"))
⇒    ("wendy l. milner" "john d. milner" "susan j. miller"
      "robert m. dale")


(defun sort-names (seq)
  (sort
    (map 'list #'change-name seq)
    #'string<))
⇒    SORT-NAMES


(sort-names names)
⇒    ("DALE, Robert M." "MILLER, Susan J."
      "MILNER, John D." "MILNER, Wendy L.")
```

# CHAPTER 16

## Exercise 16-1

This exercise creates a library catalog system. There is a title catalog and an author catalog.

```
author-catalog (authors (author1 author2 ...))
title-catalog (titles (title1 title2 ...))
```

Each author has a property list that consists of a list of titles by that author. Each title has a property list that consists of information about the book.

```
author (titles (title1 title2 ...))
title (publisher name date year author name)
```

**1.** Write a function that adds a title to the title catalog. Add the following four titles to the catalog:

```
lisp
lisp-a-gentle-introduction
common-lisp-a-tutorial
common-lisp-the-language

(defun add-title (title)
  (setf (get 'title-catalog 'titles)
        (push title (get 'title-catalog 'titles))))
⇒    ADD-TITLE

(add-title 'lisp)
⇒    (LISP)

(symbol-plist 'title-catalog)
⇒    (TITLES (LISP))

(add-title 'lisp-a-gentle-introduction)
⇒    (LISP-A-GENTLE-INTRODUCTION LISP)

(add-title 'common-lisp-a-tutorial)
⇒    (COMMON-LISP-A-TUTORIAL LISP-A-GENTLE-INTRODUCTION LISP)

(add-title 'common-lisp-the-language)
⇒    (COMMON-LISP-THE-LANGUAGE COMMON-LISP-A-TUTORIAL
      LISP-A-GENTLE-INTRODUCTION LISP)
```

**2.** Write a function that creates a property list for a title. The function should take the title, publisher, date, and author as arguments. Add the following entries:

```
lisp (publisher addison-wesley date 1984 author winston)

lisp-a-gentle-introduction
      (publisher harper&row date 1984 author touretzky)

common-lisp-a-tutorial
      (publisher prentice hall date 1988 author milner)

common-lisp-the-language
      (publisher digital-press date 1984 author steele)

(defun make-title-entry (title pub date author)
  (setf (get title 'publisher) pub)
  (setf (get title 'data) date)
  (setf (get title 'author) author))
⇒    MAKE-TITLE-ENTRY
```

```
(make-title-entry 'lisp 'addison-wesley '1984 'winston)
⇒   WINSTON


(symbol-plist 'lisp)
⇒   (AUTHOR WINSTON DATA 1984 PUBLISHER ADDISON-WESLEY)


(make-title-entry 'lisp-a-gentle-introduction 'harper&row
                  '1984 'touretzky)
⇒   TOURETZKY


(make-title-entry 'common-lisp-a-tutorial 'prentice-hall
                  '1988 'milner)
⇒   MILNER


(make-title-entry 'common-lisp-the-language 'digital-press
                  '1984 'steele)
⇒   STEELE
```

**3.** Write a function that returns the author of a book.

```
(defun get-author (title)
  (get title 'author))
⇒   GET-AUTHOR


(get-author 'lisp)
⇒   WINSTON
```

**4.** Write a function that creates an author catalog using the titles in the title catalog. The author catalog contains a list of author names.

```
(defun make-author-catalog ()
  (dolist (title (cadr (symbol-plist 'title-catalog))
                (symbol-plist 'author-catalog))
    (setf (get 'author-catalog 'authors)
          (cons (get-author title) (get 'author-catalog 'authors)))))
⇒   MAKE-AUTHOR-CATALOG


(make-author-catalog)
⇒   (AUTHORS (WINSTON TOURETZKY MILNER STEELE))
```

**5.** Write a function that adds an author to the author catalog if the author is not already in the catalog.

```
(defun add-author (author)
  (if (not (member author (cdr (get 'author-catalog 'authors))))
      (setf (get 'author-catalog 'authors)
            (cons author (get 'author-catalog 'authors)))))
⇒   ADD-AUTHOR
```

```
(add-author 'melvil)
⇒    (MELVIL WINSTON TOURETZKY MILNER STEELE)
```

**6.** Write a function that adds a title to the author property list if the title does already exist in the list.

```
(defun make-author-entry (title author)
  (if (not (member title (cdr (get author 'titles))))
      (setf (get author 'titles)
            (cons title (get author 'titles)))))
⇒   MAKE-AUTHOR-ENTRY

(make-author-entry 'common-lisp-a-tutorial 'milner)
⇒    (COMMON-LISP-A-TUTORIAL)

(symbol-plist 'milner)
⇒    (TITLES (COMMON-LISP-A-TUTORIAL))
```

**7.** Write a function that adds a book to both catalogs and makes appropriate entries for title and author symbols.

```
(defun add-book (title pub date author)
  (add-title title)
  (add-author author)
  (make-title-entry title pub date author)
  (make-author-entry title author))
⇒   ADD-BOOK

(add-book 'the-c-programming-language 'prentice hall
          '1978 'kernighan)
⇒    (THE-C-PROGRAMMING-LANGUAGE)

(symbol-plist 'author-catalog)
⇒    (AUTHORS (KERNIGHAN MELVIL WINSTON TOURETZKY MILNER STEELE))

(symbol-plist 'title-catalog)
⇒    (TITLES (THE-C-PROGRAMMING-LANGUAGE COMMON-LISP-THE-LANGUAGE
        COMMON-LISP-A-TUTORIAL LISP-A-GENTLE-INTRODUCTION LISP))

(symbol-plist 'kernighan)
⇒    (TITLES (THE-C-PROGRAMMING-LANGUAGE))

(symbol-plist 'the-c-programming-language)
⇒    (AUTHOR KERNIGHAN DATA 1978 PUBLISHER PRENTICE-HALL)
```

# CHAPTER 17

**Exercise 17-1**

Now that you have been overloaded with all the possible options available in `defstruct`, you should try them on your own.

```
(defstruct auto
           make
           model
           year
           color)
```

Using the auto structure as a beginning point, modify it as follows:

1. The make of the auto can be only one of the following: chevy, dodge, ford, or am (American Motors). Write a function that determines if the car is an American auto. Use this function in the definition of auto as the type of the make.

```
(defun am-car-p (make)
  "Is the car American Made"
  (member make '(chevy dodge ford am)))
⇒   AM-CAR-P
```

```
(defstruct auto
           (make 'chevy :type (satisfies am-car-p))
           model
           year
           color)
⇒   AUTO
```

```
(setq my-car (make-auto :make 'dodge))
⇒   #S(AUTO MAKE DODGE MODEL NIL YEAR NIL COLOR NIL)
```

```
(setq foreign (make-auto :make 'toyota))
⇒   !!!!! Error: The argument TOYOTA is not of type
             (SATISFIES AM-CAR-P).
```

2. The year must be a number.

```
(defstruct auto
           (make 'chevy :type (satisfies am-car-p))
           model
           (year 1980 :type number)
           color)
⇒   AUTO
```

```
(setq new-car (make-auto :year 1987))
⇒    #S(AUTO MAKE CHEVY MODEL NIL YEAR 1987 COLOR NIL)
```

**3.** Change the way you create a new object. Instead of make-auto, use new-car.

```
(defstruct (auto
            (:constructor new-car))
            (make 'chevy :type (satisfies am-car-p))
            model
            (year 1980 :type number)
            color)
⇒    AUTO


(setq jerrys (new-car :make 'ford :model 'mustang :year 1970
                                  :color 'red))
⇒    #S(AUTO MAKE FORD MODEL MUSTANG YEAR 1970 COLOR RED)
```

**4.** Rather than use keywords to enter the slot values, put them in a lambda list.

```
(defstruct (auto
            (:constructor new-car
                          (&optional make model year color)))
            (make 'chevy :type (satisfies am-car-p))
            model
            (year 1980 :type number)
            color)
⇒    AUTO


(setq roberts (new-car 'am 'gremlin))
⇒    #S(AUTO MAKE AM MODEL GREMLIN YEAR 1980 COLOR NIL)
```

**5.** When accessing a value, use the term car instead of auto.

```
(defstruct (auto
            (:constructor new-car
                          (&optional make model year color))
            (:conc-name car-))
            (make 'chevy :type (satisfies am-car-p))
            model
            (year 1980 :type number)
            color)
⇒    AUTO


(setq wendys (new-car 'chevy 'corvette 1987 'silver))
⇒    #S(AUTO MAKE CHEVY MODEL CORVETTE YEAR 1987 COLOR SILVER)

(car-model wendys)
⇒    CORVETTE
```

**6.** Write a function that takes four arguments, the four slot values. The function returns a structure. Create several owners for these autos.

```
(defun fun-car (make model year color)
  (new-car make model year color))
⇒    FUN-CAR

(setq karens (fun-car 'dodge 'lincoln '1974 'black))
⇒    #S(AUTO MAKE DODGE MODEL LINCOLN YEAR 1974 COLOR BLACK)

(setq toms (fun-car 'ford 'pinto '1979 'blue))
⇒    #S(AUTO MAKE FORD MODEL PINTO YEAR 1979 COLOR BLUE)

(setq richards (fun-car 'chevy 'camaro '1984 'grey))
⇒    #S(AUTO MAKE CHEVY MODEL CAMARO YEAR 1984 COLOR GREY)

(setq sarahs (fun-car 'chevy 'citation '1980 'blue))
⇒    #S(AUTO MAKE CHEVY MODEL CITATION YEAR 1980 COLOR BLUE)

(setq andys (fun-car 'dodge 'fury '1984 'black))
⇒    #S(AUTO MAKE DODGE MODEL FURY YEAR 1984 COLOR BLACK)
```

**7.** Write a function that, given a slot name and owner name, returns the value for that slot.

```
(defun get-slot-value (owner slot)
  "get the value of the slot for the specified owner"
  (cond ((eq slot 'make)(car-make owner))
        ((eq slot 'model)(car-model owner))
        ((eq slot 'year)(car-year owner))
        ((eq slot 'color)(car-color owner))
        (t nil)))
⇒    GET-SLOT-VALUE

(get-slot-value sarahs 'model)
⇒    CITATION

(get-slot-value andys 'year)
⇒    1984
```

**8.** Write a function that, given an owner's name, a slot, and a value, returns nil if the owner's car does not match the value and returns non-nil if the owner's car does match.

```
(defun match-p (owner slot value)
  "does the owner have a car that matches the slot value given?"
  (eq (get-slot-value owner slot) value))
⇒    MATCH-P
```

```
(match-p richards 'make 'chevy)
⇒    T


(match-p karens 'color 'black)
⇒    T


(match-p sarahs 'color 'green)
⇒    NIL
```

9. Write a function that takes a list of owner's names, a slot name, and a value. The function returns the names of the owners who own a car with the specified value.

```
(defun get-owners (owners slot value)
  "owners is a list of symbols"
  (cond ((eq (car owners) nil) nil)
        (t (if (match-p (symbol-value (car owners)) slot value)
               (cons (car owners)
                     (get-owners (cdr owners) slot value))
               (get-owners (cdr owners) slot value)))))
⇒    GET-OWNERS


(get-owners '(sarahs richards karens andys toms) 'make 'chevy)
⇒    (SARAHS RICHARDS)


(get-owners '(sarahs richards karens andys toms) 'color 'blue)
⇒    (SARAHS TOMS)


(get-owners '(sarahs richards karens andys toms) 'year '1984)
⇒    (RICHARDS ANDYS)
```

# CHAPTER 18

### Exercise 18-1

1. Set the value of the symbol a to 100.

```
(setq a 100)
⇒    100
```

2. Create a package named test.

```
(provide 'test)
⇒    "TEST"


(in-package 'test)
⇒    #<Package TEST>
```

**3.** Evaluate the symbol a.

```
a
⇒    !!!!! Error: The symbol A has no value.
        Condition signalled in: SYMBOL-VALUE.
```

**4.** Set the value of b to "abc".

```
(setq b "abc")
⇒    "abc"
```

**5.** Return to the user package.

```
(in-package 'user)
⇒    #<Package USER>
```

**6.** Evaluate the symbol b.

```
b
⇒    !!!!! Error: The symbol B has no value.
        Condition signalled in: SYMBOL-VALUE.
```

**Exercise 18-2**

**1.** Return to the test package and evaluate the symbol a again by using the package prefix.

```
(in-package 'test)
⇒    #<Package TEST>

user:a
⇒
        !!!!! Error: The symbol "A" is not external in the package
        #<Package USER>.
        Condition signalled in: LISP::READ-TOKEN.
```

**2.** Because a is an internal symbol, you must specify a double colon between the package and the symbol.

```
user::a
⇒    USER::100
```

**3.** Make the symbol b external to the package test.

```
(export 'b)
⇒    T
```

**4.** Return to the user package and evaluate the necessary commands so that you can get the value of b without specifying a package.

```
(in-package 'user)
⇒    #<Package USER>


(require 'test)
⇒    "TEST"


(user-package 'test)
⇒    T


b
⇒    "abc"
```

## Exercise 18-3

**1.** How many external symbols would you expect to find in the user package?

    None. The user package is set up with no symbols defined in it. It is up to you to define the symbols in this package.

**2.** How many external symbols would you expect to find in the Lisp package?

    All functions in the language are external to the Lisp package. The user package requires the Lisp package, so that you can use the lisp functions.

**3.** Prove the answer to the previous question by printing the symbols.

```
(do-external-symbols (variable (find-package 'user) '**done**)
                     (print variable))

(do-external-symbols (variable (find-package 'lisp) '**done**)
                     (print variable))
```

**4.** When might you be interested in the external symbols of a package?

    If you are unsure of the names of the symbols in a package that you want to use, check what the names are and see if they conflict with any of your internal names. If they do, execute a shadowing function before you use the package.

**5.** Write a function that determines if a particular symbol is an external symbol of a package. Two functions that will help you are symbol-name, which returns the name of a symbol as a string, and string-equal, which determines if two strings are equal.

```
(defun sym-ext (sym pack)
  (setq flag nil)
  (do-external-symbols (variable (find-package pack) flag)
                       (if (string-equal (symbol-name sym)
                                         (symbol-name variable))
                           (setq flag t))))
⇒    SYM-EXT

(sym-ext 'arrayp 'lisp)
⇒    T
```

```
(sym-ext 'test 'lisp)
⇒    NIL
```

## CHAPTER 20

**Exercise 20-1**

1. Given a list of numbers, output them in fields of not more than 10 characters.

```
(format t "~{~10,f~%~}" '(123456.789 987654321987 12.99))
⇒    123456.789
     987654322000.
           12.99
     NIL

(format t "~{~10,,,'xf~%~}" '(123456.789 987654321987 12.99))
⇒    123456.789
     xxxxxxxxxx
           12.99
     NIL

(format t "~{~10,,,'x,'*f~%~}" '(123456.789 987654321987 12.99 12))
⇒    123456.789
     xxxxxxxxxx
     *****12.99
     ******12.0
     NIL

(defun 10-col (num-list)
   (format t "~{~10,,,'x,'*f~%~}" num-list))
⇒    \10-COL

(10-col '(99 123456.78912 -44.76 0 1234567891234))
⇒    ******99.0
     123456.789
     ****-44.76
     *******0.0
     xxxxxxxxxx
     NIL
```

2. Given a list of objects, output them two at a time. Left justify the first, and right justify the second. Do not assume there is an even number of objects.

```
(format t "~{~10<~a~;~a~>~%~}" '(a b cc dd))
⇒    A         B
     CC        DD
     NIL
```

```
(format t "~{~10<~a~;~^~a~>~%~}" '(a b cc dd e))
⇒     A          B
      CC         DD
                 E
      NIL
```

```
(defun just (just-list)
   (format t "~{~10<~a~;~^~a~>~%~}" just-list))
⇒    JUST
```

```
(just '(john a mary a kerry ? tim))
⇒    JOHN       A
     MARY       A
     KERRY      ?
           TIM
     NIL
```

**Exercise 20-2**

**1.** Write a function that asks for input from the operator and then retrieves that input.

```
(defun get-input (message)
  (write message)
  (read))
⇒    GET-INPUT
```

```
(get-input "Input the next letter")
⇒    "Input the next letter"
```

```
a
⇒    A
```

**2.** Write a function that opens a file and asks the operator for data to be put in the file. Read until the operator inputs some end value.

```
(defun write-to-file (file-name)
  (with-open-stream (file-stream (open file-name :direction :output
                                    :if-exists :supersede))
    (write "Ready to receive data for the file")
    (loop
      (let ((line (read)))
           (if (equal 'eof line) (return 'end))
           (write line :stream file-stream)
           (write-char #\return file-stream)))))
⇒    WRITE-TO-FILE
```

```
(write-to-file "/users/wendy/temp/write-test")
⇒    "Ready to receive data for the file"
first
second
third
eof
⇒    END
```

**3.** Write a function that reads each line of a file and prints the results.

```
(defun read-from-file (file-name)
  (with-open-stream (file-stream (open file-name :direction :input
                                        :if-does-not-exist :error))
    (loop
      (let ((line (read file-stream nil 'end)))
        (if (equal line 'end)(return 'end))
        (print line)))))
⇒    READ-FROM-FILE
```

```
(read-from-file "/users/wendy/temp/write-test")
⇒    FIRST
     SECOND
     THIRD
     END
```

# CHAPTER 21

### Exercise 21-1

**1.** Set the default components of a pathname to be your home directory, your host, and device type.

```
(setq *default-pathname-defaults*
  (merge-pathnames (user-homedir-pathname)
                   (make-pathname :host "HP-UX" :device "S320")))
⇒    #.(make-pathname :host "HP-UX" :device "S320"
                      :directory '("" "users" "wendy") :name NIL
                      :type NIL :version NIL)
```

**2.** Create a pathname that has a file name test and all other components nil.

```
(make-pathname :name "test" :host nil :device nil :directory nil)
⇒    #.(make-pathname :host NIL :device NIL :directory NIL
                      :name "test" :type NIL :version NIL)
```

**Exercise 21-2**

**1.** Create a file name "test".

```
(setq temp (open "/users/wendy/temp/test" :direction :output
            :if-does-not-exist :create :if-exists :supersede))
⇒    #<File Stream /users/wendy/temp/test>

(close temp)
⇒    T
```

**2.** Probe the file to see if it exists.

```
(probe-file "/users/wendy/temp/test")
⇒    #.(make-pathname :host "HP-UX" :device "S320"
                      :directory '("" "users" "wendy" "temp")
                      :name "test" :type NIL :version NIL)

(open "/users/wendy/temp/test" :direction :probe)
⇒    #<File Stream /users/wendy/temp/test>
```

**3.** Open the file and write three lines of data to it.

```
(setq out-stream (open "/users/wendy/temp/test"
                       :direction :output
                       :if-exists :supersede))
⇒    #<File Stream /users/wendy/temp/test>

(write-line (read-line) out-stream)
first line
⇒    "first line "

(write-line (read-line) out-stream)
second line
⇒    "second line "

(write-line (read-line) out-stream)
third line
⇒    "third line "

(close out-stream)
⇒    T
```

**4.** Write a function that reads all the lines in the file and writes them to the display.

```
(defun write-file (name)
  (catch 'end
    (setq file (open name :direction :input
                          :if-does-not-exist :error))
    (loop
     (setq line (read-line file nil 'eof))
     (if (equal line 'eof) (throw 'end "end of file"))
     (write-line line)))
  (close file))
⇒  WRITE-FILE


(write-file "/users/wendy/temp/test")
⇒    first line
     second line
     third line
     T
```

# Appendix B

## Quick Reference

This appendix is a reference to the syntax of the nearly 700 functions, macros, special forms, variables, constants, and symbols in Common Lisp. You will find most of them described elsewhere in this book.

A specific format is used to show the syntax of the forms. In order for you to understand the forms, you must understand the symbols and type fonts used to show the syntax. The following symbols are used to describe the syntax in this manual.

```
This font indicates that an item must be typed exactly
as you see it.
```
*This font indicates a descriptive name for a form. You can choose any name or replace the name with a value.*

There are several elements to the format used to describe a function. The function name appears in `this type font`. Parameters to the function appear in *this type font*. Keywords appear in `this type font`. Lambda keywords (&key, &optional, &rest) appear in the normal text font. The symbols used to describe the syntax are described in the following list.

**448**

```
(example-function parameter1 parameter2 &key :key1 :key2)
```

&optional    Indicates that all parameters that follow are optional. When you
             type the function, do not type the word &optional. The optional
             parameters have default values. If you do not specify an optional
             parameter, the optional parameter's default value is used by the
             function.

&rest        Indicates that the parameter that follows can be repeated an
             indefinite number of times. Whatever values appear are collected
             in a list and given to the function.

&key         Indicates that keywords are accepted. The accepted keywords are
             given. You type the keyword and a value. You do not have to
             specify all the keywords, nor do you have to specify them in the
             order shown. Keywords that are not specified have a default
             value.

             If &optional parameters precede &key parameters, the
             &optional parameters **must** be specified in order to specify the
             &key parameters

{ }          Braces surround an item or set of items that can be followed by an
             asterisk or plus, and can contain a bar. Do not type the braces.

*            An asterisk indicates that the preceding item can be repeated zero
             or more times. Do not type the asterisk.

+            A plus indicates that the preceding item can be repeated one or
             more times. Do not type the plus.

[ ]          Brackets indicate that the enclosed item can appear zero or one
             time. Do not type the brackets.

|            A bar indicates that the items it separates are mutually exclusive.
             Only one of the items can appear. Do not type the bar.

## Syntax Symbols

The rest of this appendix contains an alphabetical reference to the functions, macros, special forms, variables, constants, and symbols in Common Lisp.

( * &rest *numbers* )

The * function returns the product of the arguments.

*

The * variable is bound to the result of the form evaluated in the previous iteration of the listener read-eval-print loop.

**

The ** variable is bound to the result produced two iterations before. It contains the previous value of *.

\*\*\*

The \*\*\* variable is bound to the result produced three iterations before. It contains the previous value of \*\*.

(+ &rest *numbers*)

The + function returns the sum of its arguments.

+

The + variable is bound to the previously evaluated form while the current form is being evaluated.

++

The ++ variable is bound to the form evaluated two iterations before while the current form is being evaluated. It holds the previous value of +.

+++

The +++ variable is bound to the form evaluated three iterations before while the current form is being evaluated. It holds the previous value of ++.

(− *number* &rest *more-numbers*)

The − function negates a single argument or successively subtracts its arguments.

−

The − variable is bound to the current form being evaluated. Its value is given to + once the evaluation is complete.

(/ *number* &rest *more-numbers*)

The / function returns the reciprocal of a single argument or successively divides its arguments.

/

The / variable is bound to the list of results produced by evaluation of the form in the previous iteration of the listener read-eval-print loop.

//

The // variable is bound to the list of results of the form evaluated two iterations before. It contains the previous value of /.

///

The /// variable is bound to the list of results of the form evaluated three iterations before. It contains the previous value of //.

(/= *number* &rest *more-numbers*)

The /= predicate determines if the numerical arguments are all different.

(1+ *number*)

The 1+ function adds 1 to its argument.

(1- *number*)

    The 1- function subtracts 1 from its argument.

(< *number* &rest *more-numbers*)

    The < predicate determines if the numerical arguments are monotonically increasing.

(<= *number* &rest *more-numbers*)

    The <= predicate determines if the numerical arguments are monotonically non-decreasing.

(= *number* &rest *more-numbers*)

    The = predicate determines if the numerical arguments are equal.

(> *number* &rest *more-numbers*)

    The > predicate determines if the numerical arguments are monotonically decreasing.

(>= *number* &rest *more-numbers*)

    The >= predicate determines if the numeric arguments are monotonically nonincreasing.

(abs *number*)

    The abs function returns the absolute value of the argument.

(acons *key datum a-list*)

    The acons function returns an association list constructed by adding a new association pair to an existing association list.

(acos *number*)

    The acos function returns the arc cosine of the argument.

(acosh *number*)

    The acosh function returns the hyperbolic arc cosine of the argument.

(adjoin *item list* &key :test :test-not :key)

    The adjoin function adds an element to a list if the element is not already a member of the list.

```
(adjust-array array new-dimensions &key :element-type
                                        :initial-element
                                        :initial-contents
                                        :fill-pointer
                                        :displaced-to
                                        :displaced-index-offset)
```

    The adjust-array function alters the size, shape, or displacement of an existing adjustable array.

(adjustable-array-p *array*)

The adjustable-array-p predicate determines if an array is adjustable.

(alpha-char-p *character*)

The alpha-char-p predicate determines if an object is an alphabetic character.

(alphanumericp *character*)

The alphanumericp predicate determines if a character is either alphabetic or numeric.

(and *types-list*)

The and type creates a type specifier that is the intersection of the specified types.

(and {*form*}*)

The and macro evaluates each form and returns NIL if any form is NIL. It returns the value of the last form if no form is NIL.

(append &rest *lists*)

The append function concatenates the argument lists into one list. The argument lists are not modified.

(apply *function argument* &rest *more-arguments*)

The apply function returns the value obtained from applying *function* to a list of arguments.

\*applyhook\*

The \*applyhook\* variable when non-nil causes eval to pass functions to the *apply-hook-function*.

(applyhook *function arg-list eval-hook-function apply-hook-function* &optional *env*)

The applyhook function applies a function to a list of arguments.

(apropos *string* &optional *package*)

The apropos function prints all available symbols whose print name contains the specified string. If the symbol has a value, the value is output. If the symbol has a special form, a macro or a function definition, that is stated.

(apropos-list *string* &optional *package*)

The apropos-list function returns a list of all available symbols whose print name contains the specified string. If the symbol has a value, the value is output. If the symbol has a special form, a macro or a function definition, that is stated.

(aref *array* &rest *subscripts*)

The aref function returns a specified element of an array.

{array|(array {*element-type* {*dimension*}}) }

> The array type specifies the type of arrays of varying dimension and element type.

(array-dimension *array axis-number*)

> The array-dimension function returns the length of the specified dimension of the array.

array-dimension-limit

> The array-dimension-limit is the upper exclusive bound on the size of each dimension.

(array-dimensions *array*)

> The array-dimensions function returns a list whose elements are the dimensions of an array.

(array-element-type *array*)

> The array-element-type function returns a type specifier for the set of objects that can be stored in a specified array.

(array-has-fill-pointer-p *array*)

> The array-has-fill-pointer-p predicate determines if an array has a fill pointer.

(array-in-bounds-p *array* &rest *subscripts*)

> The array-in-bounds-p predicate determines the validity of specified subscripts for a specified array.

(array-rank *array*)

> The array-rank function returns the number of dimensions of a specified array.

array-rank-limit

> The array-rank-limit is the exclusive upper bound for the rank of an array.

(array-row-major-index *array* &rest *subscripts*)

> The array-row-major-index function returns an index that identifies an element in the row major ordering of the elements.

(array-total-size *array*)

> The array-total-size function returns the number of elements in a specified array.

array-total-size-limit

> The array-total-size-limit is the exclusive upper bound for the number of elements in an array.

(arrayp *object*)

> The arrayp predicate determines if an object is an array.

(ash *integer count*)

> The ash function arithmetically shifts the bits of an integer.

(asin *number*)

> The asin function returns the arc sine of the argument.

(asinh *number*)

> The asinh function returns the hyperbolic arc sine of the argument.

(assert *test-form* [ ({*place*}*) [{*symbol* | *format-string* {*arguments*}*}]])

> The assert macro signals a continuable error when the value of a specified test-form is NIL.

(assoc *item alist* &key :test :test-not :key)

> The assoc function returns the first (leftmost) pair of an association list whose car satisfies the specified test.

(assoc-if *predicate alist*)

> The assoc-if function returns the first (leftmost) pair of an association list whose car satisfies the test.

(assoc-if-not *predicate alist*)

> The assoc-if-not function returns the first (leftmost) pair of an association list whose car does not satisfy the test.

(atan *y* &optional *x*)

> The atan function returns the arc tangent of the argument.

(atanh *number*)

> The atanh function returns the hyperbolic arc tangent of its argument.

atom

> The atom type specifies the type atom that is any object that is not a cons.

(atom *object*)

> The atom predicate determines if an object is an atom.

bignum

> The bignum type specifies the type bignum that is any integer that is not a fixnum.

bit

> The bit type specifies the type bit that is the integer 0 or 1.

(bit *bit-array* &rest *subscripts*)

> The bit function returns the specified element of a bit array.

(bit-and *bit-array1 bit-array2* &optional *result-bit-array*)

> The bit-and function returns a bit array that results from anding each bit of the first array with the corresponding bit of the second array.

(bit-andc1 *bit-array1 bit-array2* &optional *result-bit-array*)

> The bit-andc1 function returns a bit array that results from anding the complement of each bit of the first array with corresponding bit of the second array.

(bit-andc2 *bit-array1 bit-array2* &optional *result-bit-array*)

> The bit-andc2 function returns a bit array that results from anding each bit of the first array with the complement of the corresponding bit of the second array.

(bit-eqv *bit-array1 bit-array2* &optional *result-bit-array*)

> The bit-eqv function returns a bit array that results from exclusively noring each bit of the first array with the corresponding bit of the second array.

(bit-ior *bit-array1 bit-array2* &optional *result-bit-array*)

> The bit-ior function returns a bit array that results from inclusively oring each bit of the first array with the corresponding bit of the second array.

(bit-nand *bit-array1 bit-array2* &optional *result-bit-array*)

> The bit-nand function returns a bit array that results from nanding each bit of the first array with the corresponding bit of the second array.

(bit-nor *bit-array1 bit-array2* &optional *result-bit-array*)

> The bit-nor function returns a bit array that results from noring each bit of the first array with the corresponding bit of the second array.

(bit-not *bit-array* &optional *result-bit-array*)

> The bit-not function returns a bit array that results from complementing each bit in the argument bit array.

(bit-orc1 *bit-array1 bit-array2* &optional *result-bit-array*)

> The bit-orc1 function returns a bit array that results from inclusively oring the complement of each bit of the first array with the corresponding bit of the second array.

(bit-orc2 *bit-array1 bit-array2* &optional *result-bit-array*)

> The bit-orc2 function returns a bit array that results from inclusively oring each bit of the first array with the complement of the corresponding bit of the second array.

{bit-vector|(bit-vector {*size*})}

> The bit-vector type specifies the type bit-vectors that are vectors whose elements are either of the integers 1 or 0.

(bit-vector-p *object*)

The bit-vector-p predicate determines if an object is a bit vector.

(bit-xor *bit-array1 bit-array2* &optional *result-bit-array*)

The bit-xor function returns a bit array that results from exclusively oring each bit of the first array with the corresponding bit of the second array.

(block *name {form}*)

The block special form evaluates a series of forms, returning the value of the last form as its value.

(boole *operation integer1 integer2*)

The boole function returns an integer produced by applying the specified logical operation on the two integer arguments.

boole-1

The boole-1 constant, when specified as the operation to the boole function, causes boole to return the first integer.

boole-2

The boole-2 constant, when specified as the operation to the boole function, causes boole to return the second integer.

boole-and

The boole-and constant, when specified as the operation to the boole function, causes boole to return the logical and of the two integers.

boole-andc1

The boole-andc1 constant, when specified as the operation to the boole function, causes boole to return the logical and of the complement of the first integer with the second integer.

boole-andc2

The boole-andc2 constant, when specified as the operation to the boole function, causes boole to return the logical and of the first integer with the complement of the second integer.

boole-c1

The boole-c1 constant, when specified as the operation to the boole function, causes boole to return the logical complement of the first integer.

boole-c2

The boole-c2 constant, when specified as the operation to the boole function, causes boole to return the logical complement of the second integer.

boole-clr

The boole-clr constant, when specified as the operation to the boole function, causes boole to return zero.

`boole-eqv`

> The `boole-eqv` constant, when specified as the operation to the `boole` function, causes `boole` to return the logical equivalence (exclusive nor) of the two integers.

`boole-ior`

> The `boole-ior` constant, when specified as the operation to the `boole` function, causes `boole` to return the logical inclusive or of the two integers.

`boole-nand`

> The `boole-nand` constant, when specified as the operation to the `boole` function, causes `boole` to return the logical not and of the two integers.

`boole-nor`

> The `boole-nor` constant, when specified as the operation to the `boole` function, causes `boole` to return the logical not or of the two integers.

`boole-orc1`

> The `boole-orc1` constant, when specified as the operation to the `boole` function, causes `boole` to return the logical or of the complement of the first integer with the second integer.

`boole-orc2`

> The `boole-orc2` constant, when specified as the operation to the `boole` function, causes `boole` to return the logical or of the first integer with the complement of the second integer.

`boole-set`

> The `boole-set` constant, when specified as the operation to the `boole` function, causes `boole` to return 1.

`boole-xor`

> The `boole-xor` constant, when specified as the operation to the `boole` function, causes `boole` to return the logical exclusive or of the two integers.

(`both-case-p` *character*)

> The `both-case-p` predicate determines if a character has an uppercase equivalent if it is lowercase and a lowercase equivalent if it is uppercase.

(`boundp` *symbol*)

> The `boundp` predicate determines if a dynamic variable has a value.

(`break` &optional {*symbol* | *format-string* &rest *arguments*})

> The `break` function prints an error message and calls the debugger without permitting interception.

`*break-on-warnings*`

The `*break-on-warnings*` variable acts as a flag and causes `warn` to enter a break loop when it is non-nil.

(`butlast` *list* &optional *n*)

The `butlast` function returns a copy of the argument with the last *n* elements removed.

(`byte` *size position*)

The `byte` function returns a byte specifier for use in byte manipulation functions.

(`byte-position` *byte-specifier*)

The `byte-position` function returns the position of the byte specifier.

(`byte-size` *byte-specifier*)

The `byte-size` function returns the size of the byte specifier.

(`caaaar` *list*)

The `caaaar` function is equivalent to (`car` (`car` (`car` (`car` x)))). See `car`.

`call-arguments-limit`

The `call-arguments-limit` constant returns the exclusive upper bound for the number of arguments that can be passed to a function.

(`car` *list*)

The `car` function returns the first element of a cons.

Each composition of up to four `car` and `cdr` operations is supported. Each composition can be used with `setf`. They are:

```
caar    ≡ (car (car x))
cadr    ≡ (car (cdr x))
cdar    ≡ (cdr (car x))
cddr    ≡ (cdr (cdr x))
caaar   ≡ (car (car (car x)))
caadr   ≡ (car (car (cdr x)))
cadar   ≡ (car (cdr (car x)))
cdaar   ≡ (cdr (car (car x)))
caddr   ≡ (car (cdr (cdr x)))
cdadr   ≡ (cdr (car (cdr x)))
cddar   ≡ (cdr (cdr (car x)))
cdddr   ≡ (cdr (cdr (cdr x)))
caaaar  ≡ (car (car (car (car x))))
caaadr  ≡ (car (car (car (cdr x))))
caadar  ≡ (car (car (cdr (car x))))
cadaar  ≡ (car (cdr (car (car x))))
cdaaar  ≡ (cdr (car (car (car x))))
caaddr  ≡ (car (car (cdr (cdr x))))
```

```
caddar  ≡(car (cdr (cdr (car x))))
cddaar  ≡(cdr (cdr (car (car x))))
cadadr  ≡(car (cdr (car (cdr x))))
cdadar  ≡(cdr (car (cdr (car x))))
cdaadr  ≡(cdr (car (car (cdr x))))
cadddr  ≡(car (cdr (cdr (cdr x))))
cdaddr  ≡(cdr (car (cdr (cdr x))))
cddadr  ≡(cdr (cdr (car (cdr x))))
cdddar  ≡(cdr (cdr (cdr (car x))))
cddddr  ≡(cdr (cdr (cdr (cdr x))))
```

(case *keyform* { (( ({*key*}*) | *key*} {*form*}*) }*)

The case macro compares the value of a given form with constant keys and then evaluates the forms in the remainder of the clause that matches.

(catch *tag* {*form*}*)

The catch special form is a target for transfer of control from a throw.

(ccase *keyform* { (( ({*key*}*) | *key*} {*form*}) }*)

The ccase macro is similar to the case macro, except it signals a continuable error if none of the clauses is chosen.  T and otherwise clauses are not allowed.

(cdr *list*)

The cdr function returns the second element of a cons.

(ceiling *number* &optional *divisor*)

The ceiling function returns the smallest integer not less than its argument.

(cerror  { *continue-format-string error-format-string* &rest *arguments*)

The cerror function signals a continuable error.

(char *string index*)

The char function returns a character of a string.

(char/= *character* &rest *more-characters*)

The char/= predicate determines if the character arguments are distinct.

(char< *character* &rest *more-characters* )

The char< predicate determines if the codes representing the character arguments are monotonically increasing.

(char<= *character* &rest *more-characters*)

The char<= predicate determines if the codes representing the character arguments are monotonically nondecreasing.

(char= *character* &rest *more-characters*)

    The char= predicate determines if the character arguments are all the same.

(char> *character* &rest *more-characters*)

    The char> predicate determines if the codes representing the character arguments are monotonically decreasing.

(char>= *character* &rest *more-characters*)

    The char>= predicate determines if the codes representing the character arguments are monotonically nonincreasing.

character

    The character type specifies the type of all single characters known to Lisp.

(character *object*)

    The character function coerces its argument to a character. If coercion is not possible, an error is signaled.

(characterp *object*)

    The characterp predicate determines if an object is a character.

(char-bit *character character-bit*)

    The char-bit function determines if a character bit is set for the specified character.

(char-bits *character*)

    The char-bits function returns the value of the bits attribute of its argument.

char-bits-limit

    The char-bits-limit is the upper exclusive limit of values returned by char-bits.

(char-code *character*)

    The char-code function returns the value of the code attribute of its argument.

char-code-limit

    The char-code-limit is the upper exclusive limit of values produced by char-code.

char-control-bit

    The char-control-bit constant is the weight of the control bit.

(char-downcase *character*)

    The char-downcase function returns the lowercase equivalent of its argument.

(char-equal *character* &rest *more-characters*)

    The char-equal predicate determines if the character arguments are all the same while ignoring differences in case and bits.

(char-font *character*)

    The `char-font` function returns the value of the font attribute of its argument.

char-font-limit

    The `char-font-limit` is the upper exclusive limit of values produced by `char-font`.

(char-greaterp *character* &rest *more-characters*)

    The `char-greaterp` predicate determines if the character arguments are monotonically decreasing. It ignores character case and bits.

char-hyper-bit

    The `char-hyper-bit` constant is the weight of the hyper bit.

(char-int *character*)

    The `char-int` function returns the integer encoding of its argument.

(char-lessp *character* &rest *more-characters*)

    The `char-lessp` predicate determines if the character arguments are monotonically increasing. It ignores character case and bits.

char-meta-bit

    The `char-meta-bit` constant is the weight of the meta bit.

(char-name *character*)

    The `char-name` function returns the name of the character. It returns `NIL` if the character has no name.

(char-not-equal *character* &rest *more-characters*)

    The `char-not-equal` predicate determines if the character arguments are distinct. It ignores character case and bits.

(char-not-greaterp *character* &rest *more-characters*)

    The `char-not-greaterp` predicate determines if the character arguments are monotonically nondecreasing. It ignores character case and bits.

(char-not-lessp *character* &rest *more-characters*)

    The `char-not-lessp` predicate determines if the character arguments are monotonically nonincreasing. It ignores character case and bits.

char-super-bit

    The `char-super-bit` constant is the weight of the super bit.

(char-upcase *character*)

    The `char-upcase` function returns the uppercase equivalent of its argument.

(check-type *place typespec* &optional {*symbol* | *string*})

    The `check-type` macro signals a continuable error when the contents of a specified place are not of a specified type.

(cis *radians*)

> The cis function returns a complex number whose real part is the cosine of the argument and whose imaginary part is the sine.

(clear-input &optional *input-stream*)

> The clear-input function clears any buffered input in the input stream.

(clear-output &optional *output-stream*)

> The clear-output function clears any buffered output from the output stream.

(close *stream* &key :abort)

> The close function closes the specified stream.

(clrhash *hash-table*)

> The clrhash function clears all entries from a hash table. The value returned is the empty hash table.

(code-char *code* &optional *bits font* )

> The code-char function returns a character if one can be made from the arguments.

(coerce *object result-type*)

> The coerce function converts an object to an equivalent object of another type.

common

> The common type specifies the type that encompasses all the types defined in Common Lisp except the type t which may also contain types outside the definition.

(commonp *object*)

> The commonp predicate determines if an object is of a standard Common Lisp data type.

(compile *name* &optional *definition*)

> The compile function compiles a function according to a specified definition.

(compile-file *input-pathname* &key :output-file)

> The compile-file function compiles the contents of a file and stores the compiled code as an object file.

compiled-function

> The compiled-function specifies a function that consists of compiled code.

(compiled-function-p *object*)

> The compiled-function-p predicate determines if an object is a compiled code object.

(compiler-let  ({*var*| (*var value*) }*) {*form*}*)

> The compiler-let special form binds special variables to the indicated values in the execution context of the compiler.

{complex| (complex {*type*}) }

> The complex type specifies the type of complex numbers.

(complex *realpart* &optional *imagpart*)

> The complex function constructs and returns a complex number.

(complexp *object*)

> The complexp predicate determines if an object is a complex number.

(concatenate *result-type* &rest *sequences*)

> The concatenate function returns a sequence of the specified type that contains all elements of the argument sequences in order.

(cond { (*test* {*form*}*) }*)

> The cond macro conditionally evaluates zero or more clauses that contain zero or more forms.

(conjugate *number*)

> The conjugate function returns the complex conjugate of a number.

cons

> The cons type specifies the type cons, which is any object that has both a car and a cdr and is not NIL.

(cons *first-element rest-of-list*)

> The cons function creates a new cons cell.

(consp *object*)

> The consp predicate determines if an object is a cons.

(constantp *object*)

> The constantp predicate determines if an object will always return the same value when evaluated.

(copy-alist *list*)

> The copy-alist function returns a list that is a copy of the argument.

(copy-list *list*)

> The copy-list function returns a copy of the argument list that is equal to the argument but is not eq.

(copy-readtable &optional *from-readtable to-readtable*)

> The copy-readtable function makes a copy of a readtable.

(copy-seq *sequence*)

> The copy-seq function returns a copy of the specified sequence.

(copy-symbol *symbol* &optional *copy-properties*)

> The copy-symbol function returns a new and uninterned symbol that has the same print name as that of a given symbol.

(copy-tree *object*)

> The copy-tree function copies a tree of conses.

(cos *radians*)

> The cos function returns the cosine of the argument.

(cosh *number*)

> The cosh function returns the hyperbolic cosine of the argument.

(count *item sequence* &key :from-end :test :test-not
                       :start :end :key)

> The count function returns a nonnegative integer specifying the number of elements in a sequence that satisfy a test.

(count-if *test sequence* &key :from-end :start :end :key)

> The count-if function returns a nonnegative integer specifying the number of elements in a sequence that satisfy a test.

(count-if-not *test sequence* &key :from-end :start :end :key)

> The count-if-not function returns a nonnegative integer specifying the number of elements in a sequence that do not satisfy a test.

(ctypecase *keyplace* { (*type* {*form*}*) }*)

> The ctypecase macro is similar to the typecase macro, except it signals a continuable error when none of the clauses is chosen.

*debug-io*

> The *debug-io* variable is a stream used for interactive debugging.

(decf *place* [*delta*])

> The decf macro decrements a generalized variable.

(declaration *name1 name2* ... )

> The declaration symbol advises the compiler that each name is a valid but nonstandard declaration name. This kind of declaration can only be used via a proclaim.

(declare {{*decl-spec*}* | {*name symbol*}*})

> The declare special form embeds declarations within executable code.

(decode-float *float*)

The decode-float function returns three values specifying a floating-point number.

(decode-universal-time *universal-time* &optional *time-zone*)

The decode-universal-time function returns the universal time in decoded time format.

*default-pathname-defaults*

The *default-pathname-defaults* variable contains the defaults used in creating pathnames.

(defconstant *constant-name initial-value* [*documentation*])

The defconstant macro defines the use of named constants.

(define-modify-macro *name lambda-list function* [*doc-string*])

The define-modify-macro macro defines a new generalized variable manipulating macro.

(define-setf-method *access-fn lambda-list* {*declarations|doc-string*}*{*form*}*)

The define-setf-method macro defines how to setf a generalized variable reference.

(defmacro *name lambda-list* {*declaration | doc-string*}* {*form*}*)

The defmacro macro defines a macro.

(defparameter *variable-name initial-value* [*documentation*])

The defparameter macro declares the use of a special variable in a program.

(defstruct {*structname | (structname* {*options*}*) }
                  [*doc-string*]
                  {*slot-name | (slot-name* [*default-initial-value*]
                                 {*slot-option slot-option-value* }*)}+)

The defstruct macro defines a new structure.

(deftype *name lambda-list* {*declaration | doc-string*}*{*form*}*)

The deftype macro defines a new type specifier abbreviation. The *name* of the type is returned as the value of the deftype form.

(defun *name lambda-list* {*declaration | doc-string*}*{*form*}*)

The defun macro defines a named function. The name of the function is the value returned by defun.

(defvar *variable-name* [*initial-value* [*documentation*]])

The defvar macro declares the use of a special variable in a program.

(delete *item sequence* &key :from-end :test :test-not
                        :start :end :count :key)

> The delete function returns the argument sequence with elements satisfying a test deleted.

(delete-duplicates *sequence* &key :from-end :test :test-not
                            :start :end :key)

> The delete-duplicates function returns a sequence with all duplicate elements deleted.

(delete-file *file*)

> The delete-file function deletes the specified file.

(delete-if *test sequence* &key :from-end :start :end :count :key)

> The delete-if function returns the argument sequence with elements satisfying a test deleted.

(delete-if-not *test sequence* &key :from-end :start :end
                              :count :key)

> The delete-if-not function returns the argument sequence with elements not satisfying a test deleted.

(denominator *rational*)

> The denominator function returns the denominator of a rational number.

(describe *object*)

> The describe function prints information about an object to the *standard-output* stream.

(deposit-field *newbyte byte-specifier integer*)

> The deposit-field function returns the results of replacing a byte of an integer with the same byte from a different integer.

(digit-char *weight* &optional *radix font*)

> The digit-char function returns a character object representing a digit with the specified weight in the specified radix.

(digit-char-p *character* &optional *radix*)

> The digit-char-p predicate determines if a character represents a digit.

(directory *pathname* &key)

> The directory function returns a list of pathnames. Each pathname specifies a file that matches the given *pathname*.

(directory-namestring *pathname*)

> The directory-namestring function returns a string for just the directory-name part of a specified pathname.

(disassemble *name-or-compiled-function*)

>   The disassemble function prints the reverse-assembled code in symbolic format.

(do  ({( *var* [ *init* [ *step*] ]) | *var*}*)   (*end-test* {*result*}*)
>         {*declaration*}* {*tag* | *statement*}*)

>   The do macro does iteration with an arbitrary number of variables.  The variables are bound in parallel.

(do*  ( { (*var* [*init* [*step* ]]) | *var*}*)   (*end-test* {*result*}*)
>         {*declaration*}* {*tag* | *statement*}*)

>   The do* macro does iteration with an arbitrary number of variables.  The variables are bound sequentially.

(do-all-symbols  (*var* [*result-form*])  {*declaration*}* {*tag* | *statement*}*)

>   The do-all-symbols macro provides iteration for every symbol contained in every package.

(documentation *symbol doc-type*)

>   The documentation function returns the documentation string for the specified symbol.

(do-external-symbols  (*var* [ *package* [ *result-form* ]])
>                            {*declaration*}* {*tag* | *statement*}*)

>   The do-external-symbols macro provides iteration over the external symbols of a package.

(dolist  (*var* *listform* [ *resultform*])  {*declaration*}*{*tag* | *statement*}*)

>   The dolist macro evaluates a set of forms once for each element in a list.

(do-symbols  ( *var* [ *package* [*result-form* ]])  {*declaration*}*{*tag* | *statement*}*)

>   The do-symbols macro provides iteration over the accessible symbols of a package.

(dotimes  (*var* *countform* [*resultform*])  {*declaration*}*{*tag* | *statement*}*)

>   The dotimes macro evaluates a set of forms for each value in a range of integers.

{double-float | (double-float {*low* {*high*}}) }

>   The double-float type specifies the type of numbers normally thought of as floats and can provide extended precision on some machines.

double-float-epsilon

>   The double-float-epsilon constant is a small positive value in double floating-point format.

`double-float-negative-epsilon`

> The `double-float-negative-epsilon` constant is a small positive value in double floating-point format.

(dpb *newbyte byte-specifier integer*)

> The `dpb`, deposit byte, function returns the result of replacing a byte of an integer with the rightmost byte from a different integer.

(dribble &optional *pathname*)

> The `dribble` function rebinds `*terminal-io*` in such a way that all iterations with the terminal is also saved to *pathname*. When no arguments are specified, `dribble` is terminated.

(ecase *keyform* { (({ ({*key*}*) | *key*} {*form*}) }*)

> The `ecase` macro is similar to the `case` macro, except it signals a noncontinuable error if none of the clauses is chosen.

(ed &optional *x*)

> The `ed` function invokes the editor.

(eighth *list*)

> The `eighth` function returns the eighth element of a list.

(elt *sequence index*)

> The `elt` function returns an element of a sequence.

(encode-universal-time *second minute hour date month year*
&optional *time-zone*)

> The `encode-universal-time` returns the specified time in universal time format.

(endp *object*)

> The `endp` predicate determines if an object is the end of a list.

(enough-namestring *pathname* &optional *defaults*)

> The `enough-namestring` function returns an abbreviated namestring that is sufficient to identify the file named by a given pathname, considered relative to a specified default.

(eq *object1 object2*)

> The `eq` predicate determines if two objects are identical.

(eql *object1 object2*)

> The `eql` predicate determines if two objects are `eq`, if two numbers of the same type have the same value, or if two character objects represent the same character.

(equal *object1 object2*)

> The equal predicate determines if two objects are structurally similar.

(equalp *object1 object2*)

> The equalp predicate determines if two objects are equal. If they are characters, they must satisfy char-equal. If they are numbers, they must have the same value even if they are of different types. equalp is applied recursively to components of the objects.

(error {*symbol* | *format-string*} &rest *arguments*)

> The error function signals a noncontinuable error.

*error-output*

> The *error-output* variable is a stream used for reporting error messages.

(etypecase *keyform* { (*type* {*form*}*) }*)

> The etypecase macro is similar to the typecase macro, except it signals a noncontinuable error if none of the clauses is chosen.

(eval *form*)

> The eval function evaluates a form and returns its value.

*evalhook*

> The *evalhook* variable, when non-nil, causes eval to pass a form to the *eval-hook-function*.

(evalhook *form eval-hook-function apply-hook-function* &optional *environment*)

> The evalhook function evaluates a form sent to it by eval.

(eval-when ({*situation*}*) {*form*}*)

> The eval-when special form specifies when a portion of code is to be executed.

(evenp *integer*)

> The evenp predicate determines if an integer is even.

(every *predicate sequence* &rest *more-sequences*)

> The every predicate applies a function to arguments constructed from the argument sequences. It returns a non-nil value if all arguments satisfy the test, and NIL otherwise.

(exp *number*)

> The exp function returns *e* raised to a power.

(export *symbols* &optional *package*)

> The export function makes a symbol or list of symbols available in a given package.

(expt *base-number power-number*)

> The expt function returns the result of a number raised to a power.

(fboundp *symbol*)

> The fboundp predicate determines if a symbol has a global function definition.

(fceiling *number* &optional *divisor*)

> The fceiling function returns the smallest integer, in floating point format, not less than the argument.

\*features\*

> The \*features\* variable holds a list of features provided by an implementation.

(ffloor *number* &optional *divisor*)

> The ffloor function returns the largest integer, in floating point format, not greater than the argument.

(fifth *list*)

> The fifth function returns the fifth element of a list.

(file-author *file*)

> The file-author function returns the name of the author of a file.

(file-length *file-stream*)

> The file-length function returns the length of the file associated with the file stream.

(file-namestring *pathname*)

> The file-namestring function returns a string for just the name, type, and version of a specified pathname.

(file-position *file-stream* &optional *position*)

> The file-position function returns the current position in a file if the optional parameter is not specified and sets the position in a file if the optional parameter is specified.

(file-write-date *file*)

> The file-write-date function returns the time at which the file was created or last written to.

(fill *sequence item* &key :start :end)

> The fill function returns the argument sequence in which the specified elements have been replaced by the item.

(fill-pointer *vector*)

> The fill-pointer function returns the value of a vector's fill pointer.

(find *item sequence* &key :from-end :test :test-not
                    :start :end :key)

The find function returns the first element of a sequence that satisfies a test. It returns NIL if no element is found.

(find-all-symbols *string-or-symbol*)

The find-all-symbols function searches all packages in the system, finds specified symbols, and returns them in a list.

(find-if *test sequence* &key :from-end :start :end :key)

The find-if function returns the first element of a sequence that satisfies a test. It returns NIL if no element is found.

(find-if-not *test sequence* &key :from-end :start :end :key)

The find-if-not function returns the first element of a sequence that does not satisfy a test. It returns NIL if no element is found.

(find-package *name*)

The find-package function returns an existing package with the given name or nickname.

(find-symbol *string* &optional *package*)

The find-symbol function searches a given package for a symbol.

(finish-output &optional *output-stream*)

The finish-output function sends all buffered output to the output stream. It returns NIL when the output is sent.

(first *list*)

The first function returns the car of a list.

fixnum

fixnum specifies the type fixnum which is any integer that is not of a size large enough to be a bignum.

(flet ({ (*name lambda-list* {*declaration* | *doc-string*}*{*form*}*) }*) {*form*}*)

The flet special form defines locally named functions.

{float | (float {*low* {*high*}}) }

The float type specifies the type of numbers normally thought of as floating-point numbers and includes the types single-float, double-float, short-float, and long-float.

(float *number* &optional *other-number*)

The float function converts any noncomplex number to a floating-point number.

(float-digits *float*)

> The float-digits function returns a nonnegative integral number of radix digits used in the representation of the floating-point number.

(floatp *object*)

> The floatp predicate determines if an object is a floating-point number.

(float-precision *float*)

> The float-precision function returns a nonnegative integral number of significant radix digits in the floating-point number.

(float-radix *float*)

> The float-radix function returns the integral radix (base) of the floating-point number.

(float-sign *float1* &optional *float2*)

> The float-sign function returns a floating-point number with the same sign as the first number and the same absolute value as the second number.

(floor *number* &optional *divisor*)

> The floor function returns the largest integer not greater than the argument.

(fmakunbound *symbol*)

> The fmakunbound function unbinds a global function.

(force-output &optional *output-stream*)

> The force-output function sends all buffered output to the output stream. It returns NIL immediately.

(format *destination control-string* &rest *arguments*)

> The format function produces formatted output.

(fourth *list*)

> The fourth function returns the fourth element of a list.

(fresh-line &optional *output-stream*)

> The fresh-line function outputs a new line to the output stream if the stream is not already at the start of a new line.

(fround *number* &optional *divisor*)

> The fround function returns the result of rounding its argument in floating-point format.

(ftruncate *number* &optional *divisor*)

> The ftruncate function returns the integer portion of an argument in floating-point format.

(ftype *type function1 function2 ...* )

    The ftype declaration specifier specifies that the named functions will be of the functional type *type*.

(funcall *fn* &rest *arguments*)

    The funcall function returns the value obtained by applying a function to the arguments.

(function *name arglist result-type1 result-type2 ...* )

    The function declaration specifier is a way of declaring functions to be of a specified type.

{function|(function (*arg-type\**) *value-type*)}

    The function specifies the function type which includes the type of the arguments to the function and the type of the value or values returned.

(function *fn*)

    The function special form returns the functional interpretation its argument.

(functionp *object*)

    The functionp predicate determines if an object can be applied to arguments with funcall or apply, for instance.

(gcd &rest *integers*)

    The gcd function returns the greatest common divisor of the integer arguments.

(gensym &optional *x*)

    The gensym function creates and returns a new uninterned symbol.

(gentemp &optional *prefix package*)

    The gentemp function creates and returns a new interned symbol.

(get *symbol indicator* &optional *default*)

    The get function returns the value corresponding to the indicator on the symbol's property list.

(get-decoded-time)

    The get-decoded-time function returns the current time in decoded time format.

(get-dispatch-macro-character *dispatch-character sub-character*
&optional *readtable*)

    The get-dispatch-macro-character function returns the function associated with the dispatch macro character.

(getf *place indicator* &optional *default*)

    The getf function returns the value corresponding to the indicator on the symbol's property list.

(gethash *key hash-table* &optional *default-value*)

The gethash function returns the associated value of the specified key in a hash table. When used with setf, it can add values to the hash table.

(get-internal-real-time)

The get-internal-real-time function returns the current time in internal time format.

(get-internal-run-time)

The get-internal-run-time function returns the current time in internal time format.

(get-macro-character *character* &optional *readtable*)

The get-macro-character function returns the function associated with a macro character and the *non-terminating-p* value for that character.

(get-output-stream-string *string-output-string*)

The get-output-stream-string function returns a stream given it by make-string-output-stream.

(get-properties *place indicator-list*)

The get-properties function searches a property-list, that is stored in a given place for any of the indicators in a given indicator-list until it finds the first property whose indicator is an element of the given indicator-list.

(get-setf-method &optional *form environment*)

The get-setf-method function returns five values that constitute the setf method for form, where form must be a generalized-variable reference.

(get-setf-method-multiple-value &optional *form environment*)

The get-setf-method-multiple-value function is the same as the get-setf-method function, except that it does not check the number of stored values.

(get-universal-time)

The get-universal-time function returns the current time in universal time format.

(go *tag*)

The go special form transfers control to a specified tag within the enclosing tag-body.

(graphic-char-p *character*)

The graphic-char-p predicate determines if a character is a printing character.

`hash-table`

> The `hash-table` type specifies a hash-table type as created by `make-hash-table`.

(`hash-table-count` *hash-table*)

> The `hash-table-count` function returns the number of entries in a hash table.

(`hash-table-p` *object*)

> The `hash-table-p` predicate determines if an object is a hash table.

(`host-namestring` *pathname*)

> The `host-namestring` function returns a string for the host-name part of a specified pathname.

(`identity` *object*)

> The `identity` function returns its argument.

(`if` *test then* [*else*])

> The `if` special form evaluates an initial form and returns the value of a second form when the initial form returns non-nil. Otherwise, `if` returns `NIL` or, when present, the value of a third form.

(`ignore` *var1 var2 ...* )

> The `ignore` declaration specifier specifies that the bindings of the named variables are not used in the scope of this declaration.

(`imagpart` *number*)

> The `imagpart` function returns the imaginary part of a number.

(`import` *symbols* &optional *package*)

> The `import` function makes a symbol or list of symbols available as internal symbols in a given package.

(`incf` *place* [*delta*])

> The `incf` macro increments a generalized variable.

(`inline` *function1 function2 ...* )

> The `inline` declaration specifier tells the compiler to open-code, if possible, calls to the specified functions. An `inline` declaration specifier for a function achieves the same effect as setting the quality *speed* to 3 in `optimize`.

(`in-package` *package-name* &key `:nicknames` `:use`)

> The `in-package` function loads a subsystem into a designated package.

(`input-stream-p` *stream*)

> The `input-stream-p` predicate determines if its argument can handle input operations.

(inspect *object*)

> The inspect function displays information about an object and allows the user to modify parts of it.

(int-char *integer*)

> The int-char function returns the character object encoded by the integer argument. It returns NIL if no character object is specified by the integer argument.

{integer|(integer {*low* {*high*}})}

> The integer type specifies the type of numbers normally thought of as integers and consists of exactly the set of fixnums and bignums.

(integer-decode-float *float*)

> The integer-decode-float function returns three values specifying a floating-point number.

(integer-length *integer*)

> The integer-length function determines the number of bits required to store the integer value.

(integerp *object*)

> The integerp predicate determines if an object is an integer.

(intern *string* &optional *package*)

> The intern function searches a given package for a symbol and creates it if it is not found.

internal-time-units-per-second

> The internal-time-units-per-second constant is an integer that represents the number of internal time units in a second.

(intersection *list1* *list2* &key :test :test-not :key)

> The intersection function returns a list of all elements included in both argument lists.

(isqrt *integer*)

> The isqrt function returns the greatest integer less than or equal to the positive square root of an argument.

keyword

> The keyword type specifies the type of object that is a symbol and whose home package is the keyword package.

(keywordp *object*)

> The keywordp predicate determines if an object is a symbol that belongs to a keyword package.

(labels ({ (*name lambda-list* {*declaration* | *doc-string*}\*{*form*}\*) }\*) {*form*}\*)

The labels special form defines locally named functions.

(lambda *lambda-list . body*)
(lambda ({*var*}\*
       [&optional {*var* | (*var* [*initform* [*svar*]]) }\*]
       [&rest *var*]
       [&key {*var* | ({*var* | (*keyword var*) } [*initform* [*svar*]]) }\*
            [&allow-other-keys]]
       [&aux {*var* | (*var* [*initform*]) }\*])
       {*declaration* | *documentation-string*}\*
       {*form*}\*)

The lambda expression defines a form that is executed with the variables bound to the corresponding parameters.

lambda-list-keywords

The lambda-list-keywords constant contains the list of all lambda-list keywords.

lambda-parameters-limit

The lambda-parameters-limit constant is a positive integer that specifies the maximum number of parameters that can appear in a single lambda-list.

(last *list*)

The last function returns the last cons of a list.

(lcm *integer* &rest *more-integers*)

The lcm function returns the least common multiple of the integer arguments.

(ldb *byte-specifier integer*)

The ldb, load byte, function returns a number representing a byte of the specified integer.

(ldb-test *byte-specifier integer*)

The ldb-test predicate determines if the value returned by ldb is nonzero.

(ldiff *list sublist*)

The ldiff function returns a copy of the elements of a list that appear before the specified sublist.

least-negative-double-float

The least-negative-double-float constant is the negative value closest to zero in double floating-point format.

least-negative-long-float

The least-negative-long-float constant is the negative value closest to zero in long floating-point format.

`least-negative-short-float`

> The `least-negative-short-float` constant is the negative value closest to zero in short floating-point format.

`least-negative-single-float`

> The `least-negative-single-float` constant is the negative value closest to zero in single floating-point format.

`least-positive-double-float`

> The `least-positive-double-float` constant is the positive value closest to zero in double floating-point format.

`least-positive-long-float`

> The `least-positive-long-float` constant is the positive value closest to zero in long floating-point format.

`least-positive-short-float`

> The `least-positive-short-float` constant is the positive value closest to zero in short floating-point format.

`least-positive-single-float`

> The `least-positive-single-float` constant is the positive value closest to zero in single floating-point format.

(`length` *sequence*)

> The `length` function returns the number of elements in a sequence.

(`let`  ({*var*|(*var value*) }*) {*declaration*}* {*forms*}*)

> The `let` special form evaluates a series of forms with specified variables bound to specified values.  Variable assignments are made in parallel.

(`let*`  ({*var*|(*var value*)}*) {*declaration*}* {*forms*}*)

> The `let*` special form evaluates a series of forms with specified variables bound to specified values.

(`lisp-implementation-type`)

> The `lisp-implementation-type` function returns a string identifying the type of Common Lisp implemented.

(`lisp-implementation-version`)

> The `lisp-implementation-version` function returns a string identifying the version of Common Lisp implemented.

`list`

> The `list` type specifies a type that contains any object that is NIL or a cons whose cdr is a list.

(list &rest *arguments*)

>    The list function constructs and returns a list of its arguments.

(list* *argument* &rest *more-arguments*)

>    The list* function constructs and returns a list of its arguments.  The last argument is the cdr of the last cons constructed.

(list-all-packages)

>    The list-all-packages function returns a list of all packages that currently exist in the system.

(listen &optional *input-stream*)

>    The listen predicate determines if there is a character immediately available from the input stream.

(list-length *list*)

>    The list-length function returns the top-level length of a list.

(listp *object*)

>    The listp predicate determines if an object is a list.

(load *filename* &key :verbose :print :if-does-not-exist)

>    The load function loads the specified file into the Lisp environment.

*load-verbose*

>    The *load-verbose* variable provides the default :verbose argument to load.

(locally {*declarations*}* {*form*}*)

>    The locally macro makes local pervasive declarations.

(log *number* &optional *base*)

>    The log function returns the logarithm of a number in the specified base.

(logand &rest *integers*)

>    The logand function returns the logical and of its argument.

(logandc1 *integer1* *integer2*)

>    The logandc1 function returns the logical and of the complement of its first argument with its second argument.

(logandc2 *integer1* *integer2*)

>    The logandc2 function returns the logical and of its first argument with the complement of its second argument.

(logbitp *index integer*)

>    The logbitp predicate determines if the specified bit in an integer is set.

(logcount *integer*)

> The logcount function returns the number of bits in the argument.

(logeqv &rest *integers*)

> The logeqv function returns the logical equivalence of its arguments.

(logior &rest *integers*)

> The logior function returns the logical inclusive or of its arguments.

(lognand *integer1 integer2*)

> The lognand function returns the logical nand of the arguments.

(lognor *integer1 integer2*)

> The lognor function returns the logical nor of its arguments.

(lognot *integer*)

> The lognot function returns the logical not of its argument.

(logorc1 *integer1 integer2*)

> The logorc1 function returns the logical or of the complement of its first argument with the second argument.

(logorc2 *integer1 integer2*)

> The logorc2 function returns the logical or of the first argument with the complement of the second argument.

(logtest *integer1 integer2*)

> The logtest predicate determines if any of the bits designated by 1s in the first argument are 1s in the second argument.

(logxor &rest *integers*)

> The logxor function returns the logical exclusive or of the arguments.

{long-float|(long-float {*low* {*high*}}) }

> The long-float type specifies the type of numbers normally thought of as floats and can provide extended precision on some machines.

long-float-epsilon

> The long-float-epsilon is a small positive value in long floating-point format.

long-float-negative-epsilon

> The long-float-negative-epsilon is a small positive value in long floating-point format.

(long-site-name)

> The long-site-name function returns a string identifying the physical location of the hardware.

(loop {*form*}*)

> The loop macro repeatedly evaluates a series of forms.

(lower-case-p *character*)

> The lower-case-p predicate determines if a character object is lowercase.

(machine-instance)

> The machine-instance function returns a string identifying the instance of the hardware.

(machine-type)

> The machine-type function returns a string identifying the type of hardware.

(machine-version)

> The machine-version function returns a string identifying the version of hardware.

(macroexpand *form* &optional *environment*)

> The macroexpand function provides a means of expanding a macro call.

(macroexpand-1 *form* &optional *environment*)

> The macroexpand-1 function provides a means of expanding a macro call.

*macroexpand-hook*

> The *macroexpand-hook* variable is a global variable whose value provides the expansion interface hook for macroexpand-1.

(macro-function *symbol*)

> The macro-function examines a symbol and returns NIL when the symbol does not name a macro; otherwise, it returns its expansion function.

(macrolet ({ (*name lambda-list* {*declaration* | *doc-string*}* {*form*}*) }*) {*form*}*)

> The macrolet special form defines locally named macros.

(make-array *dimensions* &key :element-type :initial-element
                              :initial-contents :adjustable
                              :fill-pointer
                              :displaced-to :displaced-index-offset)

> The make-array function creates an array.

(make-broadcast-stream &rest *streams*)

> The make-broadcast-stream function creates and returns a stream that works only in the output direction.

(make-char *character* &optional *bits font*)

> The make-char function constructs a character object similar to the character argument.

(make-concatenated-stream &rest *streams*)

> The make-concatenated-stream function creates and returns a stream that works only in the input direction.

(make-dispatch-macro-character *character*
                                              &optional *non-terminating-p readtable*)

> The make-dispatch-macro-character function causes a character to be a dispatching macro character in the readtable.

(make-echo-stream *input-stream output-stream*)

> The make-echo-stream function returns a bidirectional stream that gets its input from *input-stream* and sends its output to *output-stream*, and echoes input from *input-stream* to *output-stream*.

(make-hash-table &key :test :size
                            :rehash-size :rehash-threshold)

> The make-hash-table function creates and returns a hash table.

(make-list *size* &key :initial-element)

> The make-list function returns a list of the specified length.

(make-package *package-name* &key :nicknames :use)

> The make-package function creates and returns a new package that has a specified package name.

(make-pathname &key :host :device :directory
                          :name :type :version :defaults)

> The make-pathname function constructs and returns a pathname.

(make-random-state &optional *state*)

> The make-random-state function returns an object of type random-state.

(make-sequence *type size* &key :initial-element)

> The make-sequence function returns a sequence of the specified type and size.

(make-string *size* &key :initial-element)

> The make-string function returns a simple string of the specified length.

(make-string-input-stream *string* &optional *start end*)

> The make-string-input-stream function returns an input stream.

(make-string-output-stream)

> The make-string-output-stream function returns an output stream that accumulates output given it for the benefit of get-output-stream-string.

(make-symbol *symbol*)

> The make-symbol function creates a new and uninterned symbol for a given printname with an empty property list and unbound value and function binding.

(make-synonym-string *symbol*)

> The make-synonym-stream function creates and returns a synonym stream.

(make-two-way-stream *input-stream output-stream*)

> The make-two-way-stream function returns a bidirectional stream that gets its input from *input-stream* and sends its output to *output-stream*.

(makunbound *symbol*)

> The makunbound function unbinds the given dynamic variable.

(map *result-type function sequence* &rest *more-sequences*)

> The map function returns a sequence of the specified type formed by applying a function to arguments constructed from the argument sequences.

(mapc *function list* &rest *more-lists*)

> The mapc function works like the mapcar function, but it returns the second parameter.

(mapcan *function list* &rest *more-lists*)

> The mapcan function works like the mapcar function, but it combines the values returned by a function according to nconc instead of list.

(mapcar *function list* &rest *more-lists*)

> The mapcar function applies a function to each element of each list in a series of lists.

(mapcon *function list* &rest *more-lists*)

> The mapcon function works like the maplist function, but it combines the values returned by a function according to nconc instead of list.

(maphash *function hash-table*)

> The maphash function applies the given function to each entry in the hash table. The function is passed the key for the entry and the value of that entry. maphash always returns NIL.

(mapl *function list* &rest *more-lists*)

> The mapl function works like the maplist function, but it returns the second parameter.

(maplist *function list* &rest *more-lists*)

> The maplist function applies a function to each list and to the successive cdrs of the list.

(mask-field *byte-specifier integer*)

> The mask-field function returns the specified byte of the integer argument in the same position as in the integer with zeros in all other bit positions.

(max *number* &rest *more-numbers*)

> The `max` function returns its largest argument.

(member *object-list*)

> `member` creates a type specifier from a list of specific objects.

(member *item list* &key :test :test-not :key)

> The `member` function determines if there is an element, x, of a list, such that item and x satisfy the test.

(member-if *predicate list* &key :key)

> The `member-if` function determines if an element of a list satisfies a test.

(member-if-not *predicate list* &key :key)

> The `member-if-not` function determines if an element of a list does not satisfy a test.

(merge *result-type sequence1 sequence2 predicate* &key :key)

> The `merge` function returns a sequence that contains the elements of two sorted sequences in sorted order.

(merge-pathnames *pathname* &optional *defaults default-version*)

> The `merge-pathnames` function returns a pathname by filling in unspecified components of the argument from default values.

(min *number* &rest *more-numbers*)

> The `min` function returns its smallest argument.

(minusp *number*)

> The `minusp` predicate determines if a number is less than zero.

(mismatch *sequence1 sequence2* &key :from-end :test :test-not :key :start1 :start2 :end1 :end2)

> The `mismatch` function returns an index into *sequence1* at the point where it no longer matches *sequence2*.

(mod *modulus*)

> The `mod` type specifies the type of numbers normally thought of as mods and consists of exactly the set of fixnums and bignums.

(mod *number divisor*)

> The `mod` function returns the remainder of a `floor` operation.

*modules*

> The `*modules*` variable is a list of the names of modules currently loaded into the system.

more-detail

> The more-detail function displays the chain of active lexical environments for an interpreted function.

most-negative-double-float

> The most-negative-double-float constant is the value closest to negative infinity in double floating-point format.

most-negative-fixnum

> The most-negative-fixnum constant is the smallest fixnum.

most-negative-long-float

> The most-negative-long-float constant is the closest value to negative infinity in long floating-point format.

most-negative-short-float

> The most-negative-short-float constant is the closest value to negative infinity in short floating-point format.

most-negative-single-float

> The most-negative-single-float constant is the closest value to negative infinity in single floating-point format.

most-positive-double-float

> The most-positive-double-float constant is the closest value to positive infinity in double floating-point format.

most-positive-fixnum

> The most-positive-fixnum constant is the largest fixnum.

most-positive-long-float

> The most-positive-long-float constant is the closest value to positive infinity in long floating-point format.

most-positive-short-float

> The most-positive-short-float constant is the closest value to positive infinity in short floating-point format.

most-positive-single-float

> The most-positive-single-float constant is the closest value to positive infinity in single floating-point format.

(multiple-value-bind ({*var*}*) *value-form* {*declaration*}* {*form*}*)

> The multiple-value-bind macro evaluates the form with each of the variables bound to respective values returned by the *value-form*.

`(multiple-value-call` *function* {*form*}\*)

> The `multiple-value-call` special form applies the specified function to the values returned by the forms.

`(multiple-value-list` *form*)

> The `multiple-value-list` macro evaluates a form and returns the multiple values returned by the form as a list.

`(multiple-value-prog1` *form* {*form*}\*)

> The `multiple-value-prog1` special form evaluates a series of forms, returning all values returned by the first form.

`(multiple-value-setq` *variables form*)

> The `multiple-value-setq` macro sets the variables to the respective values returned by the form.

`multiple-values-limit`

> The `multiple-values-limit` function returns an integer for the upper exclusive number of values a function can return.

`(name-char` *name*)

> The `name-char` function returns the character object named by the argument. It returns `NIL` if the argument does not name a character object.

`(namestring` *pathname*)

> The `namestring` function returns the full form of a specified pathname as a string.

`(nbutlast` *list* &optional *n*)

> The `nbutlast` function returns the argument list with the last *n* elements removed.

`(nconc` &rest *lists*)

> The `nconc` function destructively concatenates its arguments together.

`nil`

> The `nil` type specifies the type nil which is a subtype of all types and nothing is of this type.

`nil`

> The `nil` constant has a value of `NIL`. This is the logical false value.

`(nintersection` *list1 list2* &key `:test` `:test-not` `:key`)

> The `nintersection` function returns a list containing all the elements that appear in both argument lists.

(ninth *list*)

The ninth function returns the ninth element of a list.

(not *type*)

The not type creates a type specifier whose members are not those of a given type.

(not *argument*)

The not function inverts the Boolean value of an object.

(notany *predicate sequence* &rest *more-sequences*)

The notany predicate applies a function to arguments constructed from the argument sequences. It returns a non-nil value if none of the arguments satisfies the test, and returns NIL otherwise.

(notevery *predicate sequence* &rest *more-sequences*)

The notevery predicate applies a function to arguments constructed from the argument sequences. It returns a non-nil value if at least one of the arguments does not satisfy the test, and returns NIL otherwise.

(notinline *function1 function2 ...* )

The notinline declaration specifier tells the compiler not to compile the specified functions in-line.

(nreconc *x y*)

The nreconc function concatenates its second argument to the reverse of its first argument. The first argument is modified.

(nreverse *sequence*)

The nreverse function returns a sequence in the reverse order of the argument sequence. The argument can be modified.

(nset-difference *list1 list2* &key :test :test-not :key)

The nset-difference function returns a list of the elements of the first argument list that are not in the second argument list.

(nset-exclusive-or *list1 list2* &key :test :test-not :key)

The nset-exclusive-or function returns a list of the elements that appear in only one of the argument lists.

(nstring-capitalize *string* &key :start :end)

The nstring-capitalize function returns the argument string with the first character of each word in the specified substring capitalized, provided it is case-modifiable. All other case-modifiable characters are converted to lowercase.

(nstring-downcase *string* &key :start :end)

The nstring-downcase function returns the argument string with all case-modifiable characters in lowercase.

(nstring-upcase *string* &key :start :end)

The nstring-upcase function returns a string with all case-modifiable characters in uppercase.

(nsublis *alist tree* &key :test :test-not :key)

The nsublis function returns the argument list with subtrees and leaves replaced.

(nsubst *new old tree* &key :test :test-not :key)

The nsubst function returns the argument list in which *new* has been substituted for every leaf or subtree x, such that *old* and x satisfy the test.

(nsubst-if *new test tree* &key :test :test-not :key)

The nsubst-if function returns the argument list in which *new* has been substituted for every subtree and leaf.

(nsubst-if-not *new test tree* &key :key)

The nsubst-if-not function returns the argument list in which subtrees and leaves have been replaced by *new*.

(nsubstitute *newitem olditem sequence*
    &key :from-end :test :test-not :start :end :count :key)

The nsubstitute function returns the argument sequence with *newitem* substituted for every element x, such that *olditem* and x satisfy the test.

(nsubstitute-if *newitem test sequence*
    &key :from-end :start :end :count :key)

The nsubstitute-if function returns the argument sequence with *newitem* substituted for every element of the sequence that satisfies the test.

(nsubstitute-if-not *newitem test sequence*
    &key :from-end :start :end :count :key)

The nsubstitute-if-not function returns the argument sequence with *newitem* substituted for every element that fails the test.

(nth *n list*)

The nth function returns the specified element of a list.

(nthcdr *n list*)

The nthcdr function returns the nth cdr of a list.

null

The null type specifies the type null, which is a subtype of symbol, and only NIL is of this type.

(null *object*)

The null function returns true if its argument is nil.

number

> The `number` type specifies the type of all numeric objects in Lisp and includes exactly the members of rational, float, and complex.

(numberp *object*)

> The `numberp` predicate determines if an object is a number.

(numerator *rational*)

> The `numerator` function returns the numerator of a rational number.

(nunion *list1 list2* &key `:test` `:test-not` `:key`)

> The `nunion` function returns a list that contains the elements of the argument lists.

(oddp *integer*)

> The `oddp` function determines if an integer is odd.

(open *filename* &key `:direction` `:element-type`
                      `:if-exists` `:if-does-not-exist`)

> The `open` function returns a file stream that is connected to a specified file.

(optimize  (*quality1 value1*)  (*quality2 value2*) ( ... ) )

> The `optimize` declaration tells the compiler that each *quality* should be given attention according to a specified *value*.

(or *types-list*)

> The `or` type creates a type specifier that is the union of the given types.

(or {*form*}*)

> The `or` macro evaluates forms and returns the first non-nil value. If all forms evaluate to `NIL`, `NIL` is returned.

(output-stream-p *stream*)

> The `output-stream-p` predicate determines if its argument can handle output operations.

package

> `package` specifies the type that contains all packages.

*package*

> The `*package*` type variable must have a value that is a package, which is designated as the current package.

(package-name *package*)

> The `package-name` function returns the string that names a given package.

(package-nicknames *package*)

> The `package-nicknames` function returns a list of strings for nicknames for a given package, not including the package name.

(packagep *object*)

> The packagep predicate determines if an object is a package.

(package-shadowing-symbols *package*)

> The package-shadowing-symbols function returns a list of symbols declared as shadowing symbols for a given package.

(package-used-by-list *package*)

> The package-used-by-list function returns a list of other packages that use a given package.

(package-use-list *package*)

> The package-use-list function returns a list of other packages used by a given package.

(pairlis *key data* &optional *a-list*)

> The pairlis function returns an association list that associates elements of the first argument list with the corresponding elements in the second argument list.

(parse-integer *string* &key :start :end :radix :junk-allowed)

> The parse-integer function reads a string and returns the integer represented in the string.

(parse-namestring *thing* &optional *host defaults*
  &key :start :end :junk-allowed)

> The parse-namestring function converts its argument to a pathname via parsing.

pathname

> The pathname type specifies the type that contains all objects that represent filenames.

(pathname *pathname*)

> The pathname function converts its argument to a pathname.

(pathname-device *pathname*)

> The pathname-device function returns the device component of a specified pathname.

(pathname-directory *pathname*)

> The pathname-directory function returns the directory component of a specified pathname.

(pathname-host *pathname*)

> The pathname-host function returns the host component of a specified pathname.

(pathname-name *pathname*)

The pathname-name function returns the name component of a specified pathname.

(pathnamep *object*)

The pathnamep predicate determines if its argument is a pathname.

(pathname-type *pathname*)

The pathname-type function returns the type component of a specified pathname.

(pathname-version *pathname*)

The pathname-version function returns the version component of a specified pathname.

(peek-char &optional *peek-type input-stream eof-error-p eof-value recursive-p*)

The peek-char returns the next character to be read from the input stream.

(phase *number*)

The phase function returns the angle part of a number's polar representation in complex-number format.

pi

The pi constant returns an approximation of $\pi$.

(plusp *number*)

The plusp predicate determines if a number is greater than zero.

(pop *place*)

The pop macro expands into forms that remove the first element from a list and return the removed element.

(position *item sequence* &key :from-end :test :test-not
                             :start :end :key)

The position function returns the index into a sequence of the first element that satisfies a test.

(position-if *test sequence* &key :from-end :start :end :key)

The position-if function returns the index into a sequence of the first element that satisfies a test.

(position-if-not *test sequence* &key :from-end :start :end :key)

The position-if-not function returns the index into a sequence of the first element that does not satisfy a test.

(pprint *object* &optional *output-stream*)

The pprint function outputs a new line followed by the printed representation of an object using print-pretty format.

(prin1 *object* &optional *output-stream*)

> The `prin1` function outputs the printed representation of an object using escape characters as appropriate.

(prin1-to-string *object*)

> The `prin1-to-string` function returns the characters produced by `prin1` in a string.

(princ *object* &optional *output-stream*)

> The `princ` function outputs an object, omitting escape characters.

(princ-to-string *object*)

> The `princ-to-string` function returns the characters produced by `princ` and made into a string.

(print *object* &optional *output-stream*)

> The `print` function outputs a new line followed by the printed representation of an object and a space.

*print-array*

> The `*print-array*` variable specifies whether or not the printer outputs the contents of arrays.

*print-base*

> The `*print-base*` variable specifies the radix the printer uses to print rational numbers.

*print-case*

> The `*print-case*` variable specifies the letter case in which the printer outputs symbols. The value of `*print-case*` should be one of the keywords: `:upcase`, `:downcase`, or `:capitalize`.

*print-circle*

> The `*print-circle*` variable specifies whether or not the printer tests for a circular structure before printing the structure.

*print-escape*

> The `*print-escape*` variable specifies whether or not the printer outputs escape characters.

*print-gensym*

> The `*print-gensym*` variable specifies whether or not the printer outputs the prefix #: when a symbol has no home package.

*print-length*

> The `*print-length*` variable specifies the number of elements at each level the printer outputs.

`*print-level*`

> The `*print-level*` variable specifies the number of levels deep a nested object will be printed.

`*print-pretty*`

> The `*print-pretty*` variable specifies the amount of white space the printer outputs.

`*print-radix*`

> The `*print-radix*` variable specifies whether or not the printer indicates the radix when outputting rational numbers.

(`probe-file` *file*)

> The `probe-file` function determines if the specified file exists.

(`proclaim` *declaration-specifier*)

> The `proclaim` function accepts a declaration-specification and establishes it globally.

(`prog`  ({*var*|(*var* [*init*]) }*)  {*declaration*}* {*tag*|*statement*}*)

> The `prog` macro establishes an implicit `block` named `NIL`, initializes local variables, and then executes a body as an implicit `tagbody`.

(`prog*`  ({*var*|(*var* [*init*]) }*)  {*declaration*}* {*tag*|*statement*}*)

> The `prog*` macro works like `prog`, except that the initialization of local variables occurs sequentially instead of in parallel.

(`prog1` *first* {*form*}*)

> The `prog1` macro executes the forms sequentially and returns the value of the first form.

(`prog2` *first second* {*form*}*)

> The `prog2` macro executes the forms sequentially and returns the value of the second form.

(`progn` {*form*}*)

> The `progn` special form  executes the forms sequentially and returns the value of the last form.

(`progv` *symbols values* {*form*}*)

> The `progv` special form binds dynamic variables whose names can be determined at run time.

(`provide` *module-name*)

> The `provide` function adds a new module name to the current list of modules in `*modules*`.

(psetf {*place newvalue*}*)

The psetf macro assigns values to generalized variables in parallel.

(psetq {*var form*}*)

The psetq macro assigns values to variables in parallel.

(push *item place*)

The push macro expands into forms that cons an item onto the front of a list held in a generalized variable.

(pushnew *item place* &key :test :test-not :key)

The pushnew macro expands into forms that conditionally concatenate an item onto the front of a list held in a generalized variable.

*query-io*

The *query-io* variable is a stream used for asking questions of users.

(quote *object*)

The quote special form returns its argument unevaluated.

(random *number* &optional *state*)

The random function returns a pseudo-random number.

random-state

The random-state type specifies the type random-state which is the type of an object used to store the state of an internal random-number generator.

*random-state*

The *random-state* variable holds a random-state data structure.

(random-state-p *object*)

The random-state-p predicate determines if an object is of type random-state.

(rassoc *item alist* &key :test :test-not :key)

The rassoc function returns the first (leftmost) pair of an association list whose cdr satisfies the test.

(rassoc-if *predicate alist*)

The rassoc-if function returns the first (leftmost) pair of an association list whose cdr satisfies the test.

(rassoc-if-not *predicate alist*)

The rassoc-if-not function returns the first (leftmost) pair of an association list whose cdr does not satisfy the test.

ratio

The ratio type specifies the type of numbers normally thought of as rational numbers that are stored as the ratio of two numbers.

(rationalp *object*)

> The rationalp predicate determines if an object is a rational number (a ratio or an integer).

{rational|(rational {*low* {*high*}})}

> The rational type specifies the type of numbers normally thought of as rational numbers and includes the types ratio and integer.

(rational *number*)

> The rational function converts a non-complex number to a rational number. This function assumes that the floating-point number is completely accurate and returns a rational number mathematically equal to the precise value of the floating-point number.

(rationalize *number*)

> The rationalize function converts a non-complex number to a rational number. This function returns the best available rational approximation of the floating-point argument; in doing so, it attempts to keep both numerator and denominator small.

(read &optional *input-stream eof-error-p eof-value recursive-p* )

> The read function reads an object from an input stream.

*read-base*

> The *read-base* variable contains the radix in that integers and ratios are to be read.

(read-byte *binary-input-stream* &optional *eof-error-p eof-value*)

> The read-byte function reads one byte from an input stream and returns it as an integer.

(read-char &optional *input-stream eof-error-p eof-value recursive-p*)

> The read-char function reads a character from an input stream.

(read-char-no-hang &optional *input-stream eof-error-p eof-value recursive-p*)

> The read-char-no-hang function determines if there is a character in the input stream.  It returns the character if there is one, or returns NIL.

*read-default-float-format*

> The *read-default-float-format* variable specifies the format the reader uses to read floating-point numbers that do not have an exponent marker.

(read-delimited-list *character* &optional *input-stream recursive-p*)

> The read-delimited-list function reads objects from an input stream until the specified delimited character is read.

(read-from-string *string* &optional *eof-error-p eof-value*
                          &key :start :end :preserve-whitespace)

The read-from-string function reads a Lisp object from a string.

(read-line &optional *input-stream eof-error-p eof-value recursive-p*)

The read-line function reads an input stream until an end-of-line is read. It returns the character string without the new-line character.

(read-preserving-whitespace &optional *input-stream eof-error-p*
                                      *eof-value recursive-p*)

The read-preserving-whitespace function reads an input stream and returns the object. It does not discard white space.

*read-suppress*

The *read-suppress* variable determines if the reader suppresses certain operations.

readtable

The readtable type specifies the type readtable which is the type of an object used to store the information used by the system reader in parsing its input.

*readtable*

The *readtable* variable contains the readtable that controls the syntax the reader uses.

(readtablep *object*)

The readtablep predicate determines if an object is a readtable.

(realpart *number*)

The realpart function returns the real part of a number.

(reduce *function sequence* &key :from-end
                                 :start :end :initial-value)

The reduce function returns the result of successively applying a binary function to the elements of a sequence.

(rem *number divisor*)

The rem function returns the remainder of the truncate operation.

(remf *place indicator*)

The remf macro removes a property that is stored in the generalized variable that has an indicator eq to a given indicator.

(remhash *key hash-table*)

The remhash function removes an entry from a hash table.

(remove *item sequence* &key :from-end :test :test-not :start :end
:count :key)

The remove function returns a copy of the argument sequence with specified elements removed.

(remove-duplicates *sequence* &key :from-end :test
:test-not:start :end :key)

The remove-duplicates function returns a sequence from which duplicate elements have been removed.

(remove-if *test sequence* &key :from-end :start :end :count :key)

The remove-if function returns a copy of the argument sequence with elements satisfying a test removed.

(remove-if-not *test sequence* &key :from-end :start :end
:count :key)

The remove-if-not function returns a copy of the argument sequence with elements not satisfying a test removed.

(remprop *symbol indicator*)

The remprop function removes the property from the symbol's property list that has an indicator eq to the given indicator.

(rename-file *file new-name*)

The rename-file function renames the specified file.

(rename-package *package new-name* &optional *new-nicknames*)

The rename-package function changes the name of a package.

(replace *sequence1 sequence2* &key :start1 :end1 :start2 :end2)

The replace function replaces elements in the first sequence with elements in the second sequence and returns the modified first sequence.

(require *module-name* &optional *pathname*)

The require function loads a module if it is not currently present.

(rest *list*)

The rest function returns the cdr of a list.

(return [*result*])

The return macro exits from a lexically visible block named NIL. The result is used as the value of the block.

(return-from *name* [*result*])

The return-from special form exits from a lexically visible block with the given name. The result is used as the value of the block.

(revappend *x y*)

> The `revappend` function returns a list in which the second argument is appended to the reverse of the first argument.

(reverse *sequence*)

> The `reverse` function returns a sequence containing the same elements as in the argument sequence, but in reverse order. The argument is not modified.

(room &optional *x*)

> The `room` function prints information about the state of internal storage.

(rotatef {*place*}*)

> The `rotatef` macro rotates the values in the generalized variables specified to the left.

(round *number* &optional *divisor*)

> The `round` function rounds its argument to the nearest integer.

(rplaca *x y*)

> The `rplaca` function replaces the car of the first argument with the second argument and returns the modified argument.

(rplacd *x y*)

> The `rplacd` function replaces the cdr of the first argument with the second argument and returns the modified argument.

(satisfies *predicate-name*)

> The `satisfies` type creates a type specifier from a predicate.

(sbit *simple-bit-array* &rest *subscripts*)

> The `sbit` function returns the specified bit of a simple bit array.

(scale-float *float integer*)

> The `scale-float` function accepts a floating-point number $f$ and an integer $k$ and returns (*f (expt (float b f) k)).

(schar *simple-string index*)

> The `schar` function returns a character in a simple string

(search *sequence1 sequence2* &key :from-end :test :test-not :key
                              :start1 :start2 :end1 :end2)

> The `search` function returns an index into *sequence2* of the first element, which begins a subsequence that matches the elements in *sequence1*. If there is no such subsequence, `search` returns NIL.

(second *list*)

The second function returns the second element of a list.

sequence

The sequence type specifies the type of objects that deal with ordered sets of elements and includes vectors and lists.

(set *symbol value*)

The set function alters the value of a dynamic variable. The value is returned.

(set-char-bit *character character-bit new-value*)

The set-char-bit function creates a character object identical to *character*, except possibly in the character-bit position.

(set-difference *list1 list2* &key :test :test-not :key)

The set-difference function returns a list of the elements of the first argument list that do not appear in the second argument list.

(set-dispatch-macro-character *dispatch-character sub-character function*
&optional *readtable*)

The set-dispatch-macro-character function associates a function with a dispatch macro character.

(set-exclusive-or *list1 list2* &key :test :test-not :key)

The set-exclusive-or function returns a list of the elements which appear in only one of the two argument lists.

(setf {*place newvalue*}*)

The setf macro updates a generalized variable with a new value.

(set-macro-character *character function non-terminating-p readtable*)

The set-macro-character function associates a function with a character.

(set-syntax-from-char *to-char from-char*
&optional *to-readtable from-readtable*)

The set-syntax-from-char function makes the syntax of a character in one readtable the same as a character in another readtable.

(setq {*var form*}*)

The setq special form assigns values to variables. It returns the last value assigned.

(seventh *list*)

The seventh function returns the seventh element of a list.

(shadow *symbols* &optional *package*)

The shadow function searches for a given symbol in a specified package and creates the symbol if it does not currently exist, placing symbols in the shadowing list.

(shadowing-import *symbols* &optional *package*)

The shadowing-import function makes a symbol or list of symbols available as internal symbols in a given package.

(shiftf {*place*}⁺ *newvalue*)

The shiftf macro shifts the values of the generalized variables to the left, gives the last location a new value, and returns the first location's value.

{short-float|(short-float {*low* {*high*}})}

The short-float type specifies the type of numbers normally thought of as floats and can provide extended precision on some machines.

short-float-epsilon

The short-float-epsilon constant is a small, short floating-point number.

short-float-negative-epsilon

The short-float-negative-epsilon constant is a small value in short floating-point format.

(short-site-name)

The short-site-name function returns the physical location of the hardware.

{signed-byte|(signed-byte *num-bits*)}

The signed-byte type specifies the type of the integers that can be represented in s-bit two's complement number, that is from $-2^{(s-1)}$ to $2^{(s-1)}-1$.

(signum *number*)

The signum function returns the sign of a number.

{simple-array|(simple-array {*element-type* {*dimension*}})}

The simple-array type specifies the type of simple-arrays of varying dimension and element type.

{simple-bit-vector|(simple-bit-vector {*size*})}

The simple-bit-vector type specifies the type simple-bit-vectors, which are vectors whose elements are either integer 1 or 0.

(simple-bit-vector-p *object*)

The simple-bit-vector-p predicate determines if an object is a simple bit vector.

{simple-string|(simple-string {*size*})}

The simple-string type specifies the type simple-string, which is a simple-array of elements of type string-char.

(simple-string-p *object*)

The simple-string-p predicate determines if an object is a simple string.

{simple-vector│(simple-vector {*size*})}

> The simple-vector type specifies the type simple-vector, which are vectors whose elements can be of any type and whose array structure is simple.

(simple-vector-p *object*)

> The simple-vector-p predicate determines if an object is a simple vector.

(sin *radians*)

> The sin function returns the sine of the argument.

{single-float│(single-float {*low* {*high*}})}

> The single-float type specifies the type of numbers normally thought of as floats and can provide extended precision on some machines.

single-float-epsilon

> The single-float-epsilon is a small value in single floating-point format.

single-float-negative-epsilon

> The single-float-negative-epsilon is a small value in single floating-point format.

(sinh *number*)

> The sinh function returns the hyperbolic sine of the argument.

(sixth *list*)

> The sixth function returns the sixth element of a list.

(sleep *seconds*)

> The sleep function causes execution to cease for the specified number of seconds.

(software-type)

> The software-type function returns a string which identifies the supporting software.

(software-version)

> The software-version function returns a string that identifies the version of the supporting software.

(some *predicate sequence* &rest *more-sequences*)

> The some predicate applies a function to arguments constructed from the argument sequences. It returns the first non-nil value which results from the function application or NIL if no function application is non-nil.

(sort *sequence predicate* &key :key)

> The sort function returns the argument sequence in sorted order.

(special *var1 var2* ... )

>The `special` declaration specifier specifies that all variables named are to be considered *special*.

(special-form-p *symbol*)

>The `special-form-p` predicate determines if a symbol globally names a special form.

(sqrt *number*)

>The `sqrt` function returns the principal square root of a number.

(stable-sort *sequence predicate* &key :key)

>The `stable-sort` function returns the argument sequence in a sorted order.

standard-char

>The `standard-char` type specifies the type of all single standard-chars known to Lisp.

(standard-char-p *character*)

>The `standard-char-p` predicate determines if an object is of type `standard-char`.

*standard-input*

>The `*standard-input*` variable is the default stream for input.

*standard-output*

>The `*standard-output*` variable is the default stream for output.

(step *form*)

>The `step` macro allows you to step through a form.

stream

>The `stream` type represents the type of special object that can act as a source or destination for data, such as a file or device.

(stream-element-type *stream*)

>The `stream-element-type` function returns a type specifier that indicates what objects can be read from or written to a specified stream.

(streamp *object*)

>The `streamp` predicate determines if its argument is a stream.

{string|(string {*size*})}

>The `string` type specifies the type string which is an array of elements of type string-char.

(string *x*)

>The `string` function coerces its argument to a string.

(string/= *string1 string2* &key :start1 :end1 :start2 :end2)

> The string/= predicate determines if two strings are not lexicographically equal.

(string< *string1 string2* &key :start1 :end1 :start2 :end2)

> The string< predicate determines if the first string is lexicographically less than the second string.

(string<= *string1 string2* &key :start1 :end1 :start2 :end2)

> The string<= predicate determines if the first string is lexicographically less than or equal the second string.

(string= *string1 string2* &key :start1 :end1 :start2 :end2)

> The string= predicate determines if two strings are lexicographically equal.

(string> *string1 string2* &key :start1 :end1 :start2 :end2)

> The string> predicate determines if the first string is lexicographically greater than the second string.

(string>= *string1 string2* &key :start1 :end1 :start2 :end2)

> The string>= predicate determines if the first string is lexicographically greater than or equal the second string.

(string-capitalize *string* &key :start :end)

> The string-capitalize function returns a string with the first character of each word in the specified substring capitalized, provided it is case-modifiable. All other case-modifiable characters are converted to lowercase.

string-char

> The string-char type specifies the type of all single characters known to Lisp that can appear in a string.

(string-char-p *character*)

> The string-char-p predicate determines if a character can be stored in a string.

(string-downcase *string* &key :start :end)

> The string-downcase function returns a string with all case-modifiable characters in lowercase.

(string-equal *string1 string2* &key :start1 :end1 :start2 :end2)

> The string-equal predicate determines if two strings are equal while ignoring case.

(string-greaterp *string1 string2* &key :start1 :end1 :start2 :end2)

> The string-greaterp predicate determines if the first string is greater than the second string while ignoring case.

(string-left-trim *character-bag string*)

The string-left-trim function returns a substring with all characters in the specified character set removed from the beginning of the string.

(string-lessp *string1 string2* &key :start1 :end1 :start2 :end2)

The string-lessp predicate determines if the first string is less than the second string while ignoring case.

(string-not-equal *string1 string2* &key :start1 :end1
                                         :start2 :end2)

The string-not-equal predicate determines if two strings are not equal while ignoring case.

(string-not-greaterp *string1 string2* &key :start1 :end1
                                            :start2 :end2)

The string-not-greaterp predicate determines if the first string is less than or equal, not greater than, the second string while ignoring case.

(string-not-lessp *string1 string2* &key :start1 :end1
                                         :start2 :end2)

The string-not-lessp predicate determines if the first string is greater than or equal, not less than, the second string while ignoring case.

(stringp *object*)

The stringp predicate determines if an object is a string.

(string-right-trim *character-bag string*)

The string-right-trim function returns a substring with all characters in the specified character set removed from the end of the string.

(string-trim *character-bag string*)

The string-trim function returns a substring with all characters in the specified character set removed from the beginning and end of the string.

(string-upcase *string* &key :start :end)

The string-upcase function returns a string with all case-modifiable characters converted to uppercase.

(sublis *alist tree* &key :test :test-not :key)

The sublis function returns a copy of the argument list in which subtrees or leaves have been replaced as specified by an association list.

(subseq *sequence start* &optional *end*)

The subseq function returns a copy of a portion of the specified sequence.

(subsetp *list1 list2* &key :test :test-not :key)

The subsetp predicate determines if the first argument list is a subset of the second argument list.

(subst *new old tree* &key :test :test-not :key)

> The subst function returns a copy of *tree* with *new* substituted for every leaf or subtree x such that *old* and x satisfy the test.

(subst-if *new test tree* &key :key)

> The subst-if function returns a copy of *tree* with *new* substituted for every leaf or subtree that satisfies the test.

(subst-if-not *new test tree* &key :key)

> The subst-if-not function returns a copy of *tree* with *new* substituted for every leaf or subtree which does not satisfy the test.

(substitute *newitem olditem sequence* &key :from-end :test :test-not :start :end :count :key)

> The substitute function returns a copy of the argument sequence with *newitem* substituted for every element x such that *olditem* and x satisfy the test.

(substitute-if *newitem test sequence*
                    &key :from-end :start :end :count :key)

> The substitute-if function returns a copy of the argument sequence with *newitem* substituted for every element that satisfies the test.

(substitute-if-not *newitem test sequence*
                    &key :from-end :start :end :count :key)

> The substitute-if-not function returns a copy of the sequence with *newitem* substituted for every element that fails the test.

(subtypep *type1 type2*)

> The subtypep predicate determines if one data type is a subset of another data type.

(svref *simple-vector index*)

> The svref function returns the specified element of a simple-vector.

symbol

> The symbol type specifies the type symbol that is any named data object.

(sxhash *object*)

> The sxhash function computes a hash code for the given object. The hash code generated is a non-negative fixnum.

(symbol-function *symbol*)

> The symbol-function function returns the current global-function definition of the argument.

(symbol-name *symbol*)

> The symbol-name function returns the print-name of a given symbol.

(symbol-package *symbol*)

> The symbol-package function returns the package object of a package cell for a given symbol.

(symbol-plist *symbol*)

> The symbol-plist function returns the property list of the symbol.

(symbol-value *symbol*)

> The symbol-value function returns the current value of the dynamic variable.

(symbolp *object*)

> The symbolp predicate determines if its argument is a symbol.

t

> The t type specifies the type t which is a supertype of all types and as such contains all objects of any type.

t

> The constant t has a value of T (true).

(tagbody {*tag* | *statement*}*)

> The tagbody special form allows control of execution via labels and the go special form.

(tailp *sublist list*)

> The tailp predicate determines if a sublist is a cons of a list.

(tan *radians*)

> The tan function returns the tangent of its argument.

(tanh *number*)

> The tanh function returns the hyperbolic tangent of its argument.

(tenth *list*)

> The tenth function returns the tenth element of a list.

*terminal-io*

> The *terminal-io* variable is a stream usually connected to a user's console.

(terpri &optional *output-stream*)

> The terpri function outputs a new line to the output stream.

(the *value-type form*)

> The the special form returns the value of the form and allows certain assumptions about its type.

(third *list*)

> The third function returns the third element of a list.

(throw *tag result*)

>   The throw special form transfers execution to a matching catch.

(time *form*)

>   The time macro evaluates the form and prints timing information to *trace-output*.

(trace {*function-specifier*}*)

>   The trace macro prints information about the specified function whenever calls are made to it.

*trace-output*

>   The *trace-output* variable is the stream on which information about traced functions is printed.

(tree-equal *x y* &key :test :test-not)

>   The tree-equal predicate determines if the two arguments are isomorphic trees with identical leaves.

(truename *pathname*)

>   The truename function returns a pathname that contains the "true name" of a file associated with a specified pathname.

(truncate *number* &optional *division*)

>   The truncate function returns the integer portion of the argument.

(type *type var1 var2* ... )

>   The type declaration specifier specifies that all of the variables named will take on values only of the specified type.

(typecase *keyform* { (*type* {*form*}*) }*)

>   The typecase macro compares the type of a given form with type specifiers and evaluates the forms in the matching clauses.

(type-of *object*)

>   The type-of function returns a type specifier describing the type of a given object.

(typep *object type*)

>   The typep predicate returns true if an object is of the specified type and NIL otherwise.

(unexport *symbols* &optional *package*)

>   The unexport function converts a symbol or list of symbols to internal symbols in the given package.

(unintern *string* &optional *package*)

> The unintern function removes a given symbol from a package.

(union *list1 list2* &key :test :test-not :key)

> The union function returns a list containing the elements of the two argument lists.

(unless *test {form}\**)

> The unless macro evaluates an initial form. If the returned value is non-nil, then unless returns NIL and the remaining forms are not evaluated. Otherwise, the remaining forms are evaluated as an implicit progn.

(unread-char *character* &optional *input-stream*)

> The unread-char function places the previously read character back on the input stream.

{unsigned-byte| (unsigned-byte *num-bits*) }

> The unsigned-byte type specifies the type of the nonnegative-integers that can be represented in an s bit two's complement number, that is, from 0 to $2^s-1$.

(untrace *{function-specifier}\**)

> The untrace macro causes the specified function to no longer be traced.

(unuse-package *packages-to-unuse* &optional *package*)

> The unuse-package function removes a list of package names or packages from the package use-list of a specified package.

(unwind-protect *protected-form {cleanup-form}\**)

> The unwind-protect special form guarantees execution of "cleanup forms" however it terminates.

(upper-case-p *character*)

> The upper-case-p predicate determines if a character object is uppercase.

(use-package *packages-to-use* &optional *package*)

> The use-package function adds a list of package names or packages to the use list of the specified package.

(user-homedir-pathname &optional *host*)

> The user-homedir-pathname function returns a pathname for the user's home directory on a specified host.

(values &rest *args*)

> The values function returns the first value of each of its arguments as multiple values.

(values-list *list*)

The values-list function returns all elements of a list as multiple values.

(var *lisp-type non-lisp-type*)

The var symbol is used in defexternal to specify a parameter whose corresponding argument can be changed by the non-Lisp code.

{vector|(vector {*element-type* {*dimension*}})}

The vector type specifies the type of vector of varying dimension and element type.

(vector &rest *objects*)

The vector function creates a simple vector with the specified initial contents.

(vectorp *object*)

The vectorp predicate determines if an object is a vector.

(vector-pop *vector*)

The vector-pop function decrements the fill pointer and returns the vector element designated by the new value of the fill pointer.

(vector-push *new-element vector*)

The vector-push function stores the new element in the element designated by the fill pointer and increments the fill pointer by 1. It returns the index of the new element.

(vector-push-extend *new-element vector* &optional *extension*)

The vector-push-extend function stores the new element in the location designated by the fill pointer, increments the fill pointer by 1, and returns the index of the new element. If the vector is already full, it is extended first.

(warn {T|NIL})

The warn declaration allows you to turn off or turn on compiler warnings.

(warn {*symbol*|*format-string* &rest *arguments*})

The warn function prints a warning message.

(when *test* {*form*}*)

The when macro evaluates an initial form and then evaluates a series of forms, returning the value of the last form when the value of the initial form is non-nil. Otherwise, when returns NIL.

(with-input-from-string  (*var string* {*keyword value*}*)
            {*declaration*}* {*form*}*)

The with-input-from-string macro executes a body with a specified variable bound to an input stream that supplies successive characters from a specified string.

(with-open-file  (*stream filename {options}\**) *{declarations}\* {form}\**)

    The `with-open-file` macro evaluates a body with a stream bound to a file.

(with-open-stream  (*var stream*) *{declaration}\* {form}\**)

    The `with-open-stream` macro executes a body with a specified variable bound to the stream.

(with-output-to-string  (*var [string]*) *{declaration}\* {form}\**)

    The `with-output-to-string` macro executes a body with a specified variable bound to an output stream and saves outputs to the stream in a string.

(write *object* &key :stream :escape :radix :base :circle :pretty
                         :level :length :case :gensym :array)

    The `write` function outputs a printed representation of an object.

(write-byte *integer binary-output-stream*)

    The `write-byte` function writes one byte to the output stream.

(write-char *character* &optional *output-stream*)

    The `write-char` function outputs a character to the output stream.

(write-line *string* &optional *output-stream* &key \*:start :end)

    The `write-line` function outputs a string and a new line to the output stream.

(write-string *string* &optional *output-stream* &key \*:start :end)

    The `write-string` function outputs a string to the output stream.

(write-to-string *object*)

    The `write-to-string` function returns the characters produced by `write` in a string.

(y-or-n-p &optional *format-string* &rest *arguments*)

    The `y-or-n-p` predicate sends a message to `*query-io*` and reads back a single character. The function returns `T` if a "y" or "Y" was input, `NIL` if an "n" or "N" was input, and keeps prompting otherwise.

(yes-or-no-p &optional *format-string* &rest *arguments*)

    The `yes-or-no-p` predicate sends a message to `*query-io*` and reads back an answer. The function returns `T` if a "yes" or "YES" was input, `NIL` if a "no" or "NO" was input, and keeps prompting otherwise.

(zerop *number*)

    The `zerop` predicate determines if a number is zero

# Index

Each of the functions in Lisp appear in `computer typeface`. Pages on which functions are defined appear in **boldface** type.